THE ARDEN SHAKESPEARE

THIRD SERIES

General Editors: Richard Proudfoot, Ann Thompson,
David Scott Kastan and H.R. Woudhuysen

MACBETH

D1117682

THE ARDEN SHAKESPEARE

ALL'S WELL THAT ENDS WELL	edited by G.K. Hunter*
ANTONY AND CLEOPATRA	edited by John Wilders
AS YOU LIKE IT	edited by Juliet Dusinberre
THE COMEDY OF ERRORS	edited by R.A. Foakes*
CORIOLANUS	edited by Peter Holland
CYMBELINE	edited by J.M. Nosworthy*
DOUBLE FALSEHOOD	edited by Brean Hammond
HAMLET	edited by Ann Thompson and Neil Taylor
JULIUS CAESAR	edited by David Daniell
KING HENRY IV PART 1	edited by David Scott Kastan
KING HENRY IV PART 2	edited by A.R. Humphreys*
KING HENRY V	edited by T.W. Craik
KING HENRY VI PART 1	edited by Edward Burns
KING HENRY VI PART 2	edited by Ronald Knowles
KING HENRY VI PART 3	edited by John D. Cox and Eric Rasmussen
KING HENRY VIII	edited by Gordon McMullan
KING JOHN	edited by E.A.J. Honigmann*
KING LEAR	edited by R.A. Foakes
KING RICHARD II	edited by Charles Forker
KING RICHARD III	edited by James R. Siemon
LOVE'S LABOUR'S LOST	edited by H.R. Woudhuysen
MACBETH	edited by Sandra Clark and Pamela Mason
MEASURE FOR MEASURE	edited by J.W. Lever*
THE MERCHANT OF VENICE	edited by John Drakakis
THE MERRY WIVES OF WINDSOR	edited by Giorgio Melchiori
A MIDSUMMER NIGHT'S DREAM	edited by Harold F. Brooks*
MUCH ADO ABOUT NOTHING	edited by Claire McEachern
OTHELLO	edited by E.A.J. Honigmann
PERICLES	edited by Suzanne Gossett
SHAKESPEARE'S POEMS	edited by Katherine Duncan-Jones and H.R. Woudhuysen
ROMEO AND JULIET	edited by René Weis
SHAKESPEARE'S SONNETS	edited by Katherine Duncan-Jones
THE TAMING OF THE SHREW	edited by Barbara Hodgdon
THE TEMPEST	edited by Virginia Mason Vaughan and Alden T. Vaughan
TIMON OF ATHENS	edited by Anthony B. Dawson and Gretchen E. Minton
TITUS ANDRONICUS	edited by Jonathan Bate
TROILUS AND CRESSIDA	edited by David Bevington
TWELFTH NIGHT	edited by Keir Elam
THE TWO GENTLEMEN OF VERONA	edited by William C. Carroll
THE TWO NOBLE KINSMEN	edited by Lois Potter
THE WINTER'S TALE	edited by John Pitcher

* Second series

THE ARDEN SHAKESPEARE

MACBETH

Edited by

SANDRA CLARK
and
PAMELA MASON

THE ARDEN SHAKESPEARE

LONDON • NEW YORK • OXFORD • NEW DELHI • SYDNEY

THE ARDEN SHAKESPEARE
Bloomsbury Publishing Plc
50 Bedford Square, London, WC1B 3DP, UK
1385 Broadway, New York, NY 10018, USA
29 Earlsfort Terrace, Dublin 2, Ireland

BLOOMSBURY, THE ARDEN SHAKESPEARE and the Arden Shakespeare
logo are trademarks of Bloomsbury Publishing Plc

This edition of *Macbeth*, edited by Sandra Clark and Pamela Mason,
first published 2015 by the Arden Shakespeare
Reprinted by Bloomsbury Arden Shakespeare 2015, 2016 (twice), 2017 (twice)
2018, 2019 (twice), 2020, 2021

Editorial matter © Sandra Clark and Pamela Mason, 2015

The general editors of the Arden Shakespeare have been
W. J. Craig and R. H. Case (first series 1899–1944)

Una Ellis-Fermor, Harold F. Brooks, Harold Jenkins and
Brian Morris (second series 1946–82)

Present general editors (third series)
Richard Proudfoot, Ann Thompson, David Scott Kastan
and H. R. Woudhuysen

A catalogue record for this book is available from the British Library.

A catalog record for this book is available from the Library of Congress.

ISBN: HB: 978-1-9042-7140-6
PB: 978-1-9042-7141-3
ePDF: 978-1-4081-5373-4
eBook: 978-1-4081-5374-1

Series: The Arden Shakespeare Third Series

Typeset by Graphicraft Limited, Hong Kong

Printed and bound in India

To find out more about our authors and books visit www.bloomsbury.com
and sign up for our newsletters.

Sandra Clark is a Senior Research Fellow at the Institute of English Studies, University of London, and Professor Emeritus of Renaissance Literature at Birkbeck, University of London, where she taught for many years. She is the author of several books including *The Plays of Beaumont and Fletcher: Sexual Themes and Dramatic Representation* and *Women and Crime in the Street Literature of Early Modern England*, and the editor of *Amorous Rites: Elizabethan Erotic Verse* and *Shakespeare Made Fit: Restoration Adaptations of Shakespeare*. She is also Series Editor of the Arden Shakespeare Dictionaries.

Pamela Mason was formerly a Fellow of the Shakespeare Institute and Lecturer in English, The University of Birmingham. She is the co-editor of *Shakespeare in Performance* and the author of *Text and Performance: Much Ado About Nothing*, *Shakespeare's Early Comedies: A Casebook* and the *Cambridge Shakespeare Student Guide to* Othello.

CONTENTS

Contents

LIST OF
ILLUSTRATIONS

GENERAL EDITORS' PREFACE

The earliest volume in the first Arden series, Edward Dowden's *Hamlet*, was published in 1899. Since then the Arden Shakespeare has been widely acknowledged as the pre-eminent Shakespeare edition, valued by scholars, students, actors and 'the great variety of readers' alike for its clearly presented and reliable texts, its full annotation and its richly informative introductions.

In the third Arden series we seek to maintain these well-established qualities and general characteristics, preserving our predecessors' commitment to presenting the play as it has been shaped in history. Each volume necessarily has its own particular emphasis which reflects the unique possibilities and problems posed by the work in question, and the series as a whole seeks to maintain the highest standards of scholarship, combined with attractive and accessible presentation.

Newly edited from the original documents, texts are presented in fully modernized form, with a textual apparatus that records all substantial divergences from those early printings. The notes and introductions focus on the conditions and possibilities of meaning that editors, critics and performers (on stage and screen) have discovered in the play. While building upon the rich history of scholarly activity that has long shaped our understanding of Shakespeare's works, this third series of the Arden Shakespeare is enlivened by a new generation's encounter with Shakespeare.

THE TEXT

On each page of the play itself, readers will find a passage of text supported by commentary and textual notes. Act and scene divisions (seldom present in the early editions and often the product of eighteenth-century or later scholarship) have been retained for ease of reference, but have been given less prominence than in previous series. Editorial indications of location of the action have been removed to the textual notes or commentary.

In the text itself, elided forms in the early texts are spelt out in full in verse lines wherever they indicate a usual late twentieth-century pronunciation that requires no special indication and wherever they occur in prose (except where they indicate nonstandard pronunciation). In verse speeches, marks of elision are retained where they are necessary guides to the scansion and pronunciation of the line. Final -ed in past tense and participial forms of verbs is always printed as -ed, without accent, never as -'d, but wherever the required pronunciation diverges from modern usage a note in the commentary draws attention to the fact. Where the final -ed should be given syllabic value contrary to modern usage, e.g.

> Doth Silvia know that I am banished?
>
> *(TGV* 3.1.214)

the note will take the form

214 **banished** banishèd

Conventional lineation of divided verse lines shared by two or more speakers has been reconsidered and sometimes rearranged. Except for the familiar *Exit* and *Exeunt*, Latin forms in stage directions and speech prefixes have been translated into English and the original Latin forms recorded in the textual notes.

COMMENTARY AND TEXTUAL NOTES

Notes in the commentary, for which a major source will be the *Oxford English Dictionary*, offer glossarial and other explication of verbal difficulties; they may also include discussion of points of interpretation and, in relevant cases, substantial extracts from Shakespeare's source material. Editors will not usually offer glossarial notes for words adequately defined in the latest edition of *The Concise Oxford Dictionary* or *Merriam-Webster's Collegiate Dictionary*, but in cases of doubt they will include notes. Attention, however, will be drawn to places where more than one likely interpretation can be proposed and to significant verbal and syntactic complexity. Notes preceded by * discuss editorial emendations or variant readings.

Headnotes to acts or scenes discuss, where appropriate, questions of scene location, the play's treatment of source materials, and major difficulties of staging. The list of roles (so headed to emphasize the play's status as a text for performance) is also considered in the commentary notes. These may include comment on plausible patterns of casting with the resources of an Elizabethan or Jacobean acting company and also on any variation in the description of roles in their speech prefixes in the early editions.

The textual notes are designed to let readers know when the edited text diverges from the early edition(s) or manuscript sources on which it is based. Wherever this happens the note will record the rejected reading of the early edition(s) or manuscript, in original spelling, and the source of the reading adopted in this edition. Other forms from the early edition(s) or manuscript recorded in these notes will include some spellings of particular interest or significance and original forms of translated stage directions. Where two or more early editions are involved, for instance with *Othello*, the notes also record all important differences between them. The textual notes take a form that has been in use since the nineteenth century. This comprises, first: line reference, reading adopted in the text and closing square bracket; then: abbreviated reference, in italic, to the earliest edition to adopt the accepted reading, italic semicolon and noteworthy alternative reading(s), each with abbreviated italic reference to its source.

Conventions used in these textual notes include the following. The solidus / is used, in notes quoting verse or discussing verse lining, to indicate line endings. Distinctive spellings of the base text follow the square bracket without indication of source and are enclosed in italic brackets. Names enclosed in italic brackets indicate originators of conjectural emendations when these did not originate in an edition of the text, or when the named edition records a conjecture not accepted into its text. Stage directions (SDs) are referred to by the number of the line within or immediately after which they are placed. Line numbers with a decimal point relate to centred entry SDs not falling within a verse line and to SDs more than one line long, with the number after the point indicating the line within the SD: e.g. 78.4 refers to the fourth line of the SD following line 78. Lines of SDs at the start of a scene are numbered 0.1, 0.2, etc. Where only a line number precedes a square bracket, e.g. 128], the note relates to the whole line; where SD is added to the number, it relates to the whole of a SD within or immediately following the line. Speech prefixes (SPs) follow similar conventions, 203 SP] referring to the speaker's name for line 203. Where a SP reference takes the form e.g. 38+ SP, it relates to all subsequent speeches assigned to that speaker in the scene in question.

Where, as with *King Henry V*, one of the early editions is a so-called 'bad quarto' (that is, a text either heavily adapted, or reconstructed from memory, or both), the divergences from the present edition are too great to be recorded in full in the notes. In these cases, with the exception of *Hamlet*, which prints an edited text of the quarto of 1603, the editions will include a reduced photographic facsimile of the 'bad quarto' in an appendix.

INTRODUCTION

Both the introduction and the commentary are designed to present the plays as texts for performance, and make appropriate reference to stage, film and television versions, as well as introducing the reader to the range of critical approaches to the plays. They discuss the history of the reception of the texts within the theatre and scholarship and beyond, investigating the interdependency of the literary text and the surrounding 'cultural text' both at the time of the original production of Shakespeare's works and during their long and rich afterlife.

PREFACE

This edition has been long in the making, and both editors wish to acknowledge the contributions of scholars and friends along the way. We have been grateful for the wise guidance provided by the General Editors and for the support of the publishing team led so sympathetically by Margaret Bartley. Ann Thompson has been judicious and supportive throughout; her penetrating questions and comments have done much to improve the Introduction and commentary notes. We are profoundly grateful to Jane Armstrong for the meticulous attention with which she has worked on our text while guiding us through the final stages of preparing the edition. Emily Hockley has been most helpful in obtaining the illustrations.

While we have both been involved in the preparation of the edition as a whole, Sandra Clark is mainly responsible for the Introduction, commentary notes and appendices, and Pamela Mason for the text and textual notes, and Part 1 of Appendix 1.

Sandra Clark writes as follows:
I have amassed many debts while preparing this edition. I have worked mainly at Senate House Library, University of London, where staff have always been kind and efficient, and also at the British Library and the library of Birkbeck, University of London. The Librarian at the Garrick Club, Marcus Risdell, the Archivist at the National Theatre, Gavin Clarke, and the staff at the Shakespeare Centre Library, Stratford-upon-Avon, and at Smallhythe, Ellen Terry's house, have given me access to important materials. The support of colleagues at the Institute of English Studies, University of London, especially Marcus Dahl and Brian Vickers, who have been generous with their time, has been invaluable.

I would like to thank the following people for many kinds of help and encouragement: in correspondence, conversations, loans of books and programmes, suggestions, and advice, some-times sage, sometimes provocative, sometimes both: Jennifer Barnes, Tony Bromham, Warren Chernaik, Anthony Dawson, Gabriel Egan, John Fullman, Sujata Iyengar, Andrew McKinnon, Deborah Sacks, Jim Shapiro, Michael Slater, Jerry Sokol, Boika Sokolova.

I have been fortunate to draw on the learning of Shake-speareans who have much more of it than I. Tom Craik has read nearly everything I have written, and, although he may not like everything that is in it, this edition would be the poorer without his wise advice. Richard Proudfoot has run his critical eye over parts of the introduction, much to my benefit, and also given me help and friendly encouragement. The Introduction has also been improved by Henry Woudhuysen's meticulous reading of a section, and I have enjoyed, and profited from, my correspondence with George Walton Williams. Jonathan Hope has always been quick to answer email queries about matters linguistic. Gary Taylor kindly allowed me to see an article of his before it was published.

Conversations with theatre directors Rupert Goold and Declan Donnellan gave me inspiration at an early stage. It has been useful to try out ideas about *Macbeth* in seminars at the Shakespeare Association of America and the International Shakespeare Conference, Stratford-upon-Avon. I can hardly fail to mention my sense of being a dwarf on the shoulders of giants; recently there have been many fine editions of *Macbeth*, but I have learnt most from those of G.K. Hunter and A.R. Braunmuller.

My greatest debts are sometimes the hardest to define. Many decades ago, I studied Shakespeare with one of the finest of editors, the late Harold Jenkins, who represents standards of scholarship that I cannot hope to achieve. More than anything, I wish I could have talked about my work with him. Nearer to earth, I want to thank my son, Oliver Clark, who has dealt patiently with computer-associated traumas, and my husband,

Mike Holmes, who has done so much to improve my life over the many years of *Macbeth*'s gestation, not least by accompanying me without complaint to more productions of *Macbeth* than anyone should have to see.

Pamela Mason writes as follows:
I do wish to thank Kate McLuskie for her intellectual generosity in the early years of the work. I have been grateful for the insights and stimulus provided by several RSC actors and many students over the years, especially when I was a Fellow of the Shakespeare Institute in Stratford-upon-Avon: 'Honest company, I thank you all'. I owe unbounded love to my husband, Keith Parsons, and to my daughter, Elinor, for their forbearance and for sharing their perception.

Sandra Clark
Institute of English Studies, School of Advanced Study
University of London

Pamela Mason
Sometime Fellow of the Shakespeare Institute,
Stratford-upon-Avon
University of Birmingham

INTRODUCTION

This introduction consists of six sections: *Macbeth*: the tragedy, *Macbeth* in its context, language in *Macbeth*, *Macbeth* and time, *Macbeth* and its sources and *Macbeth* on the stage. Textual matters are dealt with in Appendix 1.

MACBETH: THE TRAGEDY

Macbeth is a play which attracts superlatives: it is Shakespeare's shortest tragedy and the fastest moving, the most economical of the tragedies in its use of language and thematic integration (Knights, *Themes*, 112); it has the most pronounced atmosphere of evil of any of his plays, but also contains 'the most insistent religious language' (Stachniewski, 169); it may be 'the greatest of morality plays', and was once thought 'the most instructive tragedy in the world';[1] it has been called his most timely, his darkest, his most poetic, most 'philosophically ambitious' play, 'fantastical and imaginative beyond other tragedies' (Wilson Knight, *Wheel*, 140). Its imagery has been termed 'more rich and varied, more highly imaginative . . . than that of any other single play' (Spurgeon, 324). While it is said to depict 'the happiest married couple in all his work' (Bloom, 318),[2] it is the

---

1 Muir, lxv; James Beattie, *Essays. On Poetry and Music* (1776), in Vickers, *Critical*, 6.152.

2 Bloom is not alone in this view. Moulton (156) thought the happiness of the marriage due to Lady Macbeth's unselfish devotion to her husband. Ian McKellen, one of the best Macbeths of the twentieth century, in a question-and-answer session after his one-man show *Acting Shakespeare* (Playhouse Theatre, London, 1987), cited the Macbeths as the only happily married couple in Shakespeare after the Hotspurs in *1 Henry IV*. (He could also have mentioned Paulina and Antigonus in *Winter's Tale*.) Harriet Walter, who played Lady Macbeth in 1999 to Antony Sher's Macbeth, calls the play 'the portrait of a *folie à deux*' (Walter, 18). Macbeth's devotion to his wife has been shown in some recent productions (Goold, 2007/8, Cheek by Jowl, 2010) when he addresses 'Tomorrow, and tomorrow, and tomorrow' directly to her body as an elegy. See also pp. 111–12.

play in which Shakespeare addresses himself most 'pervasively to tragic action' (Calderwood, 33). 'No other tragedy has so many strange, disturbing phenomena' (Jorgensen, 13). In the theatre, it has accrued a unique aura of superstition, and has often to be referred to as 'the Scottish play'.[1] Alone of Shakespeare's great tragedies, *Macbeth* features a hero who is also a criminal. Shakespeare had tried this before, in *Richard III*, with which *Macbeth* has often been compared, but the great difference is that he makes Macbeth a character whose commitment to evil causes him enormous suffering, and it is partly through the depiction of this suffering that the audience's sympathy is engaged. This engagement is distinctive and, in the circumstances, paradoxical. For Macbeth becomes a killer early in the play, overcoming strong moral scruples to do so, and having killed once finds himself obliged to continue in order to hold on to the power he has gained. He misuses this power tyrannically, destroying the well-being of his country; the movement of the action culminates, as it must, in his death. The tragic effect is created because, in all this, Shakespeare does not allow his audience to become alienated from his protagonist. It is appropriate for Malcolm at the end to dismiss his father's murderer as 'this dead butcher', but the phrase jars with the audience's perception. Macbeth is in an odd sense, 'one of us', as Stephen Booth says, 'the only character . . . who is our size' (Booth, *'King Lear'*, 110), who stands apart from those around him because he sees and feels more deeply than anyone else, and because from the start the audience is encouraged into a kind of complicity with him. The play 'puts us inside Macbeth's head' (Goldman, 110).

---

1   On the 'curse' of *Macbeth* see Huggett and Bartholomeusz (245). Laurie Maguire and Emma Smith include as myth 23, 'Macbeth is jinxed in the theater', in *30 Great Myths about Shakespeare* (Chichester, W. Sussex, 2013). Ngaio Marsh makes fine use of the superstition in her excellent thriller about a production of *Macbeth*, *Light Thickens* (1982).

The moral sense which makes Macbeth acutely conscious of Duncan as a good man and a king to whom he owes compelling duties never leaves him. He wants to be part of an ordered society, to enjoy the 'golden opinions' which he has won through service to the state and to share them with his 'dearest partner of greatness', to 'live the lease of nature, pay his breath / To time, and mortal custom' (4.1.98–9), only dying after an old age accompanied by 'honour, love, obedience, troops of friends' (5.3.25). He allows himself to become a murderer but is filled with horror at what he has done and at once wishes it undone, recognizing that through the deed he has irrevocably corrupted a sacramental part of his innermost self ('Put rancours in the vessel of my peace . . . and mine eternal jewel / Given to the common enemy of man' (3.1.66–8)). He tries to escape thinking of himself as responsible for what he has done, and pursues 'fantasies of invisibility' (Tilmouth, 512); his eye must 'wink at the hand' that wields the knife. As far as he can, he tries to disclaim agency. The dagger which he hallucinates becomes stained with blood apparently of its own volition, and seems to guide him on his way to Duncan's chamber. As he goes, he begs that the 'sure and firm-set earth' not hear his steps.

Not only is the audience made privy to Macbeth's state of mind from the first, but he is also a character who has an extraordinary susceptibility to strong feeling. This he registers both through his body and in language of powerful emotional affect, as in his reaction to the Sisters' prophecies. He starts fearfully, as Banquo observes. Then he tries to analyse his reaction:

> This supernatural soliciting
> Cannot be ill; cannot be good. If ill,
> Why hath it given me earnest of success,
> Commencing in a truth? I am Thane of Cawdor.
> If good, why do I yield to that suggestion
> Whose horrid image doth unfix my hair,

> And make my seated heart knock at my ribs,
> Against the use of nature? Present fears
> Are less than horrible imaginings.
> My thought, whose murder yet is but fantastical,
> Shakes so my single state of man
> That function is smothered in surmise,
> And nothing is, but what is not.

> (1.3.132–44)

Macbeth's exploration of his own emotional response to what he immediately identifies as a key event in his life contributes significantly to the play's larger tragic effect. He thinks constantly about what he is feeling, and the destructive effects of his chosen course of action are recorded in both mental and physical terms. He cannot sleep and is shaken nightly by 'terrible dreams', his mind is 'full of scorpions', his looks are 'rugged', he has fits, flaws and starts, and his heart throbs. His intense self-consciousness and his ability to draw the audience into his own perceptual system are largely responsible for the fact that he comes across not just as a villain but also as a suffering hero, constantly exposing his own emotional vulnerability. His despair in the final scenes is heightened by his inability to feel as he once did:

> I have almost forgot the taste of fears.
> The time has been, my senses would have cooled
> To hear a night-shriek, and my fell of hair
> Would at a dismal treatise rouse and stir
> As life were in't. I have supped full with horrors:

> (5.5.9–13)

Audience collusion with Macbeth is encouraged by the way in which he shares impulses and feelings which are commonplace, even if they are not always laudable: the worry and fear of exposure, the sense of having made a bad bargain, the wish to present oneself publicly in the best possible light. His loss of control in the banquet scene creates what Emrys Jones has called 'a feeling of acute tragic embarrassment' (Jones, *Scenic*, 217); the risks he takes in 2.3, when Duncan's murder is brought to light, arouse anxiety as to whether he can, as Robert Heilman (31) puts it, 'bring it off'. Macbeth is not shown in the act of killing until the end of the play, and after the deaths of Duncan and Banquo it is his anguish that is stressed above anyone else's. His lack of hesitation about ordering the slaughter of Macduff's family marks the emotional and moral distance he has travelled since the painful vacillation before Duncan's murder.

The motivation for Macbeth's criminal career is a central issue. Hazlitt, like other Romantics, saw him as 'driven along by the violence of his fate like a vessel drifting before a storm' (13), but this sidesteps the important roles of the women in his life, the Sisters and his Lady,[1] and the larger questions about choice and agency that their roles open up. In the opening scene the Sisters are already planning an assignation with Macbeth, and they are waiting for him when he first appears. His first line echoes their chant. Their soliciting, as he calls it, may be 'supernatural', and it does appear to chime with his own desires, but at this point he is ambivalent about their ontological status, and inclined not to take any action: 'If chance will have me king, why chance may crown me, / Without my stir' (1.3.146–7). Nonetheless he is so strongly affected by the coincidence between their predictions for his future and his recent promotion that his 'single state of man' is shaken to the core. In the letter to his wife he reports that 'they have more in them than mortal knowledge' (1.5.2–3); further evidence of their powers appears in the conjuring scene, when they summon up their 'masters', whose oracular injunctions fill Macbeth with disastrous self-confidence. Their final gesture exhibits high-level fortune-telling powers in producing the 'show of kings' that represents

---

1   For the speech prefix 'Lady', see Appendix 1.

1 *The Weird Sisters* (1785), by John Raphael Smith (1752–1812), after
Henry Fuseli (1741–1825)

the future Stuart dynasty; it incites Macbeth, impotent in the
face of a future in which he can have no part, to murderous
rage, which he vents on the family of Macduff. This act makes
Macduff into the revenger who in turn brings about Macbeth's
own death.

While the Sisters are 'withered' and 'wild in their attire'
(1.3.40) like the old women accused of witchcraft in early modern
England (see Fig. 2),[1] and their malice, spells and doggerel
chanting are as much childish and grotesque as frightening,

---

1 The standard histories of the witchcraft phenomenon in England are Macfarlane
and Thomas (*Religion*). The latter gives a detailed account of the social environment
of the early modern English witch (599–680). Rosen reprints the major sources for
English and Scottish witchcraft. Clark, *Thinking*, is the definitive study of how a
range of phenomena and cultural practices, including witchcraft, were conceptual-
ized as demonology. It illustrates the fluidity and porous boundaries of the concept.
Gibson & Esra is an illuminating source of information on Shakespeare's repres-
entations of demonology in his plays, in which *Macbeth* features prominently.

2   Woodcut from the title-page of *The Wonderful Discoverie of the Witchcrafts of Margaret and Phillip Flower* (1618)

they are also undeniably figures of mysterious power, operating outside of nature and society, with some kinship to the three Fates.[1] They can 'look into the seeds of time', but their prophecies have all the ambiguity of the oracle that led Oedipus to his destruction in the belief that he had outwitted fate. It is Macbeth's (somewhat selective) account of his meeting with them that inspires his Lady to call on the spirits who 'tend on mortal thoughts', as the Sisters do, to transform her from a natural woman into someone capable of murder. Macbeth realizes too late how they have been instrumental in his downfall when he calls them, reductively, 'juggling fiends . . . That palter with us in a double sense'. In this speech (5.8.17–22) he implicitly acknowledges that he had a choice, that he interpreted the Sisters' predictions in a certain way and conducted his life accordingly. Yet the background against which his course of action is played out is emphatically not one where all events are explicable and

1   On the Sisters' language, see pp. 46–51.

normal social order prevails. On the night of Duncan's death, 'Lamentings [are] heard i'th' air, strange screams of death, / And prophesying, with accents terrible' (2.3.56–7). Night takes over from day, animals behave unnaturally, and Duncan's horses turn cannibal, 'as they would / Make war with mankind' (2.4.17–18). Creation is animated by terrifying power: 'Stones have been known to move, and trees to speak' (3.4.121). Although there was a time 'Ere humane statute purged the gentle weal' and the dead stayed dead, now 'they rise again / With twenty mortal murders on their crowns, / And push us from our stools' (3.4.74, 78–80). Banquo, like the Lady, is conscious of living in a world where evil spirits 'wait on nature's mischief' and are all too ready to engage with human activity: 'The instruments of darkness tell us truths, / Win us with honest trifles, to betray's / In deepest consequence' (1.3.126–8). In such a world, how free is Macbeth to determine his own choices? Are the cards stacked against him from the start? He is, it appears, more susceptible to the Sisters than Banquo; is this because their predictions awaken 'dark and deep desires' he has already

3   Macbeth and Banquo encountering the Witches, *Holinshed's Chronicles* (1577)

felt?[1] The play raises such questions but leaves them open. It offers the possibility 'of a world in which the balance has been tipped imperceptibly towards evil' (Sanders, 282),[2] but this depends on the extent to which the play's conclusion is considered to right that balance.

Macbeth's choice to murder Duncan is the tragic action that sets his course thereafter, a choice prompted by his wife, at whose door the responsibility for much that follows has often been laid.[3] It is she who not only determines that he will become

---

1   This is an interpretation sometimes drawn on in the theatre, e.g. by Olivier and Jacobi (see p. 106). On the question of Macbeth's 'innocence' see also Bradley (287–8 and note CC, 'When was the murder of Duncan first plotted?').

2   Sanders counters the schematic Christian readings (e.g. by R. Walker, Elliott, Curry) current in the 1950s and 1960s, and powerfully rejects the idea that theological explanations for the problem of evil in the play are adequate. His analysis of key moral points is one of the most subtle and perceptive in *Macbeth* criticism in its time.

3   The reputation of Macbeth's Lady has gone through many vicissitudes since Charles Gildon (*Remarks on the Plays of Shakespeare* (1710), in Vickers, *Critical*, 2.257) pronounced her (and her husband) 'too monstrous for the stage', and Johnson referred dismissively to her as 'merely detested'. For Hazlitt she was 'a great bad woman', and for Jameson one 'doubly, trebly dyed in guilt and blood' (323) who drives her husband on to crime, even if it is 'less through her pre-eminence in wickedness than through her superiority of intellect' (325). Sarah Siddons, whose performance in the role influenced a generation (including Hazlitt, Coleridge and Jameson) thought her 'a perfectly savage creature', in pursuit of the ambitious plans she has for her husband ('Remarks on the character of Lady Macbeth', in Thomas Campbell, *The Life of Mrs Siddons* (1834), 2 vols, 2.10 (in *Var*, 473)). Joseph Comyns Carr wanted to challenge the view, current in the later nineteenth century, that Macbeth's 'enfeebled virtue was overborne by the satanic strength of her will' (*Macbeth and Lady Macbeth: An Essay* (1889), 13), and for Edward Dowden among others she was surpassed in evil by the witches (*Shakespere: A Critical Study of his Mind and Art* (1875), 245). But Christian interpreters of the mid-twentieth century like R. Walker and Coursen thought she played a part tantamount to that of the serpent in Eden, and for pre-feminist critics such as Matthew Proser (*The Heroic Image in Five Shakespearean Tragedies* (Princeton, 1965) and D.W. Harding ('Woman's fantasy of manhood: a Shakespearean theme', *SQ*, 20.3 (1965), 245–53) it was her destructive pursuit of false ideals of masculinity that brought about her husband's ruin. More recently, however, responsibility for Macbeth's career of crime has been displaced onto the distortions that patriarchal society brings about for men's sense of self-identity, and thus their inability to develop a psychically satisfactory relationship with women and the feminine (for examples, see Adelman, and Berger, 'Text').

what the Sisters have 'promised' but also that this should come about 'the nearest way'. She is confident of her own power over him and how to wield it:

> Hie thee hither,
> That I may pour my spirits in thine ear,
> And chastise with the valour of my tongue
> All that impedes thee from the golden round,
> Which fate and metaphysical aid doth seem
> To have thee crowned withal.

$$(1.5.25-30)^1$$

When he hesitates, overcome with fears and scruples, to proceed with the euphemistically named 'business', she knows that she can win him over by questioning his masculinity. Her plan for the murder and especially for deflecting 'the guilt of our great quell' onto others fills him with admiration. All vacillation dismissed, he bursts out with the alarming accolade: 'Bring forth men-children only; / For thy undaunted mettle should compose / Nothing but males' (1.7.73–5). The doubts he had entertained about undertaking Duncan's murder are expressed in a speech of such imaginative complexity and power that there can be no doubt of their seriousness; hence, his wife's success in getting him to change his mind makes her a significant agent in the tragic course of events. Her frightening invocation of the spirits connects her with the Sisters,[2] and she is at her

---

1   In Barnabe Barnes, *The Divil's Charter* (1607), a play possibly influenced by *Macbeth*, Lucretia Borgia similarly desires to cast off womanly weakness and invokes diabolical assistance, in this case, to murder her husband: 'You griesly Daughters of grimme Erebus, / Which spit out vengeance from your viperous heires, / Infuse a three-fold vigor in these armes; / I[m]marble more my strong indurate heart, / To consumate the plot of my revenge' (601–5).

2   For discussions of her association with the Sisters from feminist perspectives see Adelman (134–7), Dolan (226–7) and Stallybrass (196–8). Wills (80–3) summarizes opinion as to whether this connection identifies Macbeth's Lady as a witch, as has been suggested (e.g. by Rose, 88) but concludes that 'in any technically legal

10

most powerful in the scenes leading up to Duncan's murder. Adelman (138) argues that her importance is in willing Macbeth into a 'bloodthirsty masculinity'; this is not only a means for him to escape her taunts of cowardice, but also a shaping of his future identity. In taking it on, he rejects his own sense of 'all that may become a man'. After the murder she still for a time plays a vital role in supporting her more volatile husband both in public and in private, but he is now empowered to continue on his criminal path alone. They discuss together the dangers posed by Banquo and Fleance, but Macbeth does not choose to reveal to her his plans for their dispatch: 'Be innocent of the knowledge, dearest chuck, / Till thou applaud the deed' (3.2.46–7). Her work done, she dwindles into a helpless wife, in her last scene displaying through her 'broken discourse' (Charney & Charney, 458) all the symptoms of psychic distress, the 'torture of the mind', the sleeplessness, the guilt and fear, that had previously been Macbeth's.[1] Her little statement 'Hell is murky' may suggest a retributive link back to the powers of darkness from which she had earlier derived her strength.

The scene of the Lady's collapse follows immediately after Malcolm's assertion that 'Macbeth / Is ripe for shaking, and the powers above / Put on their instruments' (4.3.240–2) heralding the play's final movement, which is shaped by elements of nemesis and destiny.[2] In 4.3 Macduff, the last and most

---

or theological sense' she was not (83). But Bradbrook (20) says Macbeth's Lady's invocation to the spirits is 'as much as any witch could do by way of self-dedication' and Callaghan states firmly that 'By seventeenth-century standards Lady Macbeth is a witch' (359).

1   This transference between husband and wife is used by Freud in his brief notes on the play to support the idea of the Macbeths as 'two disunited parts of a single psychical individuality' (Freud, 308).

2   Nemesis and destiny are terms used by Moulton in his Aristotelian account of the plot in *Macbeth* which he analyses on the lines of a classical tragedy. This is illuminating if ultimately simplistic. According to him, it is Macbeth's mistaken choices to shut himself up in Dunsinane (and thus make himself vulnerable to the coming of Birnam Wood) and then to confront Macduff which bring about his downfall.

egregiously wronged of all Macbeth's victims, emerges as the challenger who will enact revenge on behalf of his 'poor country' as well as his family against 'this fiend of Scotland'. Macbeth's hubris is punished as the two prophecies which had shored up his sense of invulnerability are fulfilled, and he finally understands that he has been fatally deceived. Macduff's dramatic revelation about the circumstances of his birth brings Macbeth the realization that the wheel of his fate has, as Edmund in *King Lear* puts it in similar circumstances, 'come full circle', but, a fighting man to the last, he cannot surrender to the ignominy of a coward's death. Alone of Shakespeare's tragic heroes, he has no dying speech, but instead a last, long, and of course, hopeless, fight. Malcolm, defined as the true king of Scotland through his newly asserted authority in 4.3, assesses the state of the battlefield and accepts Macduff's salutation before making the first moves of his reign. The extent to which this ending is restorative has been debated. How significant are the echoes of early scenes in the play? Do the repetitions of 'Hail' recall the Sisters' greeting to Macbeth and Banquo? Are Malcolm's use of his father's image of planting and his promises of rewards and titles to his supporters ominously reminiscent of his father's speeches in 1.4? How strong are the indications of a 'cycle of trust and betrayal' beginning again?[1] The play is built around ambiguities, starting with the Sisters' chant in 1.1, 'Fair is foul, and foul is fair', and continuing through the prophecies that keep Macbeth moving forward, and its ending is open to more than one reading. It may be restorative, with 'order emerging from disorder, truth emerging from behind deceit' (Knights, 'How many', 36) and Malcolm and Macduff bringing back 'security and peace' to war-torn Scotland as 'the instruments of God's all-inclusive

---

1   Braunmuller's phrase (5.9.31–2n.). Critics who regard the ending as cyclic include Booth, *'King Lear'*, and Berger, 'Text'. The films of Welles (1948) and Polanski (1971) also suggest this. See pp. 120–21.

order'.[1] But it may reflect the play's many ambiguities, with suggestions that the violence and bloodshed are recurrent features of the political process in Scotland and that in Malcolm's concluding speech there are implications that, as Harry Berger puts it, 'the old cycle is starting over again'.[2]

This is not to deny the play a structural shapeliness. The tripartite movement, through actions dominated successively by Macbeth's relations with Duncan, Banquo and Macduff, works alongside a regular iteration of the number three (Sisters, prophecies for Macbeth, Apparitions). Macbeth achieves the throne unhindered, but in the central scene when he prepares to ratify his new regime in public with a formal banquet the news of Fleance's escape signals the beginning of his decline. As nemesis unfolds, Macbeth returns to his first role of warrior, suffering, like the former Thane of Cawdor, the traitor's ignominious fate. Yet this ending may not be without some element of tragic catharsis. Macbeth is killed, justly, by the destined adversary, avoiding the humiliation of playing the 'Roman fool'. The moral sense that made his surrender to crime so painful does not desert him.

MACBETH IN ITS CONTEXT

Date

There seems no good reason to doubt the generally accepted view that *Macbeth* was written in 1606, three years after the accession of James VI of Scotland to the English throne as James I and some months after the discovery of the Gunpowder

---

1   Wilson Knight, *Imperial*, 129, Tillyard, 321.
2   Berger's view of the cyclic nature of the political process ('Text', 49–79) has been highly influential, if not universally accepted (not by Levin, 'New', for example). So too has Booth's account of Macbeth as a play pervaded by 'a sense of limitlessness' and a lack of finality (*'King Lear'*, 99).

Plot, although exactly when remains impossible to establish. That it was a Jacobean play is confirmed by the reference at 4.1.120 to the 'twofold balls and treble sceptres' which must signify the Union of England and Scotland, and it was seen at the Globe Theatre by Simon Forman on 20 April 1611, which gives us a *terminus ante quem*. Among many reasons for supposing it to date from 1606 are possible links with other plays written or performed around that time: John Marston's *Sophonisba* (printed 1606), Thomas Tomkis's *Lingua* (entered in the Stationers' Register 23 February 1607) and Francis Beaumont's *The Knight of the Burning Pestle* (printed 1612, but probably written 1607). Tomkis and Beaumont had evidently seen *Macbeth* performed. *The Knight of the Burning Pestle* probably refers to the appearance of Banquo's ghost in the banquet scene, in a way that suggests this was a particularly striking moment onstage. Here, Jasper, his face whitened with flour, pretends to be a vengeful ghost appearing to the Merchant, who has wronged him:

> When thou art at thy table with thy friends,
> Merry in heart, and filled with swelling wine,
> I'll come in midst of all thy pride and mirth,
> Invisible to all men but thyself,
> And whisper such a sad tale in thine ear
> Shall make thee let the cup fall from thy hand,
> And stand as mute and pale as Death itself.

(5.1.22–8)[1]

Tomkis had been impressed by another scene, and in the denouement of his allegorical play he comically parodies the unconscious betrayal of her crimes by Macbeth's Lady to two

---

1 Francis Beaumont, *The Knight of the Burning Pestle*, ed. Michael Hattaway (1969). This cup was dropped by Garrick as well as many others, and perhaps appeared in the original production of *Macbeth* (Rosenberg, 463).

14

4   Ellen Terry as Lady Macbeth sleepwalking

observers while sleepwalking. In 5.18 Lingua, who has been induced to sleep by Somnus, unconsciously reveals to the listeners the plot she has hatched against the five senses. Phantastes comments: 'Here's the notablest peece of treason discovered, how say you Lingua set all the senses at ods, she hath confest it to me in her sleep'. Lingua then gets up and walks while still asleep, and in the ensuing dialogue imagines herself to be conversing with Mendatio, her page and partner in crime, just as Macbeth's Lady imagines herself to be talking to Macbeth. In the next scene, Lingua is woken and her behaviour condemned by Phantastes and Commun Sense, who tells her,

'In my conceipt Lingua, you should seale up your lippes when you go to bed, these Feminine tongues be so glibbe'.[1]

In the case of Marston's *Sophonisba*, entered in the Stationers' Register on 17 March 1606 and so likely to be the earlier, Shakespeare may be the debtor. In Geoffrey Bullough's opinion (7.425), had Marston been imitating Shakespeare, he 'would probably have done more than take a few words here and there'. The main resemblance occurs in 1.2 of *Sophonisba*, where the wedding night of Sophonisba and Massinissa is interrupted by the sudden entrance of a wounded soldier, Carthalon, with a narrative of a battle between Carthage and Rome. The Romans are led by Scipio, 'like the God of blood'. Carthalon describes the might of Rome:

> Three hundred saile
> Upon whose tops the *Roman* eagles streachd
> Their large spread winges, which fan'd the evening ayre
> To us cold breath, for well we might discerne
> *Rome* swam to Carthage.[2]

In the course of his long account of the changing fortunes of the two sides, the soldier observes that 'doubtfull stood the fight'. Finally he runs out of breath: 'No more. I bleede'. Not only are there close verbal parallels between Carthalon's speeches and those of the Captain in *Macbeth* in 1.2, but the situation of the wounded messenger reporting from the battlefield is very similar. Shakespeare may also have taken note of some later scenes in the play. In 4.1 Syphax conjures up the witch Erictho, to assist him in gaining the love of Sophonisba. Erictho commands him, 'Here Syphax here, quake not, for know / I know thy thoughts'. In *Macbeth* 4.1 the First Witch

---

1 Boas notes further verbal recollections of *Macbeth* in *Lingua*, calling the resemblances 'remarkable' (519).
2 John Marston, *Sophonisba*, in *The Plays of John Marston*, ed. H. Harvey Wood, 3 vols (1938), vol. 2.

tells Macbeth, 'He knows thy thought: / Hear his speech, but say thou nought.' In *Sophonisba*, 5.1, the ghost of Asdruball rises up to Syphax, who insists that, manlike, he is not afraid: 'Our flesh knows not ignoble tremblinges'. A connection between the two plays seems undeniable.

Support for the view that it was Shakespeare who borrowed from Marston, as he may well have done earlier, taking ideas for *Hamlet* from *Antonio's Revenge*,[1] may come from the play's links with the Gunpowder Plot of November 1605 and its aftermath, which would make the date of composition after May 1606, when the last of those tried in connection with the Plot, Father Henry Garnet, was executed. Much has been made of *Macbeth* as a 'Gunpowder play',[2] adducing the Porter's scene and Macduff's Wife's dialogue with her son about the traitors who swear and lie and must be hanged. Among the imaginary crew of damned souls whom the Porter welcomes mockingly through his 'Hell Gate' is 'a farmer that hanged himself on th'expectation of plenty', which could be a topical reference to Father Garnet, the mastermind of the plot, who used the name Farmer as an alias (Wills, 96). After the farmer, the Porter welcomes another character: 'Faith, here's an

---

1   The relative dating of these two plays is still open to question. Thorndike first put forward the view that *Antonio's Revenge* precedes *Hamlet* (200–1). Chambers (*ES*, 3.429–30) also dates the Antonio plays early. But Jenkins, who examines the case thoroughly (8–10), believes Marston to have been the borrower. Another play once considered as a possible source for *Macbeth* but almost certainly earlier is Middleton's *The Puritan Widow* (entered in the Stationers' Register 6 August 1607). In this play Sir Godfrey promises a banquet to celebrate the restoration of his stolen chain, saying that 'instead of a jester, we'll ha' the ghost i'th' white sheet sit at upper end o'th' table' (4.2.353–5). While this is suggestive of *Macbeth* 3.4, Holdsworth (*Macbeth*) argues that Middleton is referring back to his own earlier works. The latest editor of *The Puritan Widow*, Donna B. Hamilton, supports a date of composition in 1606, but probably before 30 July, the last date when performances by Paul's Boys, who acted this play, were recorded (Taylor & Lavagnino, *Textual Culture*, 359).

2   Especially by Wills, whose term this is (9).

5   *The Gunpowder Plot Conspirators* (*c.* 1605), by Crispijn de Passe the
     Elder (*c.* 1565–1637)

equivocator that could swear in both the scales against either
scale, who committed treason enough for God's sake, yet could
not equivocate to heaven' (2.3.8–11). The term 'equivocation'
and its cognates were not new in 1606, but the Porter's use of
them seems conspicuous in the context. He is not a learned
man, nor one who generally uses a Latinate vocabulary; on the
surface, he seems to allude to the popular interpretation of this
idea as prevarication or two-faced behaviour, and mocks it
again in describing how drink 'may be said to be an equivocator
with lechery'. But after Garnet's trial and execution this term
gained a new significance. Garnet had written a *Treatise of
Equivocation* (*c.* 1598) in which he defended the doctrine of
mental reservation, by which a Roman Catholic under inter-
rogation was permitted to withhold a part of a truth which
might incriminate him, or to speak in ambiguous terms, as
long as he acknowledged the whole of the truth in his heart.[1]
On the scaffold, Garnet was urged not to equivocate with his
dying breath. He said, according to the official account of the

---

1   The treatise, edited by David Jardine, was first published in 1851.

proceedings, 'It is no time now to equivocate: How it was lawfull, and when, he had showed his mind elsewhere'.[1] In this context, Macbeth's use of the word in his expression of self-doubt towards the end of the play – 'I pull in resolution, and begin / To doubt th'equivocation of the fiend, / That lies like truth' (5.5.41–3) – sounds pointed.[2] The theme of double-speak and linguistic ambiguity pervades the whole play.

It has often been assumed – and even, particularly in the wake of Henry N. Paul's book *The Royal Play of Macbeth*, stated as a fact[3] – that the play had its first performance during the state visit in July and August of James's brother-in-law, King Christian of Denmark, and that it was commissioned for the occasion. No clear evidence supports this view, which is largely based on the conjecture that the play was written as a compliment to the King.[4] True, the King's Men did perform at Greenwich in July and at Hampton Court on 7 August, but what plays they performed are not recorded. Braunmuller (8) points out that the King's Men received only the usual payment of £10 per play, and comments that more might have been expected for a royal performance of *Macbeth*, which 'would probably have required some unusual costumes, props, and machinery'. *Macbeth* was not named among the plays performed at court during the winter season of 1606/7, when *King Lear* was staged

---

1 *A True and Perfect Relation of the Whole proceedings against the late most barbarous Traitors, Garnet a Jesuite, and his Confederats* (1606), as quoted in Paul, 243.

2 It is interesting to compare the use of 'equivocation' in a reference to the fate of Father Garnet in a letter of 2 May 1606 written by Dudley Carleton to John Chamberlain: '[Garnet] hath been since often visited and examined by the attorney, who find him shifting and faltering in all his answers, and it is looked he will equivocate at the gallows, but he will be hanged without equivocation' (*Dudley Carleton to John Chamberlain 1603–1624: Jacobean Letters*, ed. Maurice Lee, Jr (1972), 80–1. See also Rogers, 'Garnet'.

3 E.g. by Mullaney, *Stage*, 122, and Orgel, 143–54.

4 Others making this assumption include Kernan, Greenblatt and Goldberg. Orgel even asserts that the play was 'prepared for a single, special occasion' with the King in the audience (144).

on 26 December. As no performance date can be assigned to *The Knight of the Burning Pestle* and *Lingua* may never have been performed, they cannot help to determine exactly when the play was first staged, though it was presumably before February 1607. The only direct early reference to an actual performance is Simon Forman's of 1611.

References to the Macbeth story in two contemporaneous works of British history do not necessarily clarify the question of dating. In 1606 William Warner published *A Continuance of Albion's England*, adding three new books, 14–16, to his long poem *Albion's England*, originally published in 1586.[1] In Book 15, ch. 94, Warner traces King James's Stuart ancestry from Fleance's brief love affair with the daughter of King Gruffyth of Wales, which produced a son. References to Macbeth as a treacherous usurper, tormented by his guilty conscience and driven 'to proceede in blood' in a desperate attempt to find safety, may suggest that Warner had seen Shakespeare's play, and Braunmuller (6, 10) considers that his additions to his poem may contain echoes of it, though this is by no means certain. Paul (404) argues that the wording of the dedication of the *Continuance* to Sir Edward Coke demonstrates publication between 30 June 1606 and 25 March 1607. Paul also suggests (406–7) that William Camden's additions to *Britannia*, in the new version published in 1607, which mention Macbeth's failed attempt to thwart the Witches' prophecy that Banquo's issue would rule Scotland (or Lochabria, as he calls it), constitute a reference to *Macbeth*; but they may simply capitalize on current interest in the King's ancestry.

Macbeth *in its historical moment*

The view that *Macbeth* was written to please the King, whose recent accession to the throne of England had been rapidly

---

1   Bullough (7.335–6) prints a passage from this as a possible source for *King Lear*.

followed by his taking over the patronage of Shakespeare's company, hitherto the Lord Chamberlain's Men, has enjoyed long – and often vehement – support.[1] Its first expression was by Lewis Theobald in 1733, who believed that Shakespeare 'inserted Compliments . . . upon his Royal Master' relating to the union of the thrones of England and Scotland and to James's touching for the King's Evil. While Shakespeare's choice of an episode from Scottish history featuring the character of Banquo whom James believed to be his ancestor can hardly be accidental,[2] it can also be argued that the play is at the least ambivalent in its handling of topics close to the King's heart; and recent work on its Scottish context, particularly in relation to the King's vision of the Union, suggests that complex issues are involved. The rise of Scottish nationalism in the 1990s and 2000s may well have helped to focus attention on them.[3] It is no longer the case that 'Scotland remains relatively hidden from view' in *Macbeth* criticism, as claimed by the editors of a recent collection of essays entitled *Shakespeare and Scotland* (Maley & Murphy, 8). The early seventeenth century has been termed a time of transformation in the life of the nation, and *Macbeth* was written at 'a critical juncture in the development of the unification project' (Alker & Nelson, 380).

There had been a number of plays featuring Scottish characters, and some specifically about Scottish history, before *Macbeth*. Some, tantalizingly, are known only by name: 'a tragedie of

---

1 Paul, whose book was highly influential in promoting this view, concludes it with reference to a letter (sadly lost) supposedly written by King James to Shakespeare which he thinks 'not at all unlikely' to have expressed the King's satisfaction with the play. His evidence is the statement of the printer Bernard Lintott in his 1709 edition of Shakespeare's poems that such a letter did exist and was once owned by Davenant (414).

2 See pp. 37–8, 90.

3 Recent work drawing attention to Scottish themes in Shakespeare includes Marshall, McEachern, Maley & Murphy, Hopkins, Floyd-Wilson, Alker & Nelson, Baldo and Kerrigan.

the King of Scottes', performed in 1567 by the Children of the Queen's Chapel, *The Scots Tragedy* (or *Robert II, King of Scots*) (1599) by Ben Jonson, Henry Chettle, Thomas Dekker and others, *Malcolm King of Scots* (1602), by Charles Massey,[1] and the notorious *Tragedy of Gowrie*, put on by the King's Men in 1604 and evidently suppressed.[2] The last is of particular interest in that it dramatized recent history, and may have represented the King onstage. The so-called Gowrie Plot took place in 1600 and was described in a pamphlet called *Gowries Conspiracy*, issued a few weeks later, as an assassination attempt on the King (whether or not it did in fact take this form).[3] The Earl of Gowrie and his brother, members of a family with a history of hostility towards James and the house of Stuart, died in an armed struggle with the King's followers. Plays called *The Scots Tragedy* and *Malcolm King of Scots* might well have had some bearing on the context of *Macbeth*. James Shapiro speculates that a play about Robert II, the first Stuart king and an ancestor of James, might have touched on the question of succession, an important matter in 1599 when anxieties about the prospect of a foreign successor to Queen Elizabeth, and dislike of the Scots, were rife in England. Bullough suggests that *Malcolm King of Scots* was 'probably about Malcolm III and his Queen Margaret, an English princess' and that 'it may have included Macbeth and Edward the Confessor' (Bullough, 7.428).[4] Several extant plays predating *Macbeth* included unattractive, ludicrous and even villainous Scottish characters: *The Pinner of Wakefield* (*c.* 1587),

---

1 See Foakes & Rickert, 199, 200, for *Malcolm King of Scots*.

2 Chambers, *ES*, 1.328. See also Knutson's account (126–7).

3 Stewart gives an account of the event and its aftermath in *Cradle*, 150–6. Kozikowskj's argument for the pamphlet as a major source for *Macbeth* is unsupportable ('The Gowrie conspiracy against James VI: a new source for Shakespeare's *Macbeth*', *SSt*, 13 (1950), 197–212).

4 Henslowe records lending the sum of 30 shillings for 'a sewt of motley for the scotchman' in this play (Foakes & Rickert, 200).

Robert Greene's *James IV* (*c.* 1591), George Peele's *Edward I* (*c.* 1590) and *Edward III* (1593/4?) in which Shakespeare is believed to have collaborated.

Before James came to the English throne, Shakespeare had included Scottish characters in *Edward III* (if he was indeed a co-author), *1 Henry IV* and *Henry V*. In *Edward III*, the Scottish King David (whose actions onstage are unhistorical additions to the plot or conflations of material from the chronicles) embodies 'the traitorous Scot' (1.1.155) taking advantage of Edward's military withdrawal to invade the border towns in breach of his league with England. He besieges in her castle the Countess of Salisbury, whose view of him and his countrymen as uncouth and barely civilized reflects the contemporary English stereotype of the Scots. She derides the 'broad untuned oaths' with which he attempts to woo her, and the 'rough insulting barbarism' of his behaviour. David, shown as both venal and boastful, is also a coward. His last appearance in the play is at Calais as the silent captive of the squire John Copland; the Scots no longer pose any threat to England here. In the *Henry* plays the disunited kingdom much resembles the condition of Scotland in James's time, and the need of the English to bring their northern neighbours under control reflects problems that James confronted in his efforts to bring together the two countries whose thrones he held after 1603. *1 Henry IV* begins with news of conflict on the borders of England, and rebellions against the King by the Welsh as well as the Scots. At the end, the rebel forces, which by now include the Percy faction, are defeated. When rebellion can be contained, it is possible to represent individual rebels in a good light. In this play, the Scots are led by Douglas, 'that ever-valiant and approved Scot' (1.1.54). Although intent on killing the King at Shrewsbury, Douglas is nonetheless delivered from captivity 'ransomless and free' (5.5.28) and admired on all sides for his valour. But in *Henry V* (1599) there is no such 'noble Scot', and in this play Scotland is initially characterized as England's 'giddy neighbour' (1.2.145), a 'weasel' ready to suck the 'princely eggs' of the 'eagle' England (169–71) if the nest is left unguarded. The general view of the Scots is similar to that in *Edward III*, which was reprinted in 1599 (with the teasing misprint of 'King of Sots' for 'Scots' at 5.1.64).[1] This potential for hostility from the Scots is never realized in *Henry V*, and gets subsumed into what has been called the 'proto-Britishness' (Rhodes, 48) of the play. Once the King has eliminated the internal threat to his country posed by the three home-grown traitors in the pay of France, the stress is rather on the unity of the component parts of the kingdom. The short scene in the Folio text (3.2.75–142) which brings together Fluellen from Wales, Macmorris from Ireland and the interestingly named Jamy from Scotland, all speaking broad dialect, with the English Captain Gower, seems to have no other purpose than to demonstrate how people from the wilder outposts of the British Isles come together to fight with the English against their common foe, the French. The use of regional dialect helps to define the Welsh and Irish captains as comic characters, but there are distinctions; Fluellen calls Macmorris an ass, but Jamy the Scot is 'a marvellous falorous gentleman . . . of great expedition and knowledge in th'anchient wars' (3.2.77–9). However, Jamy and Macmorris are absent from the quarto published in 1600, either because they were cut to avoid giving offence to James as Elizabeth's likely successor, or because they are additions later in date than the quarto. In earlier plays Shakespeare may have been less concerned about giving offence, with Dromio

1 Melchiori in his edition of *Edward III* conjectures that it was a performance of this play which caused offence to King James and the Scots in 1598. He quotes a letter of 15 April 1598 from George Nicolson, Queen Elizabeth's agent in Edinburgh, to Lord Burghley in London: 'It is regrated [regretted] to me in quiet sort that the comedians of London should in their play scorn the King and people of this land and wished that it may be speedily amended and stayed, lest the worst sort getting understanding thereof should stir the King and country to anger thereat' (12).

of Syracuse's joke about the barrenness of Scotland in *The Comedy of Errors* (3.2.119–21) and Portia's about antagonism between the English and the Scots in *The Merchant of Venice* (1.2.72–6).[1]

Although James's accession was accompanied by much official propaganda promoting him as a prince of peace – *rex pacificus* – responsible for '*The Ioiefull and Blessed Reuniting the two mighty & famous kingdomes, England & Scotland into their ancient name of great Britaine*', to quote the title of a celebratory poem of 1605 (Kinney, *Lies*, 88), this by no means mitigated popular attitudes of hostility towards Scotland and the Scots, which, despite censorship, found regular expression on the London stage. *Eastward Ho* (1605), by Jonson, George Chapman and Marston, *The Isle of Gulls* (1606), by John Day, *The Fleire* (1605/6), by Edward Sharpham, and *Michaelmas Term* (1605/6), by Thomas Middleton, all included anti-Scots gibes, some, like the references in *The Isle of Gulls* to Duke Basilius's fondness for hunting and his lavish generosity to unworthy favourites, aimed at the King,[2] others directed more broadly at the Scots and indicative of English anxieties about the relationship between the two peoples. James's Scottishness itself became an object of satire. As Chambers says, 'The uncouth speech of the Sovereign, his intemperance, his gusts of passion, his inordinate devotion to the chase, were caricatured with what appears incredible audacity, before audiences of his new subjects' (*ES*, 1.325). The personal unpopularity of the King, who was regarded by his English subjects as a foreign prince, and the intense English dislike of the Scots, were, at the time when *Macbeth* was written, not just 'an irritant . . . but a

---

1   Shakespeare did not deal overtly with Scottish topics in plays before *Macbeth*, but it has been argued that Scottish themes are present in *Hamlet* and *King Lear*, both plays written around the critical time just before and just after James's accession, involving questions of succession and right rule. On *Hamlet* see Hadfield (100) and on *King Lear* see Rhodes (50).

2   Discussed in Clare, 125–6.

significant political reality' (Wormald, 163),[1] to the extent that they have been regarded as motives for the Gunpowder plotters, Roman Catholics who hoped to return England to their faith. Jenny Wormald also argues that they disliked James's cherished project for the union of the two kingdoms, and hoped to draw on the equal dislike of this by the Protestant English to support their endeavour. Their failure made no change in popular attitudes either to the Scots or to the King's plan for the Union. The proposals for a Union bill, which James had been pushing for since his first parliament in 1604, were still decisively rejected by Parliament in May 1607.[2] Hence Shakespeare's Scottish play came into being at a critical time for Anglo-Scottish relations in general and for the fate of the King's unification policy in particular.

The material of Macbeth

Many writers assume that Shakespeare based his play on a considerable knowledge of Scottish history and also an interest in the politics of its historiography.[3] David Norbrook, for instance, believes that Shakespeare was familiar enough with the political controversies informing the histories of Scotland by Hector Boece and George Buchanan, as well as the better-known material in Holinshed, and thus capable of a 'drastic revision' of the political viewpoint of the play's sources (Norbrook, 78–116). Stewart Gillespie allows that Shakespeare may have made 'some sort of effort to research the subject', including reading Buchanan as well as Holinshed (Gillespie, 'Buchanan',

1 Kurland's well-documented article demonstrates that James's succession was not achieved without a struggle, and makes a good case for reading *Macbeth* against a background of 'uncertainty and fear surrounding the succession issue' (286).

2 See the account of this, and of the anti-Scots feeling expressed in Parliament between 1604 and 1607, in Stewart (*Cradle*, 209–16).

3 Clark, *Murder*, is perhaps the most extreme of these, assuming that Shakespeare knew material in manuscript form as well as various pieces of legislation by the Scottish Parliament.

73). Hence he would have been aware, for instance, of the view that in some circumstances regicide might be a politically preferable alternative to rule by a tyrannous but legitimate monarch (and that a monarch could be both these things); also that primogeniture was not regarded by all as the ideal model of succession. Though we cannot be certain of the extent of Shakespeare's reading, he had already shown interest both in Scotland and in the politics of the succession. It is also important that what has been termed 'the Macbeth myth', a multi-faceted story/legend built around the historical Macbeth, created from the eleventh century onwards out of a variety of material, historical and pseudo-historical, some of it in verse, was flexible enough to permit of its 'being tailored to convey contemporary political messages' of diverse kinds (Aitchison, 116).

The long history of the Macbeth story has been traced by Nick Aitchison in *Macbeth: Man and Myth*, from the poetic traditions beginning in the time of the historical Macbeth, who reigned 1040–57 and, it appears, commissioned at least one verse account of his own reign, up to the chronicles of Holinshed in the second edition of 1587. Many elements in this story lend it the character of a myth, and the earlier works owe as much to folklore as to history. Accounts of Macbeth's reign and his killing of Duncan appear in a series of chronicle histories, including the *Chronica Gentis Scotorum* (*c*. 1363), by John of Fordun, the *Orygynale Cronykil of Scotland* (*c*. 1406), by Andrew of Wyntoun, the *Historia Majoris Britanniae* (1521), by John Mair (or Major), the *Scotorum Historiae* (1526), by Hector Boece, and its English version by John Bellenden, *Croniklis of the Scots* (1536), William Stewart's *Buik of the Croniklis of Scotland* (completed *c*. 1535), a verse translation of Boece, John Leslie's *De Origine, Moribus et Rebus Gestis Scotorum* (1578) and George Buchanan's *Rerum Scoticarum Historiae* (1582). Since we know that Shakespeare used Holinshed as his major source, and Holinshed's work, building particularly on Boece and Bellenden, subsumed much of the extensive earlier tradition, it is not necessary here to trace the development of this story in detail. Shakespeare used many elements from this material but discarded others. His choices are discussed in '*Macbeth* and its sources' (see pp. 82–97).

The realization of Scotland in Macbeth

The accession of James ensured topicality for a Scottish play. But this is not to say that Shakespeare necessarily presented his subject so as to promote any viewpoint or put forward a political message in alignment with the views and policies of the King. Indeed, the capability of Shakespeare's plays 'to offer (even affirm) simultaneously, without contradiction, contradictory themes, messages and ideological stances' (Bruster, 3) can be regarded as an essential feature of his dramaturgy.

By contrast with his other writing about Scotland, it is clear that in *Macbeth* Shakespeare takes pains to avoid any stereotyped anti-Scottish sentiments. The identity of Scotland is established by quite other means. There is no obtrusive local colour. Perhaps the heath where the Sisters plan to meet Macbeth, along with the reference to bad weather, might have suggested Scotland, and it may appear as an appropriately wild and inhospitable location for Macbeth and Banquo to traverse on their way to Forres, but otherwise Shakespeare relies at the beginning of his play on names of people and geographical references to establish the location of the action. In 1.2 this is indicated by reference to the participants in the rebellions against King Duncan – the 'kerns and galloglasses' from the Hebrides who fight on the side of the rebel Macdonald and the forces of Sweno, King of Norway, supported by another rebel, the Thane of Cawdor, who have been defeated in eastern Scotland by Macbeth. No more is heard of Macdonald or his army, but in the vivid account given by the '*bleeding* Captain', they seem to represent a Gaelic enemy; and in seventeenth-century England the Macdonald clan was still regarded as a force to be contended with (Highley, 61). In 1.3 Banquo's first line (39) is the question, 'How far is't called to Forres?' The place-name reinforces the location, and perhaps also the unusual form of expression.[1] One or two other possible Scottish locutions have been noticed in the text, such as 'loon' for rogue (5.3.11), but overall Shakespeare avoids linguistic indications of Scottish identity, such as the risible Scottish accents and expressions that were deliberately used in comedies like *James IV* and *Eastward Ho*. We cannot know how the play would have sounded onstage. How much the costumes would have indicated regional dress is also hard to assess. Clan tartans did not appear until the eighteenth century.[2] Malcolm's remark on the appearance of Ross in 4.3, that he is 'My countryman, but yet I know him not' (4.3.160), and his wish that Ross 'remove / The means that makes us strangers' (162–3) might suggest that Ross is disguised for safety, yet wears something identifying him as Scottish.[3]

The Scotland of the play is both a primitive, pre-modern world and also a place where notions of kingship and power reflect recognizably Jacobean concerns. The names in the second scene establish a sense of geographical remoteness, at least for a London audience, and the nature of the action suggests a violent and turbulent kingdom. An armed rebellion, supported by treacherous Scottish thanes, is in progress, with assaults from both east and west. It is eventually subdued, not by the King himself, who acts only as an observer, but by his generals,

1 Braunmuller notes this as 'a Scotticism'.
2 'Stage-Scottishness' in general did not appear till the eighteenth century. Rogers, whose term this is, associates it with the mid-century reformulation of the national identities of the two countries (Rogers, 'Scottish', 104–13). Macklin's 'Old Caledonian' production of *Macbeth* (1773) was the first to use Highland dress, including tartan, to set the play in Scotland in the middle ages. See p. 121.
3 Braunmuller, 260, quotes a passage from John Taylor, *The Penyles Pilgrimage* (1618), which makes it clear that a distinctive Highland costume for men was already known at the time, including 'a plead about their shoulders, which is a mantle of divers colours . . . [and] blue flat caps on their heads' (John Taylor, *Works* (1630), 135).

whose relish for 'bloody execution' and readiness to deal in 'reeking wounds' is stressed. Many of the English saw the Scots as an inherently violent people. In 1607 Sir Christopher Piggott outraged the King in an attack on the Scots during a series of parliamentary debates on the union of the kingdoms, when he declared what was generally believed, that the Scots 'have not suffered above two kings to die in their beds, these two hundred years'.[1] In the play Scotland is quickly established as a wild and dangerous place, from which the King's sons must flee to the safety of England and Ireland after his murder. Some scholars have seen the play's setting in terms of a border land, both geographically, since it evokes the untamed frontier territory which James strove by violent means to pacify,[2] and more generally, in relation to boundaries such as those between a Christian present and a part-pagan past.

While Duncan is a Christian king, and Macbeth is tormented by the guilt of a Christian conscience, there are significant traces of a warrior ethic which dates from the pre-Christian era. The Lady fears that her husband is 'too full o'th' milk of human kindness, / To catch the nearest way' to the throne (1.5.17–18). Duncan in Holinshed (and all the Scottish chronicle histories of the period) is similarly incapacitated; he has 'too much of clemencie' to rule effectively, and the rebellious Makdowald (Shakespeare's Macdonald) calls him a 'faint-hearted milksop, more meet to governe a sort of idle moonks in some cloister, than to have the rule of such valiant and hardie men of warre as the Scots were' (Bullough, 7.488, 489). Macbeth, by contrast, is 'somewhat cruell of nature' but also valiant, and manages to overthrow Makdowald and his forces, defeat Sueno's troops and a subsequent Danish invasion, and restore peace to Scotland.

1 Quoted by Braunmuller, 13. The incident is recorded in the *Journal of the House of Commons*, 1.333–5.
2 See George MacDonald Fraser, *The Steel Bonnets: The Story of the Anglo-Scottish Border Reivers* (1971), for a lively history of the feuding border families up to the reign of James.

6   *Pity* (*c.* 1795), by William Blake (1757–1827); for discussion of Blake's
use of *Macbeth*, see Bate (125–6)

The contrast between a Christian Duncan and a part-pagan
Macbeth is not made explicitly by Shakespeare, but Macbeth's
credentials as a warrior of heroic cast are established early in
the play. His responses to the murders of Duncan and Banquo
show him torn between two different ethical systems. After the
death of Duncan, he is conscious of his desperate need for
spiritual atonement and perturbed by his inability to pronounce
the word 'Amen'. But after the appearance of Banquo's blood-
stained ghost, he responds quite differently. His thought is now
to look back, to regret the passing of a time when killing had
no repercussions, 'th' olden time, / Ere humane statute purged
the gentle weal', a time when, if 'the brains were out, the man
would die, / And there an end' (3.4.73–4, 77–8). David Garrick
gave Macbeth a dying speech, in which he saw himself as
damned; but in Shakespeare's play Macbeth dies as a warrior in

31

battle, dismissing the option of suicide. His momentary pang of conscience when confronted with Macduff – 'But get thee back, my soul is too much charged / With blood of thine already' (5.8.5–6) – is quickly overcome by horror at the thought of dishonourable surrender to 'young' Malcolm.

The warrior ethic is not systematically developed, but England and Scotland are to an extent contrasted in terms of a country strengthened and civilized by Christianity and one weakened by primitivism and violence. The contrast comes into force in 4.3, where Malcolm and Macduff discuss how to bring aid to their 'downfall birthdom'. Scotland is no longer their 'mother' but instead 'our grave': 'The deadman's knell / Is there scarce asked for who, and good men's lives / Expire before the flowers in their caps, / Dying or ere they sicken' (4.3.166, 170–3), an expression which recalls accounts of the plague of 1603. Scotland is also like a creature being slowly tormented to death: 'It weeps, it bleeds, and each new day a gash / Is added to her wounds' (40–1). It is a 'sickly weal' (5.2.27), and the cure must come through the assistance of 'gracious England' (a phrase repeated twice), which is offering 'goodly thousands' of troops to Malcolm to launch an attack on his homeland. This is in no sense a hostile intervention: Scotland welcomes Malcolm as its saviour.[1] England's image is Christianized through the account of 'the most pious Edward' (3.6.27) and his 'miraculous' ability to heal the sick with his royal touch, a form of virtuous magic in contrast with the Sisters' malevolent powers, conferred on him by his status. England is a country empowered by its monarchy. King Edward has received Malcolm at his court, and the large army he provides for Malcolm's aid brings life to a diseased and dying Scotland. In the words of Menteith, even the 'mortified [insensible or dead] man' would come to life

---

1   Attackers of their own country are frequent in Shakespeare, especially in plays close in time to *Macbeth*; Cordelia, Caesar and Antony, Timon, Coriolanus and Posthumus all fall into this category, which Richard Proudfoot observes (private communication) is a notable motif in later Shakespeare.

when excited by the 'dear causes' (5.2.3–5) of Malcolm and Macduff. Malcolm, the man who enlists English support, is historically half-English on the side of his mother, characterized as an ultra-saintly woman who 'Oft'ner upon her knees than on her feet, / Died every day she lived' (4.3.110–11). Siward, the Earl of Northumberland, 'An older and a better soldier, none / That Christendom gives out' (4.3.192–3), is Malcolm's uncle.[1] Malcolm's gesture at the end of the play in conferring the English title of Earl on the Scottish thanes who have supported him seems clearly to suggest the idea of the union of the kingdoms.

Relations between Scotland and England become significant in the latter part of the play. Scotland is at its lowest ebb in Act 4, when Malcolm and Macduff have fled to England while helpless women and children, like Macduff's wife and her family, are left behind to be slaughtered. At the end of 4.3 Malcolm and Macduff prepare to return to their country, with reinforcements lent by England. In 5.2, the Scottish thanes await a combined army, 'The English power . . . led on by Malcolm, / His uncle Siward and the good Macduff' (5.2.1–2). The importance of the English element in the army is highlighted by the prominence given to Siward and his self-sacrificing son. Malcolm as heir to the throne of Scotland cannot claim his inheritance without English aid. His national identity as part-English seems to make him a figure for the Union, apparently confirmed by his action at the end of the play in converting the Scottish thanes to earls, 'the first that ever Scotland / In such an honour named' (5.9.29–30). Yet there is debate as to how far the play can be seen as pro-Union, and hence in line with James's policies, as the once-favoured view of *Macbeth* as a 'royal' play would seem to suggest. Bullough, who believes the play to be written

---

1 Historically Siward was probably Danish in origin, and he may have been Malcolm's grandfather rather than uncle. But in the play he is twice called 'uncle' (5.2.2, 5.6.2), and leads the English army.

33

with 'an eye on court performance' (7.427), sees in it 'a composite picture of the darkest side of Scottish medieval history as viewed from the happy present in James's reign of unity and concord' (7.448). But Malcolm can also be seen in a more ambivalent light; as the 'embryonic Anglo-Scot' (Alker & Nelson, 389) his politics may not have appealed to English audiences suspicious of their northern neighbours, and his ability to seem what he is not, as demonstrated by his testing of Macduff in 4.3, might hint at a potential for duplicity, although this is not a reading accepted by everyone.[1] His gesture in giving away titles may recall his father's act of naming him Prince of Cumberland, in which case, Kinney suggests, 'The play has come full circle; Malcolm seems to have learnt nothing' (Kinney, 'Scottish', 51). He adds: 'This is surely meant to be the case in Holinshed, where in time Donalbain will attack his brother and seize the throne and new cycles of bloodshed and regicide will take over the annals of Scottish history once again'.[2]

Kinney and others see in the play not an endorsement of James's unionist policies through the figure of an emollient Malcolm, but warnings, to a degree coded, for the new regime and particularly the English, of the dangers of 'imperialist and absolutist thought' (Kinney, 'Scottish', 39), and of 'the hazards of joining with a nation with Scotland's violent history' (Baldo,

1 Critics inclined to stress Malcolm's potential for duplicity include Floyd-Wilson, Lemon (especially 95–100), and especially Riebling. Mullaney (*Stage*, 126) considers that the 'mask of misrule' whch Malcolm dons to test Macduff 'leaves a lasting impression' on his face. Braunmuller is more neutral on this point but allows that Malcolm may appear ambiguous in 4.3, and cites a performance of the role by Ian Richardson in 1967 which 'offered an unconventional Malcolm with an inkling of evil deep inside' (92, fn. 1, quoting Leiter, 378). Leggatt (94) notes that in the RSC production of 2004 (dir. Dominic Cooke), 'Malcolm in the England scene was not a noble prince waiting for his country's call but a dishevelled figure who seemed to have spent his exile drinking in a garret'.

2 The ending of Polanski's film, where Donalbain is seen riding in search of the Sisters' cave, follows this line.

91), of the potentially disastrous consequences of obliterating national boundaries under the rule of a Scottish king (Hopkins, 80). The two nations, English and Scots, are contrastingly characterized, and it is hard not to feel that the play registers differences between them at the same time as trying to find a conclusion that will submerge them.[1]

Genealogy and succession

Tied in to the tensions that the play registers about the concept of union is its handling of the question of royal succession. In medieval Scotland the monarchy had been elective and largely governed according to the process of tanistry, whereby royal successors were named from a collateral rather than a direct branch of the family, kingship passing not from father to son but from brother to brother, uncle to nephew or cousin to cousin. During the period of Duncan's reign this system was being replaced by succession according to the early modern European dynastic norm, namely primogeniture. James believed strongly in the divine right of kings and in succession by primogeniture, and his views leave their mark on the play. Divine kingship is assumed at several points: in Macduff's description of the body of Duncan as 'the Lord's anointed temple' (2.3.68) and Macbeth's of 'His silver skin laced with his golden blood' (113), and in the English Doctor's account of the way that King Edward's miraculous touch – 'Such sanctity hath heaven given his hand' (4.3.144) – will be transmitted 'To the succeeding royalty'. But the shadow of the older system of elective monarchy lingers. When Duncan gathers his men around him to announce the conferring of a title on his elder son, his action has more than one layer of meaning. He is creating Malcolm Prince of

---

1 Kerrigan implies almost a perversity of intent here, in that Shakespeare dramatizes material 'that is calculated to explore the heterogeneity of the archipelago at the very moment (1605–6) when James VI and I was trying to go beyond regal union and develop an integrated British state' (92).

Cumberland, the title given to the heir apparent, but he is also alerting Macbeth and those 'whose places are the nearest' that he may be preparing for a dynastic succession. This is a big moment; Duncan does not honour his son alone, but confers titles more generally (as James did after his accession to the throne of England): 'signs of nobleness, like stars, shall shine / On all deservers' (1.4.41–2). Macbeth, who had been encouraged to regard the conferring of the title of Thane of Cawdor as 'an earnest of a greater honour' (1.3.105), is taken by surprise: 'The Prince of Cumberland: that is a step / On which I must fall down, or else o'er-leap, / For in my way it lies' (1.4.48–50). In Holinshed's account of the incident Macbeth's reaction is due to causes other than disappointment at the apparent thwarting of the Witches' prophecy.

> Mackbeth [was] sore troubled herewith, for that he saw by this means his hope sore hindered (where, by the old lawes of the realme, the ordinance was, that if he that should succeed were not of able age to take the charge upon himselfe, he that was next of bloud unto him should be admitted) he began to take counsel how he might usurpe the kingdome by force, having a just quarell so to doo (as he tooke the matter) for that Duncane did what in him lay to defraud him of all maner of title and claime, which he might in time to come, pretend unto the crowne.[1]

Shakespeare's Malcolm is not, as in Holinshed, a minor, and Macbeth does not then proceed to kill Duncan in a conspiracy with 'his trustie friends, amongst whome Banquho was the chiefest'. But an audience aware of the current debates around the subject of monarchical systems, and the objections to absolutism made by Scottish historians such as John Mair, Boece and Buchanan, might be conscious of some mystification

---

1 Holinshed, *Scotland*, 171, in Bullough, 7.496.

in the play's ideology.[1] Once Macbeth has disposed of Duncan and his sons have fled the country, Macbeth's succession to the crown appears to be accepted as the obvious next step by most of the nobles. At this point in the play no voice is raised in support of Malcolm's claim. Macbeth disables himself as an acceptable king through his descent into tyranny, which is in part the result of his insecure, and ideologically contradictory, position as king; as Claire McEachern puts it, 'he arrives at the throne by objecting to patrilineal succession, but then wishes to embrace it' (105). It is the parts of the Sisters' prophecies relating to succession that cause him the greatest agony; the thought that Banquo is destined to become the 'father to a line of kings' while his own 'barren sceptre' will be 'wrenched with an unlineal hand, / No son of mine succeeding' (3.1.59, 61–3) cuts him to the heart. The sight of this spectral line stretching out 'to th' crack of doom' (4.1.116) drives him on to the worst excesses of tyranny.

This stress on lineal descent as key to the future history of Scotland takes over the latter part of the play. Indeed, this may have been a theme newly available for dramatization now that a king with two apparently thriving sons had succeeded to the throne so long occupied by a childless woman, a situation unprecedented in the experience of most English men and women at this time.[2] The show of kings includes some 'That twofold balls and treble sceptres carry' (4.1.120), almost certainly referring to rulers of England who also have dominion over Scotland, like James, and the King's concern with his own genealogical descent seems to inform this scene. James believed

---

1 Norbrook, in his seminal article '*Macbeth* and the politics of historiography', illuminates the ideological problems that faced Shakespeare in dramatizing the story of Macbeth.

2 I owe this suggestion to Richard Proudfoot (private communication). Grace Tiffany, in 'Macbeth, paternity, and the anglicization of James I', *SSt*, 23.2 (1996), argues that Shakespeare makes childlessness in the play 'a mark of demonic resistance', in order to capitalize on the succession anxiety created by Elizabeth and to compliment the new king as the father of heirs (149).

himself descended from Banquo, Thane of Lochaber, a character invented by Boece in his *Scotorum Historiae* as 'the beginner of the Stewarts in this realm, from whom our King now present [James V, grandfather to James VI and I] by long and ancient lineage is descended'.[1]

While the histories of Scotland from Boece up to Holinshed describe Banquo as participating with Macbeth in the killing of Duncan, Shakespeare could not depict the King's ancestor in this way. Yet many see his Banquo as 'a shadowy and ambiguous figure' (Norbrook, 94), not indifferent to what the Sisters have to offer him or free of personal ambition. Although after Fleance's escape from his father's murderers he is never referred to again,[2] the principle of patrilineal descent is reaffirmed with Malcolm's accession at the end of the play. There are many and diverse elements which inform the Scottish background to the play, and they do not combine in a way that endorses any clear political position. The play deals in matters topical in the new regime, yet there are, as Norbrook puts it, 'subtextual pressures' (101), vestiges of worldviews and ideologies that run counter to prevailing royalist orthodoxies, and these disrupt any easy resolution.

LANGUAGE IN *MACBETH*

In all his plays Shakespeare was concerned to make his dramatic language, in the words of Booth, 'exciting to listening minds',[3] to create verbal textures that activate the imagination and

---

1 Quoted in Aitchison, 117. A family tree illustrating this descent was published in John Leslie's *De Origine, Moribus, et Rebus Gestis Scotorum* (1578) (see Fig. 8). According to Paul, 152, Banquo's lack of historicity was first asserted by Richard Hay, *An Essay on the Origin of the Royal Family of the Stewarts* (1722).

2 He does not appear to be included in the '*show of eight kings*' in 4.1. These are usually reckoned to be Robert II, Robert III, James I, James II, James III, James IV, James V and James VI and I, excluding Mary, Queen of Scots.

3 Booth, 'Shakespeare's', 5.

engage the intellect through the auditory medium. The language of *Macbeth* provides this linguistic excitement to an extra-ordinary degree, sometimes displaying features that have met with critical disapproval, such as the bombast to which John Dryden drew attention in one of the first critical comments on the play.[1] Yet it is compact language, often complex and cryptic, but also memorable. The play contains a host of phrases and expressions that are alive in the popular imagination: 'the seeds of time', 'the milk of human kindness', 'golden opinions', 'light thickens', 'all our yesterdays', 'vaulting ambition', 'the wine of life', 'fatal vision', 'night's black agents', 'all my pretty ones', 'she should have died hereafter', 'out damned spot', 'Who would have thought the old man to have had so much blood in him?'. And so on.[2] It is a play that testifies to the intense interest in the English language during the period in a number of ways. At the most basic level this appears in words newly invented, for example, 'yeasty', 'slab', 'skirr', 'compunctious', and a phrase now fully part of present-day English, 'be-all and end-all'. There are also others newly formed out of existing ones – 'unsex', 'unprovoked', 'unbend', 'unfix', 'unspeak', 'dauntless', 'darefull', 'direness' and 'marrowless'. Some of the play's most striking passages feature individual words which were either very new to the language or specifically coined.

Macbeth begins one of his most discussed speeches as follows:

> If it were done, when 'tis done, then 'twere well
> It were done quickly. If th'assassination
> Could trammel up the consequence, and catch

---

1   In *A Defence of the Epilogue, Or, An Essay on the Dramatique Poetry of the Last Age* (1672) Dryden discussed failures of expression in Shakespeare and cited Jonson's view: 'In reading some bombast speeches of *Macbeth*, which are not to be understood, [Jonson] us'd to say that it was horrour, and I am much afraid that this is so' (Vickers, *Critical*, 1.147).

2   A website listing titles from *Macbeth* (www.barbarapaul.com/shake/macbeth.html) includes more than sixty expressions from the play that have been used to create titles of literary works.

> With his surcease, success: that but this blow
> Might be the be-all and the end-all, here,
> But here, upon this bank and shoal of time,
> We'd jump the life to come.

$$(1.7.1-7)$$

His language is compressed and euphemistic, the diction simple, but the semantics complex. It seems as if the pronoun 'it', effectively repeated four times in the first sentence, has no referent, which is startling in the opening lines of a scene. But the second sentence, opening with another conditional 'If', clarifies the subject of the first sentence with the strikingly polysyllabic noun 'assassination'. This usage is the first recorded in the *OED*. Shakespeare may have come across the word 'assassin' in Richard Knolles, *The Generall History of the Turkes* (1603), which he had certainly read for *Othello*, where it refers to 'a company of most desperate and dangerous men among the Mahometans'. It was obviously a novel word at the time. Henry Estienne, in *A World of Wonders* (1607), mentions 'the Italian trade in hyring assassins (for I must use new words to expresse new wickednesse) to cut men's throtes'.[1] A related noun form, 'assassinate', meaning the act of killing, appears in Philemon Holland's translation of Pliny's *Natural History* (1600), which Shakespeare also knew (and used for *Othello*), but he did not choose this form for *Macbeth*. The verb, to assassinate, is not recorded before 1619. Shakespeare could presumably have called the act which Macbeth contemplates an 'assassinate', but he needed five syllables to complete his line, so he made his own variant.[2] The word stands out dramatically in its context, and no doubt sounded strange to the play's first

---

1 The word 'assassin' entered the language by way of Old French, but originally from Arabic. It is first recorded in Celio Augustino, *A Notable Historie of the Saracens* (1575).

2 The earliest record in *EEBO* for 'Assassination' is Thomas Pelletier, *A Lamentable Discourse, upon the Paricide and bloudy assassination: committed on the person of Henry the fourth . . .* (1610).

40

audiences, covering in its strangeness the bald fact of murder. It contrasts in both rhythm and sound quality with the words just spoken, a series of monosyllables, repeating certain sounds and words (it, were, done), and ending on a two-syllable word ('quickly'). Then follows the thrillingly high-register polysyllable, with its introduction of the sibilant sound which is quickly caught up in the next lines: 'If th'asassination / Could trammel up the consequence, and catch / With his surcease, success'. All the nouns here are of non-native derivation, and thus the more conspicuous. 'Surcease', meaning 'bringing or coming to an end' is a rare word, not used anywhere else in Shakespeare. An auditory pun or paronomasia (the likeness of sound between two different words) is produced by 'success', here used for the fourth time in the play, and perhaps to be noticed on this account by the audience, particularly since its different meanings – prosperous achievement, succession of heirs – intertwine so ironically in the course of the play.

In a later speech about the murder Shakespeare again gives Macbeth a polysyllabic coinage. Confronting his wife in the aftermath of the killing, he cries:

> What hands are here? Ha: they pluck out mine eyes.
> Will all great Neptune's ocean wash this blood
> Clean from my hand? No, this my hand will rather
> The multitudinous seas incarnadine,
> Making the green, one red.

(2.2.60–4)

Murderers before Macbeth lamented their inability to eradicate the evidence of their crimes – for example, Claudius in *Hamlet* and Hercules in Seneca's *Hercules Furens*, a possible source – and the notion of seas dyed red with blood was not new. There was even a current proverb, 'All the water in the sea cannot wash out this stain' (Dent, W85). But Shakespeare gives new life to the hyperbole with his two bold Latinisms.

'Multitudinous', meaning vast or boundless, is not his coinage. It appears in 1603, in *The Magnificent Entertainment* by Dekker and Jonson, produced to celebrate King James's coronation procession through London, where the 'multitudinous press' of people was blamed for hindering the King on his way, and also in Dekker's *The Wonderful Year* (1603). But it was a new word and Shakespeare had not used it before, although he was to do so again in *Coriolanus*, there meaning 'belonging to the multitude' (3.1.157). 'Incarnadine', as a verb meaning to redden with dye, stain or pigment, gets its first recorded usage here. It appears as an adjective in Joshua Sylvester's translation of *Du Bartas his Divine Weeks and Works* of 1591, which Shakespeare may have seen, though this is not certain. He had experimented earlier with the word, or at least its cognates, in the form of malapropisms, having Sir Andrew Aguecheek in *Twelfth Night* blunder in his description of Sebastian as 'the very devil incar-dinate' and Lancelot Gobbo in *The Merchant of Venice* speak of Shylock as 'the very devil incarnation'. These two words are compressed in Macbeth's 'incarnadine', where the thought of the seas made the colour of blood underlies the image.

But it is much more than individual examples of unusual vocabulary that give *Macbeth* its very special verbal texture. What Frank Kermode calls its 'lexical habit' (203) is created by many stylistic features: rhetorical forms of ambiguity, puns and double meanings, echoes and repetitions, euphemism and circumlocutions. Russ McDonald identifies 'unremitting repetition' as 'the auditory pattern that overrides all others' in *Macbeth* (*Late*, 47) and a major example of this involves play on some of the commonest words in the language, 'do' and its cognates 'deed', 'done' and 'undone'. A simple neutral monosyllable, particularly common in early modern English through its use as an auxiliary verb,[1] 'do' begins to take on dark

---

1   Hope (137–8) notes changes in the use of 'do' as an auxiliary, observing that it became very common as an unemphatic auxiliary around 1600.

colouring in the play's third scene, when repeated three times by the First Witch as she sums up her malevolent intentions towards the sailor's wife:

> Her husband's to Aleppo gone, Master o'th' Tiger:
> But in a sieve I'll thither sail,
> And like a rat without a tail,
> I'll do, I'll do, and I'll do.

$$(1.3.7–10)$$

While this passage is often glossed with sexual implications, which the word 'do' could carry, the language may be more potently suggestive if kept vague. Deeds and doing figure in two proverbs current at the time: 'The thing done has an end' and 'Things done cannot be undone',[1] and also in the words of Jesus to Judas at the last supper, which early modern audiences familiar with the Bible may have known: 'That thou doest, do quickly'. When Macbeth's Lady at her first appearance starts to play on ideas of doing, the words take on specific significance. She sums up her sense of her husband's ambivalent attitude towards ambition:

> Thou'dst have, great Glamis,
> That which cries, 'Thus thou must do', if thou have it;
> And that which rather thou dost fear to do,
> Than wishest should be undone.

$$(1.5.22–5)$$

Her repetition of the nominal phrase 'that which' and the delay in naming what is to be 'done' initiate a euphemistic habit observed by both Macbeths when referring to Duncan's murder, which they refer to as 'this business', 'this enterprise' or 'our great quell'. The word 'done' resounds, three times repeated, in the first sentence of Macbeth's soliloquy in 1.7: 'If it were done,

---

1 Dent, T149 and T200.

43

when 'tis done, then 'twere well / It were done quickly.' As Simon
Palfrey says, we may hear in this clumsily repetitive phrasing,
'a nervous stutter, an evasive circumlocution, a thumping
palpitation' (69).[1] The significance of 'doing' is further developed
by the occurrence of the cognate 'deed' later in the speech, as
Macbeth begins to realize that what he has in mind (but can't
name) can't be 'done' in the sense of over and done with. The
doing will have repercussions:

> He's here in double trust:
> First, as I am his kinsman, and his subject,
> Strong both against the deed. Then, as his host,
> Who should against his murderer shut the door,
> Not bear the knife myself.

$$(1.7.12–16)$$

So great are the sanctions against it, that 'pity, like a naked
new-born babe . . . Shall blow the horrid deed in every eye, /
That tears shall drown the wind' (21, 24–5).

This is the first use of 'deed' in the play, but many are to
follow. With the exception of *Richard III*, which is much longer
(approximately 1,224 lines as against *Macbeth*'s 765), *Macbeth*
has more uses of this word than any other play. They are mostly
to be found in the speeches of Macbeth and his Lady, and all
refer without exception to acts of blood. They proliferate in the
scene after the murder of Duncan. She, nervously awaiting the
arrival of her husband from Duncan's chamber, hears him
coming: 'Alack, I am afraid they have awaked, / And 'tis not
done. The attempt, and not the deed / Confounds us' (2.2.10–12).
He announces heavily, 'I have done the deed.' Later she
attempts to stem his guilt-ridden outburst over his inability to
say 'Amen': 'These deeds must not be thought / After these
ways; so, it will make us mad.' Urged to return the daggers to

---

1   See Palfrey's excellent discussion of this repetition (68–71).

the bloody room, Macbeth refuses: 'I am afraid to think what I have done'. His wife takes over, and returns, displaying her own bloody hands with bravado: 'A little water clears us of this deed. / How easy is it then.' She urges him to regain his self-control: 'Be not lost / So poorly in your thoughts.' But for Macbeth being 'lost' is preferable to any other state of mind: 'To know my deed, 'twere best not know myself'. Macbeth owns the deed only once, but 'the deed' becomes the preferred term for outsiders to use in referring to Duncan's murder. The Old Man in 2.4 comments on the strange events taking place on the night of the murder, ''Tis unnatural, / Even like the deed that's done.' Ross asks, 'Is't known who did this more than bloody deed?' Malcolm replies that it is on Malcolm and Donalbain that 'Suspicion of the deed' has fallen.

Once crowned king, Macbeth becomes bolder, and comes to know both his deed and the self that did it. He also recognizes that the doing was not 'done', and that 'To be thus is nothing, but to be safely thus' (3.1.47). Preparing to secure his position by another murder he tells his wife that before another night is over, 'there shall be done / A deed of dreadful note'. 'What's to be done?' she asks, and he replies, 'Be innocent of the knowledge, dearest chuck, / Till thou applaud the deed' (3.2.44–7). The rising again of the dead Banquo shows Macbeth that there can be no end of 'deeds'. At the end of 3.4 he tells his wife that his panicked reaction to the Ghost is that of a beginner in the business of killing: 'My strange and self-abuse / Is the initiate fear, that wants hard use. / We are yet but young in deed' (3.4.140–2). When he then visits the Sisters to discover what the future has in store for him, he finds them at their black arts: 'What is't you do? / A deed without a name' (4.1.48).[1] After the

---

1   'Deed' seems to be Shakespeare's preferred term for acts of bloodshed. It occurs most frequently in plays with violent scenarios, such as *Richard III* and *Titus Andronicus*, which together with *Macbeth* have the highest totals. A synonym, 'action', appears only twice in *Macbeth*, but not used by Macbeth himself or referring to bloodshed. At some points the legal meaning of the word 'deed' may also be in play.

show of kings Macbeth becomes reckless. Hearing of Macduff's defection, his next step requires no planning:

> The flighty purpose never is o'ertook
> Unless the deed go with it. From this moment
> The very firstlings of my heart shall be
> The firstlings of my hand. And even now,
> To crown my thoughts with acts, be it thought and done.
>   . . . No boasting like a fool;
> This deed I'll do before this purpose cool.

(4.1.144–8, 152–3)

The deed without a name recurs for the last time in the sleep-walking scene, 5.1. 'Unnatural deeds / Do breed unnatural troubles', comments the Doctor as the Lady relives the ringing of the bell on the night of the murder: 'One; two. Why then 'tis time to do't.' As she prepares to return to bed she delivers her summary: 'What's done, cannot be undone.' The phrasing recalls Macbeth's soliloquy on the meanings of doing and doneness as well as her own firm assertions that the deed could be cleared away with a little water and that 'Things without all remedy / Should be without regard: what's done, is done' (3.2.12–13). It also recalls the proverbial utterances behind them all.

Shakespeare's uses of 'do' and related terms, which function both on auditory and intellectual levels, link the language of the Macbeths with that of the Sisters. The Sisters' characteristic idiom makes a strong appeal to the listening mind. It draws on many devices: rhyme, which produces effects of incantation, doggerel and childish musicality; alliteration; repetition; ant-ithesis and inversion; paradox. They may be 'imperfect speakers' but they do not lack command of their language. They begin the play – the only one of Shakespeare's to open with a rhyming dialogue – with a ten-line scene establishing a strongly rhythmic pattern and involving four rhyme sounds ending the lines ('again'/'rain', 'done'/'won'/'sun', 'heath'/'Macbeth', 'fair'/ 'air'), plus others within them ('we'/'three', 'hurly'/'burly', 'where'/'there'). Their typical metrical form is the heavily stressed trochaic tetrameter. The normative metrical form of the play's verse is unrhymed iambic pentameter, so this deviant form draws attention to itself; it is a deliberate device, creating an effect of otherness, its strange musicality recalling primitive forms such as nursery rhymes and doggerel verse.[1] Rhyme pervades the play. *Macbeth* has the highest proportion of couplet endings to scenes of any tragedy except *Richard II*, which is a largely verse play, and a high number of rhyming lines overall.[2] The verbal collocation in 1.1.3–4, 'done'/'lost'/ 'won', is ominously echoed at the end of 1.2, where Duncan tells Ross to greet Macbeth with the title Thane of Cawdor. Ross replies, 'I'll see it done.' Duncan then ends the scene with the line, ironic in a number of ways, 'What he hath lost, noble Macbeth hath won.' Macbeth regularly ends his scenes on a rhyming couplet: 'Away, and mock the time with fairest show: / False face must hide what the false heart doth know' (1.7.82–3) or 'My strange and self-abuse / Is the initiate fear, that wants hard use' (3.4.140–1). At some points he even uses two couplets: 'Good things of day begin to droop and drowse, / Whiles night's black agents to their preys do rouse. / Thou marvell'st at my words: but hold thee still; / Things bad begun, make strong themselves by ill' (3.2.53–6). Such couplets may function primarily as dramatic punctuation, but they also work in other ways. He uses rhyme in his private communing:

> Stars, hide your fires,
> Let not light see my black and deep desires.
> The eye wink at the hand; yet let that be
> Which the eye fears, when it is done, to see.

> (1.4.50–3)

1   Krantz analyses the Sisters' rhythms in detail (352–3). This discussion is strongly indebted to him.
2   See Doran, 156. Flint (15) calculates that there are 290 rhyming lines in the play, and out of thirty-one scenes only five contain no rhyme.

After the encounter with the Apparitions, Macbeth has a sequence of four rhymed couplets. The linkage between his mode of speech and that of the Apparitions, whose speech, distinctive from that of the Sisters, is in rhymed pentameters, is strengthened by the fact that his first couplet completes the short final line of the Third Apparition:

3 APPARITION

    Macbeth shall never vanquished be, until
    Great Birnam Wood to high Dunsinane Hill
    Shall come against him.

MACBETH   That will never be.
    Who can impress the forest, bid the tree
    Unfix his earth-bound root? Sweet bodements, good.
    Rebellious dead, rise never till the Wood
    Of Birnam rise, and our high-placed Macbeth
    Shall live the lease of nature, pay his breath
    To time, and mortal custom. Yet my heart
    Throbs to know one thing: tell me, if your art
    Can tell so much, shall Banquo's issue ever
    Reign in this kingdom?

                       (4.1.91–102)

David L. Krantz (355) calls this a 'musical yoking', relating it back to the 'selfsame tune' which Banquo heard in the Sisters' prophecies in 1.3.[1]

The Sisters' speech uses other forms of repetition. It is conspicuously alliterative, another linguistic feature which draws attention to itself and links their verbal style with Macbeth's. In 1.1 the fricatives in their concluding couplet are chanted in unison: 'Fair is foul, and foul is fair, / Hover through the fog and filthy air.' In 1.3 the First Witch relishes her recollection of the sailor's wife who refused to give her the food she asked for:

1 For other useful accounts of language in the play, see Dean, Flint and Williams, 'Time'.

' "Aroynt thee, witch," the rump-fed ronyon cries.' The strong *r*
sounds draw attention to the unusual words 'aroynt' and 'ronyon'.
They combine alliteration with repeated words, as in the first 35
lines of 1.3, which contain the following: 'munched' (3 times),
'I'll do' (3), 'Show me' (2), 'drum' (2), 'hand' (2), 'about' (2),
'thrice' (3). Repetition becomes formulaic in their greetings to
Macbeth and Banquo:

1 WITCH
    All hail Macbeth, hail to thee, Thane of Glamis.
2 WITCH
    All hail Macbeth, hail to thee, Thane of Cawdor.
3 WITCH
    All hail Macbeth, that shalt be king hereafter.

(1.3.48–50)

1 WITCH
    Lesser than Macbeth, and greater.
2 WITCH
    Not so happy, yet much happier.
3 WITCH
    Thou shalt get kings, though thou be none:
    So all hail Macbeth, and Banquo.
1 WITCH
    Banquo, and Macbeth, all hail.

(65–9)

Macbeth himself speaks a language that often resembles this,
especially in his private utterances; his soliloquy at 1.7.1–28,
where the repetitions ('If'/'If'), echoes ('were done'/'were
done', 'here, / But here', 'teach'/'taught') and alliterations
('consequence'/'catch', 'surcease'/'success', 'but'/'blow',
'be-all'/'end-all') create what have been called 'thick clusters
of repeated sounds' that 'help express whatever it is the witches
represent and serve' (Krantz, 348).

49

The speech of both Macbeth and the Sisters is also characterized by rhetorical figures which work to complicate meaning. In 1.1 the Sisters expect to meet again 'When the battle's lost, and won'; their chant 'Fair is foul and foul is fair', mingling paradox and chiasmus (a criss-cross structure, involving inverted parallelism), is echoed in Macbeth's first line, 'So foul and fair a day I have not seen' (1.3.38). Their predictions for Macbeth and Banquo are similarly shaped: 'Lesser than Macbeth, and greater', 'Not so happy, yet much happier'. They weave a web of ambiguity and double meaning, in which Macbeth seems trapped. As he tells himself, 'This supernatural soliciting / Cannot be ill; cannot be good.' He is so bewildered by the attempt to make sense out of what he has been foretold, that he can only sum it up in another chiasmic paradox: 'nothing is, but what is not'. Banquo reminds him:

> But 'tis strange:
> And oftentimes, to win us to our harm,
> The instruments of darkness tell us truths,
> Win us with honest trifles, to betray's
> In deepest consequence.

> (1.3.124–8)

But Macbeth does not realize this until too late. When he hears that, contrary to reason, the Wood of Birnam *is* coming towards Dunsinane, he begins finally to see what it is the Sisters have done to him: 'I pull in resolution, and begin / To doubt th'equivocation of the fiend, / That lies like truth' (5.5.41–3). Confronted by his antagonist Macduff, who is, in a sense that Macbeth never entertained, 'not of woman born', being born by what we would call caesarean section, he understands at last how it is that the Sisters' language has operated to trick him:

> And be these juggling fiends no more believed
> That palter with us in a double sense,

> That keep the word of promise to our ear,
> And break it to our hope.

(5.8.19–22)

'Juggling' for Shakespeare meant playing magic tricks, a term associated with witchcraft; 'palter' meant prevaricate or equivocate. But there is also an underlying hint of something childish, the trickery that a malevolent child might play on an adult. The Sisters in their riddling speech, their 'duplicitous semantics' (Krantz, 370), are like sinister children, dancing in circles, making spells and playing games with words. They have, as Banquo says, betrayed Macbeth 'in deepest consequence', but they have also made him look like a fool.

The Sisters' strongly individualized speech is only one example of the play's linguistic variety and its movement between contrasted registers: its language can be simple or densely figurative, proverbial or magniloquent, Senecan or colloquial. At times Macbeth's language seems to verge on rant: in his addresses to Banquo's ghost, for instance, or his extravagant speech to the Sisters in 4.1, the scene where he has gone to seek them out. According to John Porter Houston, rant typically is characterized by 'invocation, imperatives and hyperbole' as well as the 'personification of great forces', all features that appear here (Houston, *Rhetoric*, 150). But this manner, of almost exaggerated high style, escapes absurdity because of its appropriateness to Macbeth's extreme state of mind. The speech is highly rhetorical:

> I conjure you, by that which you profess,
> Howe'er you come to know it, answer me;
> Though you untie the winds and let them fight
> Against the churches, though the yeasty waves
> Confound and swallow navigation up,
> Though bladed corn be lodged and trees blown down,
> Though castles topple on their warders' heads,

Though palaces and pyramids do slope
Their heads to their foundations, though the treasure
Of Nature's germen tumble altogether
Even till destruction sicken, answer me
To what I ask you.

(4.1.49–60)

This powerful utterance consists of a single sentence, which takes the form of a command, 'I conjure you', followed by two adverbial elements and a subordinate sentence with a series of further adverbial elements, with the subordinate verb and object repeated at the end.[1] Between the two instances of the subordinate verb, 'answer me', are sandwiched six parallel clauses beginning with the concessive 'though', marking a series of hypothetical possibilities. The figure here is parison, a device used to create an effect of massing or accumulation.[2] The clauses share the same structure but are varied in length and rhythmic effect, and each has a different subject, moving through individual elements (the Sisters, waves, corn, castles, palaces and pyramids) to a general summation ('the treasure / Of Nature's germen'). The specificity of the cataclysmic events that Macbeth imagines, partly created by the visual quality of the words ('yeasty', 'bladed', 'topple', 'slope their heads') contrasts with the deliberate vagueness attributed to the Sisters' powers: 'that which you profess', 'Howe'er you come to know it'. Macbeth's speech is carefully structured to suggest control, but the intensity of the repetition also conveys his determination to assert it. He understands the seriousness of what he is about to ask. His speech is more than a command, it is a solemn conjuration, in which the repetitive clause structure mimics the mode of an incantation.

1   According to the punctuation in F, followed here, though some editors put a full stop after 'answer me' (50).
2   Russ McDonald ('Compar or parison: Measure for Measure', in Adamson *et al.*, 39–58) gives a useful account of it.

The syntax and manner of conjuration appear elsewhere as features of the grander *Macbeth* style. Macbeth envisages the circumstances in which his 'deed of dreadful note' is to be carried out, again using parallel clauses:

> ere the bat hath flown
> His cloistered flight, ere to black Hecate's summons
> The shard-born beetle, with his drowsy hums,
> Hath rung night's yawning peal

> (3.2.41–4)

and he invokes the powers of the night to carry out his commands as he does the Sisters:

> Come, seeling night,
> Scarf up the tender eye of pitiful day
> And with thy bloody and invisible hand
> Cancel and tear to pieces that great bond
> Which keeps me pale.

> (47–51)

In this speech the distinctive epithets ('cloistered', 'shard-born', 'drowsy', 'yawning', 'seeling', 'bloody and invisible') combine with densely packed metaphor to produce a hypnotic quality. Macbeth's ruthless determination to get what he wants is variously conveyed: through the temporal emphasis – this deed must happen before regular and normal ('drowsing', 'yawning') nocturnal activities get under way, the incantatory rhythms and repeated phrasing ('ere . . . ere'), the violent images. To different effect, his Lady draws on the language of conjuration in her speech to the spirits as she prepares for Duncan's arrival:

> Come you spirits
> That tend on mortal thoughts, unsex me here,
> And fill me from the crown to the toe, top-full
> Of direst cruelty. Make thick my blood,
> Stop up th'access and passage to remorse,

> That no compunctious visitings of nature
> Shake my fell purpose, nor keep peace between
> Th'effect and it. Come to my woman's breasts,
> And take my milk for gall, you murdering ministers,
> Wherever, in your sightless substances,
> You wait on nature's mischief. Come thick night,
> And pall thee in the dunnest smoke of hell,
> That my keen knife see not the wound it makes,
> Nor heaven peep through the blanket of the dark
> To cry, 'Hold, hold'.

(1.5.40–54)

'Come' is repeated three times at irregular intervals; the syntax of the speech is less formal and more varied than in Macbeth's conjuration of the Sisters, and thus perhaps less open to the charge of rant. There is nothing in it of excess or repetitiveness. The first command to the spirits, divided into two sentences, makes four claims on them (that they should unsex her, fill her with cruelty, thicken her blood and stop up in her the access to remorse), but they are not expressed in parallel clauses. The second command has the form of two main verbs ('Come . . . and take') spoken before the description of the spirits completes the sentence. The third invocation is to night, also coupling the verb 'come' with another ('pall thee'), bringing the speech to its conclusion with two subordinate clauses of consequence ('That my keen knife see not' and 'Nor heaven peep through'). Johnson thought the speech appropriate to a murderer (though he attributed it to Macbeth), and said that it 'exerted all the force of poetry'; yet he felt its force to be weakened by inappropriate diction, objecting particularly to low terms such as 'dunnest' and 'knife' and the expression 'peep through the blanket of the dark'.[1] But to a modern ear the variation in

---

1 See Johnson's discussion of 'low terms' in *The Rambler*, 168 (1751) (*Rambler*, 92–4). He was less critical of these words when defining them in his *Dictionary* (1755).

register, from the grand alliterative phrases – 'murdering ministers', 'sightless substances' – to the plain native diction of the Lady's summons to 'thick night' is thrilling, and the images in the last sentence, with the agency for the killing deferred to the non-seeing knife, and heaven relegated to an outsider's role, appear boldly evocative rather than, as Johnson deemed them, 'risible'.

Like this 'demonic invocation', many aspects of the play's language have been thought Senecan.[1] The stylistic peculiarities of the scene with the bleeding Captain (1.2) have often been ascribed to Senecan influence.[2] Robert Miola considers that Macbeth 'in his worst moments . . . sounds like Clytemnestra, Atreus or Medea, urging the self to unspeakable crimes', citing his use of 'that form of hyperbole that lists extreme cataclysmic events', such as his speech daring Banquo's ghost to approach him (3.4.98–102) or his address to the Sisters in 4.1. And it is clear that terms of particular significance in Seneca, such as 'night', 'darkness', 'murder', 'fear' and 'hell', make important contributions to the play's linguistic density.[3] Senecan body terms such as 'hand', 'heart' and, crucially, 'blood', pervade *Macbeth*.[4] Blood is a keynote of the play struck in Duncan's first line: 'What bloody man is that?' (1.2.1). In this scene Macbeth's sword 'smoked with bloody execution' and he and Banquo acted as if they 'meant to bathe in reeking wounds / Or memorize another Golgotha' (18, 39–40). Miola notes the importance of blood-stained hands in Seneca's *Hercules* plays, where the hand is used as a metonym for strength and great

1 The term is that of Merchant, 75. Ewbank, 'Fiend-like', quotes C. Mendell, *Our Seneca* (1941), who says that '*Macbeth* without Seneca would have been impossible' (53). She relates this speech to several passages in Seneca's *Medea*, which she considers Shakespeare may have known in Studley's translation. Paul calls *Macbeth* 'the most Senecan of all Shakespeare's plays' (48). For fuller discussion of Senecan elements in Shakespeare, see Cunliffe, Lucas, and pp. 91–4.

2 Especially by Nosworthy ('Bleeding').

3 See Doran, 157, on these terms and the play's 'necrophilous vocabulary'.

4 See Jones, *Origins*, Appendix A, 'Shakespeare and Seneca'.

deeds. He connects with this Macbeth's attitude to the relation between his deeds, represented by his hand, and his mental acknowledgment of them. Initially Macbeth desires a disjunction, for the eye to 'wink at the hand' (1.4.52), and after Duncan's murder, in a particularly Senecan passage (2.2.59–64), he is terrorized by the sight of his bloody hands – 'What hands are here? Ha: they pluck out mine eyes.' Here his hands seem to act as if independent of his control. But later mind and hand act together: 'Strange things I have in head, that will to hand, / Which must be acted, ere they may be scanned' (3.4.137–8), and 'From this moment / The very firstlings of my heart shall be / The firstlings of my hand' (4.1.145–7). The nouns ('head'/ 'hand', 'heart'/'hand') are forced into conjunction by the strongly rhythmic and repetitive patterning. Such noun-based concreteness – sometimes quite extravagant – is a distinctive feature of the play's linguistic character.

Equally important and expressive are forms of language owing more to indirectness and complication, for which the Sisters' paradoxical manner in the first scene sets the tone. Macbeth's inner confusion is displayed in a language of paradox and antithesis, as when (in 1.3.132–44) he tries to define for himself the meaning of the 'supernatural soliciting' which 'Cannot be ill; cannot be good', because in either case there are contraindications. He concludes this speech in despairing illogic: 'nothing is, but what is not'. The convoluted grammar of the line 'My thought, whose murder yet is but fantastical', which introduces the idea of murder to the play, personifies the 'thought' as victim of a murder,[1] but the murder is as yet the product of fantasy, and the real victim cannot even be referred to, let alone named. His opening soliloquy in 1.7 is full of paradox, in the 'Bloody instructions, which being taught, return / To plague th'inventor', the 'even-handed justice' which commends the ingredients of the poisoned chalice to the

---

1 Brooke, however, paraphrases 'whose murder' as 'the thought of murder'.

poisoner, the 'naked new-born babe' who is yet powerful enough to ride the winds.[1] Shocking moments in the play are captured through qualities of paradox. Banquo's ghost glares at Macbeth, but with eyes lacking the power of 'speculation'; its appearance bespeaks a time when dead men no longer stay in their graves but 'rise again / With twenty mortal murders on their crowns, / And push us from our stools' (3.4.93, 78–80). The Lady's condition in her sleepwalking scene embodies paradox; her actions display 'A great perturbation in nature, to receive at once the benefit of sleep and do the effects of watching' (5.1.9–11). She walks carrying a light that she cannot see, and she is obsessed with attempting to rub out invisible bloodstains. Only unreality is real to her now; nothing is but what is not.

At the end of the play Macbeth at last realizes how the Sisters have dealt with him: 'juggling fiends . . . That palter with us in a double sense, / That keep the word of promise to our ear, / And break it to our hope' (5.8.19–22). The 'double sense' behind their utterances, their skill in equivocation, has led him to a series of fatal misreadings; it has also, by what has been called 'verbal contagion' (Katherine Rowe, 49), infected his own way of thinking about his actions, and that of his wife. They equivocate from the start about the idea of murdering Duncan, and, as their circumlocutions around 'deed' and the other evasive expressions ('this business', 'this enterprise') show, avoid the reality of what they are to do. The Lady's circumlocutions in the soliloquy after she has read the letter (1.5.15–30) have often been remarked. She appears 'incapable of making a direct statement' (Badawi, 29), avoiding the word 'king' and substituting referents and careful phrases ('What

---

1   Brooks comments on this passage: 'Is Pity like the human and helpless babe, or powerful as the angel that rides the winds? It is both; and it is strong because of its very weakness. The paradox is inherent in the situation itself; and it is the paradox that will destroy the overbrittle rationalism on which Macbeth founds his career' (45).

thou wouldst highly, / That wouldst thou holily', 'catch the nearest way', 'that which rather thou dost fear to do, / Than wishest should be undone') so as not to name the act of killing. Macbeth resorts to similar linguistic strategies in 'If it were done' (1.7.1–28). Sometimes the Lady draws on aggrandizing epithets to bestow a heroic dimension on the murder, which she calls 'our great quell', to be enacted in defiance of Duncan's 'spongy officers' lying helpless in 'swinish sleep'. Her lines at the end of 1.5 typify the euphemistic manner: 'He that's coming / Must be provided for; and you shall put / This night's great business into my dispatch' (1.5.66–8). She does not name Duncan or give him his title; 'provided for' and 'my dispatch' are sinisterly ambiguous, suggesting as they do the service due to the King from his hostess rather than the treatment intended. It is indeed, as the Sisters say, 'a deed without a name'.

It is perhaps not coincidental that the language of hospitality, as used in exchanges between Duncan and Macbeth at 1.4.16–27 and Duncan and the Lady at 1.6.10–19, is also one of indirection and circumlocution. Duncan thanks Macbeth for his services in battle in an idiom of elaborate self-deprecation:

> Thou art so far before,
> That swiftest wing of recompense is slow
> To overtake thee. Would thou hadst less deserved,
> That the proportion both of thanks, and payment,
> Might have been mine. Only I have left to say,
> More is thy due, than more than all can pay.

(1.4.16–21)

Macbeth responds in the same style:

> The service and the loyalty I owe,
> In doing it, pays itself. Your highness' part
> Is to receive our duties; and our duties
> Are to your throne and state, children and servants,

> Which do but what they should, by doing everything
> Safe toward your love and honour.

(22–7)

Each tries to outdo the other in postures of humility and unworthiness. Duncan's speech is what it seems, the gracious language of the monarch honouring a deserving servant, but Macbeth's, while observing the linguistic conventions of such dialogue, is underlaid with ironic double meaning. His Lady's speech, also responding to a tortuous compliment from Duncan, is more conspicuously loaded:

> All our service,
> In every point twice done, and then done double,
> Were poor and single business, to contend
> Against those honours deep and broad wherewith
> Your majesty loads our house. For those of old,
> And the late dignities heaped up to them,
> We rest your hermits.

(1.6.14–20)

Although this is a public language of conventional politeness, in the context more private languages are recalled: 'service' and 'business' are reminders of the euphemisms exchanged between the couple; and the idiom of doubling and multiplying reappears in the style of the Sisters ('Double, double, toil and trouble').

Language in *Macbeth* does not always achieve its effects through surface complexity, as the speech of the Sisters shows. The exchange between the couple after Macbeth's entrance with the bloody daggers in 2.2 creates tension through its terse simplicity, and throughout this scene the Lady's speech is noticeably plain in diction and syntax. Macbeth's lament in 5.3.22–8 for his failed life gains its resonance from the single image he uses, somewhere between a simile and a metaphor – 'my way of life / Is fallen into the sere, the yellow leaf' – and the simple listing of what he has lost in pursuit of his ambition – 'honour, love, obedience, troops of friends'. But undeniably the play's most memorable passages are usually those involving a degree of figurative complexity, as well as rhetorical devices which link them with patterns of language more broadly deployed. Macbeth's speech on learning of his wife's death is one of the best known in Shakespeare, with an immediate emotional impact, and also one where it is the density of the figuration, not the diction or syntax, that defies analysis:

> Tomorrow, and tomorrow, and tomorrow,
> Creeps in this petty pace from day to day,
> To the last syllable of recorded time;
> And all our yesterdays have lighted fools
> The way to dusty death. Out, out, brief candle,
> Life's but a walking shadow, a poor player,
> That struts and frets his hour upon the stage,
> And then is heard no more. It is a tale
> Told by an idiot, full of sound and fury
> Signifying nothing.

(5.5.18–27)

The theme of time pervades the play,[1] and Macbeth's sense that all that now remains for him is worthless looks back to his epitaph for Duncan: 'Had I but died an hour before this chance, / I had lived a blessed time' (2.3.92–3).[2] Brian Cummings observes of figures of speech piled up in the first three lines:

> [Macbeth] refers overtly to the mathematical reckoning
> of time, measured in terms of speed ('this petty pace').
> Time passes by inexorably, indifferent to the course of

---

1   See pp. 62–82.
2   Dean (219) discusses this as part of the play's pervasive echoic patterning focused on 2.3.

a single life. Macbeth longs for the space to mourn his wife but time will not let him. This figure is conflated with a figure of an individual lifetime made up like a book with 'syllables', in particular the book of record which the angel keeps at the last judgment. Time itself seems infinite but each life within it is limited, like a sentence that must end in its own period. These are perhaps the primary figures we have to keep in mind. Yet we also note that there is no explicit connection between them. The figure transfers itself from one referent to the other without elucidation.[1]

And there are, as he says, other 'figurative undercurrents'; as Brooke notes,[2] 'in this petty pace' might mean '1. at this meaningless pace; 2. in this petty way; 3. in this narrow passage', referring to the contemporary meaning of 'pace' as a narrow passage. The word could also mean a journey, the gait (of a horse) used figuratively, and the passage between pews in a church. Cummings introduces further ideas, of burial 'perhaps in a catacomb' and of one's past as a funeral procession – 'the way to dusty death' that concludes the sentence. The succession of images of transience, each of which though poignantly simple could be subjected to a similar level of interpretation, invokes the actor's very speech as the epitome of meaninglessness. The aural echo of 'Struts and frets' in 'sound and fury' emphasizes Macbeth's pathetic self-importance. The complex rhythm of the long line '**Told** by an **id**iot, **full** of **sound** and **fu**ry' culminates in the falling assonantal cadence of '**Sig**nifying **noth**ing'. This is language at its most dense, concentrated and hard-working. It is fully adjusted to the situation of the speaker but at the same time operational within the play's larger meaning. It does not typify that kind of language towards

---

1 Cummings, 'Metalepsis' (Adamson *et al.*, 217–18).
2 Brooke calls l. 20 'a line too complex in its resonances for commentary to be anything but reductive'.

which Shakespeare seems to be moving later in his career, of 'difficult' verse, where prosody and syntax become looser and the effect on the ear of the listener is perhaps more subtle but harder to evaluate. It is not language where 'effects of clash and discontinuity' are displayed, although these are not absent from the play as a whole.[1] But it is dramatic language at its most expressive, which brilliantly creates the effect of Macbeth's subjectivity at work during a moment of emotional crisis.

MACBETH AND TIME

From at least Coleridge onwards, critics have drawn attention to the ways in which time is a major aspect, not to say a governing principle, of the play. Coleridge's view that 'of all Shakespeare's plays, *Macbeth* is the most rapid'[2] has been developed in a huge variety of ways. *Macbeth* readily presents itself as a play in which time and its passage are central. From its opening with the First Witch's question, 'When shall we three meet again?', to its closing with Malcolm's reassurance that 'What's more to do, / Which would be planted newly with the time . . . We will perform in measure, time and place' (5.9.30–1, 39), it is permeated with time references. 'The density of terms measuring and positioning things in time'[3] has often been noticed; this is not just a matter of the great abundance of temporal terminology, of terms relating to the timing of human activity – 'when', 'now', 'tonight', 'tomorrow', 'yesterday', 'forever', 'hereafter', 'late', 'timely' – but also of more complex

---

1 For such views of Shakespeare's later language, see McDonald, *Late*, and Houston, *Rhetoric*, 158.

2 Coleridge, 1.49.

3 Craig, *Of Philosophers*, 59. The word 'time' (including 'times') is used 49 times in the play; occurrences of 'oftentimes', 'sometime', 'timely', 'untimely' and 'betimes' add another 10 to the total.

evocations of the markers and rhythms of time in the natural world. Thus Macbeth prepares himself for the murder of Banquo with a series of elaborate periphrases:

> ere the bat hath flown
> His cloistered flight, ere to black Hecate's summons
> The shard-born beetle, with his drowsy hums,
> Hath rung night's yawning peal, there shall be done
> A deed of dreadful note.

(3.2.41–5)

In contrasting mood the First Murderer describes the approach of nightfall:

> The west yet glimmers with some streaks of day.
> Now spurs the lated traveller apace
> To gain the timely inn

(3.3.5–7)

Such passages as these, and there are several of them, function most obviously in the creation of the intensity of mood and atmosphere; they can appear conspicuously expansive in this compact play, the 'lightning-swift economy' (Brennan, 160) of which has been remarked by many. Time, its delineation in action and its conceptualization, has a special role in *Macbeth*. Molly Mahood (131) refers to time as 'a predominant element' in the play's 'pattern of ideas'. T. McAlindon (214) sums up what many have said: 'In no other tragedy of Shakespeare is time so comprehensive in its significance or so conspicuously implicated in what is said and done', and this view has not been challenged. Put another way, 'the play seems to be dominated by an obsession with time' (Guj, 175). This obsession extends to the protagonist's own relation with time; Macbeth's 'nervous urgency' (Turner, 143) in the first part of the play gives way to a nihilistic sense of 'limitless and directionless time' (Booth, *'King Lear'*, 94) in his response to the news of his wife's death.

No succession of tomorrows will ever bring on that future for which the two of them plotted and longed.

Time and structure

The action of the first part of the play seems from the very start to take place within a carefully delineated, and rapidly unfolding, temporal structure. As it begins, the Sisters are already setting up their next meeting, within specific parameters: it will take place before sunset, 'when the battle's lost and won', on the heath and there they will meet Macbeth. This meeting comes about in the third scene, where Ross and Angus greet Macbeth with news of his promotion to Thane of Cawdor; in 1.4 they bring him to receive the honour at Duncan's hands. In 1.5 Macbeth's Lady reads her husband's letter and hears from the Messenger that the arrival of Duncan, who will honour the Macbeths by staying in their house, is imminent. A keynote sounded early is hurry. 'Characters rush about in frantic haste, the action strains forward, the present is only a stepping stone to the future' (Harcourt, 396). The sense is created not just of a gathering momentum but of a rush of events coming one of top of another. Already, things are beginning to happen out of turn. Macbeth should have been the one to announce Duncan's coming. His wife is so surprised by the Messenger's news that he has to explain it:

> So please you, it is true: our thane is coming.
> One of my fellows had the speed of him,
> Who, almost dead for breath, had scarcely more
> Than would make up his message.

> (1.5.34–7)

Yet the news is also ominously timely, for in her thoughts Duncan is already present in the shape of 'all that impedes thee from the golden round' that she wishes for Macbeth. Her greeting to her husband suggests an impatience for the fulfilment

64

of the Sisters' prophecies so great that she longs to jettison
temporal order:

> Great Glamis, worthy Cawdor,
> Greater than both, by the all-hail hereafter,
> Thy letters have transported me beyond
> This ignorant present, and I feel now
> The future in the instant.

(54–8)

Macbeth shares his wife's eagerness to be in charge of the
movement of time. He wants the assassination 'done quickly',
and ideally in such a way as to have no consequences, stopping
up the flow of time's river so that his act can be 'the be-all
and the end-all' and he can 'jump the life to come' (1.7). The
Macbeths cannot live in accord with time; preparing to receive
Duncan, Macbeth's Lady urges her husband 'to beguile the
time', to 'Look like the time', to deceive it by simulating
expected appearances. They will 'mock the time with fairest
show'. This temporal chaos in the lives of the Macbeths is
further defined by the play's focus in Acts 2 and 3 on the rapid
succession of events taking place on two action-packed nights.
On the first, Duncan arrives at the castle at Inverness (1.6) very
soon after Macbeth, having 'coursed him at the heels', and
almost immediately goes to dinner. Macbeth and his Lady, in
whispered exchanges outside the dining chamber (1.7), make
their plans while waiting for him to go to the bed 'Whereto . . . his
day's hard journey / Soundly invite[s] him'. The beginning of
Act 2 is explicitly located in the temporal sequence by Banquo's
dialogue with Fleance; it is late, after midnight, but the castle's
inhabitants are wakeful. Banquo remarks on the fact that
Macbeth is 'not yet at rest'. His Lady too is awake, ready to
give the signal for action. The knocking that brings to an end
the fearful scene of *post mortem* moves the action seamlessly
into an early morning (2.3) where the Porter is rudely awoken

from a drunken sleep after 'carousing till the second cock'. Macduff arrives to give Duncan his 'timely' morning call, afraid of being late. 'This sore night' as the Old Man calls it, is slow to end: 'By th' clock 'tis day, / And yet dark night strangles the travelling lamp' (2.4.6–7). But Macbeth has wasted no time, and no sooner than Malcolm and Donalbain have 'stolen away and fled', as Macduff wryly observes, 'He is already named, and gone to Scone / To be invested' (31–2).

Act 3 opens with Macbeth's preparations for a second bloody night, for which he and his Lady are preparing a 'solemn supper', another display of the obsequious hospitality which characterized Duncan's arrival under their battlements. This time the chief guest is to be Banquo, whose presence is solicited with fawning affability by his hosts. Banquo, however, insists on preceding the feast with an afternoon excursion, almost as if he had had some sixth sense that it might be better not to return. The numerous references to his plans by Macbeth – 'Ride you this afternoon?', 'Is't far you ride?', 'Goes Fleance with you?', 'Adieu, till you return at night' – draw attention to this intermission almost as a gap in the passage of time which the new king wants filled. After a ceremonial entrance with his royal entourage in the first scene, he sweepingly dismisses the assembled company:

> Let every man be master of his time
> Till seven at night; to make society
> The sweeter welcome, we will keep ourself
> Till supper time alone.

(3.1.40–3)

Time references permeate the first two scenes of this act. The feast is precisely scheduled. Macbeth fills in the afternoon making his plans with the two Murderers, even, unbeknownst to them, arranging for a third, but he can hardly wait for the onset of darkness. Hinting to his wife of the 'deed of dreadful note' that will take place before 'black Hecate's summons', he calls urgently on 'seeling night' to replace 'pitiful day', thus empowering him and authorizing, with its 'bloody and invisible hand', the murder he has arranged. But this time the night does not go according to plan (3.3). Not only does Fleance escape, but the murdered Banquo does not behave like a dead man, biding safe in the ditch where he was hacked down. The appearance of his bloodstained ghost at the banquet (3.4) makes Macbeth feel that the time is seriously out of joint:

> The times have been,
> That when the brains were out, the man would die,
> And there an end. But now they rise again
> With twenty mortal murders on their crowns,
> And push us from our stools.

> (3.4.76–80)

After hurried goodnights, the guests are dismissed and the scene ends with the Macbeths alone together. 'What is the night?', Macbeth asks his wife. Her response, 'Almost at odds with morning, which is which', suggests exhaustion. She longs for the natural rhythms of life, of sleeping and waking, to reassert themselves. But although Macbeth agrees to go to bed, he is already planning the next step: 'I will tomorrow, / And betimes I will, to the weïrd sisters. / More shall they speak' (130–2).

The sense of temporal momentum in the sequence of the play's events is maintained, even accelerated. No time must be lost, and Macbeth will be up early to call on the Sisters. But it is at this meeting (4.1) that he is faced with devastating evidence that his efforts to control time and tamper with natural sequence will, *sub specie aeternitatis*, come to nothing. The line of kings descended from Banquo, conjured up at his own insistence, does indeed stretch out to the crack of doom. Yet this seems only to strengthen his compulsion to be constantly moving ahead, 'to crown my thoughts with acts', and the destruction of Macduff's family takes place immediately (4.2). But this is a futile act of revenge; just as in the previous two killings the people who really mattered, the sons of Duncan and Banquo, escaped, so this time Macduff remains at large. In his desperation for hasty action, Macbeth involves himself in yet more killing – of Macduff's wife and family – that will achieve nothing, since the real enemy, Macduff, is absent.

But now, as the focus of the action shifts, from Scotland to England and from Macbeth to Malcolm and Macduff, its helter-skelter pace comes almost to a halt in the long scene of reflection and recuperation (4.3). Malcolm's desire to take stock and indulge in a period of grieving is reproved by Macduff, who feels that time is passing without positive action: 'Each new morn / New widows howl, new orphans cry, new sorrows / Strike heaven on the face' (4–6). But Malcolm is conscious of the need to wait for the right moment, 'as I shall find the time to friend', and by the end of the scene it seems to have arrived:

> our power is ready,
> Our lack is nothing but our leave. Macbeth
> Is ripe for shaking . . .
> The night is long that never finds the day.

> (239–41, 243)

Scenes in the last act showing the orderly progress of Malcolm and his English allies, joining up with the Scottish army, are intercut with scenes showing Macbeth in his increasingly disordered relationship with time. He is impatient for battle, calling several times for armour, yet giving out contradictory signals, outwardly full of nervous energy but inwardly exhausted. He senses that his life has been wasted, that he has never captured the present moment. For all his hurry, life has passed him by; he has lived not just 'long enough' but too long, approaching old age but without any prospect of its proper consolations. 'Endlessly relegating value to the future' (Zamir, 533), he has reached the recognition (5.5) that the time to come points to nothing beyond itself: only 'Tomorrow, and tomorrow, and tomorrow'. Even his wife's death is outside of temporal order: 'She should have died hereafter'. He is finally overcome by Macduff, the man who owes his life to an accident of time, being 'untimely ripped' from his mother's womb. The play ends with Malcolm's assertions of the re-establishment of temporal order. The sight of 'Th'usurper's cursed head' prefaces Macduff's claim that 'the time is free'. Malcolm will set about establishing himself as king with a series of acts carried out carefully, 'in measure, time and place'.

Chronology

This apparently clear and intelligible linear sequence is complicated in various ways. There are some temporal oddities which may be explicable in terms of textual problems, for example, the inconsistency between 3.6 and 4.1. In 3.6, in a dialogue between Lennox, clearly here an opponent of Macbeth to whom he refers as 'the tyrant', and another Lord, it appears that Macduff, having failed to attend Macbeth's feast in 3.4, has fled to England and that Macbeth knows this. But in 4.1 Lennox, here apparently serving Macbeth, brings him this very news and Macbeth is taken by surprise. Many editors find some kind of explanation for this in terms of textual corruption or revision.[1] While the suggestion that 'the impossible temporality just might be a daring structural embodiment of a dominant theme in the play' (Richardson, 288) implies a deliberately deceptive style of time management uncharacteristic of Shakespeare, there are undoubtedly temporal anomalies, or instances of temporal uncertainty, at several points. In the exchange between

---

1 Though Braunmuller tentatively suggests a rather elaborate timetable that would resolve the narrative inconsistency (261–2). See also Appendix 1, pp. 322–3.

Lennox and the Lord in 3.6 it is unclear if Macduff has arrived in the English court or is only on his way. Lennox prays that 'Some holy angel / Fly to the court of England and unfold / His message ere he come' (3.6.46–8), though King Edward's preparations for war (39) imply that he has already heard this message.[1] Indeed, in 4.3 Malcolm tells Macduff that 'before thy here-approach, / Old Siward, with ten thousand warlike men / Already at a point, was setting forth' (4.3.133–5). The Lord also tells Lennox how Macduff responded to Macbeth's invitation to the feast 'with an absolute, "Sir, not I" '. In 3.4 Macbeth is incredulous that 'Macduff denies his person / At our great bidding'. When his wife asks, 'Did you send to him, sir?', he replies, 'I hear it by the way; but I will send. / There's not a one of them but in his house / I keep a servant fee'd' (3.4.126–7, 128–30). This passage demonstrates another kind of temporal anomaly. As Marvin Rosenberg observes (478), 'An astonishing trick is played by Shakespeare here. Suddenly in the present a history has been inserted into the past' – the history, that is, of Macbeth's tyrannical practices, already established, although his reign seems only just to have begun. Other such instances slip easily into the text, creating a back-story for the characters and thickening the narrative. Act 2 clearly takes place immediately after the end of Act 1, Duncan having gone to bed after 'his day's hard journey' (1.7.63) to Macbeth's castle. Having told Macbeth that the King has gone to bed 'in unusual pleasure' (2.1.13), Banquo then goes on to say that he 'dreamt last night of the three weïrd sisters', but again, the action leaves no clear space when this dream could

---

1　The ambiguity of 37–9 does not help matters. In F, as here, they read: 'And this report / Hath so exasperate their king, that he / Prepares for some attempt of war.' Since they are immediately followed by Lennox's question 'Sent he to Macduff?', it appears at first that 'he' in 38 must be the same as 'he' in 40, that is, Macbeth; 'their' has sometimes been emended to 'the' (e.g. by Hanmer) to strengthen this reading. But the Lord is talking about King Edward, despite the difficulty of the abrupt change of referent.

have occurred. More contentious is the moment in 1.7 when Macbeth's Lady upbraids her husband for cowardice with reference to an occasion when he was fully prepared to undertake the murder of Duncan:

> What beast was't then
> That made you break this enterprise to me?
> When you durst do it, then you were a man;
> And to be more than what you were, you would
> Be so much more the man. Nor time nor place
> Did then adhere, and yet you would make both;

$$(1.7.47–52)$$

Her temporal indicators – 'When', 'then . . . then' – appear so specific that critics have used the passage to support the theory of a lost scene, or even of a plan to kill the King conceived before Macbeth met the Sisters.[1] But there is no need to resort to such suppositions here. Events can take place in the offstage lives of the characters to speed up and contextualize the onstage action, and to enrich it with subsequent ironies: Macbeth's wife in her sleepwalking scene clearly knows what has happened to Macduff's wife, though no one has been seen to tell her.

However it cannot be denied that, particularly in the first part of the play, linear time is handled with some complexity. The inconsistency between 1.2 and 1.3 suggests a certain temporal confusion. In 1.2 Ross describes the victory of Macbeth, 'Bellona's bridegroom', over the treacherous Thane of Cawdor, but in 1.3 Macbeth seems completely to have forgotten his feat and to believe the Thane of Cawdor to be still alive as a 'prosperous gentleman'. The many explicit temporal indicators

---

1 Muir (xlviii–xlix) discusses these possibilities, referring to the views of Coleridge, who conjectured that the Macbeths had discussed killing Duncan before the action of the play begins, and also of Bradley. But he rightly dismisses Dover Wilson's theory of an earlier version of the play in which this 'missing scene' was present (xxxiv–xxxviii).

in Acts 2 and 3 draw attention to the fact that the actual passage of time as represented onstage is 'logically impossible',[1] in that long hours – in the case of 3.4 an evening and a whole night – pass with such speed. This 'unnatural temporality' (Richardson, 287) is reflected in Macbeth's own confused and internally contradictory attitudes to time. The drive towards the future implicit in the play's opening line begins to infiltrate his consciousness as soon as he has heard the Sisters' predictions for him (1.3) 'Of noble having and of royal hope'. Once assured that the first two predictions have achieved the status of fact, Macbeth comments that 'The greatest is behind', presumably meaning 'still to come' (though 'behind' could mean 'in the past').[2] The 'Two truths' already told seem like 'happy prologues' to a greater action, but he is uncertain how to regard the prophecy as a whole. The future is balanced between conditionals (here italicized):

> This supernatural soliciting
> Cannot be ill; cannot be good. *If* ill,
> Why hath it given me earnest of success,
> Commencing in a truth? I am Thane of Cawdor.
> *If* good, why do I yield to that suggestion
> Whose horrid image doth unfix my hair,
> And make my seated heart knock at my ribs,
> Against the use of nature? . . .
>
> *If* chance will have me king, why chance may
>   crown me,
> Without my stir.

$$(1.3.132-9, 146-7)$$

---

1 Richardson, 285. Richardson is illuminating on the attention to temporality in the play, but his view that *Macbeth* is a 'radical experiment' in narrative structure (284) ignores the fact that time in tragedy is rarely realistically indicated and that double time-schemes (as notoriously in *Othello*), and the compression of temporal sequence (as in the final scene of Marlowe's *Dr Faustus* or Middleton and Rowley's *The Changeling*, 5.1) are not uncommon.

2 See *OED* behind *adv*. 1c.

At this point it seems as if he is willing to accept that the Sisters' predictions will come to pass without any intervention on his part, and that he has a choice in the matter. Yet his attitude to them is unstable. At first he is filled with terror at the 'horrid image' created by the temptation to make the murder something more than just 'fantastical'; further possibilities expressed through conditional phrasing prevent him from having a clear view of what lies ahead:

> *If* it were done, when 'tis done, then 'twere well
> It were done quickly. *If* th'assassination
> Could trammel up the consequence, and catch
> With his surcease, success: *that but* this blow
> Might be the be-all and the end-all, here,
> But here, upon this bank and shoal of time,
> We'd jump the life to come.

$$(1.7.1–7)$$

The complicated play of verb tenses and moods in this passage, and the speech as a whole, has often been discussed.[1] Macbeth mixes subjunctives and indicatives, contriving to identify the future with the present and 'converting what is to be done into what is already done' (Sypher, 101). This typifies that destructive longing he shares with his wife to be forever moving forward. Although none of the objections he makes to the murder in this passage is ever met, he still proceeds with it, apparently now believing – or at least persuaded by his wife to believe – that chance will *not* crown him without his stir. He is desperate to control time. The action against Banquo and Fleance is undertaken in a compulsion to counteract what has been predicted. His actions are without logic: he 'tries to create the future while simultaneously and contradictorily considering it as predetermined' (Waller, 131). Macbeth will challenge fate

---

1   See especially Berry, 52–3, and Sypher, 100–1.

to a contest[1] rather than accept that all he has done will be for the benefit of Banquo's issue, 'To make them kings, the seeds of Banquo kings'. He continues to act as if he can exercise some power over the future, determined after the banquet to get to the Sisters as soon as possible, force them to render up their secrets, and do whatever it takes to secure his position: 'for mine own good, / All causes shall give way' (3.4.133–4). Characteristically, the Sisters again palter with him (4.1), on the one hand showing him an apparently predetermined vision of a line of Banquo's descendants stretching out 'to th' crack of doom', but on the other offering advice for the future. The First Apparition urges him to 'Beware Macduff, / Beware the Thane of Fife', but the Second seems to counter this with his injunction to 'Be bloody, bold and resolute: laugh to scorn / The power of man, for none of woman born / Shall harm Macbeth' (4.1.78–80). Macbeth wants to take this for reassurance that the future is predetermined to his advantage, yet again he feels he cannot leave things to chance:

> Then live, Macduff: what need I fear of thee?
> But yet I'll make assurance double sure,
> And take a bond of fate: thou shalt not live,
> That I may tell pale-hearted fear it lies
> And sleep in spite of thunder.

$$(81-5)$$

By killing Macduff he will, as it were, take out a guarantee that fate will keep what he sees as an agreement made by the Second Apparition. Yet he finds himself constantly in a struggle to keep ahead. No sooner has he made the plan to secure his future by killing Macduff than he is informed that Macduff has eluded him by fleeing to England. Macbeth is in a race with time, which is always ahead: 'Time, thou anticipat'st my dread

---

1 See 3.1.70n., 71n. The lines have been read in different ways.

exploits. / The flighty purpose never is o'ertook / Unless the deed go with it' (143–5). There is a logical impossibility in these lines, as editors have noted; as Capell says, 'if purpose and deed go together, *o'ertaking* can not be predicated of either'.[1] But this is in keeping with the inner contradictions created by Macbeth's conflicted attitude towards time.

This conflict has sometimes been interpreted in terms of the simultaneous operation in the play of two time-schemes: most simply put, that of objective time, as measured by the natural progression of hours and seasons, and subjective, or personal, time, as perceived by Macbeth.[2] As has been shown, the play has a carefully signposted linear structure, and this does not only enforce the rapidity with which events move forward in a world apparently dominated by the actions of Macbeth, but also provides a sense that there is an alternative world in which events take place in a natural progression. Macbeth's evil progress is measured against what David Kastan (*Shapes*, 92) calls 'an objective temporal order'. Images of organic growth fill out the representation of this alternative, for instance the idea of time as a plant, expressed in Banquo's address to the Sisters as beings who can 'look into the seeds of time, / And say which grain will grow, and which will not' (1.3.58–9). Duncan draws on the same idea, envisaging his followers as crops which his benevolent nurture will bring to a harvest (1.4.28–9, 32–3), and is echoed by Malcolm (5.9.31). Macbeth, 'ripe for shaking', sees his wasted life as a dying tree, 'fallen into the sere, the yellow leaf'. The 'bloody stage' on which the ending of Duncan's life is played out is depicted against a background of life in the animal world; while Duncan and Banquo admire the delicacy of the air around Macbeth's castle and the contribution to it of the 'temple-haunting martlet', on

1 Capell, *Notes*, 23, cited by Braunmuller.
2 Sypher (94–107) articulates these in relation to Henri Bergson's theories about time and consciousness, opposing what he calls chronometric time to psychic time.

the night of the murder nature revolts, owls attack falcons and horses eat one another. That night was unnaturally prolonged; but at the end of Act 4, Malcolm perceives a reassertion of the regular diurnal rhythms: 'The night is long that never finds the day.'

Macbeth's early half-couplet, 'Come what come may, / Time, and the hour, runs through the roughest day' (1.3.149–50), acknowledges this rhythm, but it is not long before he is seeking to construct a 'fantasy time-world' (Waller, 131) within which to orchestrate a temporal momentum of his own. His wife looks forward to a future of their own devising; her 'dispatch' of the night's 'great business' will 'to all our nights and days to come, / Give solely sovereign sway and masterdom' (1.5.68, 69–70). She 'trusts the mechanism of cause and effect' (Sypher, 104) and time for her is simply a succession of incidents. But Macbeth's private world is not so orderly. His desire to bring on the future becomes an obsession, and the present is overtaken by the future. As he hallucinates the dagger he will use to kill Duncan, tenses collapse into one another and he cannot distinguish between the real and the imaginary: 'Thou marshall'st me the way that I was going, / And such an instrument I was to use' (2.1.42–3). At the end of the soliloquy he asserts, 'I go, and it is done'. Present and future become one. Harold Bloom writes of the play as 'a tragedy of the imagination', and characterizes Macbeth's imagination as fatally proleptic, always leaping forward to the consequences of an act not yet committed (517).[1] While for Bloom this marks Macbeth out as something of a seer, and contributes to a quality in him that critics from the Romantics onwards have called sublime, it is also part of his surrender to a world of disjointed time in which his efforts to take control of the future are constantly thwarted. Killing

1   Calderwood uses the same notion: 'The present is by no means an end in itself but a launching point for the future' (29).

Duncan is not enough, because it brings no security; he must then kill Banquo, and as soon as possible, since 'every minute of his being thrusts / Against my near'st of life' (3.1.119–20). But this murder has a result he has not planned on, Banquo is not, as Macbeth, proleptically perhaps, puts it, 'safe', and his ghost appears to take its place at the banquet. Macbeth's sense of order is outraged: when time took its normal course, as in the past, the dead stayed dead,

> But now they rise again
> With twenty mortal murders on their crowns,
> And push us from our stools. This is more strange
> Than such a murder is.

> (3.4.78–81)

He had thought to control the future by obliterating his rival, but the operations of time have taken a form he did not predict. His response is not to review his past actions but to move on faster and faster; his forward planning becomes hectically accelerated. But his constant plotting is never conclusive. He strives for mastery over his destiny, for agency, but is always thwarted, and more remains to be done. 'Finality is regularly unattainable throughout *Macbeth*', as Booth (*'King Lear'*, 93) suggestively comments.

Now Macbeth loses no time in his determination to get what he wants:

> I will tomorrow,
> And betimes I will, to the weïrd sisters.
> More shall they speak: for now I am bent to know
> By the worst means, the worst; for mine own good,
> All causes shall give way . . .
> Strange things I have in head, that will to hand,
> Which must be acted, ere they may be scanned.

> (3.4.130–4, 137–8)

77

The underlying theatrical metaphor brings out the temporal illogicality: the part is to be performed before it is learned. Macbeth wants desire and achievement to be impossibly simultaneous. In his speech at the end of 4.1, after he has witnessed the show of kings and realized that he cannot ever get anything he really wants to have, he is planning his next move:

> From this moment
> The very firstlings of my heart shall be
> The firstlings of my hand. And even now,
> To crown my thoughts with acts, be it thought and
> done.

(4.1.145–8)

Heart and hand will now act in complete concert, thinking and doing will be simultaneous. Present and future are one. Where once the doing of deeds was fraught with problems ('If it were done, when 'tis done, then 'twere well / It were done quickly'), and Macbeth begged for his eye to 'wink at the hand' so that he need not face the reality of what he was doing, now he scorns ratiocination: 'No boasting like a fool; / This deed I'll do before this purpose cool' (152–3). But what he does do is pointless; his murderers, this time more efficient, wipe out Macduff's whole family, but Macduff himself is beyond reach. It is the inverse of the situation with Banquo, although once again the person whose death would count escapes. The futility of Macbeth's murderous violence is underlined when Ross breaks the news of it to Macduff.

Time and succession

Try as he may, success always evades Macbeth. Ideas of success and succession pervade the play, helping to define its notion of futurity. There are several relevant senses: one thing happening after another, sons succeeding fathers, royal succession.

Success, a word with which Macbeth seems, to use Barbara Everett's term (96), 'infatuated', can in this period mean both good or bad fortune. Macbeth's fortunes in battle constitute 'success' in the former sense; but when he wishes that the assassination of Duncan would 'catch with his surcease, success', the word's potential for ambiguity reflects back on his belief that the predictions of the Sisters have given him 'earnest of success'. Macbeth longs to succeed as king, but to do so means he must find a means of avoiding the other part of their prophecy. Macbeth reads their prediction for Banquo, that he will 'get kings, though thou be none', to indicate that for him there will be only 'a fruitless crown . . . [and] a barren sceptre in my gripe, / Thence to be wrenched with an unlineal hand, / No son of mine succeeding' (3.1.60–3). He compliments his wife's boldness of spirit in wishing her to 'Bring forth men-children only', but the babe to which she has given suck is no part of their life, and no man child ever appears. Although he kills such sons as he can, those of Macduff and Old Siward, he fails to destroy those sons who are to succeed, Malcolm and Fleance. The process of lineal succession which Duncan initiates continues in despite of Macbeth's intervention, and in any case he has no line of his own with which to replace it.

In some ways it seems as if the regular processes of time, apparently at one with a world which is ultimately stable and predictable, will triumph. But the play's various complications of temporality discussed above, and the representation of Macbeth's subjective experience of time, allow for the possibility that a different model of the relation between time and causality may be operative. Kristen Poole plausibly suggests that the 'cosmic frame' within which Macbeth has his being owes much to Calvin's theology, whereby God's over-arching providence, and his 'arbitrary, unknowable will' supersede any construction of order and regularity in the operations of the cosmos.[1] Once crowned, Macbeth longs for future time to function in a regular and ordered way, so that he will be able to 'live the lease of nature, pay his breath / To time, and mortal custom' (4.1.98–9), according to the competing cosmological theology of Hooker based on the concept of a stable law of nature which is 'the stay of the whole world'.[2] But the world he inhabits is one of temporal chaos, in which night and day become confused, and he shares his wife's urgent longing to forego 'this ignorant present' and experience 'the future in the instant'. In the past, even in lawless ages, events took place in what Macbeth perceives as a natural order: 'The times have been, / That when the brains were out, the man would die, / And there an end' (3.4.76–8). In the radically unstable and contingent world of the present, however, it seems to him as if there is no telling what might happen: 'now they rise again / With twenty mortal murders on their crowns, / And push us from our stools' (78–80). There is no finality, no closure. Macbeth cannot say 'Amen' at the close of Duncan's life; he cannot sleep; for him, the longed-for future eventually presents itself as a series of hopeless and empty tomorrows. Macbeth's relation to time in this play which is so full of paradox and ambiguity, where what seems impossible comes regularly to pass, is appropriately fraught; and the play's own temporal disruptions suggest the experience of a period in which many people found them-selves uneasily attempting to negotiate between competing

---

1   Poole, 132. Poole gives an illuminating reading of Macbeth's situation as a dilemma arising from the failed attempt to negotiate between the opposing models of cosmology of John Calvin and Richard Hooker. She broadens her discussion of Calvin's thought in relation to *Macbeth* to take it outside the narrower stress on predestination with which some theological accounts (e.g. Stachniewski) are primarily concerned. Her lucid account of the connection between the 'volatile physics of Calvin's universe' (144) and his theory of predestination is more helpful for this play, and its problems with time, than the kind of cosmology based on Hooker that Tillyard proposes.

2   Hooker, *Sermon of Obedience* (1547), quoted by Tillyard (26).

cosmological systems and different ideas of how order and meaning were constituted in human life.

Malcolm's final speech is overtly concerned with issues of time and order. He tells his supporters that he will not 'spend a large expense of time / Before we reckon with your several loves / And make us even with you' (5.9.26–8). He knows there are many things to be done for the future good of his country 'Which would be planted newly with the time', and these he promises to 'perform in measure, time and place'. The emphases are on speed, efficient economics and good order. But the apparently restorative quality of the play's ending has not convinced everyone, and some have noticed disturbing implications of a circularity in the action. Malcolm's image for appropriate action, doing what would be 'planted newly with the time', recalls his father's unluckily worded promise to Macbeth: 'I have begun to plant thee, and will labour / To make thee full of growing'; the 'deluge of Hails' that welcomes Malcolm has been thought to invite comparison with the Sisters' greeting to Macbeth.[1] The linkage of the play's ending with its beginning has been accorded a kind of aesthetic elegance by M.J.B. Allen, who cites *Macbeth* as an exemplar of that sort of tragedy 'whose ends are fully anticipated in their beginnings' and calls it the 'most circular and self-contained' of all Shakespeare's plays (Allen, 4, 9). He shows how, for the reader, the opening scenes are re-experienced in the light of the closing ones, as prefiguring so much of what is to come, and how Macbeth re-enacts the treachery of Macdonald. Some stagings of the play have developed the disquieting implications of this circularity, bringing on the Sisters again at the end.[2] The long theatrical history of cuts to the final scene suggests dissatisfaction with what it can offer as closure.[3] As

---

1   For instance by Booth (*'King Lear'*, 96, 92).

2   See p. 102.

3   See p. 116.

king, Malcolm has not the stature of his father; Macbeth has no dying speech and his offstage death (if so presented) denies the protagonist tragic finality. But some of these objections can be made to other Shakespearean tragedies, which also suffer cuts to their original endings. What is unique to *Macbeth* is the all-pervasive theme of time, the foregrounding of it in the play's last speech and the meaning of this foregrounding as an ending.

MACBETH AND ITS SOURCES

As Miola has observed in his study of Seneca's influence on Shakespeare, sources may take different forms, and the traditional view of the source as 'a prior text that shapes a present one through authorial reminiscence and . . . manifests itself in verbal iteration' (*Classical*, 7) is not the only one. Sources may leave their traces in trains of association, affinities or what one critic has called 'resonances';[1] as Jones says, they may take the form of 'glancingly rapid effects [rather] than of a laborious working out of correspondences' (Jones, *Origins*, 272). Their uses may be more or less conscious. Shakespeare draws on a number of sources for *Macbeth*, and uses them in different ways. His main narrative source, the play's 'prior text', was Holinshed's *Chronicles*, which he had recently consulted when writing *King Lear*.[2] He followed Holinshed's account of Macbeth's career in considerable detail but supplemented it with material drawn from the reigns of other Scottish kings; he also used elements from the stories of the murder of King Duff by assassins hired by Donwald and his ambitious wife, of King Kenneth II's murder of his nephew Malcolm (son of King Duff)

---

1 Peyré revisits a familiar subject but provides an exceptionally sensitive and restrained account of it.

2 While it is generally assumed that Shakespeare used the 1587 edition of the *Chronicles*, I am persuaded by the argument of Kinney, 'Scottish', that he also consulted the 1577 edition on account of his apparent knowledge of illustrations which only appear there.

to ensure that his own son should succeed him, and perhaps also of the brief account of the murder of King Natholocus by one of his trusted servants who had been told by a witch that the King would meet his end in just this way. There is no doubt that the overriding influence was the atmosphere 'of violent deeds and haunting remorse' that Holinshed creates from a succession of stories 'of men driven by an irresistible impulse into deeds of treachery and bloodshed but haunted when the deed was done by spectres of conscience and superstition'.[1] In Holinshed Shakespeare found a medieval Scotland which was war-torn and primitive, desperately in need of the civilizing hand of England.

Holinshed's account of Macbeth's rise to power and fall through tyranny gave Shakespeare a clear narrative line, which he followed with considerable fidelity and largely in sequence, including the rebellions against Duncan's rule and the role of Macbeth and Banquo in quelling them, their meeting with the Sisters and the prophecies, the subsequent growth of Macbeth's ambition, fuelled by his ambitious wife, the murder of Banquo and escape of Fleance, Macbeth's development as a tyrant, his slaughter of Macduff's family, Malcolm's escape to England and his testing of Macduff, the mustering of English support for Malcolm, Macduff's killing of Macbeth and Malcolm's creation of Scotland's first earls. Shakespeare followed Holinshed at a level of some detail. For instance, he made use of Holinshed's reference to the fact that Macbeth was 'sore troubled' when Duncan created Malcolm Prince of Cumberland, and that he was swayed by the words of 'a certaine witch, whome he had in great trust' that he would not be killed by a man born of woman or vanquished till Birnam Wood came to Dunsinane. He followed Holinshed's account of the meeting between Malcolm and Macduff in England especially closely, perhaps because this is, as Kenneth Muir says, the only passage of

1   Grierson & Smith, xviii–xix.

dialogue of any length relating to Macbeth's reign.[1] Holinshed explicitly states that it is Malcolm's initial suspicions of Macduff that induce him to test his compatriot's loyalty, a fact which Shakespeare allows his audience to realize only by degrees. There are two interesting changes of emphasis in the representation of Malcolm himself: Holinshed's Malcolm accuses himself of dissimulation, making it his crowning vice, but in Shakespeare this is one vice that Malcolm does not claim; and while Shakespeare's Malcolm opens the retraction of his statement of vice by stating that he is a virgin, Holinshed's Malcolm says nothing about this. Elsewhere, Shakespeare makes changes that bear on the management of the tragedy more broadly. In Holinshed, Macbeth and Duncan are cousins of contrasted temperament, the former 'somewhat cruell', the latter 'soft and gentle', 'negligent . . . in punishing offenders', and even, in the eyes of Makdowald, 'a faint-hearted milksop, more meet to governe a sort of idle monks in some cloister, than to have the rule of such valiant and hardie men of warre as the Scots were'. His 'small skill in warlike affaires' is an important weakness in a king.[2] Although Macbeth and Duncan each acknowledge their kinship in Shakespeare, the characters are not contrasted in this way; Shakespeare redirects the idea of contrast away from that of two styles of ruler to compare Macbeth in moral terms with two rivals, shaping the action around his relations with first Banquo and then Macduff. The portrayal of Macduff as the man who will become Macbeth's nemesis is sharpened by Shakespeare's change to a crucial series of events in Macduff's life. In Holinshed, Macduff knows of the slaughter of his wife and children and goes to England to revenge it; but in Shakespeare, his poignant discovery of this

---

1 Muir, 4.3n. Kinney suggests that it was 'the congruence [of Holinshed] with the ideas of Buchanan on right rule' that made Shakespeare 'indulge in' this long dialogue ('Scottish', 48).

2 This characterization of Duncan is found in many major histories of early Scotland, including Fordun's *Chronica Gentis Scotorum* (*c*. 1370), Boece and Buchanan.

7   Slaughter of Macduff's wife and children, *Holinshed's Chronicles* (1577)

horror only takes place after he has come to England to rouse Malcolm to action. Thus, his motivation for revenge on Macbeth is charged with his sense of guilt and responsibility, and the play's handling of the themes of masculinity and fatherhood considerably complicated.

It is also key to Shakespeare's tragedy that Duncan's ineptitude as a ruler is nowhere pointed up.[1] Rather, Macbeth speaks in admiration of Duncan's style of rule when he says that the King 'Hath borne his faculties so meek, hath been / So clear in his great office'; Macduff calls him 'a most sainted king'. It is often assumed that Duncan in the play is an old man,[2] but while this is not explicit in the text, there has been some adjustment of ages, since Malcolm, 'scarce out of his childhood' at the time of Duncan's death, according to Buchanan,[3] is a young man in the play, old enough to be thought guilty along with his younger brother Donalbain of contriving the murder of their father. The

1   It is key to the influential readings of Berger, 'Early', and Booth, *'King Lear'*.
2   E.g. in the RSC productions by Nunn (1976) and Doran (1999).
3   Bullough, 7.513. Bullough includes excerpts from the English translation of T. Page (1690), and all references to Buchanan are taken from this.

kinship of Macbeth and Duncan has a political significance in Holinshed which is obscured in Shakespeare. According to the practice of tanistry, whereby royal successors were named from a collateral rather than a direct line of the family, Macbeth would have had a good claim to the throne as Duncan's cousin. Holinshed does not allude to tanistry directly, but mentions 'the old lawes of the realme' whereby if the successor was 'not of able age to take the charge upon himselfe, he that was next of bloud unto him should be admitted' (Bullough, 7.496). In Holinshed, Macbeth bears a grudge against Duncan for having robbed him of what he considered a legitimate 'hope'.[1]

Two further changes transform Macbeth's story decisively: in Holinshed, Macbeth is aided by a group of 'trustie friends, amongst whome Banquho was the chiefest' in the killing of Duncan, and subsequently he rules Scotland well for ten years, as Holinshed stresses,[2] correcting the abuses that had resulted from Duncan's ineffective regime, before he begins to display the signs of tyranny. It is characteristic of Shakespeare to condense his time-scheme in the interests of speeding up the tragic action; and for the tragic focus to centre on Macbeth the idea of Duncan's murder as part of a conspiracy among like-minded men had to be abandoned (and James's ancestor Banquo, accordingly, to be morally resuscitated). What is essential to the tragedy is that although Shakespeare appears to remove any element from his source that might have been used to justify the regicide, he still managed to create in Macbeth a protagonist who commands the audience's sympathy for much of the play. Some of the elements that complicate and enrich the character of Macbeth were imported from other stories of murder. Donwald, a trusted lieutenant of King Duff, is shamed and angered when the King executes some of his kinsmen, and,

---

1 Dover Wilson (xiii) considers that Shakespeare suppressed suggestions 'still discernible in Holinshed' of Macbeth's claim to the throne.

2 In the 1587 edition, the laws that Macbeth makes are set out in larger type.

urged on by his wife, plans to kill him when the King is a guest in his castle, 'though he abhorred that act greatlie in his owne heart' (Bullough, 7.482). The murder is carried out by Donwald's servants, and when it is discovered in the morning, the chamber covered in blood, he pretends in public to know nothing of it; behaving 'like a mad man running to and fro', he kills the King's two chamberlains. For a long period afterwards the sun and moon do not shine in Scotland, and horses 'of singular beautie and swiftnesse did eate their owne flesh' (Bullough, 7.484). The idea of the conscience-stricken murderer being reproved by a voice warning him of divine vengeance and keeping him from sleep comes from the story of King Kenneth, who killed his nephew Malcolm to prevent him succeeding to the throne. The ambiguous role of the Sisters and of supernatural prophecy in Macbeth's criminal career is adumbrated in the account of the unnamed gentleman whom King Natholocus sends to consult a witch about the outcome of a revolt against his rule. The gentleman is told that the King is soon to be murdered, not by one of his enemies but by a friend whom he especially trusts, in fact, by himself. He upbraids the witch because he has no desire to do such a deed. But on his way home he has second thoughts, once he starts to consider the likelihood of danger to himself if he tells the King what the witch has said. Eventually, 'he determined with himselfe to worke the surest way' and stabs the King to death in his privy chamber. Holinshed's marginal note is of interest: 'What happened by giving credit to the woords of a witch' (Bullough, 7.478). In most of these stories witches are involved.

In Holinshed, then, Shakespeare found a high proportion of the narrative elements from which he structured his plot. It has been suggested by many critics that he supplemented this basis with details from George Buchanan's *Rerum Scoticarum Historia* (1582), and although there was no English translation available at the time, this seems very likely. Buchanan, who had been tutor to James, was a historian of a different stamp from Holinshed, of republican persuasion, with a European reputation as a humanist scholar and a more sceptical turn of mind. Although his account of Macbeth does not ignore the supernatural aspects of the story, they are differently inflected. For instance, the Sisters are three beautiful women who appear to Macbeth in a dream, and hail him by various titles including King of Scotland, thus encouraging royal ambitions he had already begun to entertain. The prophecies about the coming of Birnam Wood to Dunsinane and the man not of woman born are nowhere mentioned, and the wood features only in the form of green boughs which Malcolm's soldiers stick up on their helmets 'representing an Army Triumphing' (Bullough, 7.516). Of Macbeth's demise, Buchanan observes that 'some of our Writers do here Record many Fables, which are like *Milesian* Tales, and fitter for the Stage, than an History; and therefore I omit them' (Bullough, 7.517). Norbrook (99) argues persuasively that Buchanan's history constituted a radical view of kingship which Shakespeare attempted to revise in *Macbeth*.[1] Yet there are aspects of Buchanan's work that may well have influenced the play in more direct ways. Buchanan characterizes Macbeth himself more fully than does Holinshed, noting that he 'was of a sharp Wit, and of a very lofty Spirit' (Bullough, 7.511) and exploring his mental turmoil at key points – suggesting, for instance, how his insecurity after the killing of Duncan (even though carried out with the aid of 'intimate Friends' including Banquo) 'hurried his Mind into dangerous Precipices, so that he converted his Government, got by Treachery, into a Cruel Tyranny' (7.514). Buchanan also stresses more than Holinshed how Macbeth comes to regard Banquo as a threat, because he is powerful and active (*'potens et industrius'* in Buchanan),[2] and

---

1   See also pp. 35–8 above.

2   Buchanan also describes Banquo as *'Regio iam sanguine imbutus'*. Page translates this as 'also of the Blood Royal', but Bullough (7.514, fn. 2) says this is 'properly "already stained with blood of a king"'. Paul (218) renders the phrase 'with royal blood in his veins', which makes more sense in the context.

invites him to supper even while planning his murder.[1] The
timing of Macduff's flight to England in Shakespeare seems to
owe more to Buchanan than to Holinshed, since in the former
the slaughter takes place after Macduff, threatened by Macbeth,
has fled Scotland for his own safety. Bullough also suggests
that Buchanan supplied the idea of the 'insane root, / That takes
the reason prisoner' (1.3.85–6) which Banquo thought might
have produced a hallucination of the Witches, in his account of
the drugged potion that Duncan had administered to the Danish
army so that Macbeth and Banquo could enter their camp by
stealth and slaughter them. The amount of detail that Buchanan
puts into his description of 'a Poysonous Herb ... called,
Somniferous Night-shade' (Bullough, 7.512) is eye-catching
enough to attract Shakespeare's attention and resurface in
another context.

John Leslie's *De Origine, Moribus, et Rebus Gestis Scotorum*
(1578) is regarded by Bullough as a possible source, and by
Paul (212) as among the histories which Shakespeare, in
his view, 'took some pains' to consult, again in Latin. Leslie
summarizes the reigns of Duncan and Macbeth without much
new detail, but what he adds to the accounts of Holinshed and
Buchanan is an emphasis on Banquo as originator of the Stuart
dynasty. In particular, he supplies genealogical tables, including
one which shows the family tree of the Stuarts with Banquo at
the base of the trunk and James VI as the uppermost branch
(see Fig. 8). But since it shows, in a prominent position, '*Maria
Jacobi V filia*', the King's mother and a figure of controversial
reputation even at the time, it is unlikely to be the inspiration
for the line of kings in 4.1, which does not include Mary Stuart.
The contemporary interest in the King's family tree and his
descent from Banquo motivated the address to James that
prefaced Matthew Gwinn's Latin play *Vertumnus Sive Annus*

---

1 Paul (218) and Bullough (7.440) note Buchanan's term '*familiariter*', meaning in a
friendly way, to describe the manner of Macbeth's invitation.

8 Banquo and his descendants, family tree from John Leslie, *De Origine, Moribus, et Rebus Gestis Scotorum* (1578). Banquo is at the foot of the tree, James VI at the top

90

Recurrens, performed at Oxford on 29 August 1605 and printed in 1607.[1] In this, three Sibyls recall Banquo, 'proud Lochaber's Thane', and the promise of 'eternal rule' to his descendants, and hail the king as 'Lord of Britain, Ireland, France'. While this little pageant has sometimes been accorded considerable importance as a source for the play, there is nothing to suggest that Shakespeare actually knew it or was even present in Oxford at the time; and the resemblances between it and the words of the Sisters may well be due to a common source in Holinshed.

Inga-Stina Ewbank distinguishes between two types of source in Shakespeare: those used as 'storehouses of plot and character material' and those suggesting 'ways of analysing and defining emotional situations' (Ewbank, 'Fiend-like', 53), and for *Macbeth*, Seneca's plays are the most important examples of the latter. She cites *Medea* as a play which Shakespeare drew on to enlarge his conception of Macbeth's Lady beyond that of the stereotype of the ambitious wife who figures several times in Holinshed. It is not only the motif of child-murder, 'the ultimate *nefas*' (Miola, *Classical*, 108), which connects the two characters, but the whole presentation of 'an obsessed woman perverting her woman's nature' in order to commit a great crime (Ewbank, 'Fiend-like', 86). Ewbank suggests that Shakespeare consulted the recent English translation of Seneca's play by John Studley in *Seneca His Tenne Tragedies* (1581), as well

---

1 The text of the address is given in Bullough, 7.470–2, with an English translation. He refers to it as an analogue. Paul, aiming to bolster his case for the 'royal play', calls it the '*fons et origo*' of *Macbeth*. Goldberg (262, n.10) notes that Bullough's text 'may not represent the exact form of the entertainment'; it has no mention of Macbeth, whereas Sir Isaac Wake in his description of the event in *Rex Platonicus* (1607) states that '*tres olim Sibyllae occurrisse duobus Scotiae proceribus* Macbetho & Banchioni, *& illum praedixisse Regem futurum, sed Regem nullum geniturum, hunc Regem non futurum, sed reges geniturum multes*' (18). This wording is quite close to that of the play, but the question of Shakespeare's access to, and knowledge of, the event remains unresolved. The King's Men were in Oxford on 9 October 1605 (Chambers, *ES*, 2.212) but there is no record of their being there in August. See also Braunmuller, 5–6.

as using a Latin text; she draws attention to Studley's stress on Medea as 'a wilfully wicked moral agent', in line with the early modern moralistic approach to Seneca, and his insertion of the word 'wicked' to 'place' Medea (as she puts it) even where there is no justification in the original for it. Several elements key to Shakespeare's presentation of the Lady appear in the soliloquy with which the vengeful Medea opens the play: the incantatory rhythms in which an address to 'threefolde shapen Hecate' is included; the vision of slain children; above all, the need to summon up strength and courage for the deed to come and to 'exile all foolish Female fear, and pity' from her mind, and the idea of hands bathed in blood. In Act 4 Medea calls upon the assistance of Hecate in making her poisons powerful, and Gillespie thinks that the Lady's invocation to the spirits in 1.5 'may be meant expressly to recall' this speech.[1] Miola (*Classical*, 106) notes in *Medea* the connection between a 'suggestive verbal cluster' around *facio* and its derivatives (*feci, perfectum*, etc.) and Shakespeare's play on the seminal terms 'do, deed, done'. A second play with abundant resonances for *Macbeth* is *Hercules Furens*, which Shakespeare may have used earlier for *Richard III* (itself in some ways a source for *Macbeth*) in its portrayal of the aspiring tyrant.[2] *Hercules*

---

1   Gillespie, 455. The extract he gives from Studley's translation is as follows: 'Breath on these venoms Hecate, with deadly myght inspyre, / Preserve the touching poulder of my secret covert fyre, / O graunt that these my cloked craftes so may bewitch theyr Eyes, / That lykelyhoode of treason none they may heerein surmyse: / So worke that they in handling it may feele no kynde of heate: / Her stewing breast, her seathing vaynes, let fervent fyer freate / And force her rosted pyning lymmes to drop and melt away'.

2   On the influence of *Hercules Furens*, see also Craig, 'Accidents', and Atkins. Macbeth and Richard III have been the subject of comparison as characters since the eighteenth century. See, for example, William Richardson, *Characters of Shakespeare* (1774), Thomas Whately, *Remarks on Some Characters of Shakespeare* (1785), Richard Cumberland in *The Observer* (1785–91) and Elizabeth Montague, *An Essay on the Writings and Genius of Shakespeare . . .* (1769). Extracts are included in Vickers, *Critical*, vols 5 and 6.

Furens includes both child-killing and the motif of bloody hands which 'vividly symbolize the untrammelled consequences of action, the moral pollution which attaches indelibly to the murderer' (Miola, *Classical*, 116).[1] Hercules' hands drip with the blood of the tyrant Lycus whom he has killed, as he feels the onset of the madness which will cause him to murder his own wife and children; the daytime sky darkens and the sun disappears. As the play ends, Hercules feels himself despised by the whole world, and, like Macbeth, cannot imagine that any sea will ever wash his hands clean of blood.

But the influence of Seneca on *Macbeth* is more diffuse than this might suggest, which has led critics to think that Shakespeare may have reread his plays while working on his own.[2] Muir suggests that the first chorus of *Agamemnon*, in Studley's translation, gave Shakespeare inspiration for some of his descriptions of chaos and disorder in the natural world,[3] while Miola (*Classical*, 87–8) finds echoes of it in Macbeth's 'Tomorrow, and tomorrow, and tomorrow' speech. It is also the source for the aphorism, familiar to playwrights of the period, '*Per scelera semper sceleribus tutum est iter*' (*Agamemnon*, 115) which Shakespeare renders in two forms: as 'Things bad begun, make strong themselves by ill' (3.2.56) and 'I am in blood / Stepped in so far, that should I wade no more, / Returning were as tedious as go o'er' (3.4.134–6). Another well-known Senecan maxim, '*Curae leves loquuntur, ingentes stupent*' (*Phaedra*, 607) appears in 4.3.210–11, when Malcolm bids Macduff 'Give sorrow words. The grief that does not speak / Whispers the o'erfraught heart and bids it break.' Numerous features of Senecan tragedy appear in the play, for example, the obsession with sacrilegious crime, vaulting ambition and the setting of personal daring against 'impossibilities in the world

---

1 Miola notes that '*manus*' occurs 55 times in *Hercules Furens*.

2 E.g. Peyré, 141, citing Muir, Ewbank, Miola.

3 See Muir, 4.1.56n. and 5.3.45n.

of nature',[1] the protagonist's self-dramatization and the 'heated rhetoric' (Atkins, 11) that characterizes Macbeth's style of speech at fraught moments. But, as many have noted, the Senecanism of the play is inflected with Christian attitudes towards the meaning of crime, informing Macbeth's sense of the consequences of killing Duncan, and the regret and awareness of loss that he experiences.

A number of other works have been proposed as possible sources for the play, including Montaigne's *Essays* (translated by John Florio in 1603), Pierre Le Loyer's *A Treatise of Specters* (published in English translation in 1605) and, for some localized instances, the anonymous pamphlet *Newes from Scotland* (1591),[2] Camden's *Remains* (1605)[3] and Samuel Daniel's *The Queenes Arcadia* (1606).[4] Montaigne's *Essays* have often been cited as a source for Shakespeare, whether in Florio's translation of 1603 (though possibly available earlier)[5] or in French, and Shakespeare probably consulted them for *King Lear*.[6] There are two specifically which relate to *Macbeth*: 'Our affections are transported beyond ourselves' (1.3) and 'Of the force of imagination' (1.20). In both cases the inspiration is general rather than particular, and there are no close verbal correspondences, but they illuminate aspects of Shakespeare's characterization of Macbeth which he did not find in Seneca or his historical sources. Macbeth's inability to live in the present

1 Craig ('Accidents', 7) compares *Hercules Furens*, 735ff., with *Mac* 3.4.98–104.
2 It is hard to imagine that Shakespeare would not have consulted this work, given that it is an account of a plot by Scottish witches against the King, the publication of which James himself commissioned. For instances in the play where it may be reflected, see 1.1.0.1, 1.3.8 and 4.1.6–8. Shakespeare may also have consulted the King's own *Daemonologie* (1597).
3 See 5.9.10–19n.
4 See 5.3.39–45n.
5 Hankins, 15. Hankins is wisely cautious about making claims for Montaigne's direct influence on Shakespeare, though he records a large number of parallels between their ideas.
6 See Bullough, 7.305.

9   Woodcut from James VI and I's *Newes from Scotland* (1591)

resonates with Montaigne's view of the destructiveness of 'gaping after future things': 'Feare, desire, and hope, draw us ever towards that which is to come, and remove our sense and consideration of that which is, to amuse us on that which shall be . . . *Calamitosus est animus futuri anxius* (SEN. *Epi.* 98). *A minde in suspense what is to come, is in a pitiful case.*'[1] The essay on imagination gives many examples of people deceived into believing what is not true through the strength of their imaginations, and Montaigne describes vividly the physical effects of the 'very great conflict and power of imagination' to which he claims himself to be susceptible: 'Wee sweat, we shake, we grow pale, and we blush at the motions of our imaginations . . . We cannot command our haire to stand on

1   Montaigne, 1.25.

end, nor our skinne to startle for desire or feare. Our hands are often carried where we direct them not. Our tongue and voice are sometimes to seeke of their faculties, the one loseth her speech, the other her nimbleness'.[1] The power of the imagination is mentioned again in Le Loyer's *Treatise of Specters*, which Muir thinks a likely source for Banquo's appearance in the banquet scene.[2] Le Loyer notes that tyrants responsible for many deaths are often 'troubled and tormented with most horrible phantosmes and imaginations', which often take the form of 'sundry visions and apparitions of those whome they have murthered'.[3] He gives the example of King Thierry, who murders Simmachus, and afterwards is haunted by his victim in circumstances very like those in which Banquo's ghost appears to Macbeth:

> On an euening as hee sate at supper . . . the face of Simmachus in a most horrible shape and fashion, with mustachoes, knitting his browes, frowning with his eyes, biting his lippes for very anger, and looking awry upon him [appeared].[4]

Le Loyer makes a distinction between what he calls 'specters' and 'phantosmes'. The former is

> an imagination of a substance without a Bodie, the which presenteth itself sensible unto men, against the order and course of nature, and maketh them afraid . . . The Specter hath a substance hidden and concealed, the which seemeth to move the fantastique body, the which it hath taken. Moreover, the Phantosme (being as it is) a thing without life, hath not any will: whereas

1 Montaigne, 1.93. Paul, 48–9, considers that Shakespeare 'seems to have pondered . . . deeply' the opening words of this essay.
2 Muir, *Sources*, 216. Paul, 57–9, had previously discussed it.
3 Le Loyer, 112, as quoted by Muir, *Sources*, 216.
4 Le Loyer, 112ᵛ, as quoted by Muir, *Sources*, 216.

the Specter, if it will, doth appeare unto us: if it will
not, it doth not appeare.[1]

Although there are no specific verbal connections to Macbeth's
speeches at the sight of Banquo's ghost, the passage might
have inspired horrified speculations about the nature of the
speechless, glaring ghost and its lifeless yet moving body.
Shakespeare clearly sought ways to delineate Macbeth's subjectivity, and these works that explore the different manifestations of the power of the imagination may have suggested
some.

MACBETH ON THE STAGE

Macbeth has enjoyed a long and full stage history, beginning
with Simon Forman's account of a production at the Globe in
1611.[2] Forman's recollections of what he saw may be mingled
with those of what he read about Macbeth in Holinshed, and
need treating with some caution. He says nothing of the actors
and little of the quality of the performance, although it is clear
that he was impressed by the banquet scene, and the 'great
passion of fear and fury' demonstrated by Macbeth at the sight
of Banquo's ghost. The play has been continuously in production
from the 1660s to the present day, and its popularity has never
waned. This history has already been described extensively.[3]
Rather than attempt yet another chronological coverage, this
brief section will consider a selection of themes and topics that
have proved significant in productions in England over a long
period, up to the present day. My hope is to provide an overview

1 Quoted from Paul, 57–8.
2 The text of Forman's account is given in Appendix 2.
3 There are three book-length studies by Bartholomeusz, Rosenberg and Kliman, and
   an edition by Wilders in the Shakespeare in Production series. Further accounts are
   given by Sprague, *Actors*, 224–81, Carlisle, *Greenroom*, 320–427, and Laury
   Magnus, in Drakakis & Townshend, 55–94.

that is both historical and comparative, and also to give a sense of some of the different ways in which the play has been interpreted for modern audiences and performance conditions. My focus is on stage productions, and films are mentioned only in passing. In Appendix 4 I list the productions referred to in this introduction.

The pre-eminence of the Witches

William Davenant's adaptation, the form in which *Macbeth* was known in the theatre from the 1660s, when Pepys wrote enthusiastically about it, to Garrick's first performance as Macbeth in 1744, gave particular prominence to the Witches. The title-page of this version, *Macbeth, A Tragaedy. With all the Alterations, Amendments, Additions, and New Songs. As it's now Acted at the Duke's Theatre*, is iconic; the '*Alterations, Amendments, Additions, and New Songs*' continued to be staged well after Garrick claimed to have returned to the play 'as written by Shakespeare'. The middle of the play was all witches: 3.6 was omitted, and the Hecate scene, 3.5, enlarged with lines and music from Middleton's *The Witch*, was followed immediately by a version of 4.1 with much extra witch business, more lines from *The Witch* and many more witches. In addition to the original three Sisters, singing witches featured regularly in cast lists from the eighteenth century to the later nineteenth. One or more verses of the song indicated in F only by the cue, '*Blacke Spirits, &c.*' in 4.1 are called for from '*all the singing witches*' in Edward Salmon and J. Lee's 1753 text *The Historical Tragedy of Macbeth*, in John Philip Kemble, in the texts of William Oxberry (1821), Charles Kean, Edwin Booth, Henry Irving and elsewhere. Matthew Locke's music, probably composed for the Davenant version, was a regular accompaniment. The Witches were sometimes given an extra scene including songs and dances, adapted from Davenant, after the discovery of Duncan's murder. This was staged at least as late as Charles Kean (1853).

Samuel Phelps had attempted to break with this tradition in his second production of the play at Sadlers Wells in 1847, announcing that he would offer 'Macbeth from the original text, dispensing with the Singing Witches', and was applauded critically for his boldness. But the pressure of custom was too great, and in 1858 five singing witches appeared, with Locke's music reinstated. Irving in 1888 regarded himself as an innovator in having female witches, and in aiming 'to divest [them] of that semi-comic element which at one time threatened to obscure, if not altogether to efface, their supernatural significance.'[1] Since Davenant's time the Witches had been played by male actors as a comic turn. Charles Macklin in 1773 made an effort to treat the Witches seriously, as did Kemble in 1794 in his staging of their scenes:

> The scenes were all new, and the witches no longer wore mittens, plaited caps, laced aprons, red stomachers, ruff, etc. (which was the dress of those weird sisters, when Mess. Beard, Champness, etc. represented them with Garrick's Macbeth) or any human garb, but appeared as preternatural beings, distinguishable only by the fellness of their purposes, and the fatality of their delusions.[2]

But neither Macklin, Kemble nor Irving attempted to pare down their parts, as Phelps had done, and Irving's production made the spectacular effects of the combined scenes 3.5 and 4.1 central to its attractions. Kemble had a chorus of fifty or sixty singing witches, and also a group of children to represent the 'Black spirits and white, / Red spirits and grey'. Irving's Hecate was attended by sixty spirits, 'clad mystically in greenish white gauze' who performed to an 'exquisite choral

---

1 Preface to the printed text as performed at the Lyceum in 1888, in Richards, 255–6.
2 W.C. Oulton, *The History of the Theatres*, 2 vols (1796), 2.139, quoted in Nagler, 413.

setting of "Black Spirits"' (Rosenberg, 508). Such spectacle lengthened the playing time; despite heavy cutting of the text itself, productions would run to three hours or more. Probably the last major *Macbeth* to take this shape was that of Herbert Beerbohm Tree in 1911. He cut 4.2 and most of 4.3, also nearly fifty lines from 4.1; but he staged the Hecate material (including 3.5) elaborately, with extra witches, songs and dances and the appearance of a 'wraith-like horde' behind the Apparitions. His staging was much admired, but not simply as spectacle; the Witches were said to represent 'the psychic realities usually glimpsed only in dream and nightmare', and contributed to the transformation of *Macbeth* into 'a dream play, as essentially unrealistic as Maeterlinck's *Pelléas et Mélisande*' (Mullin, 'Strange', 135).

In the earlier twentieth century, when it was generally taken for granted that the Hecate scenes were inauthentic and would not be staged, the supernatural element of the play was reconceptualized, and largely replaced by the psychological, with the Sisters themselves downplayed. William Poel in 1909 had included Hecate and her three attendants, dressed in masquing costumes, but this was regarded as an eccentric experiment (Moore, 32). Sir Frank Benson in a wartime touring production (1917/18) cut 3.5 but included Hecate and a chorus of witches in 4.1.[1] For most of the twentieth century, however, Hecate was rarely seen onstage. Peter Hall's production at the National Theatre in 1978, which included both songs in full, the Hecate scene (3.5) and all the Hecate and Witch lines in 4.1, appeared an aberration. 'An uncommon antiquarian gift', the critic J.C. Trewin called it, but the general impression was not favourable, despite the beauty of the young Judi Bowker as Hecate, chosen 'to make evil look as wholesome and innocent and good as

---

1   See the promptbooks held at the Shakespeare Centre, Stratford-upon-Avon (72.919 [4506] and [10725]).

possible'.[1] More typical have been stagings like that of Theodore Komisarjevsky (1933) who depicted the Witches (through judicious cutting of their lines) first as old women without any suggestion of supernatural powers, plundering corpses on the battlefield and telling the fortunes of Macbeth and Banquo through palmistry, and later as hallucinatory projections of Macbeth's diseased imagination, like Banquo's ghost.[2] In like spirit, Tyrone Guthrie in 1934 cut the opening scene completely, believing it to be unShakespearean and wanting to dispel the belief that the Sisters 'are a governing influence of the tragedy'.[3] Trevor Nunn's widely admired and minimalist RSC production (1976), which limited spectacle to effects created by means the audience would see, such as the use of a thunder-sheet, the swinging of a naked light-bulb and the production of misshapen dolls given by the Witches to a hallucinating Macbeth in the cauldron scene, suggested that the power of the Witches was in large part due to their affinity with Macbeth.[4] Bernice Kliman refers to 'the smooth integration of the natural and the supernatural' as an effect of the unified production style (129). The austere staging, in bare, black-walled auditoria with the audience gathered closely round a circle chalked on the wooden floor marking out the playing area, made the play a peculiarly intimate and intense experience, and contributed to the means whereby it evoked evil. Braunmuller (83) considers that Nunn achieved a new expression of the demonic, through effects

---

1   Trewin's review features in his article 'Shakespeare in Britain', *SQ*, 30.2 (1979), 151–8, 156. Hall's comment on Hecate comes from a note to John Bury, preserved at the National Theatre Archive. Hall defends his inclusion of the Hecate scenes in dialogue with John Russell Brown, in Brown, 242–4. He had obviously had a change of heart since his production at Stratford in 1967, which cut 3.5 and all reference to Hecate.

2   The staging of 4.1 in Mullin's account ('Augures', 28) recalls Nunn's RSC production of 1976.

3   Bartholomeusz (238) quotes Guthrie's programme note, and discusses the production at 238–40.

4   Mullin, 'Stage', gives a detailed review of this production.

10   Witches on stilts, from the Polish production by Teatr Biuro Podrozy, performed at the Edinburgh Festival in 2007

understood by the audience 'not [as] "effects", but something, some *things*, happening outside human comprehension and beyond human explanation'.

It is not uncommon nowadays to find the Sisters making extra unscheduled appearances, sometimes even returning to the stage at the end, often after having featured regularly as presences throughout the play.[1] In productions by the RSC in 2004 and 2007 and at Shakespeare's Globe in 2010 they were omnipresent, sometimes employed as servants in Macbeth's household, offering him the dagger in 2.1, presenting Banquo's bloodied ghost at the banquet, presiding over the murder of Macduff's family, carrying away Macbeth's corpse at the end. At the Globe they lurked in the background while Lady Macbeth spoke her invocation to the spirits and Macbeth called on 'seeling night'; they appeared on the battlefield in

1   Wilders, 117, and Rosenberg, 201, 315, 317, etc., give further examples.

armour, identifying themselves with the 'juggling fiends' who have deceived him throughout. In Rupert Goold's production (2007/8), with its evocations of Stalinism and the Cold War, the supernatural was in part replaced by evocations of state terror, to which the handling of the ubiquitous Witches contributed: they were sometimes nurses who killed rather than cured, and frequently domestic staff in Macbeth's household. In modern times they are less the focus for the play's representation of the supernatural than one manifestation of a pervasive evil.

Macbeth and his Lady: the relationship of power

Although it has been said that no actor has ever made his name in the part of Macbeth,[1] almost every male actor of any status has tried. Up to the end of the nineteenth century notable Macbeths on the London stage had included Thomas Betterton, Garrick, Kemble, Edmund Kean, William Charles Macready, Tommaso Salvini and Irving. Up to the present day the names of Beerbohm Tree, John Gielgud, Laurence Olivier, Michael Redgrave, Alec Guinness, Paul Scofield, Jonathan Pryce, Derek Jacobi, Antony Sher, Patrick Stewart and Kenneth Branagh might be added. Characterizations of Macbeth must negotiate the problem of what Rosenberg (63) calls 'the primary polarity . . . in Macbeth's design', that 'Macbeth is noble; Macbeth murders'. Put another way: is he strong and courageous, or weak and cowardly? Is he noble but corrupted, or evil from the start?

The earliest actor for whose performances there are substantial records, David Garrick, established an influential

---

1 Nielsen, 193. Prescott (81) lists as actors who have failed in the part Charles Macklin, both Keans, Irving, Ralph Richardson, Peter O'Toole, Derek Jacobi, Alan Howard and Mark Rylance. He might have added Sir Michael Redgrave who, describing the part as a 'teaser', said that no actor had ever 'claimed Macbeth as his own' (Sir Michael Redgrave, 'Shakespeare and the actors', in Garrett, 138).

reading of the part (1748), depicting a Macbeth who was not innately evil, but urged to deeds of violence and murder by his powerful wife, in consequence suffering intense mental torment. This interpretation capitalized on his physical attributes and also complemented that of his Lady, Hannah Pritchard. Though a small man, he was possessed of supreme vocal skills and bodily expressiveness, which enabled him to convince the audience as a man dominated by the force of imagination, and to retain their sympathy to the end. To strengthen this final impression he added a dying speech of his own composition for Macbeth.[1] Kemble followed Garrick in aiming to attract sympathy for Macbeth; he argued, as a leading man might, for Macbeth as a man of courage and ambition.[2] Sir Walter Scott admired the 'stately step' with which the tall, handsome Kemble made his first entrance (Sprague, *Actors*, 229), and his dignity and even serenity when in Duncan's presence were praised (Bartholomeusz, 126). His rendering of Macbeth's speech after hearing of his wife's death moved many, including Leigh Hunt and Scott, in rising to a 'climax of desperation'. He retained Garrick's dying speech. Macready also made Macbeth sympathetic, drawing on the expressive power of his acting and his skill in using Shakespeare's poetry to present 'the gradations of passion'[3] and his strong conception of Macbeth's nobility

---

1 In consultation with Shakespeare scholars such as Theobald, Johnson and Warburton, Garrick had devised a new text, much closer to F than audiences were then accustomed to, and advertised this in the press. His major (but far from sole) deviation from F was the dying speech: ''Tis done! The scene of life will quickly close. / Ambition's vain, delusive dreams are fled, / And now I wake to darkness, guilt, and horror; / I cannot bear it! Let me shake it off – / It will not be; my soul is clogg'd with blood – / I cannot rise! I dare not ask for mercy – / It is too late, hell drags me down; I sink, / I sink – Oh! – my soul is lost for ever!'

2 *Macbeth Reconsidered; an Essay* (1786), and the enlarged version, *Macbeth, and King Richard the Third: An Essay, in answer to some Remarks on the Characters of Shakespeare* (1817). Vickers, *Critical*, 6.430–5, gives extracts.

3 Bartholomeusz, 169, quoting Lady Juliet Creed Pollock, *Macready as I Knew Him* (1885), 104.

and courage. Unlike previous actors he strove to show the character as a whole, rather than focusing on a series of 'points'. 'I cannot act Macbeth without *being Macbeth*', he wrote in his diary for 1 March 1836, and of a performance in April 1841, 'I have improved Macbeth. The general tone of the character was lofty, manly, or indeed as it should be, heroic, that of one living to command. The whole view of the character was constantly in sight: the grief, the care, the doubt was not that of a weak person, but of a strong mind and a strong man' (Macready, 1, 282). Like Macready, Gielgud in the 1930s and 1940s used his melodious voice and feeling for poetry to enable Macbeth's suffering to reach out to the audience. When, after hearing the 'cry of women' that announces his wife's death, Macbeth says that he has 'supped full of horrors', Gielgud 'made the audience realise that this is precisely what Macbeth had been doing while he was absent from the stage'.[1] More recently, Simon Russell Beale (2005) presented Macbeth as an isolated, pitiable man, who would have liked to achieve his ends 'with the minimum of destruction', and if possible to avoid killing Fleance (Dobson, 107–8).

Reaction against the idea of Macbeth as a 'noble murderer' began early, with Macklin and Edmund Kean. Macklin, in 1773, aiming to challenge Garrick's interpretation, deliberately emphasized Macbeth's criminality over his nobility, presenting the character as innately evil.[2] Kean (in the early nineteenth century) played Macbeth initially as a dominating character, fully responsible for his own murderous choices, but also showed him in tears after the murder of Duncan, overcome with fear at the sight of Banquo's ghost, degenerating rapidly into a moral coward. Irving, in the 1870s and 1880s, saw Macbeth as one of Shakespeare's 'most bloody-minded, hypocritical villains', who had already conceived the idea of murdering Duncan

1 Bartholomeusz, 234, quoting James Agate, *Brief Chronicles* (1943), 228.
2 Kinsevik gives an extremely useful and well-researched account of this production.

before meeting the Sisters, and who resembled Richard III in that 'the mere appreciation and enjoyment of his own wickedness gave irony to his grim humor and zest to his crime'.[1] Few actors other than Donald Wolfit (in the 1940s and 1950s) have developed the 'evil Macbeth' to this extent, though several, including Olivier and Derek Jacobi, played Macbeth as having from the start thought of becoming king. Olivier (1955) played Macbeth as a complex man with a heart of darkness, yet one full of self-hatred, drawn to evil by some inner compulsion he could not resist. This conception was to be expanded in the film version he planned but never made.[2]

It may have been the modern dress productions in the first part of the twentieth century that gave impetus to the conception of Macbeth as what Rosenberg has called the 'victim of a savage time' (78). When Barry Jackson in 1928 set the play in the Great War he turned Macbeth (Eric Maturin) into a betrayer of what a postwar audience saw as the British officer's code of honour, personified by Duncan, who as a Field Marshal with his military entourage, embodied 'the calm, unheroic efficiency of a modern army' (Mullin, '*Macbeth*', 183). Macbeth as something of a modern-day tyrant has featured in productions locating the action in a militarized state by Joan Littlewood (1957), Michael Bogdanov (1992), Greg Doran (1999), Max Stafford-Clark (2004/5) and Goold (2007/8), though this has not always precluded showing him as a man torn by internal contradictions. For example, in Doran's production, which

1 Irving, *Character of Macbeth*, quoted from Furness, 470.
2 Like his stage *Hamlet*, Olivier's *Macbeth* was to have been filmed, but financial difficulties caused the cancellation of the project at a late stage. It seems that the Macbeths were to double as the First and Second Witches, Macbeth would be seen killing the Thane of Cawdor with an axe and his wife made responsible for the murder of Duncan. A dissolving shot would indicate that the Witches live inside Macbeth's head. The recently rediscovered versions of the screenplay and shooting script indicate that the production was radically re-imagined for film. A full account of the projected film is given in Barnes.

deliberately referred to topical military conflicts and conjured up the recent Balkan wars through costumes and weaponry, Macbeth (Antony Sher) made his first appearance with Banquo fresh from battle, 'mad-eyed, laughingly gung-ho', borne shoulder-high in triumph by their troops.[1] He was a career soldier who came into his own on the battlefield, but was destroyed psychologically by the guilt of murdering Duncan. Goold's production brought out the banality and normalizing of evil in a totalitarian state, as in the kitchen scene between Macbeth and the two Murderers, when Patrick Stewart as Macbeth made himself a ham sandwich while he discussed the arrangements for disposing of Banquo, then offered half of it to his accomplices who had no choice but to gulp it down. The whimsical manner in which power was exercised demonstrated that it was absolute.

Over the centuries the characterization of Macbeth has regularly been conditioned by that of his Lady. The version of their relationship initiated by Garrick and Hannah Pritchard (and so amazingly captured by Fuseli; see Fig. 11), depicting a Macbeth strongly influenced, even dominated by his wife, persisted for many years. It was developed with greater sub-tlety by Sarah Siddons, whose performance, alongside her brother, John Kemble, set the standard. In her 'Remarks on the Character of Lady Macbeth' she claimed to want to dispense with Pritchard's 'fiend-like queen', describing the ideal Lady as 'fair, feminine, nay, perhaps even fragile',[2] but accounts of her acting belie this. She could make audiences start from their seats when she commanded, 'Give *me* the daggers' or believe they could smell the blood on her hands in the sleepwalking scene (Kliman, 38–9). She was styled 'the Royal Murderess', and her invocation of the spirits in 1.5 made one observer feel

---

1 Review by Paul Taylor, *Independent*, 17 November 1999.
2 'Remarks on the character of Lady Macbeth,' in Thomas Campbell, *Life of Mrs Siddons* (1839), 170.

11 *Lady Macbeth Seizing the Daggers* (exhibited 1812), by Henry Fuseli
    (1741–1825), portraying David Garrick as Macbeth and Hannah
    Pritchard as Lady Macbeth

that 'Till then . . . a figure so terrible had never bent over the pit
of a theatre'.[1] It was in keeping with her portrayal of an iron
lady that, after trying out different intonations for the words
'We fail' (1.7.60), she opted for what Anna Jameson (327)
called 'the dark fatalism' of 'a simple period, which settled the
issue at once, as if she had said, "If we fail, why then we fail,
and all is over"'. Sian Thomas, playing the part in 2004, aimed
to copy Siddons's appearance in the sleepwalking scene, and
followed her intonation on 'We fail' (Dobson, 96–7). One of
the most dominating Ladies of the twentieth century is surely
Lady Asaji in Kurosawa's film adaptation of *Macbeth*, *Throne*

1   James Boaden, *Memoirs of Mrs Siddons* (1827), 1.37, and see Rosenberg, 225.

of Blood (1957).[1] This terrifying figure, still and almost expressionless for most of the film, persuades her husband to murder his lord Tsuzuki to ensure his own survival and in the same way turns him against his friend Miki (Banquo); her belief in a dog-eat-dog world where self-interest is the only consideration overcomes his more principled vision.

Many actors in the role have shown a Lady motivated by wifely ambition for her husband's success, which allows for an interweaving of good and evil in the character. Helen Faucit and then Ellen Terry did it this way.[2] Faucit's 'ill-suppressed anguish' at Macbeth's alarmingly self-revelatory behaviour in the banquet scene was thought poignant, and her interpretation of the role seemed revelatory. 'I began to feel as if I had never seen Lady Macbeth's true character before', wrote one observer. 'This woman is simply urging her husband forward through her love for him' (Carlisle, 'Faucit', 210). Terry's approach is encapsulated in her regular insertion of the word 'woman', heavily underlined, in her annotated copy of the play (Irving's acting version, 1888). At the end of 1.7 she wrote, 'She loved her babies and she could not kill the man who looked like her father, (Woman)'. After Lady Macbeth's invocation to the powers of darkness in 1.5 Terry wrote, 'she feels she has only a woman's strength & calls on "spirits"'.[3] She deployed her legendary beauty to advantage and created a memorable stage picture when she fainted in 2.3, and 'was raised and carried out with her fair head thrown back over a thane's shoulder, and her red hair streaming in the torchlight'.[4]

---

1   For fuller accounts of Kurosawa's much-admired film, see Mullin, 'Film', which compares Kurosawa's film with those of Welles and Polanski; also Davies, 152–66, Donaldson, 71–91, and Goodwin, 169–91.

2   Carlisle, 'Faucit', gives the fullest account of Faucit in the role, including a useful scene-by-scene reconstruction.

3   Terry's comments are recorded in two copies of *Macbeth* kept at her house, Smallhythe Place, in Kent.

4   *Liverpool Daily Post*, 31 December 1888, quoted in Sprague, *Actors*, 247.

12   *Ellen Terry as Lady Macbeth* (1889), by John Singer Sargent (1856–1925)

Macbeth's wife's ambition for her husband has sometimes been translated into passionate love. Judi Dench (RSC, 1976) saw her as 'totally besotted with Macbeth' and desperate to ensure that his career did not 'lack fulfilment' (Jacobs, 90). Dench's Lady Macbeth, in the tradition of Ellen Terry, was a nervous and vulnerable figure, so passionately eager for her husband's success that she had learnt his letter almost off by heart, but had to struggle to find within herself a commitment to the forces of evil, crying out in horror at the word 'cruelty'. Initially the Macbeths' need for one another was mutual. His

13 Ian McKellen as Macbeth and Judi Dench as Lady Macbeth, directed by Trevor Nunn, RSC, 1976

assurance in public contrasted with dependence on his wife in their early scenes where their relationship was intense and passionate. She welcomed him with joyful rapture at his return from battle, and the plan to kill Duncan was hatched while the two were in a close embrace. But Ian McKellen was a Macbeth who grew stronger with success, and once his masterly display of feigned grief and his quick thinking had paid off in the scene of the discovery of the murder, he had less need for her.

The Macbeths' passion was made mutual in the Cheek by Jowl production of 2010, which took its cue from Freud's notion of the couple as a single consciousness. Lady Macbeth (Anastasia Hille) was present in ghostly form, pressed against her husband (Will Keen), 'mutely smiling' as he stroked her cheek, even as her suicide was announced by the cry of women.[1] For Sinead Cusack (RSC, 1986) they were a 'golden couple', and until the killing of Duncan completely 'in tune with each other's minds'. Her Lady was young and vulnerable, and her recognition in the banquet scene that she had lost her husband (Jonathan Pryce) sent her irrevocably mad (Rutter, 53–72). The marital relationship was central to the Olivier production, which utilized what has been called the 'chiasmus effect' to create the balance of power between the couple. Olivier described it as 'the passage of two people, one going up and one going down' (Olivier, 87). His performance had a quiet opening and a slow burn, allowing Vivien Leigh (who was of course his wife in real life) to come to the fore in the first two acts, before he gave full force to the power of his acting in the banquet scene.[2] The moment when he leapt on the banquet table to confront Banquo's ghost, a crimson cloak swirling around him, was astonishing. From then on his momentum increased relentlessly. Tynan saw the virtues of this approach:

> He begins in a perilously low key, the reason for which is soon revealed. This Macbeth is paralysed with guilt before the curtain rises, having already killed Duncan time and time again in his mind. Far from recoiling and popping his eyes, he greets the air-drawn dagger with sad familiarity. Uxoriousness leads him to the act, which unexpectedly purges him of remorse. Now

1 Kate Bassett, *Independent on Sunday*, 28 March 2010.
2 It does seem to have demanded something of a sacrifice of effect on his part, and was not universally approved. Milton Shulman, in the *Evening Standard*, 8 June 1955, talked of 'restraint run amok'.

14   Laurence Olivier as Macbeth and Vivien Leigh as Lady Macbeth in 3.2, directed by Glen Byam Shaw, RSC, 1955

the portrait swells . . . At the heart we find, beautifully projected, the anguish of the *de facto* ruler who dares not admit that he lacks the essential qualities of kingship.

(Tynan, *View*, 157)

This gradual building up of Macbeth avoids the problem whereby the play itself can seem to fall off in dramatic excitement from its mid-point, especially if the character is at his most complex and exciting in the first two acts. It appears to have been a special part of Olivier's achievement that he made Macbeth moving in decline, so that the audience came almost to sympathize with him. His reception of the news of his wife's death was so full of 'poetic weariness, [that] pity could hardly be withheld'.[1] When he questioned the Doctor earlier as to his ability to 'minister to a mind diseased', he made a movement with his hands 'gesturing dumbly and half-consciously towards his own breast' that seemed to include himself with his wife in a 'plea for mercy' (David, 125). Just as the chiasmic pattern gave scope for this storing up of emotion to evoke tragic pity for the damned and despairing Macbeth in his final scenes, so at the beginning of the play it allowed for Lady Macbeth to create a strong impression from the start. Her 'force and drive' were praised, along with the intensity with which she upbraided her husband when he returned from Duncan's bloody chamber: 'Infirm of purpose, / Give me the daggers' (2.2.53–4) (Kliman, 71). The 'ominous' charm (Mullin, *Promptbook*, 250) with which she played the 'gracious hostess' with Duncan helped to set up the later pathos of her reversion to childishness in the sleep-walking scene.[2]

The idea of the marriage as a partnership in which the wife has a social role to further her husband's career has informed some twentieth-century productions. Sibyl Thorndike, in the 1920s, apparently regarded the Macbeths as 'big capitalists' in a tragic partnership (Bartholomeusz, 226); Vivien Merchant (RSC, 1967) and Harriet Walter (RSC, 1999), both handsome and commanding women, played society wives who knew how to manipulate their husbands as well as those around them to achieve what they wanted. Walter played the Lady as a military wife from a high social level, gaunt and elegant, contrasting

---

1 Patrick Gibbs, *Daily Telegraph*, 8 June 1955, quoted in Kliman, 77. Harold Hobson's comment on the delivery of this speech, that it held 'tones . . . like the notes of some divine music: echoes of years of departed happiness' (Kliman, 77), intimates the resonance of the emotion with something in Olivier's own experience of happiness lost.

2 Maxine Audley, who played Lady Macduff, commented on the chiasmus effect: 'The whole thing about Macbeth is that he starts off rather quietly and gets madder and madder the more murders he commits, and she starts off on a high note and gradually crumbles, after the first murder. She goes to pieces and he gets stronger – madder but stronger. They change places.' (Vickers, *Vivien Leigh*, 225–6).

15   Patrick Stewart as Macbeth and Kate Fleetwood as Lady Macbeth,
     directed by Rupert Goold, Chichester Festival Theatre, 2007, 2008

physically with her 'swarthy little husband' (Sher, 343). They
were intensely convincing as partners, united in ambition.
Walter delivered the invocation to the spirits on her knees 'in
a vile travesty of prayer'[1] and greeted the return of Macbeth
from war by wiping his face clean of blood and dirt. In Goold's
2007/8 production the dynamic between the Macbeths was
strikingly defined by their age difference, with the beautiful and
strongly sexual Kate Fleetwood as the trophy wife, decades
younger than her grizzled husband (Patrick Stewart), who was
totally in thrall to her. Her vocal stresses brought out her power
and confidence – 'You would be / *So* much more the man',
'Give *me* the daggers'. Their identity as a couple was marked
by many exits hand in hand, even, unusually, at the end of
the banquet scene when they have shared a moment together.
This Macbeth was devastated by his wife's death. He spoke
'Tomorrow, and tomorrow, and tomorrow' over her body,

1   *Mail on Sunday*, 21 November 1999.

which had been brought in on a hospital trolley, uncovering her face to address her directly and giving the lines a poignant note of personal desolation.

Endings

Garrick's addition of a Faustian dying speech, used later by Kemble and Kean,[1] suggests that he found Shakespeare's ending unsatisfactory, as have many subsequent actors and directors. McKellen shared this view, and praised his director, Trevor Nunn, for cutting down the lines given to the invading army so as to focus on Macbeth.[2] Nunn was by no means the only director to truncate the play's ending. Charles Kean omitted the last scene completely, so as to end with Macbeth's death; Kemble, Phelps, Macready, Tree and Johnston Forbes-Robertson kept something of Malcolm's summarizing speech but made considerable cuts (often including the vilification of the Macbeths as 'the dead butcher and his fiend-like queen'); so too Komisarjevsky, Anthony Quayle (RSC, 1949), whose promptbook notes at the end, 'Quick curtain down', and more recently Adrian Noble (RSC, 1986), Doran and Dominic Cooke (RSC, 2004). The heroic death of Young Siward and his father's reaction was first cut by Davenant, and subsequently by many, including Phelps, Macready, Nunn, Noble and Declan Donnellan (Cheek by Jowl, 2010). Although the leafy screens of Malcolm's army made part of the spectacle in the nineteenth century, Komisarjevsky dispensed with them, and so, more recently did Donnellan, the 2010 production at Shakespeare's Globe and the Liverpool Everyman production in 2011. It is a rare production now that leaves the last scene as Shakespeare wrote it.[3]

---

1   Peter Holland compares the different attitudes of the three actors to this speech in his chapter 'The Romantic stage' (Bate & Jackson, 100–1).

2   In *Shakespeare on Stage*, ed. Julian Curry (2010), 147.

3   Michael Blakemore's long and lightly cut production (National Theatre, 1972) did so.

16 The set of the 1933 RSC production of *Macbeth* directed by Theodore Komisarjevsky

The stage directions for the final encounter of Macbeth and Macduff are textually problematic,[1] but it is commonly assumed that if Macbeth's head is to be brought on in the last scene – itself a difficulty – he must die offstage. Clearly Garrick, Kemble and Kean felt this dramatically inappropriate, and many actors have taken the opportunity to die onstage in spectacular fashion. Kean's Macbeth died displaying a desperate courage that waned only from bodily exhaustion, as when, 'after falling he crawls on the floor to reach again his sword and dies as he touches it'.[2] Macready fought on to the last, and finally, 'thrusting his own sword into the ground, [he] raises himself by its help to his knees where he stares full in the face of his vanquisher with a resolute and defiant gaze of concentrated majesty, hate, and knowledge, and instantly falls

1 See notes to stage directions at 5.8.34.
2 Henry Crabbe Robinson, *The Diary, Reminiscences and Correspondence of Henry Crabbe Robinson*, ed. T. Sadler, 2 vols (1872), 1.241, quoted in Bartholomeusz, 148.

dead' (Downer, 338). Irving, having played Macbeth, controversially, as a coward, at the last stressed his warrior nature and courage in defeat, dying heroically onstage: 'at once brave and prescient of evil . . . the great famished wolf fought out his splendid despair'.[1]

Twentieth-century and later productions have treated Macbeth's death more ambivalently. Some Macbeths have fought heroically, but died offstage. Olivier did so, to the disappointment of Kenneth Tynan, who felt that ' "Exeunt, fighting" was a poor end for such a giant warrior. We wanted to see how he would die; and it was not he but Shakespeare who let us down' (Tynan, *Curtains*, 99). As John Westland Marston said of Phelps's brave decision to die offstage in 1847, it was for the actor 'a piece of self-sacrifice . . . that cannot well be overrated'.[2] But offstage dying can prove unfortunately anticlimactic, as in the RSC production with Ralph Richardson (1952), whose exit, 'chased off the stage by a sword-brandishing Macduff . . . was more ludicrous than tragic'.[3] However, not all Macbeths have been defiant to the end; some have emphasized instead Macbeth's sense of despair and loss over his assertion of courage. Jacobi (1993), having contemplated suicide at 'I have lived long enough', at last pulled his own sword into his body, accepting that, as the one who 'first cries, "Hold, enough" ', he is damning himself.[4] Russell Beale (2005) thought Macbeth 'almost wholly inactive' at the end of the play, even tricking Macduff 'into helping him with a sort of assisted suicide' (Dobson, 107–8). He repunctuated Macbeth's last line as 'Hold. Enough', with a pause for fighting between the two words and a final stress on his desire to make an end. Patrick Stewart (2007/8) divided the

---

1 Rosenberg, 645, quoting *Saturday Review*. Sprague, *Actors*, 278–9, and Wilders, 214, give more such examples.
2 Marston, 2.472. Rosenberg (648) gives further examples of actors who died offstage but without loss of spectacle.
3 Wilders, 214, quoting the *New Statesman*, 21 June 1952.
4 Jacobi, in Smallwood, 210.

line in the same way. The more conventionally warrior-like Elliot Cowan (Shakespeare's Globe, 2010) threw away his armour on hearing of Macduff's caesarean birth; Will Keen (Cheek by Jowl, 2010), a Macbeth with no reason to live after the death of his wife, surrendered to Macduff and ran on his (mimed) sword.

Even when glamorizing Macbeth's dying agonies, earlier productions often ended on a triumphalist note. Alan Downer's reconstruction of Macready's handling of the ending is typical: 'Malcolm and the thanes enter with banners and accompanying trumpet flourishes. To the general cry of "Hail, King of Scotland", the curtain falls' (338). Irving ended similarly. In Tree's production, Macduff placed the crown on the head of Malcolm, who was then lifted high on the shoulders of his soldiers. The exhibiting of Macbeth's severed head (though over the years more often cut than retained) might be used to establish this as a moment when tyranny has been overcome. Rosenberg describes how it was 'jammed with effort down on the point of a lance' (652) in the RSC production with Paul Scofield (1967). Occasionally it has featured in recent productions, displayed in a bag (Liverpool Everyman, 2011), on a pole (Trafalgar Studios, 2013) or, most disquietingly, in Stafford-Clark's promenade production (Out of Joint, 2004/5) so as to ironize the triumphalism. Here, pictures of women holding the severed head were handed out to the audience, during a raucous celebration of Malcolm's accession by kilted warriors playing bagpipes; their music recalled the incantatory rituals with which the play began.

In contrast to upbeat stagings of the ending that convey restoration and closure there is a growing tradition suggesting how it may appear more ambiguous. Nunn's (1976) production ended with exhaustion and uncertainty; the RSC production of 2004 'had a limp, dispirited conclusion' (Braunmuller, 96). Suicidal Macbeths like Jacobi and Russell Beale gave more weight to loss than to gain. Malcolm is often a shell-shocked survivor rather than a victor. A highly politicized production by Michael Bogdanov (ESC, 1992) complicated the meaning of his triumph: the Scottish piping of 'O Flower of Scotland' was drowned out by a band playing 'God save the King', and Malcolm wore the velvet and ermine of England, not the yellow and red robes of his predecessors (Parsons & Mason, 129). The reappearance of the Sisters, or sometimes Fleance,[1] suggests that the past may not be past. Tree's production of 1911 was unusual for its time in making the Sisters all-pervasive, lurking in Macbeth's castle and laughing mockingly when he cursed them just before his death.[2] Mid-twentieth-century films by Orson Welles (1948) and Roman Polanski (1971) reintroduced the Sisters so as to end on a note of moral uncertainty. Although in Welles's film Christian symbolism becomes progressively more conspicuous, his ending suggests no complete victory for the forces of good. From the battlements Macbeth hurls his stave into the heart of the Holy Father, a character invented to embody Christianity in contrast to the paganism of the Witches, who is standing far below. The Witches, unseen, chant the words 'untimely ripped' as Macbeth is killed by Macduff, and the head of the clay doll that they had fashioned is lopped off. The last words spoken in the film are also given to them: 'Peace, the charm's wound up'. In Polanski's film, despite symbolic use of the natural setting, with brighter skies and the appearance of the rising sun as Malcolm's troops, an effective moving wood, appear over the horizon, the film ends without any suggestion of restoration. This is in part due to Polanski's innovative development of the character of Ross, whose ambiguity in Shakespeare is resolved by his transformation into a time-server. Initially he is Macbeth's man, informing and spying for him, acting as the Third Murderer and taking charge of the

---

1   For example, in the RSC production of 1999 and at the Liverpool Everyman in 2011. Rosenberg (653) mentions a production in Paris in 1973 when this also happened.

2   Mullin, 'Strange', describes the production in detail.

outrages at Fife. But spurned by Macbeth for promotion, he changes sides, and his final gesture of removing the crown from Macbeth's severed head and placing it on Malcolm's is opportunistic. The film ends with a solitary cloaked figure, Donalbain, riding through the mists to find the Witches' cavern. As he enters, his horse is seen tied up outside, in the same place that Macbeth's had been earlier.[1]

History vs. contemporaneity: setting and location

The earliest visual evidence we have for Macbeth's appearance in the theatre is the illustration in Rowe's edition of 1709 depicting Betterton, which makes it clear that he performed in the costume of his day. Garrick, a few decades later, was criticized for appearing as 'a modern fine Gentleman', and as such lacking dignity, but did not consider appearing in 'the old Dress' until spurred on by Macklin's example (Bartholomeusz, 71). Macklin's 'Old Caledonian' production of 1773 aimed to create a vision of medieval Scotland, barbaric and splendid, with Highland dress, tartan and bagpipes. It met with a hostile reception and Macklin's appearance was caricatured. Efforts at a historically accurate setting have been made sporadically, as by Charles Kean in 1853, but, ironically in view of the prevalent euphemism for the play's title, Macbeth's Scottishness has been gestured to rather than consistently demonstrated. Macready's tam-o-shanter, plaid scarf and curious knee-length robe (see Fig. 17) suggested to one observer 'simply a rugged, semi-barbaric chief' rather than a Scottish thane (Coleman, 221). The flowered dressing gown he wore in 2.3 over his armour, disliked by some, added to the eclectic feel. McKellen's question 'As for Macbeth's nationality, isn't it irrelevant?' has been treated as purely rhetorical. Nunn's abolition of any sense

---

1 Holland, 'Stands Scotland', is unfairly dismissive of this film, and refers to the 'banality' of the final sequence (374).

17   Full-length portrait of William Charles Macready as Macbeth. Plate in
      an edition of Shakespeare, nineteenth-century print

of geographical location was extreme and deliberate; Cheek
by Jowl's similarly dark and minimalist production (2010)
captured the same quality of nightmare.

Semi-barbaric impressionism has often been the default
option for a visual style (as in productions of Phelps, Irving,

18   Henry Irving in *Macbeth* at the Lyceum Theatre, from *Illustrated Sporting and Dramatic News*, 1888

Tree and Olivier). Welles created a distinctive look for his film, eschewing a realist location and adapting an Expressionist mode to fit a setting largely derived from the 'Voodoo' production of the play that he had staged in Harlem two years earlier.[1] The action took place in a dark and nightmarishly ambiguous space, characterized by mist and formlessness, rarely anchored in any specific geography, which helped create a kind of interiority for Macbeth and his spiritual journey. In this it was akin to Kurosawa's setting, in a labyrinthine forest, where the (single) Witch's shelter was bathed in eerie white light. Welles's Witches represented the force of a powerful paganism, also influenced by the 'Voodoo' production, which battled against a primitive

1   For the 'Voodoo' production, see France & McCloskey. Welles's handling of the text and foregrounding of the theme of good versus evil originated in this production. Kliman (112–17) compares it with the film. Newstok and Thompson list in an appendix more than 100 productions of the play with cross-racial casting.

Celtic Christianity for Macbeth's soul. In contrast, Polanski's film (1971), made on location in Wales and Northumberland to represent a wild Scottish landscape, was naturalistic in style and set the action in medieval Scotland, depicted as primitive and violent. The domestic life of Macbeth and his wife in Dunsinane castle was realized with much detail, some of it with symbolic resonances, like the scenes of bear-baiting in the courtyard watched with nervous fascination by Lady Macbeth. More distinctly historicized period settings for stagings in recent years, illuminating the religious context of the play, have included the Jacobean, as in Peter Hall's productions at the RSC (1967) and National Theatre (1978), and the aftermath of the Protestant Reformation, with broken stained glass windows and desecrated icons (RSC, 2011). But the predominant design has been military in emphasis. Barry Jackson in 1928 set the play in the Great War, using contemporary military uniforms. Though regarded as a failed experiment, this production with its defiantly contemporary application resonates with many more recent stagings of the play such as Littlewood's (1957), Bogdanov's (ESC, 1992), Doran's, (RSC, 1999), Stafford-Clark's (Out of Joint, 2004/5), Goold's (Chichester Festival Theatre, 2007/8) and Jamie Lloyd's (Trafalgar Studios, 2013).[1] A contemporary or near-contemporary setting can make the play more accessible to a modern audience, as was Jackson's intention; in Doran's production the decision to switch from a Jacobean design to modern dress was seen as key to engaging the audience with a vision of a devastated war-torn world familiar from TV images: 'impoverished, muddy, scorched, dark' (Sher, 341). In such productions Macbeth can emerge as tyrant or brutalized soldier, far from the heroic images created by star actors of the past.

---

1   For Littlewood's production, see Holdsworth, *Littlewood*, 108–12. On Doran's production, see Walter. Welles's film is regarded by Gunter (123–4) as originating in the 1930s with Nazi references.

MACBETH

Duncan, KING of Scotland		
MALCOLM	*his elder son*	
DONALBAIN	*his younger son*	
MACBETH, Thane of Glamis		
LADY	*Macbeth's wife*	5
BANQUO		
FLEANCE	*Banquo's son*	
MACDUFF, Thane of Fife		
WIFE	*Macduff's wife*	
SON	*Macduff's son*	10
LENNOX		
ROSS		
ANGUS	*Thanes of Scotland*	
MENTEITH		
CAITHNESS		15
SIWARD, Earl of Northumberland		
YOUNG SIWARD	*his son*	
FIRST WITCH		
SECOND WITCH	*three weïrd sisters*	
THIRD WITCH		20
HECATE		
Three other WITCHES		
APPARITIONS		
CAPTAIN		
SEYTON	*retainer in Macbeth's household*	25
PORTER	*in Macbeth's household*	
OLD MAN		
Three MURDERERS		
Other MURDERERS		
DOCTOR	*at the English court*	30
DOCTOR	*in Macbeth's household*	
Waiting GENTLEWOMAN	*in Macbeth's household*	

LORDS *and* THANES
SERVANTS
MESSENGERS   35
SOLDIER

Attendants, Soldiers

HISTORICAL NOTES

1 DUNCAN (Duncan I) reigned 1034–40, succeeding his grandfather, Malcolm II. His reign was marked by constant warfare against both the Orkney Vikings and enemies to the south vying for control of Cumbria. According to Holinshed and other chroniclers, he was not a strong king. Chroniclers referred to him as 'the Man of many diseases' (Watson, 193). He was probably aged about 39 when he died (Aitchison, 64).

2 MALCOLM, later known as Canmore, or 'big head', was still a minor at the time of his father's murder. As Malcolm III he reigned 1058–93. He defeated Macbeth in the Battle of the Seven Sleepers in 1054, but did not kill him, or consolidate his victory for three years. He married twice, his second wife Margaret being canonized by the pope. His eldest son, Duncan, was murdered by Donalbain on his return from Ireland, but the sons of his second wife continued his dynasty.

3 DONALBAIN, known as Donald Bane ('Donald the fair'), spent many years in Ireland. He reigned as Donald III (1093–7).

4 MACBETH, son of Findlaech, Mormaer of Moray, and like Duncan a grandson of Malcolm II, reigned 1040–57. He was killed in battle at Lumphanan in 1058. He had claims to the throne through his royal descent and also through his marriage to Gruoch, herself of royal blood. He encountered no opposition at the beginning of his reign and according to Holinshed only developed tyrannous tendencies after 10 years of good rule. During this period, in 1050, he made a pilgrimage to Rome, accompanied by his wife. His reign was a long one for a Scottish king at this time. He was briefly succeeded by his stepson

Lulach, who took over while Macbeth was still alive and reigned for less than a year before being killed probably by Malcolm (Watson, 238).

5 LADY Macbeth's wife, Gruoch, a descendant of a previous Scottish king, either Kenneth II or Kenneth III, was previously married to Macbeth's cousin Gillacomgain, who was probably murdered by Macbeth. She had a son, Lulach, by Gillacomgain, whom Macbeth made his heir. Lulach reigned for a few months only (1057–8) and was probably killed by Malcolm. Nothing is known of Gruoch's fate.

6 BANQUO, Thane of Lochaber, was not a historical figure, though portrayed as such in Holinshed, but an invention of the chronicler Hector Boece (in *Scotorum Historiae*, 1526) to provide his patron King James V with an ancestor for his dynasty.

7 FLEANCE, son of Banquo, who after his father's murder on the orders of Macbeth fled to Wales, got the Prince of Wales's daughter pregnant and was killed by the Prince on this account. His son, Walter, supposedly became Steward of Scotland.

8 MACDUFF, like Banquo not a historical figure, but presumed to be a descendant of the medieval earls of Fife

12 ROSS According to Holinshed (*Scotland*, 171), Ross was one of several thanes, including Caithness, put to death for sedition by Macbeth during his reign.

16 SIWARD, Earl of Northumbria, was closely related by marriage to Duncan, though in origin a Dane and earlier an enemy of Duncan's (Aitchison, 59–60). He died in 1055.

17 YOUNG SIWARD Two younger relatives of Siward, Earl of Northumbria, his nephew Siward and his son Osbern, died fighting against Macbeth at the Battle of the Seven Sleepers in 1054.

THE TRAGEDY OF MACBETH

1.1   *Thunder and lightning. Enter three* WITCHES.

1 WITCH

When shall we three meet again?
In thunder, lightning, or in rain?

2 WITCH

When the hurly-burly's done,
When the battle's lost, and won.

1.1 One of Shakespeare's shortest opening scenes, evoking much that is to follow: disturbances in nature, confusion and turmoil, evil ritual, and riddling language that both offers and retracts meaning.

0.1 *Thunder and lightning* Thunder effects could be produced by rolling a cannonball along the wooden trough or thunder-run above the stage, lightning perhaps by squibs. They commonly occur together in supernatural contexts (Dessen & Thomson, 'thunder and lightning', Wilson & Calore, 'thunder'). Witches were thought capable of raising storms, and had claimed to do so in *News from Scotland* (1591), sig. C1, though the sceptical Reginald Scot denies this (*The Discovery of Witchcraft* (1584), Bk 3, ch. 13). Harris (119–39) speculates that the smell of the squibs may have aroused significant cultural memories, suggestive, for example, of the Catholic past.

***three* WITCHES** Not only is three a magic number for witches, and suggestive of the Fates or the Norns of Scandinavian mythology, but the number is part of the scenic patterning: the Witches speak singly in turn three times each before chanting the final couplet in unison (Jones, *Scenic*, 210), although this is due

to a widely accepted rearrangement of lines 8–9, where in F all three speak the words, '*Padock* calls anon'. Blake ('Study', 15–16) argues for retaining F.

1 This short scene seems to form the conclusion to a longer meeting; the Witches are actively planning their next encounter, which takes place after the battle described in 1.2.

3 **hurly-burly** commotion, tumult, 'formerly a more dignified word than now' (*OED n.* 1). See *1H4* 5.1.78: 'hurly burly innovation'. Shakespeare might have noted the use of the expression in Studley's translation of Seneca's *Agamemnon*, a possible source: 'One hurley burley done, another doth begin'. It also occurs in Newton's translation of *Thebais* (or *Phoenissae*): 'a hurly burly make / Confusedly of ev'rythinge' (Seneca, *Tenne Tragedies*).

4 **battle's** 'Battle' can mean a hostile encounter, or a body of troops, even a whole army, in battle array (Edelman, 'battle'[1], 'battle'[4]). The speaker may imply both meanings.

lost, and won perhaps an echo of Dent (?)W408.1: 'The battle (field) is won and lost (lost and won)'. The riddling language of *Mac* and especially of the

TITLE] *The Tragedie of Macbeth (and in running title throughout)*
1.1] *Actus Primus. Scoena Prima.*   1 again?] again *Hanmer*   2 or] and *Hanmer, Capell*   3 hurly-burly's] *(*Hurley-burley's*)*

3 WITCH

    That will be ere the set of sun.   5

1 WITCH

    Where the place?

2 WITCH   Upon the heath.

3 WITCH

    There to meet with Macbeth.

1 WITCH

    I come, Gray-Malkin.

2 WITCH   Paddock calls.

3 WITCH   Anon.

ALL

    Fair is foul, and foul is fair,   9
    Hover through the fog and filthy air.   *Exeunt.*

Witches has been much discussed. For a metrical analysis of the Witches' verse see Krantz, 351–3, and Williams, 'Time', 153–9. The Witches may refer to the battle which Duncan's forces have won against his enemies, although Macbeth's triumph here will eventually have disastrous consequences for Duncan.

7 **meet with** Blake, *Grammar*, 1.2.2, notes that in early modern English 'meet with' is a phrasal verb which can mean 'to attack, ambush, waylay', and that *meet with* here may be distinguished from *meet* in 1. See also his comments on other phrasal verbs at 4.3.10. In Blake, 'Study' (11–17) he comments more extensively on the grammatical features of the scene as a whole.

8 **I come** Blake, *Grammar*, 2.3.2.1, notes the possibility that 'I' can stand for 'aye' in early modern spelling, and that the First Witch may be summoning her cat, rather than responding to its call.

Gray-Malkin. Paddock Gray-Malkin is a name for a cat and Paddock means a toad. Both animals were common witches' familiars.

Anon could mean soon or even immediately (*OED adv.* 5, 4). *OED* also notes that it can function as a response by a servant who is summoned (*adv.* 7), as in the comic scene of the teasing of the tapster Francis by Hal and Poins in *1H4* 2.4.26–65. The Witches have a close relationship with their familiars.

9 Similar paradoxical expressions occur in contemporary literature. See Spenser, *FQ*, 4.8.32: 'Then faire grew foul and foul grew faire in sight', where Spenser is describing the common condition of fallen humanity. See also Dent, F29: 'Fair without but foul within'.

10 **Hover** Blake, *Grammar*, 1.2.2, comments on the grammatical ambiguity of this word, and the possibility that it may be a verb, imperative or indicative, or, less likely, a noun. All Shakespeare's other uses of the word, however, are in verb forms, and the most probable mood is imperative.

10 SD In Davenant's version of *Mac* the Witches '*Exeunt flying*', and Sprague suggests that 'Perhaps there is a hint of action in that "hover" ' (*Actors*, 225).

6 heath.] heath: *Pope*   8 2 WITCH . . . Anon.] *Singer; All. Padock calls anon: faire is foule, and foule is faire, / Houer through the fogge and filthie ayre. F;* 2 Witch Padocke calls – anon. / All. Faire . . . faire *Pope*   10 the] *om. Pope*   SD] *They rise from the stage and fly away. / Rowe; Witches vanish. / Malone*

1.2　　*Alarum within. Enter* KING [Duncan,] MALCOLM,
　　　　DONALBAIN, LENNOX, *with Attendants, meeting*
　　　　　　　a bleeding Captain.

KING

What bloody man is that? He can report,
As seemeth by his plight, of the revolt
The newest state.
MALCOLM　　　　　　This is the sergeant,
Who like a good and hardy soldier fought
'Gainst my captivity. Hail, brave friend.　　　　　　　　5

1.2 The revolts against Duncan's rule are described in Holinshed, 2.168–72, where Makdowald's rebellion, put down by Macbeth, is immediately followed by an invasion by Sweno, King of Norway, whose troops are referred to indifferently as both Norwegians and Danes. Sweno's defeat results in a further invasion by his brother Canute, King of England. These campaigns are compressed into one action by Shakespeare, who also suppresses any mention of the Danes, perhaps in deference to King James's Danish wife. The scene has sometimes been regarded as textually corrupt as a result of cuts due to censorship or the anticipation of it, or else on account of Middleton's interventions. See Nosworthy, 'Bleeding', and *Shakespeare's*, 2–23, Dover Wilson, xxiv–xxvi, and Appendix 1 below. Taylor also argues for abridgement in this scene in Taylor & Lavagnino, *Textual Culture*, 386–7.

0.1 *Alarum within* The alarum (a variant spelling of 'alarm'), commonly signifying a call to arms, was sounded on drums and/or trumpets (Edelman, 'alarum'). The direction '*within*' indicates that the musicians performed offstage, within the tiring-house.

0.1–3 *Enter . . . Captain* The two groups of characters may enter from different doors, or one may meet another which has come on earlier. The latter interpretation is more characteristic of Middleton's stage directions than of Shakespeare's, and this form of 'meeting' appears at the beginning of 3.5, a scene sometimes regarded as by Middleton. For a discussion of Middleton's relationship to the text of *Mac*, see Appendix 1.

1　**bloody man** the introduction of what is to become a leitmotiv throughout this play, in which 'blood' and related terms are mentioned more than in any other of Shakespeare's plays.

2　**revolt** insurrection. Scotland is in a state of civil war.

3　**sergeant** pronounced with three syllables (Abbott, 479), and spelt 'serieant' in F. Since 'captain' is used loosely as a non-specific military title by Shakespeare, it does not necessarily conflict with the designation 'sergeant', which signifies a higher rank than nowadays. Edelman, 'sergeant', suggests it could have meant a sergeant at arms or a sergeant major, both however anachronistic in terms of the play's historical setting.

5　**captivity** being taken captive

1.2] *Scena Secunda.*　0.1 Duncan] *Capell*　1] Dun. *Capell*　5 Hail] Haile: Haile *F2;* Haile, Haile *F3–4, Rowe*

Say to the King the knowledge of the broil,
As thou didst leave it.

CAPTAIN   Doubtful it stood,
As two spent swimmers, that do cling together,
And choke their art. The merciless Macdonald
(Worthy to be a rebel, for to that   10
The multiplying villainies of nature
Do swarm upon him) from the Western Isles
Of kerns and galloglasses is supplied,
And Fortune, on his damned quarry smiling,

6 **broil** confused disturbance, tumult or turmoil (*OED n.*[1] 1)

7–23 **Doubtful ... battlements** Much has been written about the Captain's speech style, and the extent to which his odd locutions and metrical irregularities reflect his degenerating physical condition or are rather to be explained in terms of special circumstances related to performance or the condition of the text. The speech has been seen as written in a version of epic style, intended to stand out from the surrounding dialogue, like the Pyrrhus speeches in *Ham* (Nosworthy, 'Bleeding'). In function, it may be a variant on the expository Senecan messenger speech (Miola, *Classical*, 97).

7 **Doubtful** full of doubt as to the outcome

8 **spent** exhausted

9 **choke their art** impede their own functioning. Norgaard cites Daniel, *Cleopatra* (1594) as a source for this simile: 'Given that Shakespeare seems to have been preparing for the two plays at the same time, this is not improbable' (Norgaard, 395–6). See Nosworthy, *Shakespeare's*, 9–12, and Barroll, 151–68, on the relative dating of the two plays.

10 **Worthy to be** deserving to be thought
    to that to that end

11 **multiplying ... nature** may mean Macdonald's inherent and increasing villainies or the evil of the rebels who are attracted to him like swarming insects

12 **Western Isles** Hebrides

13 **kerns and galloglasses** Kerns were Irish foot-soldiers who fought in guerrilla style; the more heavily armed galloglasses with whom Shakespeare associates them were originally Scottish, and the Macdonalds were the first great galloglass family, according to Edelman, 'gallowglass' (though *OED* galloglass 1 calls them soldiers or retainers 'formerly maintained by Irish chiefs'). Galloglasses were renowned for their impressive physique. The phrase comes from Holinshed.

14–15 **Fortune ... whore** i.e. Fortune, in appearing to favour Macdonald by commending his feats of killing, behaved amorally, like a rebel's whore. See Dent, F603.1: 'Fortune is a strumpet'.

14 **damned** damnèd
    quarry often emended to 'quarrel', of which it is a variant spelling. But 'quarry' can mean 'a heap of dead men; a pile of dead bodies' (*OED n.*[1] 2b) as in *Cor* 1.1.193–4: 'And let me use my sword, / I'd make a quarry / With thousands of these quartered slaves'.

6 the knowledge] thy knowledge *W.S. Walker*   7 SP] *(Cap.);* Sergeant *Dyce*   11 villainies] *(*Villainies*);* Villaines *F3–4*   13 galloglasses] *F2–4 (*Gallow glasses*);* Gallowgrosses *F*   14 quarry] quarrel *Hanmer, Ard*[2]

Showed like a rebel's whore. But all's too weak: 15
For brave Macbeth (well he deserves that name),
Disdaining Fortune, with his brandished steel,
Which smoked with bloody execution,
Like Valour's minion, carved out his passage,
Till he faced the slave,   20
Which ne'er shook hands, nor bade farewell to him,
Till he unseamed him from the nave to th' chops,
And fixed his head upon our battlements.

KING

O valiant cousin, worthy gentleman.

CAPTAIN

As whence the sun 'gins his reflection,   25

15 **all's too weak** 'no expression is adequate'

18 **smoked** steamed, as from hot blood. Compare *KL* 5.3.222–3: 'What means this bloody knife? 'Tis hot, it smokes, / It came even from the heart of – ', and see *OED* smoke *v.* 2a: 'To give off or send up vapour, dust, spray, etc.: *esp.* to steam'.

19 **minion** favourite. In similar vein, Macbeth is later called 'Bellona's bridegroom' (55). But Valour, like Fortune, is fickle. The favour Macbeth seems to find with female figures of power (like the Witches) is always equivocal. Probably pronounced as two syllables, with disyllabic *carvèd*.

20 **the slave** term of insult, referring to Macdonald

21 i.e. who did not bother with the niceties of conduct. There may be a weary irony in the Captain's language here.
Which means 'who', referring to Macbeth. For the use of 'which' referring to human antecedents, see Hope, 1.4.2b.

22 **unseamed him** slit him open
nave ... chops i.e. bottom (navel or perhaps crotch) to top (jaws). See Marlowe and Nashe, *Dido, Queen of Carthage*,

2.1.255–6: 'Then from the navel to the throat at once / He ript old Priam'.

23 **fixed his head** Displaying the heads of defeated enemies or executed traitors in public was a common practice, as Macduff demonstrates at the end of the play.

24 **cousin** not merely a term of affection. Macbeth and Duncan were blood relations as first cousins, both grandsons of King Malcolm. See also 1.3.129. Holderness comments on these lines: 'Duncan governs his thanes through his graceful and measured language of loyalty and gratitude, service and love; but he rules Scotland through the barbaric violence of those same professional warriors' (66).

25–8 **As ... swells** a syntactically complex and ambiguous passage, perhaps denoting the Captain's exhaustion. The gist is that from an apparently favourable situation disaster may emerge. The word *reflection* may be an astronomical term (*OED n.* 4d), referring to the sun's 'turning back' at the equinox (here, the spring), a time when storms and thunder occur; but it may simply refer to the sun's shining; *spring*

15 a rebel's] *(a* Rebells*); the rebel's *Hanmer*   all's] all *Pope*   20 he] he had *Pope*   22 nave] nape *Hanmer*

Shipwrecking storms and direful thunders,
So from that spring, whence comfort seemed to come,
Discomfort swells: mark, King of Scotland, mark,
No sooner justice had, with valour armed,
Compelled these skipping kerns to trust their heels,   30
But the Norwegian lord, surveying vantage,
With furbished arms, and new supplies of men,
Began a fresh assault.

KING

Dismayed not this our captains, Macbeth and Banquo?

CAPTAIN

Yes, as sparrows, eagles, or the hare, the lion.   35
If I say sooth, I must report they were
As cannons over-charged with double cracks,

may refer to the season, continuing the astronomical metaphor, or it may more simply mean 'source'. Nosworthy (*Shakespeare's*, 21) compares *Ham* 2.2.479–84, where a simile closely resembling this is more fully worked out.

26 **Shipwrecking** participial adjective, meaning 'causing shipwrecks', the earliest recorded usage in this sense
thunders F2, adding 'breaking' to the line to even out the metre, reads 'thunders breaking'. Many modern editors following Pope add 'break' for this purpose. Cordner (107) makes a persuasive case from a theatrical perspective for retaining F1, and Blake ('Study', 26) ingeniously elucidates the grammar of the line to support F1.

29 **justice ... valour** The Captain identifies Duncan's cause with *justice*, and personifies Macbeth as the *valour* that comes to his aid.

30 **skipping** lightly armed, but may also suggest lightweight, irresponsible. See *1H4* 3.2.60: 'The skipping king, he ambled up and down'.

31 **Norwegian lord** i.e. Sweno
surveying vantage perceiving himself to have the advantage. In *OED* survey *v.* 4c, this line is given as the first occurrence of 'surveying' in the sense 'observe, perceive, see' (though *EEBO* has some earlier examples, e.g. Barnabe Barnes, *Parthenophil and Parthenope* (1593): 'But for surveying of that bewteous sort'). However, Shakespeare's use here also has something of *OED v.* 4a: 'To look at from, or as from, a height or commanding position; to take a broad, general or comprehensive view of'.

32 **furbished** replenished

35 **sparrows ... lion** Macbeth and Banquo are as little dismayed by the Norwegian attack as eagles would be by sparrows or lions by hares. For instances where the inversion of nature that the Captain refers to here in an ironic sense take place in earnest, see 2.4.

37 **over-charged ... cracks** overloaded with twice the usual amount of shot (*OED* crack *n.* 2)

26 thunders] thunders breaking *F2–4*; thunders break *Pope*   29 had,] had *F4*   34–5] *Rowe; F lines* Banquoh? / Eagles; / Lyon: / ; *Pope lines* this / yes / lion. / ; *Ard² lines* Banquo? / Yes; / lion. /

So they doubly redoubled strokes upon the foe.
Except they meant to bathe in reeking wounds,
Or memorize another Golgotha,   40
I cannot tell. But I am faint;
My gashes cry for help.

KING

So well thy words become thee as thy wounds,
They smack of honour both. Go get him surgeons.

> [*Exit Captain with Attendants.*]

Enter ROSS *and* ANGUS.

Who comes here?
MALCOLM   The worthy Thane of Ross.   45
LENNOX

What a haste looks through his eyes.
So should he look, that seems to speak things strange.

ROSS

God save the King.

---

38 **doubly redoubled** hugely increased. See *R2* 1.3.80–1: 'Let thy blows, doubly redoubled / Fall like amazing thunder'. Doubling is part of a theme of multiplication running through the play, linking the idiom of the Witches with that of mainstream characters (though Braunmuller notes that literally overloading cannon in this way would have destroyed them). The metrical irregularity of the line may be a further indication of the speaker's exhaustion.

39 **Except** unless
reeking steaming with blood

40 **memorize** keep alive the memory of (*OED* memorise *v.* 2a)

Golgotha another name for Calvary, the place where Christ was crucified; here it signifies a graveyard or charnel house.

42 His wounds are thought of as open mouths, crying out for help. See *JC* 3.1.259–60: 'thy wounds . . . / Which like dumb mouths do ope their ruby lips'.

44 **smack** savour

45 **Thane** in this period, a Scottish title denoting a rank equivalent to earl

47 **that . . . strange** 'whose appearance corresponds with the strangeness of his message' (Muir). Lennox's introduction creates excited expectation for Ross's message.

39 reeking] recking *F2–3*   40–2] *Rowe lines* tell: / help. / ; *Ard²*, *Cam¹ line* Golgotha, / tell – / help. / 44 SD] *not in F; Exeunt some with the Soldier.* / *Capell; Exit soldier attended.* / *Malone*   46–8] *Oxf¹*, *Ard²*, *Cam¹ line* look / King. /   46 What a] What *(conj. GWW)*

KING

Whence cam'st thou, worthy thane?

ROSS　　　　　　　　　　　　　From Fife, great King,

Where the Norwegian banners flout the sky, 　　　　50

And fan our people cold.

Norway himself, with terrible numbers,

Assisted by that most disloyal traitor,

The Thane of Cawdor, began a dismal conflict,

Till that Bellona's bridegroom, lapped in proof, 　　　55

Confronted him with self-comparisons,

Point against point, rebellious arm 'gainst arm,

Curbing his lavish spirit; and to conclude,

The victory fell on us.

KING　　　　　　　　　　Great happiness.

ROSS

That now Sweno, the Norways' king, craves

　　　composition. 　　　　　　　　　　　　　　60

49　**Fife** district on the east coast of Scotland

50　**flout** mock or jeer at, in the sense of being raised in insult

51　**fan ... cold** chill our supporters with fear; *fan* continues the visual imagery. This is another messenger speech, demanding a graphic style. 'Fan' could also mean 'winnow' (*OED v.* 1a), separate out the good from the bad.

52　**Norway** i.e. the King of Norway

53–4　**traitor ... Cawdor** The next Thane of Cawdor will take on the same role. See Johnson's remarks on the inconsistencies in the references to Cawdor in the play (*Miscellaneous*, Note VI, 49–50), and 1.3.71–3n.

55　**Bellona's bridegroom** spouse to the goddess of war. This is generally taken to refer to Macbeth, for instance by Muir, Brooke and Braunmuller, though Granville Barker doubts this, and Hayes, 127–8,

argues for Macduff. Although the identification of Macduff as the killer of the Thane of Cawdor clears up the apparent inconsistency at 1.3.109–10, where Macbeth is surprised to hear of Cawdor's death, the identification with Macbeth is consistent with the praise lavished on Macbeth's warlike exploits in 1.2. As Muir comments, 'There would have been no point [for Shakespeare] in making some other general responsible for the victory over Sweno, in defiance of his source'. **lapped in proof** clad in impenetrable armour

56　Macbeth faced the Thane of Cawdor with a fighting spirit equal to his own, ironic in view of his later assumption of this title.

57　**Point against point** point of one sword against the other (*OED* point *n.*[1] 19c)

58　**lavish** unrestrained or wild

60　**craves composition** asks for a treaty

51–2] *Ard²* lines himself, / numbers, / 　57 point, rebellious arm] point rebellious, arm *Theobald*; Point against point-rebellious, arm *Hunter*　60 That ... composition] *Pope*; F lines King, / composition: /

Nor would we deign him burial of his men,
Till he disbursed, at Saint Colme's Inch,
Ten thousand dollars, to our general use.

KING

No more that Thane of Cawdor shall deceive
Our bosom interest. Go pronounce his present death,   65
And with his former title greet Macbeth.

ROSS

I'll see it done.

KING

What he hath lost, noble Macbeth hath won.   *Exeunt.*

1.3   *Thunder. Enter the three* WITCHES.

1 WITCH

Where hast thou been, sister?

2 WITCH

Killing swine.

3 WITCH

Sister, where thou?

61 **deign him burial** 'Deign' means treat as worthy of (*OED v.* 3). The refusal to allow the enemy to bury his dead until a ransom has been paid reflects the battle practices of Shakespeare's day. See also Hawkins (167) on the military code in the play.

62 **disbursed** disbursèd; paid out
Saint Colme's Inch Inchcombe, a small island in the Firth of Forth near Edinburgh. Colme, referring to St Columba, is pronounced with two syllables.

63 **dollars** 'Dollar' is the English name for the German *thaler* (which did not come into existence till the sixteenth century) and also of coins of other northern countries bearing equivalent names, such

as the *rigsdaler* of Denmark and *riksdaler* of Sweden (*OED* dollar *n.* 1).

65 **bosom interest** most intimate concerns (compare 'bosom friend')
present immediate

68 Duncan unconsciously echoes the Witches' rhyme. For the proverb see Dent, M337: 'No man loses but another wins'.

1.3 This scene presumably takes place on the heath referred to by the Witches in 1.1. It meets the expectations created by the first two scenes, introducing Macbeth in person, staging his anticipated meeting with the Witches and consolidating his battlefield success.

2 **Killing swine** a practice that witches were commonly accused of, and one that might leave the hands bloody

62 Colme's] *(Colmes)*   66 greet] great *F2–4*   **1.3**] *Scena Tertia.*

1 WITCH

A sailor's wife had chestnuts in her lap
And munched, and munched, and munched.
    'Give me,' quoth I.   5
'Aroynt thee, witch,' the rump-fed ronyon cries.
Her husband's to Aleppo gone, Master o'th' Tiger:
But in a sieve I'll thither sail,
And like a rat without a tail,
I'll do, I'll do, and I'll do.   10

6   **Aroynt** avaunt, be gone. *OED* credits
    Shakespeare with the first uses of the
    word, a term of unknown origin, and
    none earlier are to be found in *EEBO*.
    Hulme, 17–19, gives evidence from
    contemporary documentation of the
    phrase 'arent the wich' (beware of the
    witch). Compare *KL* 3.4.120: 'aroint
    thee, witch, aroint thee'.

    witch used as an insult here. It is worth
    noting that the word occurs only twice in
    the dialogue in *Mac* (also at 4.1.23), and
    the Sisters do not refer to themselves in
    this way.

    rump-fed sometimes taken to mean fed
    on offal or scraps. Muir prefers 'fed on the
    best joints, pampered', citing Clarendon,
    but given the meaning of *ronyon* this
    seems unlikely. Another suggested mean-
    ing is 'fat rumped' (Kittredge). There is
    no prior recorded evidence of this term as
    an insult.

    ronyon an abusive term for a woman. See
    MW 4.2.174–5: 'Out of my door, you
    witch, you rag, you baggage, you polecat,
    you runnion'. See also Williams, *Diction-
    ary*, who defines 'runnion' as an abusive
    term meaning penis, equivalent to present
    day use of 'prick'.

7   **Aleppo** trading city in Syria
    Master o'th' Tiger There was a voyage
    to Aleppo in a ship of this name in 1583,
    as well as other examples of vessels

called 'Tiger', a name which Shakespeare
uses in *TN* 5.1.58. But, as Loomis
discovered, there had been a recent
voyage by a ship named Tiger, lasting
from 5 December 1604 to 27 June 1606,
i.e. 567 days, or 81 weeks, thus 'sennights nine times nine'. It is, however,
impossible to know if Shakespeare was
aware of this fact.

8   **in a sieve** perhaps an oblique reference to
    the exploits of the witches in *News from
    Scotland* (1591), where Agnes Tompson
    confessed 'that vpon the night of *Allhollon
    Euen* last, she was accompanied aswell
    with the persons aforesaide, as also with a
    great many other witches, to the number
    of two hundreth: and that all they together
    went by Sea each one in a Riddle or Ciue'
    (sig. A3).

9   **rat ... tail** According to Steevens (cited
    by Muir), witches were believed to be
    able to turn themselves into rats but did
    not have the body part equivalent to a tail.

10 The Witch's vagueness as to her precise
    intentions is sinister rather than sugges-
    tive of impotence. The word *do* here
    seems more likely to mean 'act' (*OED*
    act *v.* 15a) than, as has been suggested
    (e.g. by Braunmuller) fornicate (Blake,
    'Study', 18). The repeated *do* links into a
    pattern of related terms in the play, esp.
    deed and *done*. See for example 1.7.1–2,
    2.1.62, 2.2.15, 5.1.68–9.

5] *Pope; F lines* ³mounch: / I. /   6 Aroynt] Anoynt *F3–4*

137

2 WITCH

    I'll give thee a wind.

1 WITCH

    Th'art kind.

3 WITCH

    And I another.

1 WITCH

    I myself have all the other,

    And the very ports they blow,   15

    All the quarters that they know,

    I'th' shipman's card.

    I'll drain him dry as hay:

    Sleep shall neither night nor day

    Hang upon his penthouse lid: 20

    He shall live a man forbid.

    Weary sev'nights nine times nine

    Shall he dwindle, peak, and pine:

11 **give . . . wind** Witches were believed to produce winds, and often thought to sell them. See Nashe, *Summer's Last Will and Testament* (1600), in *Works*, 3, ll. 1219–20: 'in Ireland and Denmarke both / Witches for gold will sell a man a winde'. Giving them freely suggests sisterly supportiveness.

14–17 **I . . . card** The syntax is not entirely clear but the gist is that the Witches will so disorient the captain that he cannot steer his ship into safety. Blake ('Study', 17–19) explicates the lines at length.

14 **other** i.e. other winds

16 **quarters** directions, regions (*OED* quarter *n*. 12a)

17 **shipman's card** his map (*OED* card *n.²* 3b) or sea chart, or as Muir suggests, the circular card on which the 32 points of the compass were marked (*n.²* 4a)

18 **drain . . . hay** suggests sexual debilitation; the Witch is perhaps to be thought of as a succubus. See Dent, H231.1: 'As dry as hay'.

20 **penthouse lid** For the implied comparison of the eyelid to the roof of a penthouse compare Dekker, *The Gull's Horn-book* (1609), 14: 'The two Eyes are the glasse windows . . . having goodly penthouses of haire to overshadow them'. The disturbed sleep of Macbeth and his wife may be an effect not just of their crimes but also of their association with the Witches.

21 **forbid** under a curse

22 **sev'nights . . . nine** Nine, like three, is one of the Witches' spell numbers. See 35–6 below. Furness cites Ovid, *Met.*, 14.58 and 7.189–91, on the fondness of witches for multiples of three and nine. **sev'nights** weeks

23 **peak** languish

12 Th'art] Thou'rt *Capell*   15 ports] points *Pope*   22 sev'nights] *(*seu'nights*)*; sev'n nights *Johnson*; sennights *Cam¹*

138

Though his bark cannot be lost,
Yet it shall be tempest-tossed.   25
Look what I have.

2 WITCH

Show me, show me.

1 WITCH

Here I have a pilot's thumb,
Wrecked as homeward he did come.   *Drum within*

3 WITCH

A drum, a drum: 30
Macbeth doth come.

ALL

The weïrd sisters, hand in hand,
Posters of the sea and land,
Thus do go, about, about,

---

24 **bark ... lost** A *bark* is a small ship. The
Witches' power is limited, here and
elsewhere.

28 **pilot's thumb** Wilson, 131–2, makes an
elaborate case for identifying this with
the thumb of Edmund Campion, cut off at
his execution in 1581, and subsequently
venerated as a relic.

29 SD See Thomson, 143, on the cueing of
sound effects. It is not uncommon for
drums to be sounded within, rather than
onstage (Dessen & Thomson, 'drum'). As
Muir notes, 'It is curious that, though
Banquo and Macbeth are alone, their
arrival is announced by a drum', since the
sound might be expected to precede the
entry of an army. But Shakespeare is
clearly preparing a huge build-up to the
first entrance of his protagonist. Sprague,
Actors, 228, cites a copy of Kirkman's
Life of Macklin with Macklin's manuscript notes on the grand effects created
for this moment in a production of 1773.
According to Simon Forman's account,
Macbeth and Banquo are 'riding through
a wood' when they meet the Witches, but

his recollections may be supplemented
with details gleaned from Holinshed
(Scragg, 81–2, though see also Benecke,
who is more doubtful of this).

32 ***weïrd*** emendation proposed by Theobald
for F 'wayward' or 'weyard', generally
accepted, although the word does not
occur elsewhere in Shakespeare. Boece, in
his chronicle *Scotorum Historiae* (1526),
and Holinshed both refer to the 'weird
sisters' in contexts that identify them as
goddesses of destiny. Brome and Heywood,
The Late Lancashire Witches (1633), refer
to the 'Scottish wayward sisters' (447), but
Muir conjectures that they were influenced
by the spelling in F. 'Weird' comes from
OE *wyrd*, fate, and Holinshed refers to
this meaning: 'the weird sisters, that is (as
ye would say) the goddesses of destinie'.
See Braunmuller, 255–6, on the etymo-
logy. The word must be pronounced with
two syllables (Abbott, 485).

33 **Posters** travellers who post or travel
quickly (*OED* poster *n.*¹ 1)

34 **about** in a circular direction (*OED* go
about PV 1.1)

29 Wrecked] *(*Wrackt*);* wreckt *Theobald*   32 weïrd] *Theobald;* weyward *F*

Thrice to thine, and thrice to mine,   35
And thrice again, to make up nine.
Peace, the charm's wound up.

Enter MACBETH *and* BANQUO.

MACBETH
So foul and fair a day I have not seen.
BANQUO
How far is't called to Forres? What are these,
So withered and so wild in their attire,   40
That look not like th'inhabitants o'th' earth,
And yet are on't? Live you, or are you aught
That man may question? You seem to understand me,
By each at once her choppy finger laying
Upon her skinny lips. You should be women,   45

35–6 The lines suggest a circular dance, moving round nine times. On three and nine, see above, 22n.

35 **to thine ... to mine** towards you ... towards me. The Witches' movements here have been compared to those of Jonson's witches in *The Masque of Queens* (1609), 'dancing back to back, and hip to hip, their hands joined, and making their circles backward, to the left hand' (ll. 330–1). Witches were associated with the reversal of the norm. See 'Hysteron proteron', in Adamson *et al.*

37 **wound up** ready to go, perhaps a metaphor from the tightening of strings on a musical instrument to make them ready to play. Compare 1.7.61.

38 Macbeth, like Duncan earlier, sub-consciously echoes the Witches' conjunction of opposites. Palfrey and Stern comment on this, Macbeth's first line, as showing him entering in mid-conversation

on a significant day 'that already befuddles his categories of understanding' (98).

39 **How ... Forres** 'How far away is Forres?'
Forres town in the Moray Firth region. The geography of the characters' movements is not entirely clear, though Muir assumes that in 1.4 the characters have reached Forres, from where it is not too long a journey to Macbeth's castle at Inverness.

40 **So ... wild** not like the well-dressed figures in Holinshed's illustration of this encounter. See Fig. 3.

42–3 **Live ... question** i.e. are you living beings, capable of being questioned by us?

44 **at once** simultaneously (*OED adv. phr.* 3)
choppy perhaps chapped, rough-skinned; the first recorded usage in this sense. The gesture suggests that the Witches refuse to answer questions until ready to do so.

37.1 BANQUO] *Banquo with Soldiers and other Attendants. / Rowe*   39 Forres] *Rowe;* Soris *F;* Foris *Pope*

And yet your beards forbid me to interpret
That you are so.

MACBETH   Speak if you can: what are you?

1 WITCH

All hail Macbeth, hail to thee, Thane of Glamis.

2 WITCH

All hail Macbeth, hail to thee, Thane of Cawdor.

3 WITCH

All hail Macbeth, that shalt be king hereafter.   50

BANQUO

Good sir, why do you start, and seem to fear
Things that do sound so fair? – I'th' name of truth,
Are ye fantastical, or that indeed
Which outwardly ye show? My noble partner
You greet with present grace, and great prediction   55
Of noble having and of royal hope,
That he seems rapt withal. To me you speak not.

---

46 **beards** a detail added by Shakespeare to Holinshed's description, which relates to Shakespeare's exploration of gender roles in the play. Schiffer encapsulates much critical discussion on this topic. Witches were popularly believed to sport beards on occasion. See Fletcher and Massinger, *The Honest Man's Fortune* (1613), 2.1.23–5: 'The women that / Come to us, for disguises must wear beards, / And that's they say, a token of a witch'.

48 **All hail** This appears here to be a particularly respectful salutation. The word is reported in Macbeth's letter to his wife (1.5.7) and echoed in her first address to him (55). But elsewhere (*3H6* 5.7.33–4 and *R2* 4.1.169–71) the phrase is associated with Judas's betrayal of Christ.

Glamis a village in Angus, north of Dundee, site of a medieval castle. The thaneship belonged to Macbeth's family. The word sometimes has two syllables

in Shakespeare, e.g. at 3.1.1 and perhaps here and at 1.5.54, but elsewhere only one.

51–2 **fear ... fair** Banquo puns on these near-homophones. The sounds recall the *fair/foul* antithesis prominent in the play from the start.

53 **fantastical** imaginary

55–6 Banquo's alliterative patterning (*greet ... grace ... great, having ... hope*) draws attention to the double benefits apparently offered to Macbeth, in both the present and the future.

55 **present grace** immediate benefit, referring to the title Macbeth already has

56 **noble having** noble fortune or possessions

57 **rapt** absorbed, entranced (*OED adj.* 7a). Compare 145 below. Hulme, 237, suggests that F's 'wrapt' may relate to the clothing imagery in the play and that there may be a secondary meaning of 'entangled, caught, or implicated' (*OED* wrap *v.* 3b).

57 rapt] *Pope;* wrapt *F*

141

If you can look into the seeds of time,
And say which grain will grow, and which will not,
Speak then to me, who neither beg nor fear   60
Your favours, nor your hate.

1 WITCH

Hail.

2 WITCH

Hail.

3 WITCH

Hail.

1 WITCH

Lesser than Macbeth, and greater.   65

2 WITCH

Not so happy, yet much happier.

3 WITCH

Thou shalt get kings, though thou be none:
So all hail Macbeth, and Banquo.

1 WITCH

Banquo, and Macbeth, all hail.

MACBETH

Stay, you imperfect speakers, tell me more.   70
By Finel's death, I know I am Thane of Glamis,

58 **seeds of time** This is the first of the play's many images of natural growth, which critics have linked with those of children. See Brooks, 36–8, who gives the classic account of these, and above, p. 79. The Witches can predict the future.

60–1 **neither . . . hate** Banquo does not beg the Witches' favours or fear their hate. He uses the rhetorical figure hyperbaton (a figure of speech in which the customary order of words is inverted) along with alliteration. Perhaps he is implicitly contrasting himself with Macbeth in his objective attitude to the Witches.

67 **get kings** *get* means beget. The Witch refers to Banquo as the ancestor of King

James VI and I, through Fleance. A family tree, printed in John Leslie, *De Origine . . . Scotorum* (1578) depicts this descent. In fact, Banquo was a fictional character, inserted by Hector Boece into his *Scotorum Historiae* as an ancestor of James V to reinforce the Stewart line. See Aitchison, 117–18 on Boece's invention, and above, p. 38.

70 **imperfect speakers** i.e. persons who speak incompletely

71 **Finel's death** Finel (Sinell in Holinshed) was Macbeth's father. The *s/f* confusion results from the early modern use of a long *s* (∫).

71 Finel's] *Cam¹; Sinells* F

But how of Cawdor? The Thane of Cawdor lives
A prosperous gentleman: and to be king
Stands not within the prospect of belief,
No more than to be Cawdor. Say from whence   75
You owe this strange intelligence, or why
Upon this blasted heath you stop our way
With such prophetic greeting? Speak, I charge you.

Witches vanish.

BANQUO

The earth hath bubbles, as the water has,
And these are of them. Whither are they vanished?   80

MACBETH

Into the air; and what seemed corporal,
Melted, as breath into the wind.
Would they had stayed.

BANQUO

Were such things here as we do speak about?
Or have we eaten on the insane root,   85
That takes the reason prisoner?

72–3 **Thane ... gentleman** It is problematic that Macbeth can refer to Cawdor in these terms, when in the previous scene Ross has graphically described his defeat of the traitor in battle. Furness, 43–4, summarizes the efforts of earlier editors to rationalize the difficulty. Muir suggests that Cawdor's support for the King of Norway was not discovered till after Macbeth had left the battlefield, and at this point the audience does not know Cawdor is dead. The apparent inconsistency has sometimes been used to support theories of the text having been cut, and of 1.2 perhaps having been revised. See 1.2n. and Appendix 1.

74 **prospect** forethought, consideration of something in the future (*OED n.* 7a, where this is the earliest citation, though *EEBO* has examples from 1580. See also

Thomas Cooper, *Certain sermons wherein is contained the defence of the gospel now preached*: 'They have small care and prospect, howe to maytayne the state of their Countrey in safetie', 226.) It may also take in something of *OED n.* 6, 'a mental picture or vista, esp. of something future or expected'.

76 **intelligence** information, especially that obtained by spies (*OED n.* 5b)

77 **blasted** blighted, perhaps with implications of a curse

78 SD On how this might have been effected, see Wickham, 'To fly', 171–84, and 3.5.20n. The comments of Banquo and Macbeth which follow suggest an unusually dramatic mode of exit.

81 **corporal** corporeal, physically embodied

85 **insane root** root which makes an eater go insane, as hemlock was thought to do.

85 on] of *F4*

MACBETH

Your children shall be kings.

BANQUO   You shall be king.

MACBETH

And Thane of Cawdor too: went it not so?

BANQUO

To th' self-same tune and words. Who's here?

Enter ROSS *and* ANGUS.

ROSS

The King hath happily received, Macbeth,   90
The news of thy success; and when he reads
Thy personal venture in the rebels' fight,
His wonders and his praises do contend
Which should be thine, or his. Silenced with that,
In viewing o'er the rest o'th' self-same day,   95
He finds thee in the stout Norwegian ranks,
Nothing afeared of what thyself didst make,
Strange images of death. As thick as tale
Came post with post, and every one did bear

Nosworthy (*Shakespeare's*, 10) finds here one of several pieces of evidence for Shakespeare's preparing for *AC* while he was also writing *Mac*, in a passage from Plutarch's *Life of Antony* about Roman soldiers tasting strange roots: 'Among the which there was one that killed them, and made them out of their wits. For he that had once eaten of it, his memorye went from him, and he knew no manner of thing'. For a possible source for the idea, see p. 97.

92 **fight** often emended to 'sight' though *fight* makes sense. For a similar 'sight'/'fight' ambiguity, resolved in favour of 'sight', see *Ham* Q1 17.132 and n.

93 **His wonders . . . praises** 'There is a conflict in Duncan's mind between his astonishment at the achievement and his

admiration for Macbeth' (Muir). This is yet another example of the convoluted language of compliment.

96 **stout** 'valiant, brave, undaunted, vigorous in conflict' (*OED adj.* 3a), or perhaps 'formidable, menacing, terrible in appearance' (*adj.* 2b *obs.*)

97 **Nothing afeard** not in the least deterred by or afraid

98–9 **As . . . with post** 'Tale' is often emended to 'hail' but need not be. 'Thick' can mean 'fast' in this period (*OED* thick *adj.* 5b *obs.*). See *2H4* 2.3.24, where Hotspur is described as 'speaking thick'. Ross means that Macbeth killed men so rapidly that it was like posts (couriers) arriving so fast that they could not be counted. 'Tale' means tally, enumeration

92 fight] sight *Oxf, Cam*[1]   99 Came] *Rowe;* Can *F*

Thy praises in his kingdom's great defence   100
And poured them down before him.

ANGUS   We are sent
To give thee from our royal master thanks,
Only to herald thee into his sight
Not pay thee.

ROSS

And for an earnest of a greater honour,   105
He bade me, from him, call thee Thane of Cawdor:
In which addition, hail most worthy thane,
For it is thine.

BANQUO   What, can the devil speak true?

MACBETH

The Thane of Cawdor lives. Why do you dress me
In borrowed robes?

ANGUS   Who was the Thane lives yet,   110
But under heavy judgement bears that life
Which he deserves to lose.
Whether he was combined with those of Norway,
Or did line the rebel with hidden help
And vantage, or that with both he laboured   115
In his country's wrack, I know not,

(*OED* tale *n.* 7). Johnson paraphrases: 'Posts arrived as fast as they could be counted'. *Came* is Rowe's emendation for F 'can', now generally accepted. See Hulme, who defends *tale* but not 'can' (24–6). as does Sisson (2.193).

105 **earnest** pledge (as of something more significant to come)

107 **addition** title. See *Cor* 1.9.62–5: 'for what he did before Corioles, call him . . . / Martius Caius Coriolanus! / Bear th'addition nobly ever!'

110 **borrowed robes** The play's proliferation of images of clothing, borrowed, stolen,

ill-fitting, has been much discussed, initially by Spurgeon, 325–7, and also Brooks, 25–30.

111 **judgement** sentence

112 This is a short line in F, and retained as such by some recent editors, e.g. Brooke, Braunmuller. But the efforts of others, e.g. Muir, Hunter, Oxford, to relineate this speech have not been notably successful.

114 **line** strengthen, reinforce (*OED v.*[1] 2)
    rebel i.e. Macdonald

115 **vantage** support

116 **wrack** destruction

103 herald] *F4; harrold F; herrald F2–3*   109–10] *Capell; F lines* lives: / Robes? / yet, /   110 borrowed] his borrowed *F2–4*   114 Or] Or else *F2–4*   116 wrack] wreck *Theobald*

But treasons capital, confessed and proved
Have overthrown him.
MACBETH [*aside*]   Glamis and Thane of Cawdor:
The greatest is behind. – Thanks for your pains.
[*to Banquo*] Do you not hope your children shall
   be kings   120
When those that gave the Thane of Cawdor to me
Promised no less to them?
BANQUO   That, trusted home,
Might yet enkindle you unto the crown,
Besides the Thane of Cawdor. But 'tis strange:
And oftentimes, to win us to our harm,   125
The instruments of darkness tell us truths,
Win us with honest trifles, to betray's
In deepest consequence.
Cousins, a word, I pray you.
MACBETH [*aside*]   Two truths are told
As happy prologues to the swelling act   130

---

117 **capital** punishable by death

119 **The ... behind** The most important (i.e. the title of king) is still to come. No aside is marked in F, but Macbeth is clearly musing to himself, as he is again at 129–31. See Dent, B318: 'The best (?greatest) is behind'.

121 **those that gave** i.e. the Witches. Macbeth seems reluctant to name them.

122 **home** to its ultimate extent, fully (*OED adv.* 4a)

123 **enkindle** inflame with desire (*OED v.* 2b); Banquo may or may not be suspicious of Macbeth's motives yet. Coleridge, 1.62, suggests a hint of the meaning of 'kindle' as 'to bring forth, give birth to' (*OED* kindle *v.*[2]).

126 Muir cites James VI and I's *Daemonologie*, 8: 'For that old and craftie Serpent

being a Spirit, he easilie spyes our affections, and so conformes himself thereto to deceave us to our wracke'. See Dent, D266: 'The devil sometimes speaks the truth'.

128 to the fullest extent, or, with fatal results

129 **Cousins ... you** Banquo draws Ross and Angus aside. The word 'cousin' can refer to a wide range of collateral relatives (*OED* cousin *n.* 1).

130 **prologues** Macbeth is envisaging his future as a grand drama shortly to be enacted.
swelling growing, developing. See *H5* Prol.3–4: 'A kingdom for a stage, princes to act, / And monarchs to behold the swelling scene!'

---

118 SD] *Rowe*   119 Thanks] *To Angus* Thanks *Rowe*   120 SD] *Rowe*   122 That] *Aside* That *Capell* trusted] thrusted *Malone*   123 unto] into *F4*   129 SD] *Rowe*

Of the imperial theme. – I thank you, gentlemen. –
This supernatural soliciting
Cannot be ill; cannot be good. If ill,
Why hath it given me earnest of success,
Commencing in a truth? I am Thane of Cawdor.   135
If good, why do I yield to that suggestion
Whose horrid image doth unfix my hair,
And make my seated heart knock at my ribs,
Against the use of nature? Present fears
Are less than horrible imaginings.   140
My thought, whose murder yet is but fantastical,

131 **imperial theme** 'Imperial' means to do
with empire or reigning. 'Theme' might
mean a subject for discourse, discussion
or meditation (*OED* theme *n.* 1a), or a
subject or cause for action (*OED n.* 1c).
See *Ham* 5.1.255: 'I will fight with him
upon this theme'.

I . . . gentlemen Macbeth seems suddenly
to become conscious of the presence of
others.

132–3 **This . . . good** Knights's comment
on the irregular rhythm of these lines
suggests their powerful emotional effect:
'Its sickening see-saw rhythm completes
the impression of "a phantasma, or
a hideous dream"' (*Explorations*, 20).
Flatter, 120–2, argues effectively for F's
lineation here.

134 **success** Though Macbeth does not take
account of this, 'success' could have a
neutral meaning or even indicate a bad
outcome. See Sackville and Norton,
Gorboduc (1565), 1.1.55: 'If the end
bring forth an ill success'. It also means
'succession' as of heirs (*OED n.* 5). See
pp. 78–82.

136 **that suggestion** No literal suggestion
(of murdering Duncan) has yet been put
to Macbeth, but this phrase and what
follows in the speech testify to the
intense power of his imagination.

137 **horrid image** i.e. the image of himself of
murdering Duncan. 'Horrid', a stronger
term then than now, means 'causing
horror or aversion . . . terrible, dreadful'
(*OED adj.* 2). It is nearly synonymous
with *horrible* (140). See also 1.7.24 and
4.3.56. There may also be an implicit pun
on the root of 'horrid' from Latin *horreo*,
meaning to bristle or have one's hair
stand on end.

unfix my hair make my hair stand on
end. Compare 5.5.11–13.

138 **seated** fixed in position (*OED ppl. a.*1
cites this as the first use in this sense, and
EEBO gives none earlier)

139 **use** custom

139–40 **Present . . . imaginings** 'Real objects
of fear are less terrible than those
conjured up by the imagination.'

141–4 The complex expression suggests
Macbeth's mental agitation. He seems to
mean that the image of murder in his
mind, although still only a fantasy and
not a reality, is nonetheless so powerful
that his whole being is in a state of
turmoil.

141 The grammar of this line is disconcerting:
'first, the "thought" is personified by
being assigned the capacity to possess;
second the murder is strangely distanced
by being possessed – especially when it

131 I thank] [*To Rosse and Angus*] I thank *Johnson*   132 This] *Aside* This *Capell*   137 hair] (Heire)

Shakes so my single state of man
That function is smothered in surmise,
And nothing is, but what is not.

BANQUO

Look how our partner's rapt. 145

MACBETH [*aside*]

If chance will have me king, why chance may
crown me,
Without my stir.

BANQUO   New honours come upon him,
Like our strange garments, cleave not to their mould,
But with the aid of use.

MACBETH [*aside*]   Come what come may,
Time, and the hour, runs through the roughest day. 150

BANQUO

Worthy Macbeth, we stay upon your leisure.

---

is possessed by something we'd expect
to be co-referential (he's thinking of
murder, so murder *is* his thought)' (JH).

142 **single . . . man** 'Single' could mean 'slight,
poor, trivial' (*OED adj.* 12b). Macbeth
is concerned with the radical effect of
an imagined act on his being. See *JC*
2.1.63–9, where Brutus is similarly
conscious of the power of imagination:
'Between the acting of a dreadful thing /
And the first motion . . . the state of man,
/ Like to a little kingdom, suffers then /
The nature of an insurrection'.

143 **function** the ability to act. The word has
three syllables.
    smothered . . . surmise entirely sup-
    pressed by imagination

147 **stir** 'doing anything active about it'
(*OED n.*[1] 3, commotion, disturbance,
fuss)

148 **strange** unfamiliar. This fits into the
pattern of clothes that are for whatever
reason uncomfortable to the wearer (see
also 110n.).

149 **Come . . . may** See Dent, C529: 'Come
(Hap, Befall) what come (hap, befall,)
may'.

150 proverbial. See Dent, D90: 'The longest
day has an end'. Macbeth draws on
proverbial utterances to justify his decision at this point to take no action.
Abbott, 336, notes several examples of
two or more singular nouns followed by a
verb ending in *-s* and apparently singular.
See also Blake, *Grammar*, 6.1.1.1 on
subject/verb concord.
    runs through i.e. like sand in an hourglass

151 **stay . . . leisure** await your attention.
Banquo draws further attention to
Macbeth's distraction.

145 Look] *To Rosse* Look *Collier*   146 SD] *Rowe*   If . . . crown me] *Rowe; F lines* King, / Crowne me, /
149 SD] *Hanmer*

MACBETH

> Give me your favour. My dull brain was wrought
> With things forgotten. Kind gentlemen, your pains
> Are registered, where every day I turn
> The leaf to read them. Let us toward the King.   155
> Think upon what hath chanced; and at more time,
> The interim having weighed it, let us speak
> Our free hearts each to other.

BANQUO   Very gladly.

MACBETH

> Till then, enough: come, friends.   *Exeunt.*

1.4   *Flourish. Enter* KING [Duncan], LENNOX,
            MALCOLM, DONALBAIN *and Attendants.*

KING

> Is execution done on Cawdor? Or not
> Those in commission yet returned?

MALCOLM   My liege,

> They are not yet come back. But I have spoke
> With one that saw him die, who did report,
> That very frankly he confessed his treasons,   5

---

152 **favour** indulgence; i.e. please excuse me.
   wrought agitated, troubled (*OED adj.* 5)
154 **registered** noted, as in the pages of a book
157 **The interim** perhaps a personification, or more probably standing for 'in the interim'
   weighed considered
1.4.0.1 *Flourish* Trumpet-call indicating the arrival of a character of high status. See Long, 183–4.

1 **Or** F2 emends to 'are' but the verb may be understood after *Or*.
2 **in commission** in charge of the task
   liege i.e. liege lord, originally a term for a feudal lord, but more generally applied in Shakespeare's day: 'the superior to whom one owes feudal allegiance and service' (*OED adj.* 1b)
3 **spoke** spoken. See Abbott, 343, on participle formation. The shortened form of the past participle without the inflection *-en* is common.

152–6] *Pope; F lines* fauour: / forgotten. / registred, / Leafe, / them. / upon / time, /   153 forgotten] forgot *Pope*   156 Think] *Aside* Think *Capell;* [*To Banquo*] Think *Cam¹*   158 Very] [*Aside to Macbeth*] Very *Dyce*   159 Till] *Aside to Banquo* Till *Dyce*   **1.4**] *Scena Quarta.*   1–2] *Capell; F lines* Cawdor? / return'd /   1 Cawdor? Or not] Cawdor yet? *Pope*   Or] Are *F2–4, Oxf, Hunter*   2–8 My liege . . . died] *Pope; F lines* back. / die: / hee / Pardon, / repentance: / him, / dy'de, /

Implored your highness' pardon, and set forth
A deep repentance. Nothing in his life
Became him like the leaving it. He died
As one that had been studied in his death,
To throw away the dearest thing he owed,   10
As 'twere a careless trifle.

KING   There's no art
To find the mind's construction in the face:
He was a gentleman on whom I built
An absolute trust.

Enter MACBETH, BANQUO, ROSS *and* ANGUS.

O worthiest cousin,
The sin of my ingratitude even now   15
Was heavy on me. Thou art so far before,
That swiftest wing of recompense is slow
To overtake thee. Would thou hadst less deserved,
That the proportion both of thanks, and payment,
Might have been mine. Only I have left to say,   20
More is thy due, than more than all can pay.

---

8 **Became** befitted, suited (*OED* become *v.* 7)
9 **studied ... death** prepared for it, in the way an actor prepares for a part
10 **owed** owned
11 **As** as if (Abbott, 107)
   careless worthless, not worth caring about
11–12 **There's ... face** proverbial; Dent, F1.1: 'The face is no index to the heart', citing Juvenal, *Satire* 2: '*Frontis nulla fides*'. The lack of fit between face and heart is often remarked on in Shakespeare, for instance by Hamlet, thinking of his uncle: 'One may smile and smile and be a villain' (*Ham* 1.5.108). Like Duncan, Hastings in *R3* is deceived by a villain's countenance: 'never a man in Christendom /

Can lesser hide his love or hate than he, / For by his face straight shall you know his heart' (*R3* 3.4.51–3).
   construction interpretation (*OED n.* 8a), perhaps with overtones of analysis in the grammatical sense, construing (*OED n.* 5)
16 **so far before** i.e. in advance of my ability to reward you
18–20 **Would ... mine** In the florid style typical of courteous exchanges in this play, Duncan wishes that Macbeth's deservings had not been so great, so that he could have rewarded him adequately.
19 **proportion** apportioning, allocation (*OED n.* 4, 'The action of proportioning something', citing this line)
21 **all** i.e. all of my thanks and payment

---

6 highness'] *Pope;* Highnesse *F*   10 owed] own'd *Johnson*   17 wing] wine *F2–4;* wind *Rowe*
21] 'More ... pay'. *Oxf*   than] *F4;* then *F*

150

MACBETH

    The service and the loyalty I owe,
    In doing it, pays itself. Your highness' part
    Is to receive our duties; and our duties
    Are to your throne and state, children and servants,   25
    Which do but what they should, by doing everything
    Safe toward your love and honour.

KING   Welcome hither.

    I have begun to plant thee, and will labour
    To make thee full of growing. Noble Banquo,
    That hast no less deserved, nor must be known   30
    No less to have done so. Let me enfold thee
    And hold thee to my heart.

BANQUO   There if I grow

    The harvest is your own.

KING   My plenteous joys,

    Wanton in fullness, seek to hide themselves
    In drops of sorrow. Sons, kinsmen, thanes,   35
    And you whose places are the nearest, know:
    We will establish our estate upon
    Our eldest, Malcolm, whom we name hereafter,

22–3 **The service . . . itself** In similar idiom Macbeth says that carrying out the services he owes Duncan is its own reward. Coleridge (1.63) refers to 'the language of effort' employed by the speakers here. See Heal, 19, on hospitality and reciprocity in early modern England.

27 **Safe** Crystal and Crystal gloss this as an adverb, 'trustworthily, in an assured way', though *OED* gives no examples of adverbial uses. The expression is strained.

28 **plant** establish. Shaheen notes that 'In Scripture the righteous are frequently compared to flourishing trees that the Lord has planted', and compares Jeremiah, 12.2: 'thou hast planted them . . . they grow and bring forth fruit' (160).

31 **enfold** embrace

32–3 **There . . . own** Banquo uses the language of compliment more easily than Macbeth.

34 **Wanton** unrestrained, profuse

35–6 **Sons . . . nearest** Duncan is making a formal announcement here, and wishes to include all present. If he is not naming the groups in order of precedence, his decision to begin with the word *Sons* may prepare the hearers for what is to come.

23–7] *Pope; F lines* it selfe. / Duties: / State, / should, / Loue / Honor. / hither: /   27 Safe] Shap'd *Hanmer;* Saf'd *Malone*   30 That] Thou *Pope*   nor] and *Rowe*

The Prince of Cumberland, which honour must,
Not unaccompanied, invest him only.   40
But signs of nobleness, like stars, shall shine
On all deservers. From hence to Inverness,
And bind us further to you.

MACBETH

The rest is labour which is not used for you;
I'll be myself the harbinger, and make joyful   45
The hearing of my wife with your approach.
So, humbly take my leave.

KING   My worthy Cawdor.

MACBETH [*aside*]

The Prince of Cumberland: that is a step
On which I must fall down, or else o'er-leap,
For in my way it lies. Stars, hide your fires,   50
Let not light see my black and deep desires.
The eye wink at the hand; yet let that be
Which the eye fears, when it is done, to see.   *Exit.*

---

39 **Prince of Cumberland** title given to the heir apparent of Scotland; compare 'Prince of Wales' in British usage. The crown of Scotland was not hereditary in Macbeth's time, as Shakespeare may have known. For discussions of the systems of inheritance in Scotland, see Norbrook, 88, Hawkins, 175, and above, pp. 35–6.

40 **Not unaccompanied** not on its own. Malcolm's elevation must be accompanied by the provision of honours to the others whom Duncan addresses.

42 **Inverness** a town at the head of the Moray Firth on the eastern coast of Scotland, ancient capital of Scotland

43 **to you** Braunmuller, citing Keightley, inserts a SD to indicate that this last sentence is addressed to Macbeth specifically, but it is not clear why Banquo,

who has also been thanked for his services, should not also be included.

44 Macbeth's strained style is evident again: *rest* may mean 'leisure' or 'resting', or 'the remainder', 'anything else'. The main meaning is that only service to Duncan is of any significance, and any other action on his part is worthless.

45 **harbinger** officer of the royal household employed to go in advance of the king on journeys and prepare his lodgings

49 **o'er-leap** jump over. Macbeth's need to move ahead faster than is orderly is also reflected in his wish to 'jump the life to come' (1.7.7).

52 **wink ... hand** *wink at* here means 'fail to see' (*OED* wink *v.* 5a). Macbeth's sense of a disjunction between the actions of hands and eyes appears again in

---

40 unaccompanied] accompanied *Warburton*   42 From hence] [*To Macbeth*] From hence *Keightley*, *Cam¹*   From] *om. Pope*   48 SD] *Rowe*   51 not] no *Hanmer*   light] night *Warburton*

KING

True, worthy Banquo, he is full so valiant,
And in his commendations, I am fed: 55
It is a banquet to me. Let's after him,
Whose care is gone before to bid us welcome.
It is a peerless kinsman.   *Flourish. Exeunt.*

1.5   *Enter Macbeth's wife* [LADY] *alone with a letter.*

LADY   *They met me in the day of success, and I have*
learned by the perfectest report, they have more
in them than mortal knowledge. When I burned in
desire to question them further, they made themselves
air, into which they vanished. Whiles I stood rapt   5

2.2.60 and 3.2.48–50. But Miola, noting Senecan influence on the prominence of 'hands', comments that 'in the doing of monstrous deeds the murderer's mind and hand co-operate' (*Classical*, 115).

54 **True, worthy Banquo** Although F gives no SD for Macbeth's aside, this speech makes it clear that Duncan and Banquo are assumed to have been in conversation in praise of Macbeth while it is being spoken. See Thomson, 144, on the convention of the 'unheard conversation'. The fact that it is spoken after Macbeth's exit may emphasize the irony of the praise.

54–5 **full . . . fed** Drawing on food images, Duncan's eulogistic language conveys the idea that any praise for Macbeth is a sustenance to him.

56 **banquet** seems to play on *Banquo*, who is being addressed, though Duncan is talking about Macbeth

58 **peerless** matchless

1.5.0.1 LADY Throughout this edition the character commonly known as 'Lady Macbeth' is referred to as 'the Lady' or 'Macbeth's Lady', except where performers

or productions are referred to. The expression 'Lady Macbeth' never occurs in F. For a discussion of this decision, see Appendix 1.

alone . . . letter For discussions of letters in Shakespeare see Taylor, 'Letters', and Stewart, *Shakespeare's*, esp. 33–4.

1–14 The part of the letter read out by the Lady may well not be the whole thing. There is no mention of the Witches' appearance, or of their promises to Banquo, and no opening greeting to her. Editors have also surmised that this is not her first reading of it. See Furness for descriptions of how Sarah Siddons and Ellen Terry played this moment and also McDonald, *Look*, 44–5, on Siddons. Sprague, *Actors*, 232, cites Leigh Hunt on Siddons making a circle in the air about her head at the end of the letter.

2 **perfectest report** most reliable testimony. Macbeth called the Witches *imperfect speakers* (1.3.70), but perhaps referred to the incompletion of their prophecies rather than their unreliability.

5 **vanished** perhaps suggests stage trickery for managing their exit

56 Let's] Let us *Pope*   **1.5**] *Scena Quinta.*   1.5.0] *Enter Lady Macbeth, reading.* / *Capell*   1 LADY] Lady *M. Malone; Lady Macbeth* [*Reads*] *Cam¹*   3 than] *F4; then F*   5 Whiles] While *Pope*

153

in the wonder of it, came missives from the King,
who all-hailed me 'Thane of Cawdor', by which title
before these weïrd sisters saluted me, and referred
me to the coming on of time, with 'Hail King that
shalt be'. This have I thought good to deliver thee,   10
my dearest partner of greatness, that thou mightst
not lose the dues of rejoicing by being ignorant of
what greatness is promised thee. Lay it to thy heart,
and farewell.

Glamis thou art, and Cawdor, and shalt be   15
What thou art promised. Yet do I fear thy nature,
It is too full o'th' milk of human kindness
To catch the nearest way. Thou wouldst be great,
Art not without ambition, but without
The illness should attend it. What thou wouldst highly,   20
That wouldst thou holily; wouldst not play false,

6   ***missives*** messengers (*OED n.* 4, where
    this is the first citation in this sense),
    rather than letters. Compare *AC* 2.2.78–9:
    'with taunts / Did gibe my missive out of
    audience'.

7   ***all-hailed me*** Macbeth recalls the Witches'
    greeting, although Duncan's messengers,
    Ross and Angus, do not use the phrase.
    Florio, *A New World of Words* (1598),
    cited by Furness, has: 'Salutare, to greet,
    to salute, to recommend, to all-haile . . . to
    do reverence'.

    'Thane of Cawdor' perhaps quoted speech,
    'Thane' being picked out in a Roman
    typeface in F where the remainder of the
    letter is printed in italics

9   ***coming . . . time*** future events

12 ***dues of rejoicing*** cause for rejoicing due
    to you

17 ***milk . . . kindness*** compassion felt by
    human beings for their like. Hunter, 113,
    paraphrases: 'what binds the individual to

the order of Man'. The expression is more
complicated than first appears. 'Human'
was not distinguished from 'humane' (the
form of the word in F) at this period;
kindness may carry the sense familiar
nowadays, but more probably here means
'kinship', or 'that which is appropriate
to one's kind'. Milk in the play is concep-
tually opposed to that other significant fluid,
blood. Berger, 'Early', discusses Duncan
as source of both 'blood and manliness'
and 'the milk of human kindness' (26).

18 **nearest way** See Dent, W142.1: 'The
    shortest way is commonly the foulest, the
    fairer way not much about', which seems
    apposite here.

20 **illness** evilness, wickedness
    wouldst highly would have (or do) of
    importance or high status

21 **holily** blamelessly. The alliteration with
    highly enhances the opposed meanings of
    the words.

7 ' *Thane of Cawdor* '] *Collier;* Thane *of Cawdor* F   8 weïrd] *Theobald;* weyward F   9–10 'Hail . . . be ']
Pope subst.; haile . . . be F   12 *the*] thy *Capell*   16 do I] I do *F4*   17 human] *Rowe;* humane *F*

And yet wouldst wrongly win. Thou'dst have, great
   Glamis,
That which cries, 'Thus thou must do', if thou have it;
And that which rather thou dost fear to do,
Than wishest should be undone. Hie thee hither,   25
That I may pour my spirits in thine ear,
And chastise with the valour of my tongue
All that impedes thee from the golden round,
Which fate and metaphysical aid doth seem
To have thee crowned withal.

Enter Messenger.

What is your tidings?   30

MESSENGER
The King comes here tonight.
LADY   Thou'rt mad to say it.

---

22 **wrongly win** succeed, or get what you want, by wrongful means

23 **That which cries** It makes better sense to interpret this as the crown, which Macbeth wishes to *have*, calling to him, than (as Braunmuller suggests) as a voice.
'Thus . . . do' Pope was the first to put quotation marks round these words, extending the speech to *undone* (25). *Thus* means 'play false'.
if . . . it if you would obtain it (i.e. the crown)

24 **that** referring back to 'Thus thou must do'

26 **pour . . . ear** The introduction of substances into the ear is often associated with poison in plays of this period. See *Ham* 1.5.63–4: 'in the porches of my ears did pour / The leperous distilment', and *Oth* 2.3.351: 'I'll pour this pestilence into his ear'.

27 **chastise** in the sense of *OED v.* 4, 'To free from faults, purify, refine' (Taylor, 'Letters', 36)

valour . . . tongue A woman's tongue was regarded as her main weapon, but her excessive use of it seen as unwomanly. Findlay, 'tongue', gives many useful references.

28 **impedes** This line is *OED*'s first citation for the word in the sense of obstructing the progress of, hindering, but it is used earlier by John Knox, *An Answer to a great number of blasphemous cavillations written by an Anabaptist* (1560), 265: 'if he wold stay and impede the sinne of man . . . which he may not impede'.
golden round i.e. the crown

29 **metaphysical** supernatural (*OED* supernatural *adj.* and *n.* 4c)

31 **Thou'rt . . . it** The Lady's response may suggest that the Messenger appears to be echoing her own thoughts by referring to Macbeth as king. Soliloquies are elsewhere interrupted by intrusions of some kind, e.g. Macbeth's at 1.7.28 and 3.1.71.

22–3] *Pope; F lines* winne. / cryes, / it; /   23 'Thus . . . do'] *Pope;* Thus . . . do *F*   Thus] This *Hanmer*
25 Than] *F4;* Then *F*   Hie] *F4;* High *F*   26 pour] *F4;* powre *F*   28 impedes thee] thee hinders *F2–3*

Is not thy master with him? Who, were't so,
Would have informed for preparation.

MESSENGER

So please you, it is true: our thane is coming.
One of my fellows had the speed of him,   35
Who, almost dead for breath, had scarcely more
Than would make up his message.

LADY   Give him tending,
He brings great news.   *Exit Messenger.*
The raven himself is hoarse
That croaks the fatal entrance of Duncan
Under my battlements. Come you spirits   40
That tend on mortal thoughts, unsex me here,

33 **informed for preparation** sent word for things to be made ready

35 **had ... speed of** outstripped, got ahead of (*OED* speed *n.* 10b, the first citation in this sense, though in fact it appears in *MA* 1.1.135–6: 'I would my horse had the speed of your tongue').

38 **raven ... hoarse** The raven is commonly regarded as a bird of ill omen and herald of death. See *Tit* 2.2.96–7: 'Here never shines the sun, here nothing breeds / Unless the nightly owl or fatal raven'. Hamlet refers to 'the croaking raven' (3.2. 247). Wills, 81–2, notes that the raven was often seen as a familiar. Ravens feed on carrion. Harting, 99–110, assembles a large number of unflattering references to the bird in Shakespeare.

39 **entrance** *OED* (*n.* 1a) gives Shakespeare as the first to use the word in the sense of 'the action of coming or going in', but *EEBO* has numerous earlier examples.

40, 47, 50 **Come ... Come ... Come** Like the Witches, the Lady makes a triple invocation. See Ewbank, 'Fiend-like', on the influence of the opening invocation of

Seneca's *Medea* on this speech. Gillespie, 'Seneca, Lucius Annaeus, the Younger', considers that 'Lady Macbeth may be meant expressly to recall Seneca's Medea here'.

40–1 **spirits ... thoughts** suggests the kind of spirit Shakespeare embodies in benevolent form in Ariel (*Tem*) who can 'come with a thought' (4.1.164) to Prospero. But perhaps, as Malone thought, Shakespeare has in mind the kind of spirits described in Nashe, *Pierce Penniless his Supplication to the Devil* (1592) (*Works*, 1.130): 'The second kind of Devils, which he most imploieth, are those northerne Marcii, called the spirits of revenge, & the authors of massacres, & seedesmen of mischiefe; for they have commission to incense men to rapines, sacriledge, theft, murther, wrath, furie, and all manner of crueltries'.

41 **tend on** serve, wait on or minister to (*OED* tend *v.*[1] 4a)
mortal human
unsex take away (my) female qualities; a word apparently coined by Shakespeare

37 Than] *F4;* Then *F*   38] *Rowe; F lines* newes. / hoarse, /   40 Come you spirits] Come all you spirits *Davenant*

156

And fill me from the crown to the toe, top-full
Of direst cruelty. Make thick my blood,
Stop up th'access and passage to remorse,
That no compunctious visitings of nature   45
Shake my fell purpose, nor keep peace between
Th'effect and it. Come to my woman's breasts,
And take my milk for gall, you murdering ministers,
Wherever, in your sightless substances,

---

42 **crown ... toe** head to foot. See Dent, C864: 'From the crown of the head to the sole of the foot'.

43 **Make thick** In medical theory of the period it was held that the vital spirits passed through the blood, and that if the blood, normally 'thin and wholesome' (*Ham* 1.5.70) should become thickened, various unhealthy conditions would arise. Braunmuller cites Barrough, *The Methode of Physicke*, 168: 'There be feavers ... which are ingendered of thickening and stopping of the conduits and passages'. Feminist critics have seen a more specific application in this passage; the Lady may be asking for a suppression of her biological femininity, for 'the periodic flow to cease, the genital tract to be blocked' (LaBelle, 381). On theories about blood, see also Clark, 'Passions', 302–3.

44 **remorse** pity

45 **compunctious** having compunction, remorseful. *OED adj.* 1 cites this as the first use, and *EEBO* records none earlier.
visitings of nature perhaps her menstrual periods, or general feelings of pity. Fox (129) calls the expression 'visitings of nature' 'a common euphemism for menstruation'. LaBelle cites Thomas Brugis, *Vade Mecum: Or, A Companion For a Chyrurgion* (1652), who refers to 'the overmuch flowing of womens naturall visits'. She relates the early modern view of the consequences of amenorrhea to the Lady's subsequent behaviour, in terms of fainting, fear and melancholy (381, 383).

46 **fell** ruthless, cruel

46–7 **keep ... it** prevent my intention (*it*) from achieving its fulfilment (*Th'effect*)

48 **take ... gall** Johnson (in the notes to his edition of Shakespeare, 1765) paraphrases this: 'Take away my milk, and put gall into the place'. Rosenberg suggests 'Take my milk as your gall', implying 'an erotic image of devils suckling' (223). Adelman similarly suggests that the Lady may be 'asking the spirits to take her milk *as* gall, to nurse from her breasts and find in her milk their sustaining poison' (135). In this connection, Cavell considers that F 'murthering' may have been pronounced like 'mothering' (242). Merchant (47–8) argues that *take* here means 'blast or strike malignantly' as if by witchcraft, citing *Ham* 1.1.162: 'No fairy takes, nor witch hath power to charm'.
gall poison (*OED n.*[1] 5), but also bitterness, from the secretion of the liver (*OED n.*[1] 3a), supposedly the source of the irascible instinct. See *Ham* 2.2.511–13: 'For it cannot be / But I am pigeon-livered and lack gall / To make oppression bitter'.
ministers attendants, servants. See *OED minister n.* 1a : 'a person acting under the authority of another; one who carries out executive duties as the agent or representative of a superior', and compare *Tem* 3.3.60–1: 'I and my fellows / Are ministers of fate'.

49 **sightless substances** invisible forms

47 it] *F3–4;* hit *F1–2*

You wait on nature's mischief. Come thick night,　　　　50
And pall thee in the dunnest smoke of hell,
That my keen knife see not the wound it makes,
Nor heaven peep through the blanket of the dark
To cry, 'Hold, hold'.

Enter MACBETH.

　　　　　　　　　Great Glamis, worthy Cawdor,
Greater than both, by the all-hail hereafter,　　　　55
Thy letters have transported me beyond
This ignorant present, and I feel now
The future in the instant.

MACBETH　　　　　　　　　My dearest love,

Duncan comes here tonight.

LADY　　　　　　　　　　　And when goes hence?

MACBETH

Tomorrow, as he purposes.

50 **wait on** accompany, attend
51 **pall** wrap
　　dunnest murkiest
53 **blanket ... dark** Johnson (*Rambler*, 168) and Coleridge (1.65) both objected to this expression, and Furness lists many editorial emendations, often ludicrous, intended to polish it. But the idea of darkness as thick and muffling is in keeping with the general imagery of the play (and Johnson did not repeat the criticism in his *Dictionary*).
54–5 **Great ... hereafter** The Lady's greeting of her husband at the moment they first come face to face has generated much discussion, esp. of the stage business involved. Rosenberg, 227–34, has a good account of the range of possibilities.
55 **all-hail hereafter** The phrase recalls the Third Witch's prophecy (1.3.50), although the part of Macbeth's letter which the Lady reads aloud does not include it. She

means that Macbeth will be greater than Thane of Glamis and Cawdor by virtue of the Witches' 'all hail'. Rather than taking *all-hail* as an adjective modifying *hereafter* as a noun (Braunmuller) it is easier to read *hereafter* as adverbial, meaning 'in the future' (Muir) and *all-hail* as a noun. Compare *Cor* 5.3.138–9: 'each in either side / Give the all-hail to thee'.
56 **letters** Brooke notes that 'letters' could be used in the plural with a singular meaning, as in Latin *litterae* (*OED* letter *n.*[1] 4b). Compare *Oth* 4.1.275: 'did the letters work upon his blood ... ?'
57 **ignorant** unknowing, uninformed (*OED* adj. 1a)
58 **the future ... instant** the future, as if it were happening now. See pp. 62–82, on time in the play.
60 **Tomorrow ... purposes** part of an irregularly short line. Actors have taken

54] *Capell; F lines* hold. / Cawdor, /

LADY   O never   60
Shall sun that morrow see.
Your face, my thane, is as a book, where men
May read strange matters; to beguile the time,
Look like the time, bear welcome in your eye,
Your hand, your tongue; look like the innocent flower,   65
But be the serpent under't. He that's coming
Must be provided for; and you shall put
This night's great business into my dispatch,
Which shall to all our nights and days to come,
Give solely sovereign sway and masterdom.   70

MACBETH

We will speak further.

LADY   Only look up clear;

the opportunity offered by the comma after *Tomorrow* to add suggestive emphasis. This could be the moment at which Macbeth's Lady becomes aware of her husband's too open face.

61 **that morrow** i.e. the day when Duncan departs alive

62 **face ... book** The *face*/*book* comparison was commonplace. See *RJ* 1.3.82–9, where Capulet's wife describes 'the volume of young Paris' face', and Dent, B531.1: 'To read one like a book'. Duncan found the previous Thane of Cawdor's face deceptively innocent (1.4.11–12).

63 **beguile** divert attention from, in a pleasant way (*OED v.* 5). See *Tit* 4.1.34–5: 'Come and take choice of all my library, / And so beguile thy sorrow', and Dent, T340.1: 'To beguile the time'.

64 **Look ... time** 'Put on an expression suitable to the occasion.'

65–6 **look ... under't** The idea is ultimately derived from Vergil, *Eclogues*, 3.93: '*latet anguis in herba*' [the snake hides in the grass] (cited by Muir). It was

proverbial in Shakespeare's time. See Dent, S585: 'Snake in the grass'. Kinney, *Lies*, 123, notes that King James had a commemorative medal struck for himself after the discovery of the Gunpowder Plot, inscribed '*Detectus qui Latuit S.C. [Senatus Consulto]*', depicting a snake gliding among flowers.

67 **provided for** prepared for, but with sinister innuendo. Though neither husband nor wife has made explicit their intentions, each fully understands what is being proposed.

68 **night's great business** euphemism, characteristic of the Macbeths' language in this scene. For more on euphemism in the play, see pp. 42, 59.
dispatch management, but 'dispatch' can also mean putting to death (*OED n.* 4)

70 **solely** exclusively, for us alone

71 **further** Braunmuller punctuates with a dash at this point, suggesting that the Lady interrupts her husband, to prevent any expression of hesitation.
clear unclouded by fear or guilt, serene (*OED adj.* 2d)

63 time,] *Theobald;* time. *F*   71 further.] *Cam[1]*

To alter favour ever is to fear.
Leave all the rest to me.   *Exeunt.*

1.6   *Hautboys and Torches. Enter* KING [Duncan],
          MALCOLM, DONALBAIN, BANQUO, LENNOX,
          MACDUFF, ROSS, ANGUS *and Attendants.*

KING

This castle hath a pleasant seat, the air
Nimbly and sweetly recommends itself
Unto our gentle senses.
BANQUO   This guest of summer,
The temple-haunting martlet, does approve,

---

72 **favour** appearance, facial expression. She means that fear changes one's expression.

1.6.0.1 *Hautboys and Torches* i.e. hautboy-players and torchbearers. The Elizabethan hautboy (or hoboy) was a loud wooden instrument with finger holes, sounded by a reed; it was a member of the shawm family and not an ancestor of the modern oboe, a later instrument. It can be symbolically ominous, accompanying supernatural or sinister events as in *AC* 4.3.12, but may also signify the entrance of royalty (Wilson & Calore, 'hoboy', Dessen & Thomson, 'hoboy'). Brooke points out the incongruousness of both hautboys and torches for a scene 'emphatically located out-of-doors . . . where light is stressed', but in some productions it is treated as a night-time scene, and it can be located inside the castle. See Furness on Irving's celebrated production of 1888 depicting a night scene, and Rosenberg, 243–4, who is certain that night is at least coming on. The Jacobean stage allowed for the possibility of both lighting and location

being indeterminate or flexible that is less available to the modern stage.

1–10 **This . . . delicate** Duncan in his judge-ment of the castle again shows his inability to penetrate beneath surface appearances. Banquo on this occasion follows suit. See Innes, 'castle', on Duncan's response to Macbeth's castle as that of 'the lowlander on reaching the Highlands'.

1   **seat** situation, site (*OED n.* 18)

1–2 **the air . . . itself** Hunter paraphrases: 'The air is prompt to come forward and show its merits'.

2   **Nimbly** quickly

3   **gentle** may continue the pathetic fallacy of 1–2, in which the air is personified, signifying senses made gentle, or refined, by the action of the air. The language of compliment in this scene is character-istically elaborate. See Heal, 192–9, on the reciprocal behaviour of hosts and guests.

4   **temple-haunting** a Shakespearean coinage, meaning frequenting places of worship
     ***martlet** All editors emend F's 'Barlet', and Braunmuller notes that F prints 'martlet' in *MV* 2.9.28. The martlet is a swift, but may also mean a swallow or

1.6] *Scena Sexta.* 1–2] *Rowe; F lines* seat, / it selfe /   3 gentle senses] *general sense Warburton;* gentle sense *Capell*   4 martlet] *Rowe;* Barlet *F;* marlet *Collier*

By his loved mansionry, that the heaven's breath   5
Smells wooingly here. No jutty frieze,
Buttress, nor coin of vantage, but this bird
Hath made his pendent bed, and procreant cradle:
Where they must breed and haunt, I have observed
The air is delicate.

Enter LADY.

KING   See, see, our honoured hostess.   10
The love that follows us, sometime is our trouble,
Which still we thank as love. Herein I teach you
How you shall bid God yield us for your pains,
And thank us for your trouble.

---

house-martin; it is a bird which builds its nest attached to the walls of buildings, and is thought to bring good fortune. Daly gives an extensive discussion.

5 ***mansionry** mansions collectively. Finkenstaedt gives this (in fact, an emendation from F 'mansonry'), as the first appearance of the word in English, and this line is the first citation in *OED*. *EEBO* records none earlier.

6 **jutty** alternative form of 'jetty', 'part of a building that juttieth beyond, or leaneth over, the rest' (Cotgrave)
frieze band between the lintel of a building and the cornice, usually decorated

7 **Buttress** projecting structure erected against the side of a building to support it
coin of vantage place or point of advantage (*OED* vantage *n.* 3c). 'Quoin' is now the commoner spelling for the architectural meaning.

8 **pendent** hanging. Brooke draws attention to the appropriateness of this term to the situation of the martin's nest.

bed . . . cradle nest. Banquo's images of fertility relate to the play's themes of procreation and dynasty.

9 **must** often emended to 'most', but the sense 'are determined to' (*OED v.* 2b) suits the context

10 **delicate** soft, fragrant. See *WT* 3.1.1: 'The climate's delicate, the air most sweet'.

11–12 **The love . . . love** As Braunmuller says, this initiates a 'tortuously polite exchange' in which Duncan attempts to turn the efforts of the Macbeths to please him into a compliment, and the Lady to downplay her ability to honour him sufficiently. See also Ide, who characterizes the exchange as 'a mock-offertory' (346), drawing on language and concepts from the Offertory verses. The phrase *our trouble* may mean either 'the trouble we (as king) cause' or 'troublesome'.

12–14 **Herein . . . trouble** i.e. in this way I am showing you how to pray for the good of those who cause you trouble.

13 ***bid . . . yield** pray to God to recompense

---

5 mansionry] *Theobald;* Mansonry *F*   6 jutty frieze] jutty, frieze *Steevens;* jutting frieze *Pope*   9 must] most *Rowe;* much *Collier*   10.1 LADY] *Lady Macbeth / Capell*   11 sometime is] sometime's *Pope*   13 shall] should *Rowe*   God yield] *Johnson;* God-eyld *F;* God 'ild *Globe, Ard²;* 'God 'ield us' *Hunter*

LADY   All our service,

In every point twice done, and then done double,   15
Were poor and single business, to contend
Against those honours deep and broad wherewith
Your majesty loads our house. For those of old,
And the late dignities heaped up to them,
We rest your hermits.

KING   Where's the Thane of Cawdor?   20

We coursed him at the heels, and had a purpose
To be his purveyor. But he rides well,
And his great love, sharp as his spur, hath holp him
To his home before us. Fair and noble hostess,
We are your guest tonight.

LADY   Your servants ever,   25

Have theirs, themselves, and what is theirs in count,
To make their audit at your highness' pleasure,
Still to return your own.

KING   Give me your hand.

Conduct me to mine host: we love him highly,
And shall continue our graces towards him.   30
By your leave, hostess.   *Exeunt.*

---

16 **single** slight, trivial
  business labour, exertion, effort (*OED n.* 1.2)
19 **late** recent
  We . . . hermits 'We are bound to pray for you.' 'Hermits' could mean beadsmen, bound by vow or fee to say prayers for particular individuals (*OED* hermit *n.* 2c).
21 **coursed** chased, as in a hunt
22 **purveyor** official in a royal household who makes advance preparations for a superior. Duncan continues his style of self-deprecation.
23 **holp** helped (archaic past tense of 'help')
26 **in count** in trust
27 **audit** cut-off point where financial accounts are brought up to date. On the implications of this exchange 'in a play where the concept of reciprocity is central', see Thomas, *Political*, 'audit, auditor'.
28 **Still . . . own** ready to return (what is yours) to you

15] (In . . . double) *Pope*   17–20 Against . . . hermits] *Pope; F lines* broad, / House: / Dignities, / Ermites. /
20 hermits] *F2;* Ermites *F*   23 as] at *F2*   26 count] *(*compt*)*   27 highness'] *Pope;* Highnesse *F*
29 host:] *Collier;* Host *F*   31 SD] *He kisses her.* / *Hunter*

162

1.7   *Hautboys. Torches. Enter a Sewer and divers*
            Servants with dishes and service over the stage.

                Then enter MACBETH.

MACBETH

If it were done, when 'tis done, then 'twere well
It were done quickly. If th'assassination
Could trammel up the consequence, and catch

1.7.0.1 *Hautboys. Torches* indications of a
ceremonial scene taking place at night

0.1–2 *Enter ... service* dumb-show preceding Macbeth's entrance, suggestive of
busy activity before he is left onstage
alone, for the first time in the play, having
abruptly quit the meal and his guests (29
below)

0.1 *Sewer* from French *essayeur*, originally
a servant who tasted all the dishes for
poison, but in this period one in charge of
preparations for the meal (which is taking
place offstage)

0.2 *service* the courses of the meal, and
utensils (Dessen & Thomson, 'service')
over the stage i.e. moving from one side
of the stage to the other

1–28 If ... th'other This complex and
tortured soliloquy has occasioned much
critical comment. See, for example,
Bradshaw, 252–5, Everett, 96–7, Gardner,
52–61, Jorgensen, 53–6, Palfrey, 68–71,
Traversi, 117–18. Norbrook, discussing
Macbeth's 'unnatural relations with time',
here and elsewhere, observes that 'the
sibilants explode in his face' (101). Houston,
Shakespearean, compares the syntax and
speech patterns here with other passages
in the play (142–5). Hope analyses the
grammatical features of 1–7 in illuminating detail to demonstrate the link between
grammar and literary effect (13–16).

1–2 If ... quickly Macbeth seems to mean,
'if it (i.e. the murder) were over and done

with once it was committed, it would
be good to do it without delay', but as
Mahood, 136–9, suggests, the underlying
meaning may be more complex. 'Done'
can mean both 'ended' and 'performed'.
See also Calderwood, 36–8, on *done* in
this speech. There may be an allusion to
Judas and the last supper here. See John,
13.27: 'And after the sop, Satan entred
into hym. Then sayde Iesus unto hym,
That thou doest, do quickly' (cited in
Jones, *Origins*, 83). Proverbial expressions such as 'The thing done has an end'
(Dent, T149) and 'Things done cannot
be undone' (Dent, T200) may also have
been in Shakespeare's mind. Doing and
undoing are constant themes; see 2.2.52,
74, 3.2.13, 5.1.68–9, and Palfrey's
discussion of the repetition of 'done'
(68–71).

2   **th'assassination** 'the taking the life of
anyone by treacherous violence' (*OED*,
where this is the first citation for the
meaning. *EEBO* records none earlier.)
See Palfrey & Stern, 322–4, on the
impact of newly coined words in the
theatre, and above, pp. 38–41.

3   **trammel up** entangle, or prevent from
developing. A trammel could be a net to
catch fish or a hobble to prevent a horse
from kicking or straying. The idea is
followed up in *catch*. See also Hulme,
21–3, on 'trammel' meaning 'bound up'
(as a corpse), citing *OED* trammel *v.* 1).

1.7] *Scena Septima.*   0.1 *Hautboys*] *Malone; Ho-boyes* F

With his surcease, success: that but this blow
Might be the be-all and the end-all, here,   5
But here, upon this bank and shoal of time,
We'd jump the life to come. But in these cases,
We still have judgement here, that we but teach
Bloody instructions, which being taught, return
To plague th'inventor. This even-handed justice   10

---

4 **surcease** cessation, end (of Duncan's life). See *Luc* 1766: 'If they surcease to be that should survive'. Mahood suggests also the legal meaning of 'a temporary stopping of a lawsuit' (139).

success could mean both 'prosperous outcome' and 'succession (of heirs)'. In this period it could also mean 'that which happens in the sequel' (*OED n.* 1a), in a neutral sense, not necessarily favourable. Braunmuller draws attention to earlier uses of the word at 1.3.91, 134, and 1.5.1, pointing out emerging ironies in its uses. Everett (96) calls it 'a word and concept in the process of change'.

that but if only

5 **be-all . . . end-all** Shakespeare seems to have coined this expression. *EEBO* records no earlier examples.

6 ***bank and shoal** *shoal* (meaning shallow or sandbank) is Theobald's emendation for F 'schoole'. It functions as a hendiadys with *bank*, and fits in with Macbeth's preoccupation with the passing of time. Mahood calls this 'the momentous instant in the flux of time' (24). But 'school' (in the regular sense of a place of learning) could be spelt 'shoal' in Shakespeare's time, and 'bank' taken to mean 'bench' (*OED n.*² 1). Even if the emendation gives a meaning more resonant in the play as a whole, the other possibility may underlie it.

7 **jump** leap over (*OED v.* 6a, citing *Son* 44: 'For nimble thought can jump both

sea and land'). The river of life metaphor is still at work. Bradshaw suggests the idea of 'a man jumping into eternity, damned and lost for all time' (254).

the life to come the hereafter, life after death

8 **judgement here** Kean famously pressed his hand to his heart on 'here' (Sprague, *Actors*, 235), but rather than referring to his conscience, Macbeth may mean that in behaving in this way he will only be calling down judgement on himself in the form of those who imitate his own actions.

that in that

8–10 **teach . . . th'inventor** Sources in Seneca have been suggested for the idea that evil deeds rebound on the doer, for instance *Hercules Furens*, 735–6: '*Quod quisque fecit, patitur: auctorem scelus / Repetit suoque premitur exemplo nocens*', translated by Heywood (1561): 'What ech man one hath done, he feeles: and guilt to th'author theare / Returnes, and th'hurtful with their owne example punish bee' (Seneca, *Tenne Tragedies*). *Thyestes*, 311, is also a possible source: '*Saepe in magistrum scelera redierunt sua*' ('Crimes often return upon the teacher', Seneca, *Tragedies*). See the comments of Jacobson, who argues for *Thyestes*, and Muir on this passage.

10 **even-handed** impartial, with reference to the personification of justice as a figure holding evenly balanced scales

---

4 his] its *Pope*   surcease, success] success, surcease *Johnson*   5 be-all . . . end-all] *Pope*; be all, . . . end all *F*   end-all, here,] *Hanmer subst.* (end-all here,); end all. *Heere F*; end-all – Here, *Rowe*   6 shoal] *Theobald*; schoole *F1–2*   10 This] *om. Pope*

Commends th'ingredience of our poisoned chalice
To our own lips. He's here in double trust:
First, as I am his kinsman, and his subject,
Strong both against the deed. Then, as his host,
Who should against his murderer shut the door,   15
Not bear the knife myself. Besides, this Duncan
Hath borne his faculties so meek, hath been
So clear in his great office, that his virtues
Will plead like angels, trumpet-tongued, against
The deep damnation of his taking off;   20
And pity, like a naked new-born babe,

11 **Commends** offers
th'ingredience ingredients in the modern
sense (as at 4.1.34), but also the process
of entering in, entry (*OED* ingredience
n. 1). Brooke notes a frequent use of
the term in the second sense in theological contexts, supporting the underlying meaning of *chalice* as communion
cup.
chalice can mean simply cup, or specifically the communion cup. This may also
be the underlying significance of 'the
vessel of my peace' (3.1.66).
12 **double trust** As Braunmuller notes,
Macbeth actually cites three 'relations of
trust', which at this point he is hesitant
to violate. Doubling (and trebling) are
significant elsewhere (e.g. 1.6.15, 4.1.10,
20). See p. 59.
16 **bear** could also signify 'bare', as Mahood
notes (143), bringing in the idea of
exposure.
16–17 **Duncan ... meek** See Holinshed,
2.168 (in Bullough, 7.488): 'Duncane was
so soft and gentle of nature, that the
people wished the inclinations and maners
of these two cousins [i.e himself and

Macbeth] to have been . . . enterchange-
ablie bestowed betwixt them'.
17 **faculties** powers, both personal and those
of his office
18 **clear** pure, innocent. Compare 1.5.65.
19 **trumpet-tongued** may modify either
virtues or *angels*. The element *trumpet*
here may suggest the loudness and clarity
of a public announcement (see Wilson &
Calore, 'trumpet'). But Dover Wilson's
reference to the Last Judgement, leading
on to apocalyptic imagery (113), also
seems apt.
21–3 Brooks's discussion of the contrasting
possibilities of this passage is helpful:
'Is the babe natural or supernatural – an
ordinary helpless baby ... Or is it some
infant Hercules, quite capable of striding
the blast, but, since it is powerful and
not helpless, hardly the typical pitiable
object? ... Does Shakespeare mean for
pity or for fear of retribution to be
dominant in Macbeth's mind?' (22). But
see also Gardner's rebuttal of his reading
(61). Shakespeare seems to be reaching
after a biblical-style paradox about the
power of the powerless.

11 Commends] Commands *Davenant;* Returns *Pope* ingredience] *(* Ingredience*);* ingredients *Pope*
17 his] this *F2–3* 19 angels . . . against] *Capell;* Angels, Trumpet-tongu'd against *F;* angels trumpet-
tongued against *Pope;* angels, trumpet-tongued against, *Collier*

Striding the blast, or heaven's cherubin, horsed
Upon the sightless couriers of the air,
Shall blow the horrid deed in every eye,
That tears shall drown the wind. I have no spur   25
To prick the sides of my intent, but only

22 **Striding the blast** bestriding the wind, as if riding a horse. *Pity* may be imagined in control of the wind, like a rider. Brooks notes that 'the winds were sometimes pictured as human figures blowing invisible columns of air' (as in Botticelli's *The Birth of Venus*). The word *blast* may also refer back to *trumpet*. The imagery is suggestive, rather than precise. William Blake's illustration *Pity*, depicting a female cherub leaning down from a position on horseback to rescue a naked baby, seems to refer to this image. See Fig. 6.

cherubin collective term for a company or order of angels (*OED n.* 1d), also imagined as baby-like in form. Editors often emend F 'Cherubin' to 'cherubins' (though the correct Hebrew plural is 'cherubim'), but 'cherubin' was used as a plural in the period. See *Batman upon Bartholome* (1582): 'Duely excepted Seraphin, Cherubin are the highest companies of Angelles' (Bk 2, Ch. 9) and Shaheen, 162. This is another comparison for pity, and its mighty ability to broadcast the horror of Duncan's murder.

22–3 **horsed / Upon** riding. There is perhaps a confused recollection of Psalms, 18.10: 'He rid upon the Cherub and he did fly: he came fleeing upon the wings of the wind'.

23 **sightless . . . air** i.e. the winds. 'Sightless' may mean either invisible or blind. Blake assumed 'blind' in his painting *Pity* (1795). Bate's account of the painting (125–6) also illuminates the passage.

Sight and blindness are underlying motifs throughout the play. See, for example, 1.5.49, 53.

24 **blow** puff or propel (as the wind does a speck of dust)

25 **tears . . . wind** as Brooke in his note on the line suggests, a paradox, deriving from the proverbial phrase 'Small rain allays great winds' (Dent, R16). Macbeth's idea is that the murder will be such an outrage that tears of pity will overpower even the mighty wind.

25–8 **I . . . th'other** another metaphor from horse-riding, as earlier in the speech, but also with a recollection of the idea of a leap that goes too far, as in 1.4.48–50. Scholars have found many problems with these lines, sometimes arising from over-literal interpretation (as with the anxiety over the single spur apparently pricking both sides of the horse, cited by Furness). The main idea, that Macbeth is all too aware of the dangers of being motivated only by ambition, is clear. Shakespeare appears to combine two images: one of Macbeth's intent to murder, imagined as a horse in need of goading on, and the other of his ambition, as an over-eager rider who tries to vault into his saddle but jumps too far. Belsey (198–201) suggests a connection with the depiction in medieval literature of Pride as a vaulting figure, falling from his horse (see Hall, 'Pride'). Vaulting accurately into one's saddle was a much admired feat. See Vernon's description of Hal's grace in achieving it in *1H4* 4.1.103–9.

22 cherubin] Cherubins *Ard²*   23 sightless] silent *Theobald*   couriers] *Rowe;* Curriors *F;* coursers *Warburton*

Vaulting ambition, which o'er-leaps itself,
And falls on th'other.

Enter LADY.

How now? What news?

LADY

He has almost supped. Why have you left the
chamber?

MACBETH

Hath he asked for me?

LADY   Know you not, he has?   30

MACBETH

We will proceed no further in this business:
He hath honoured me of late, and I have bought
Golden opinions from all sorts of people,
Which would be worn now in their newest gloss,
Not cast aside so soon.

LADY   Was the hope drunk   35
Wherein you dressed yourself? Hath it slept since?

---

28 **th'other** 'side' to be understood, but the completion of Macbeth's thought is interrupted by the entrance of his wife, perhaps the spur he needs.

29 **supped** finished his supper
left the chamber Leaving before his guest is an act of discourtesy on Macbeth's part.

30 **Know . . . has** This line can be variously punctuated. Cordner (108) draws attention to Sarah Siddons's emphatic rendering: '*Know* you not he has?'.

32–3 **bought / Golden opinions** This is another in the train of clothing images initiated at 1.3.109–10. The value Macbeth puts on these *opinions* is painfully acknowledged in his awareness of their loss (5.3.22–8).

33 **sorts** kinds, ranks
34 **gloss** shine
35–8 **Was . . . freely** The Lady responds to this new situation with a mixed metaphor which quickly separates out into a single concept. The *hope* with which Macbeth formed the plan of murdering Duncan is initially an assumed attire. This is subsumed into the personification of a drunken individual, who falls asleep and wakes only to be overcome with sick nausea at his former conduct. The delusions of drunkenness are taken up by the Porter in 2.3. Miola comments on the fatal effects of Macbeth's 'immoderate hopes' (*Classical*, 110).

28 th'other.] th'other – *Rowe*   30 not, he has?] *(*not, he ha's?*); not? he has Capell conj.; not he has? Pope*
33 sorts] sort *Theobald*   34 would] should *Pope*   36 since?] since *Collier*

And wakes it now to look so green and pale,
At what it did so freely? From this time
Such I account thy love. Art thou afeared
To be the same in thine own act and valour,   40
As thou art in desire? Wouldst thou have that
Which thou esteem'st the ornament of life,
And live a coward in thine own esteem,
Letting 'I dare not', wait upon 'I would',
Like the poor cat i'th' adage?

MACBETH   Prithee, peace.   45
I dare do all that may become a man,
Who dares do more, is none.

LADY   What beast was't then
That made you break this enterprise to me?
When you durst do it, then you were a man;

37 **green and pale** i.e. nauseous with a hangover, but perhaps with overtones of girlishness, as in green sickness
39 **Such** i.e. like the worthless bravado of a drunk
   account value
39–41 **Art ... desire?** 'Are you afraid, now that you are sober, to be what you wanted to be when drunk?' Braunmuller draws attention to the 'sexualised language' of *be* (40) in conjunction with *do* and *become a man* in 46.
42 **ornament of life** highest achievement, greatness, or in this case the crown
44–5 **Letting ... adage** The *adage* (proverb) is, 'The cat wanted to eat fish but dared not get her feet wet' (Dent, C144).
44 **wait upon** accompany
46 **become** be becoming to, befit (*OED v.* III 7). Compare *TNK* 5.3.49–50: 'Melancholy / Becomes him nobly'.
47 ***do more** F has 'no more', but Rowe's emendation, followed by most editors, makes better sense. Macbeth wishes

here to assert the adequacy of his own manliness.
   none not a man, outside the bounds of humanity. Macbeth's recognition that gender roles are to be defined within limits recalls Angelo's injunction to Isabella: 'Be that you are, / That is, a woman; if you be more, you're none' (*MM* 2.4.133–4).
47–51 **What ... man** Editors have sometimes inferred from these lines that a scene has been lost in which Macbeth stated his readiness to commit the murder (see Furness, Dover Wilson, xxxiv–xxxviii, and Muir). Thaler argues cogently against this theory. For further discussion, see Appendix 1. Macbeth's Lady may well be giving her version of the discussion in 1.5.
47 **What beast** Ignoring her husband's scruples, Macbeth's Lady takes *none* as if it means an animal.
48 **break** reveal, divulge (*OED v.* 22)
   enterprise bold undertaking
49 **durst** dared (obsolete)

39 afeared] afraid *F4*   43 esteem,] *Collier;* Esteeme? *F;* esteem; *Capell*   44 'I dare not' ... 'I would']
Ard²; I dare not ... I would *F*   45 adage?] *Capell;* adage. *F*   47 do] *Rowe;* no *F*   beast] boast *Collier*

168

And to be more than what you were, you would   50
Be so much more the man. Nor time nor place
Did then adhere, and yet you would make both:
They have made themselves, and that their fitness
    now
Does unmake you. I have given suck, and know
How tender 'tis to love the babe that milks me: 55
I would, while it was smiling in my face,
Have plucked the nipple from his boneless gums,
And dashed the brains out, had I so sworn
As you have done to this.

MACBETH   If we should fail?
LADY
We fail?   60

50–1 **And ... man** In order to become
greater (*more*) than you were, you were
prepared to become even more manly.
In Goold's 2007/8 production at the
Chichester Festival Theatre Kate Fleetwood laid telling emphasis on the word *so*.
52 **adhere** fit together
    make both i.e. contrive to make them
    fit together
53 **that their fitness** 'that fitness of theirs'
    (Hunter)
54 **unmake** undo, ruin or destroy (*OED v.* 3,
    citing this passage)
54 **I ... suck** Unless Macduff's assertion
    at 4.3.219 that 'He has no children' is
    taken to refer to Malcolm, which is
    unlikely (though the interpretation has
    some supporters, for which see the note),
    this passage raises questions. Knights
    famously used it as the starting-point of
    his attack on character-based criticism as
    represented by Bradley (Knights, *Explora-
    tions*, 1–39), but more recently feminist
    critics have drawn on its evocation of
    'maternal malevolence' (Adelman, 134)
    to trace the play's suppression of the

feminine. Boece mentions the custom
of Scottish noblewomen of nursing their
own children, contrary to early modern
English practice (cited in Bullough,
7.506). The historical Lady Macbeth
had a son by a previous marriage. See
Historical Notes.
55 **milks** obtains milk by sucking. *OED*
    records this usage as *obs. rare*, and gives
    this as the first citation.
56–7 **it ... his** Braunmuller sees the transi-
    tion from an ungendered pronoun to a
    masculine one as significant. But Abbott
    notes that '*His* still represented the
    genitive of *It* as well as *He*' (228).
60 F's question mark has sometimes been
    replaced by other punctuation, especially
    in performance. Printers of the period
    used the question mark for both interroga-
    tion and exclamation. Crystal (73–4) gives
    examples of this. According to Jameson,
    Sarah Siddons tried out three possibilities:
    'At first as a quick contemptuous
    interrogation – "*we fail?*" Afterwards
    with a note of admiration, and an accent
    of indignant astonishment, laying the

51 the] than *Hanmer*   52 adhere] co-here *Pope*   58 so] but so *Rowe*   59 fail?] fail, – *Theobald*   60 fail?]
fail! *Rowe;* fail. *Capell*

But screw your courage to the sticking place,
And we'll not fail. When Duncan is asleep,
Whereto the rather shall his day's hard journey
Soundly invite him, his two chamberlains
Will I with wine and wassail so convince,   65
That memory, the warder of the brain,
Shall be a fume, and the receipt of reason
A limbeck only. When in swinish sleep
Their drenched natures lies as in a death,
What cannot you and I perform upon   70
Th'unguarded Duncan? What not put upon
His spongy officers, who shall bear the guilt
Of our great quell?

MACBETH   Bring forth men-children only;

principal emphasis on the word *we* – *we fail*! Lastly . . . we fail, with the simple period' (327). Jameson preferred the third reading. F's short line seems worth retaining here, allowing the actor scope for maximum expressiveness, whatever intonation is chosen.

61 **screw . . . place** Either, as *OED* (screw *v*. 3b) suggests, a metaphor from tightening the peg of a musical instrument until it becomes tightly fixed in the hole, or from winding up the cord on a crossbow. Macbeth's Lady urges her husband to stiffen his resolve to its furthest point.

63 **the rather** the sooner, or the more readily

64 **chamberlains** attendants who wait on the king in his bedchamber

65 **wassail** festivity, revelry
convince overpower

66–8 **memory . . . only** complex metaphor to describe drunkenness, taken from alchemy: the drink-sodden brain becomes a kind of distillery. One part of the brain (memory, which acts as a guardian against the repetition of wrongful acts previously committed) is robbed of its proper function and reduced to a vapour;

another part of the brain, the receptacle of reason, becomes a mere alembic or vessel, which fills with the fumes.

66 **warder** guardian, watchman

67 **fume** vapour, often signifying noxious vapours believed to ascend from the stomach to the brain (*OED n*. 4)
receipt receptacle

68 **limbeck** alternative word for 'alembic', a vessel used in distilling
swinish i.e. drunken. See the proverb 'As drunk as a swine' (Dent, S1042).

69 **drenched** drenchèd; sodden
lies singular verb for plural subject. See Abbott, 335.

71 **put upon** impose upon, saddle with (*OED* put *v*. 23)

72 **spongy** absorbent, i.e. of drink. Compare *MV* 1.2.108: 'I will do anything, Nerissa, ere I will be married to a sponge'.

73 **quell** slaughter (*OED n.*[1])

73–5 **Bring . . . males** Macbeth compliments his wife by accepting her valuation of manliness. The Macbeths at this point 'can think readily of having children' (Everett, 97), although they will end up without successors. See p. 37.

63 his] this *Pope*   day's] *(*dayes*)*   69 lies] lie *F2, Rowe*   72–3 officers, . . . quell?] *Ard²;* Officers? . . . quell. *F*   73 men-children] *(*Men-Children*)*

For thy undaunted mettle should compose
Nothing but males. Will it not be received,   75
When we have marked with blood those sleepy two
Of his own chamber, and used their very daggers,
That they have done't?

LADY   Who dares receive it other,
As we shall make our griefs and clamour roar,
Upon his death?

MACBETH   I am settled, and bend up   80
Each corporal agent to this terrible feat.
Away, and mock the time with fairest show:
False face must hide what the false heart doth know.

Exeunt.

2.1   *Enter* BANQUO, *and* FLEANCE, *with a torch before him.*

BANQUO
How goes the night, boy?

FLEANCE
The moon is down; I have not heard the clock.

---

74   **undaunted** intrepid. Brooke suggests a
pun on 'undented'.
mettle spirit, but perhaps with a pun on
'metal' which was an alternative spelling,
in which case *males* might also suggest
'mails', i.e. metal armour. Adelman draws
on the pun to argue that here 'Lady
Macbeth herself becomes virtually male,
composed of the hard metal of which the
armoured male is made' (139).

79   **As** inasmuch as

80   **settled** resolved
bend up tauten, strain (taking up the
metaphor from 61). In modern usage,
bend seems to be contradicted by *up*

but 'bend up' in early modern English
is a phrasal verb used of tautening
bow-strings (Blake, *Grammar*, 4.3.10).
Compare *H5* 3.1.16–17: 'bend up every
spirit / To his full height'.

81   **corporal agent** bodily faculty

82   **mock** delude

83   See Dent, F3: 'Fair face foul heart'. This
echoes the Lady's advice at 1.5.63–6.
Macbeth now speaks his wife's language.

2.1.0.1   *torch* could mean a torchbearer (often
referred to as 'Torch'), but could also
mean that Fleance carries the torch and
precedes his father, as is more probable at
3.3.14. See also the SD for 1.6.0.1.

---

74 mettle] metal *F4*   **2.1**] *Actus Secundus. Scena Prima.*   0.1] *Enter Banquo, and Fleance with a Servant
with a Torch before them. Capell; Enter Banquo, preceded by Fleance with a torch. / Dyce; Enter Banquo,
and Fleance bearing a torch before him. / Collier; Enter Banquo and Fleance with a Torch [-bearer] before
him Cam¹*

BANQUO

And she goes down at twelve.

FLEANCE   I take't 'tis later, sir.

BANQUO

Hold, take my sword. There's husbandry in heaven,
Their candles are all out; take thee that too.   5
A heavy summons lies like lead upon me,
And yet I would not sleep. Merciful powers,
Restrain in me the cursed thoughts that nature
Gives way to in repose.

Enter MACBETH *and a Servant with a torch.*

Give me my sword; who's there?   10

MACBETH

A friend.

BANQUO

What, sir, not yet at rest? The King's abed.
He hath been in unusual pleasure
And sent forth great largess to your offices.

4   **husbandry** thrift
5   **candles** stars. A common metaphor.
    Compare *RJ*: 'Night's candles are burnt
    out' (3.5.9). This scene-setting emphas-
    izes the total darkness that the audience
    is to imagine.
    take ... too implied SD, in which
    Banquo, disarming, directs Fleance to
    help remove some item such as his dagger
    or cloak
6–7 **A heavy ... sleep** Banquo is tired, but
    anxious not to allow his troubled mind
    free rein once he can no longer control it.
7   **Merciful powers** In medieval angelology,
    powers were an order of angel (*OED*
    angel *n*. 1 9b). Muir cites Curry, 81, to the

effect that they were angels 'concerned
especially with the restraint and coercion
of demons', but Banquo's invocation may
be more general. Macbeth too suffers
from *terrible dreams* (3.2.19).

8   **cursed thoughts** cursèd; may refer to
    the guilt Banquo feels in recalling the
    Witches' prophecies for him, or to the
    prophecies themselves
10 Macbeth's entrance startles Banquo, who
    is ill at ease and in the dark needs his
    weapon for protection.
14 **largess ... offices** generous gifts to the
    functionaries in Macbeth's household.
    An 'office' is here an office-holder (*OED*
    office *n*. 2c)

7–10] *Rowe; F lines* sleepe: / thoughts / repose. / ; *Ard² lines* Powers! / nature / sword, / there? / ; *Oxf lines*
powers, / nature / there? /   9.1] *opp. 10 Dyce; after* sword. *10 Capell*

This diamond he greets your wife withal,   15
By the name of most kind hostess, and shut up
In measureless content.

MACBETH   Being unprepared,
Our will became the servant to defect,
Which else should free have wrought.

BANQUO   All's well.

                       [*Exit Fleance.*]

I dreamt last night of the three weïrd sisters: 20
To you they have showed some truth.

MACBETH   I think not of them;
Yet, when we can entreat an hour to serve,
We would spend it in some words upon that business
If you would grant the time.

BANQUO   At your kind'st leisure.

15 **diamond** Banquo here acts as Duncan's emissary, delivering this royal gift on the King's behalf. As Thomson, 146, notes: 'A diamond is not a shy property'. For discussion of the culture of gift-giving and the roles of host and guest, see Heal, chs 1 and 2. The detail may come from Holinshed's account of King Duff's bestowal of 'honorable gifts' to Donwald and others on the night before Donwald murders him.

15–16 **greets ... up** This apparent change of tense has caused editorial problems, but Blake's solution (*Grammar*, 10.2e, 5.1.1), to treat *and* in this context as an adverbial rather than a conjunction, and *shut up* as a past participle, makes sense.

15 **withal** in addition (*OED adv.* and *prep.* 1)

16 **shut up** concluded (his greeting). See *OED* shut *v.* 19g, though Braunmuller takes it as a past tense, meaning 'went to bed (in a curtained bed ... within a chamber)'.

17–18 **Being ... defect** a return to the formal and convoluted language of courtesy of 1.4
unprepared i.e. unready to receive such a guest as Duncan

18–19 **Our ... wrought** 'In the circumstances, we were unable to achieve the high standards we should have liked.' *Our* may be an anticipatory use of the royal plural, or may simply refer to Macbeth and his wife. The referent of *which* is *our will*. 'Wrought' is the archaic past tense of 'work' (*OED* work *v.* A2).
defect shortcoming (*OED n.* 2)

19 SD ***Exit Fleance** F marks no exit for Fleance, and editors usually have him leave with Banquo at 30. But the latter part of the conversation between Macbeth and Banquo is more intimate and confidential, and takes a different tone from the earlier part; this distinction would be enhanced if Fleance has an exit on his own.

20 Banquo's introduction of this topic may suggest that his interest in the Sisters is not entirely an innocent one.

16–18] *Rowe; F lines* Hostesse, / content. / unprepar'd, / *; Pope lines* up / content. / unprepared, /   16 up] it up *F2–4*   19 SD] *this edn*   20 weïrd] *Theobald;* weyward *F*   23 it in] *it Rowe*

MACBETH

    If you shall cleave to my consent when 'tis,   25

    It shall make honour for you.

BANQUO   So I lose none

    In seeking to augment it, but still keep

    My bosom franchised and allegiance clear,

    I shall be counselled.

MACBETH   Good repose the while.   29

BANQUO

    Thanks, sir, the like to you.   *Exit Banquo.*

MACBETH

    Go bid thy mistress, when my drink is ready,

    She strike upon the bell. Get thee to bed.   *Exit [Servant].*

    Is this a dagger which I see before me,

    The handle toward my hand? Come, let me clutch

       thee.

    I have thee not, and yet I see thee still.   35

    Art thou not, fatal vision, sensible

---

25 **cleave . . . consent** go along with my opinion (*OED* consent *n.* 6)
when 'tis when the time comes. Macbeth is deliberately vague here; he may mean when Duncan dies (of natural causes) or when it seems appropriate to expedite the Witches' prophecies or simply when he and Banquo do find the time to talk.

28 **franchised** free, i.e. not committed to Macbeth

31 **drink** posset or nightcap, made with hot milk and ale or wine, to induce sleep

32 **strike . . . bell** perhaps a pre-arranged signal, the bell that rings at 61. For the significance of bells, sounded on many occasions in *Mac*, see Kinney, 'Bells'.

33–47 **Is . . . before** Muir, *Sources*, 213–14, suggests the influence of Cassandra's soliloquy foreseeing the murder of Agamemnon in Act 5 of Seneca's *Agamemnon* here (Seneca, *Tenne Tragedies*, 2.133*)*. Garrick's performance of this speech indicated that his visualizing of a non-existent object might be symptomatic of Satanic possession (Bartholomeusz, 58). Rosenberg, 299–307, summarizes a wide range of actors' ways of handling the dagger business. See also Innes, 'dagger', on the contemporary context of the dagger.

34 **handle . . . hand** i.e. inviting him to seize it rather than offering him a threat. The dagger is often associated with the temptation to suicide. See Spenser, *FQ*, 1.9.51–2, and Mephostophilis' offer of a dagger to Faustus (Marlowe, *Doctor Faustus*, 5.1.58); also Hattaway, 65.

36 **fatal** ominous (*OED adj.* 4c)
sensible able to be perceived by the senses. See Hope, 1.2.2b.

25–6] *Rowe; F lines* consent, / you. / none, /   30 SD] *Exeunt Banquo, Fleance, and Servant* / *Capell* 32 SD *Servant*] *Rowe*

To feeling as to sight? Or art thou but
A dagger of the mind, a false creation,
Proceeding from the heat-oppressed brain?
I see thee yet, in form as palpable   40
As this which now I draw.
Thou marshall'st me the way that I was going,
And such an instrument I was to use.
Mine eyes are made the fools o'th' other senses,
Or else worth all the rest. I see thee still,   45
And on thy blade, and dudgeon, gouts of blood,
Which was not so before. There's no such thing.
It is the bloody business which informs
Thus to mine eyes. Now o'er the one half-world
Nature seems dead, and wicked dreams abuse   50

39 **heat-oppressed** oppressèd; feverish, but perhaps with reference to Galenic theories of physiology. See also Clark, 'Passions', 305.

40 **yet** still. Macbeth expects the vision to disappear at any moment.

42 **marshall'st** direct or usher
way . . . going The moving dagger follows Macbeth's inclinations rather than directs them.

44–5 **eyes . . . rest** Macbeth is still uncertain as to the status of the dagger. If it is unreal, then his eyes are deceived, but if not, then they are more reliable than his other senses (which tell him the dagger is an illusion). For other instances of disjunction between the perceptions of the senses, see 1.4.52 and 2.2.60–2.

46 **dudgeon** originally, a kind of wood used to make the handles of daggers or knives, here, the hilt of a dagger. Braunmuller cites Cotgrave's definition of '*dague à roëlles*' as 'a Scottish dagger; or Dudgeon haft dagger' to suggest that the term is used with Scottish overtones.
gouts spots or splashes

48 **bloody business** Macbeth's euphemism for the planned murder of Duncan. Euphemistic language is common to both Macbeths. Badawi examines euphemism in the play systematically.
informs takes form, or appears in a visible shape (*OED* inform *v*.[1] 2)

49–56 **Now . . . ghost** Malone compares *Luc* 162–5: 'Now stole upon the time the dead of night, / When heavy sleep had closed up mortal eyes. / No comfortable star did lend his light, / No noise but owls' and wolves' death-boding cries.' The whole meditation on Tarquin's state of mind at this point in the poem (120–68) is relevant to Macbeth's speech in its debate on the paradoxes attending on ambition. For a useful discussion of the links between *Mac* and *Luc* see Kirsch, esp. 271–3.

49 *****half-world** hemisphere

50 **seems dead** i.e. because asleep. But when nature sleeps, the unnatural takes over. See 2.4.1–18.
abuse misuse, pervert (*OED v.* 2a)

49 half-world] *Clarendon;* halfe World *F*

The curtained sleep; Witchcraft celebrates
Pale Hecate's offerings; and withered Murder,
Alarumed by his sentinel, the wolf,
Whose howl's his watch, thus with his stealthy pace,
With Tarquin's ravishing strides, towards his design   55
Moves like a ghost. Thou sure and firm-set earth,
Hear not my steps, which way they walk, for fear
Thy very stones prate of my whereabout,
And take the present horror from the time,

51 **curtained sleep** sleep protected as if by curtains around a four-poster bed
celebrates honours with ritual and ceremony

52 **Pale Hecate's** Hecate is goddess of the moon (hence *Pale*) and also of sorcery. The name ('Hecat' in F) is pronounced with two syllables.
offerings ritual offerings made to Hecate
withered Murder murder imagined as an old man, a personification not found elsewhere in Shakespeare

53 **Alarumed** warned, readied for action

54 **howl's his watch** The wolf's howl is like a signal (*OED* watch *n.* 16) to *Murder* or a striking time-piece (*n.* 21a).
stealthy This use is *OED*'s first citation, though the word appears earlier in Marcello Palengenio Stellato, *The Zodiac of Life*, trans. Barnabe Googe (1565): 'Those monsters two, with stealthy steps that followed after there'.

55 **Tarquin's** Sextus Tarquinius, whose rape of the chaste Lucretia led to the overthrow of the monarchy in Rome and the establishment of a republic. Shakespeare's poem *The Rape of Lucrece* was in his mind during the composition of parts of *Mac.* In *Cym* Iachimo alludes to 'our Tarquin' and recalls the rape in his scene in Imogen's bedchamber (2.2).
ravishing rapacious, intent on prey (*OED adj.* and *adv.* 1). As *OED* states, this is a

transferred epithet, applying to Tarquin himself.
***strides** Pope's emendation, almost universally accepted, for F 'sides'. Murder, like Tarquin, moves with frightening rapidity towards his goal. *OED* (stride *n.* 2a) notes that the word often occurs 'with implication of haste or impetuosity . . . or of haughtiness or arrogance'.

56 **like a ghost** i.e. silently
***sure** Capell's emendation for F 'sowre', a variant spelling of 'sure' (*OED* sure *adj.* and *adv.*). Dover Wilson cites Psalms, 93.2: 'He hath made the round world so sure: that it can not be moved'.
firm-set stable

58 **prate** chatter, tell tales. Shaheen cites Luke, 19.40, on tale-telling stones ('If these holde their peace, then shall the stones crye').

59 **take . . . time** Macbeth seems to mean that the speaking stones would take away or remove the present horror, that is, the silence appropriate to the moment. Johnson in his edition of Shakespeare comments, 'Whether to *take horrour from the time* means not rather to *catch it* as communicated, than to *deprive the time of horrour*, deserves to be considered'. But Muir counters Johnson effectively, citing Dover Wilson's comment that Macbeth 'speaks as if watching himself in a dream', and adding, 'and

52 offerings] *F3–4;* Offrings *F*   55 strides] *Pope;* sides *F*   56 sure] *Capell;* sowre *F*   57 way they] *Rowe;* they may *F*

Which now suits with it. Whiles I threat, he lives;   60
Words to the heat of deeds too cold breath gives.

A bell rings.

I go, and it is done; the bell invites me.
Hear it not, Duncan, for it is a knell
That summons thee to heaven, or to hell.   *Exit.*

2.2   *Enter* LADY.

LADY

That which hath made them drunk, hath made
    me bold;
What hath quenched them, hath given me fire.
Hark, peace; it was the owl that shrieked,
The fatal bellman, which gives the stern'st good night.

in this queer state of objectivity he wants
the details of the scene to be in keeping
with the deed'.

60 **threat** threaten, that is, speak rather than
    act

61 This sounds like an aphorism, but no such
    proverbial utterance has been found.
    For a plural subject followed by a verb
    ending in *-s*, see Abbott, 333.

62 **done** Compare 1.7.1–2, and other
    significant uses of 'done' at 3.2.13 and
    5.1.68–9. See Rosenberg, 312–14, on the
    variety of ways in which actors have
    stressed the momentous quality of
    Macbeth's exit here.

63 **knell** bell rung to announce a death or
    funeral, hence an evil omen. For a
    fuller explanation, see Wilson & Calore,
    'knell'. This bell, his wife's signal (see 32
    above), is ominous to Macbeth as well as
    to Duncan.

2.2 The rapidity with which one scene
    follows another in this part of the play
    contributes much to the excitement and
    horror. The Lady's heightened state here
    contrasts with Macbeth's doom-laden

exit. The fact that her soliloquy immediately follows his may indicate their
working partnership.

1   **That . . . drunk** Actors of the part have
    capitalized on the Lady's apparent need
    for a stimulant to assist her here. Ellen
    Terry and Sarah Siddons both accentuated
    her mood by rendering the lines with a
    smile (Wilders, 118).

2   **quenched** overcome

3   **owl** bird of ill omen. In *Luc* the night
    when Tarquin goes to rape Lucrece is
    silent, with 'No noise but owls' . . . death-
    boding cries' (165).

4   **fatal** foreboding, ominous (*OED adj.* 4c)
    bellman The bellman is a town-crier,
    who walks the streets ringing a bell to
    make announcements, or a night watchman.
    See Samuel Rowlands, *Heaven's Glory*
    (1628): 'For though you lay down to
    sleepe, / The belman wakes your peace
    to keepe'. However, in 1605, a gift was
    made by Robert Dow for a bell to be
    rung outside Newgate prison on the
    night before an execution to warn the
    condemned of their impending fate (Paul,

2.2] *Scena Secunda.*   2 fire.] fire. [*An owl shrieks*] *Cam¹*

He is about it. The doors are open,   5
And the surfeited grooms do mock their charge
With snores. I have drugged their possets
That death and nature do contend about them,
Whether they live, or die.

Enter MACBETH.

MACBETH   Who's there? What ho?
LADY

Alack, I am afraid they have awaked,   10
And 'tis not done. The attempt, and not the deed
Confounds us. Hark. I laid their daggers ready;

26–9). In Webster, *The Duchess of Malfi*, Bosola describes himself as 'the common bellman / That usually is sent to condemn'd persons / The night before they suffer' (4.2.173–5).

stern'st good night i.e. the last goodnight, that is, death

5 **He .. it** another euphemism. See 2.1.48, and also 52–3 below. Neither of them dares name the deed.

6 **surfeited** over-fed. *OED* gives this line as the first citation for this meaning (*OED ppl. a.* 1) but it was used in this sense from at least 1534. See George Joye, *The Psalter of David in English, purely and faithfully translated*: 'And the Lorde awaked as thoughe he had slepte and sterte vp with great noyse from slombre as a man that had surfetted with wyne' (Psalm 78).

grooms servingmen

mock their charge pay no heed to, or flout, their obligations (*OED* mock *n.* 5)

7 **drugged** adulterated with a narcotic or poisonous drug. *OED* drug *v.* 2 gives this as the earliest use of the word in this sense and *EEBO* records none earlier. See

Fitzpatrick, 54, on the Lady as feeder and poisoner.

possets See 2.1.31n.

8 The lives of the servingmen hang in the balance, as if they are subjects of a battle between life and death.

9 **Who's there**? Macbeth's question, like Banquo's at 2.1.10, suggests his extreme nervousness. Editors have sometimes added the SD '*Within*' at this point, and delayed Macbeth's entrance till 15, to account for the fact that the Lady does not answer her husband's question, or seem to notice him until 15. On retaining F at this point, see Braunmuller (256–7) and Dessen (*Recovering*, 103–4), who suggests that this early entrance is part of a theatrical vocabulary which 'included signifiers linked to onstage figures limited in their ability to "see" important things around them' (103). By contrast, Cordner (113–15) stoutly defends the F placement on the grounds of the original staging when the convention of day-for-night was accepted without question.

12 **Hark** Listen. In her nervousness she is startled by a noise. See 17.

9 SD MACBETH] *Macbeth* (*within*) / Steevens; *Macbeth* [*above*] *Oxf;* MACBETH [*with two bloody daggers*] *Cam¹*   9 ho?] ho! *Ard²*, Hunter

He could not miss 'em. Had he not resembled
My father as he slept, I had done't.
My husband?

MACBETH   I have done the deed.   15
Didst thou not hear a noise?

LADY

I heard the owl scream and the crickets cry.
Did not you speak?

MACBETH   When?

LADY   Now.

MACBETH   As I descended?

LADY

Ay.

MACBETH   Hark, who lies i'the second chamber?

LADY

Donalbain.

MACBETH   This is a sorry sight.   20

---

13 **He ... he** She refers first to Macbeth, then to Duncan.

13–14 **Had ... done't** Although the Lady declared herself prepared to murder a suckling infant if necessary, this is one taboo she cannot break, suggesting the supreme importance of the father-king analogy.

15 **My husband?** The Lady's only use of this word. Bradbrook (17) considers this a more intimate form of address than the more usual 'my lord'. The Lady's question may be prompted by the fact that she has not yet seen Macbeth, and needs to confirm his identity, or by her wish to affirm his claim to the title of her husband. Some editors, e.g. *Riv*, Oxf, punctuate with an exclamation mark here, which would be justifiable since the question mark could be used in this way in the period.

I ... deed Actors have sometimes used Macbeth's demeanour at this point to mark the contrast between his state of mind now and his 'martial figure' in Act 1 (Wilders), for example Irving, who returned from Duncan's chamber a broken man: 'His body sways as if already hanging on a gibbet' (Sprague, *Actors*, 243).

17 **crickets** insects more commonly known for merriment (Dent, C825: 'As merry as a cricket'), but also for their shriek. See Dekker, *Lantern and Candlelight* (1609), sig. D3: 'shrieke like a cricket in the brew-house'. The cricket is sometimes regarded as a witch's familiar (*The Wonderful Discovery of the Witchcrafts of Margaret and Philip Flower* (1619), sig. B3ᵛ).

20 **sorry** painful, distressing (*OED adj*. 4)

---

14 done't.] done't. [*Enter Macbeth below*] *Oxf*; done't. [*Enter Macbeth, carrying two bloodstained daggers*] / *Hunter*   14–15 My father ... husband?] *one line Rowe*   15 husband?] husband! *Ard²*, *Hunter*   17 owl scream] owl-scream *Hunter*   19 Ay] *Rowe*; I *F*   20 MACBETH] MACBETH (*looking at his hands*) *Oxf*

LADY

A foolish thought, to say a sorry sight.

MACBETH

There's one did laugh in 's sleep,
And one cried, 'Murder', that they did wake each other.
I stood and heard them; but they did say their prayers
And addressed them again to sleep.   25

LADY

There are two lodged together.

MACBETH

One cried, 'God bless us', and 'Amen' the other,
As they had seen me with these hangman's hands.
Listening their fear, I could not say 'Amen'
When they did say, 'God bless us'.   30

LADY

Consider it not so deeply.

MACBETH

But wherefore could not I pronounce 'Amen'?
I had most need of blessing, and 'Amen'
Stuck in my throat.

LADY   These deeds must not be thought
After these ways; so, it will make us mad.   35

22–3 **one ... one** The identities of these two are ambiguous. Some editors, e.g. Braunmuller, assume them to be Malcolm and Donalbain, but it is more likely that they are the *sleepy grooms* referred to later (51), and subsequently made Macbeth's scapegoats.

25 **addressed them** prepared themselves

26 **lodged together** housed in the same room

28 **As** as if
hangman's hands The hangman had the additional duty of drawing and quartering the victim. Miola (*Classical*, 112–13) notes Hercules' self-recognition seeing

his own bloody hands, along with other parallels to this symbol for inexpiable guilt (*Hercules Furens*, 1323–9). For the bloody hand symbolizing the guilt of murder, compare *KL* 3.2.53.

29 **Listening** listening to
I ... 'Amen' 'Amen' expresses concurrence in a prayer (*OED adv. int. n.* 2a). Macbeth longs to participate in prayer but is prevented. Compare the inability of Claudius, also guilty of murder, to pray (*Ham* 3.3.97–8).

34 **thought** considered, pondered over (*OED think v.*[2] 2a)

23, 27, 29, 30, 32, 33, 42, 43–4] *inverted commas as Hanmer*   33–4] *Pope; F lines* throat. / thought /

MACBETH

Methought I heard a voice cry, 'Sleep no more.
Macbeth does murder sleep' – the innocent sleep,
Sleep that knits up the ravelled sleave of care,
The death of each day's life, sore labour's bath,
Balm of hurt minds, great Nature's second course,   40
Chief nourisher in life's feast –

LADY   What do you mean?

MACBETH

Still it cried, 'Sleep no more' to all the house;
'Glamis hath murdered sleep, and therefore Cawdor
Shall sleep no more. Macbeth shall sleep no more.'

LADY

Who was it that thus cried? Why, worthy thane,   45
You do unbend your noble strength, to think
So brainsickly of things. Go, get some water

36–44 The extent of the quoted speech here is uncertain. It may include Macbeth's speech in 36–41, but there may be more dramatic impact if this speech is rendered as Macbeth's impassioned improvisation on the theme of murdered sleep, set out starkly in the voice's injunction. 43–4 might again be Macbeth's self-condemnation, but perhaps enlarges on what the voice cried 'to all the house'. The source for this voice may be Holinshed's account of the voice which spoke to the sleepless King Kenneth, reminding him that his murder of Malcolm Duff could not be kept secret (158).

37–41 **the innocent . . . feast** Apostrophizing sleep was commonplace in the period, as Rawson observes. Muir has an extensive note, citing several parallels. For possible classical sources, see Ovid, *Met.*, 11.723–6, and Seneca, *Hercules Furens*, 1065–81.

38 **ravelled** frayed, tangled, unravelled (*OED* ravel *v.*[1] 6a)

sleave a slender filament of silk obtained by separating out a thicker thread (*OED n.* 1). But the listening audience would not have been able to distinguish this meaning from that of 'sleeve', part of a garment covering the arm.

39 **bath** i.e. soothing the tired and dusty worker

40 **second course** main (and most substantial) course in a meal

41 **Chief nourisher** main source of physical nourishment (*OED* nourisher *n.* 2)
What . . . mean Although F prints a full stop at the end of Macbeth's speech, both the context and his unfinished line suggest that his wife interrupts him, failing to understand his emotional apostrophe to sleep.

46 **unbend** relax. See 1.7.80. Strength must be maintained in a state of taut readiness.

47 **brainsickly** as if produced by a diseased mind. Shakespeare seems to have coined the adverbial form.

36–41 'Sleep . . . murder sleep' . . . feast –] *Johnson; no inverted commas F*; 'Sleep . . . feast.' *Hanmer*
38 sleave] *Steevens*; Sleeue *F*; sleeve *Cam*[1]

181

And wash this filthy witness from your hand.
Why did you bring these daggers from the place?
They must lie there. Go, carry them, and smear   50
The sleepy grooms with blood.

MACBETH   I'll go no more.
I am afraid to think what I have done;
Look on't again, I dare not.

LADY   Infirm of purpose,
Give me the daggers. The sleeping and the dead
Are but as pictures; 'tis the eye of childhood   55
That fears a painted devil. If he do bleed,
I'll gild the faces of the grooms withal,
For it must seem their guilt.   *Exit. Knock within*

---

48 **filthy witness** polluting evidence (*OED* witness *n.* 2a). The Lady's euphemism here perhaps makes her horror at the sight of the bloody and incriminating daggers more evident. Her failure to notice the daggers till this point has been variously dealt with in production. Olivier held both in one hand, blades facing down, lost in the fold of his cloak. His wife took his hands on the previous line as she urged him to wash, which prompted her exclamation, as Glen Byam Shaw, the director, described (Mullin, *Promptbook*, 89). Rosenberg suggests Shakespeare's deliberate delaying of the Lady's 'awareness of the incriminating things' (338), and Dessen (*Recovering*, 104–5) makes a good case for the delay in relation to the play's motifs of darkness and blindness, and the Lady's repeated failure to see something that the audience will have seen.

55 **as pictures** because they don't move. The Lady tries to curb Macbeth's imaginative responses.

55–6 **'tis ... devil** See the proverb 'Bugbears to scare babies' (Dent, B703). A bugbear was an imaginary creature invoked by nurses to frighten children (*OED* bugbear *n.* 2). Braunmuller notes the echo of these lines in Webster, *The White Devil*: 'Terrify babes, my lord, with painted devils' (3.2.147).

56 **If ... bleed** perhaps invoking the then current belief that corpses of the murdered bled afresh in the presence of the murderer. See *R3* 1.2.55–61. James VI and I refers to this belief in *Daemonologie* (229). Corpse-touching was used in murder trials to establish the identity of the murderer (Gaskill, 227–30).

57–8 **gild ... guilt** The Lady's alarming pun draws on the fact that old gold was red (Brooke); thus she makes the grooms into painted devils. Red and gold are often associated. See 'My red dominical, my golden letter' (*LLL* 5.2.44), 'The sun begins to gild the western sky' (*TGV* 5.1.1), and *his golden blood*, 2.3.113 below. The pun suggests impatient self-control. Read suggests that this 'gory witticism' was in Macbeth's mind in his reference to Duncan's *golden blood* at 2.3.113 (91).

58 SD ***Knock within*** Thomson, 147, suggests that audiences might have associated this

MACBETH   Whence is that knocking?
How is't with me, when every noise appals me?
What hands are here? Ha: they pluck out mine eyes.   60
Will all great Neptune's ocean wash this blood
Clean from my hand? No, this my hand will rather
The multitudinous seas incarnadine,
Making the green, one red.

Enter LADY.

LADY

My hands are of your colour, but I shame   65
To wear a heart so white. I hear a knocking   *Knock*

sound with the ominous knocking at the gate by plague-searchers. It is the first of many offstage knockings (10 such SDs in F), here conveying the sense of the outside (and everyday) world breaking in on the characters' inner space. 'The pulses of life are beginning to beat again' (De Quincey, 10.393).

59 **appals** alarms, but also, as in the etymological sense of the word, makes pale (*OED appal v.* 5)

60 **pluck . . . eyes** For the idea of the senses at odds with one another, compare 1.4.52–3. Oedipus, having blinded himself, cannot bear the sight of what he has (unwittingly) done. See also Muir on hand/eye opposition (xxix–xxx).

61–4 The idea of bloody hands that cannot be washed clean by any sea appears in Seneca, *Phaedra*, 717–18, and *Hercules Furens*, 1323–6. Miola, *Classical*, 113–14, argues strongly for *Hercules Furens* as the source of 61–4.

62–4 Compare the idea of the contaminated ocean in *Luc* 653–5.

63 **multitudinous** vast, composed of multitudes (*OED adj.* 2). The word was new in the period, first recorded in Jonson, *B. Jon: his part of King James his royall and magnificent entertainment* (1603), and would have been striking in its polysyllabic and Latinate conjunction with the rare word *incarnadine*.

incarnadine redden, as with blood. *OED* gives this as the word's first use as a verb, and *EEBO* records none earlier. It appears as an adjective in Sylvester's translation of *Du Bartas his divine weekes and workes* (1605): 'Her wings and train of fethers (mixed fine) / Of orient azure and incarnadine' (130).

64 **green, one red** The comma after *green*, following Johnson's reading, makes *one red* mean uniformly or completely red. It stresses the totality of the staining blood invoked in the previous lines. F has a comma after *one*, which Brooke suggests gives *green one* the secondary meaning of innocent.

66 **white** pale from fear or cowardice (*OED adj.* 5a)

60 Ha] *(*hah*)*   63 incarnadine] *Rowe;* incarnardine *F*   64 green, one red] *Johnson;* Greene one, Red *F;* Greene one Red *F4*   64.1] *Re-enter Lady Macbeth / Capell*   66–7] *Pope; F lines* white. / entry; / Chamber: / 66, 70, 74 SDs] *Knock within / Steevens*

At the south entry. Retire we to our chamber;
A little water clears us of this deed.
How easy is it then. Your constancy
Hath left you unattended.   *Knock*
                          Hark, more knocking.   70
Get on your nightgown, lest occasion call us
And show us to be watchers. Be not lost
So poorly in your thoughts.

MACBETH

To know my deed, 'twere best not know myself.   *Knock*
Wake Duncan with thy knocking. I would thou
    couldst.   *Exeunt.*

2.3   *Enter a* Porter. *Knocking within.*

PORTER   Here's a knocking indeed: if a man were porter
of Hell Gate, he should have old turning the key.

---

67 **south entry** The south was associated in medieval cycle plays with heaven, the north with the devil (Jones, *Scenic*, 213). Jones also notes that in the Harrowing of Hell plays the person knocking at the door is Christ. Braunmuller, however, gives examples where Shakespeare associates the southerly direction with disease (e.g. *2H4* 2.4.361–2, *TC* 5.1.18, *Cor* 1.4.31, *Cym* 4.2.349).

69–70 **Your . . . unattended** Two ideas are compressed: your firmness of purpose has deserted you, and you are left unguarded. Davenant's version of the line is: 'Your fear has left you unman'd'.

71 **nightgown** probably a dressing-gown, rather than a garment worn in bed; a garment suggesting privacy and informality. See *2H4* 3.1.0 SD: '*Enter King in his nightgown*', and *Ham* Q1 11.57 SD: '*Enter the* GHOST *in his night-gown*'. See also Dessen & Thomson, 'nightgown'.

occasion call us circumstances cause us to be called for

72 **watchers** those who keep watch (and hence are up while others sleep)

73 **poorly** abjectly, in a mean-spirited way (*OED adv*. 3). See *R2* 3.3.127–8: 'We do debase ourselves . . . / To look so poorly and to speak so fair'.

74 **know** may mean both 'acknowledge' and 'be conscious of'. Macbeth recognizes his own progressive self-alienation. 'Know thyself' (Dent, K175) is an ancient injunction for the achieving of wisdom.

2.3.0.1 *Enter a* **Porter** The Porter's part in this scene was cut for nearly two centuries after Davenant first began the practice. It was reinstated by Booth in 1868 but has sometimes been considered an interpolation, most famously by Coleridge (1.66). De Quincey's stout defence of the scene as evidence of Shakespeare's genius is justly well known. Muir in 1951 still

69 then.] *this edn;* then? *F*   74–5] *Pope; F lines* deed, / selfe. / knocking: / could'st. /   **2.3**] *Scena Tertia.*
2 Hell Gate] hell-gate *Rowe*

(*Knock*) Knock, knock, knock. Who's there, i'th'
name of Belzebub? Here's a farmer that hanged
himself on th'expectation of plenty. Come in time.   5
Have napkins enow about you; here you'll sweat
for't. (*Knock*) Knock, knock. Who's there, in th'other
devil's name? Faith, here's an equivocator that could
swear in both the scales against either scale, who

felt it necessary to argue for the scene's
authenticity (xxv–xxxii) but Harcourt,
Wickham, 'Hell Castle', and Rosenberg
(352–8) discuss it from more theatrical
angles.

1–2 **porter ... Gate** Critics have noted the
irony of the Porter's conditional phrasing.
'"If a man were porter of hell-gate". But
is this man not so? What then is hell?
And where are its gates?" (Hales, 284).
Shakespeare borrows from the medieval
cycle plays, where hell is envisaged as a
castle (Wickham, 'Hell Castle', 68–9).
For instances of devil-porter figures in
medieval art, see Braunmuller, 257, and
in medieval drama, Harcourt, 399–400.

2 **old** plenty of, more than enough. For
examples of this usage, see Crystal and
Crystal, who cite *Tem* 1.2.370, *2H4*
2.4.19, etc.

4 **Belzebub** named prince of the devils in
Matthew, 12.24, and from early on a
popular name for the devil (Hassel,
'Belzebub'). The Porter is here assuming
the role of porter of Hell Gate.
farmer The hoarding farmer who made
his gains from high prices in times of
scarcity was a popular hate-figure in
topical satire. See Sordido the farmer in
Jonson, *Everyman Out of his Humour*
(1599), characterized in the dramatis
personae as 'one that never prayed but
for a lean dearth, and even wept in a fat
harvest'. 'Farmer' was also a name by

which Father Garnet was known (Wills,
98–9). For the topicality of this speech,
see p. 17.

5 **Come in time** The word *time* here is often
emended, commonly to 'time-server' (e.g.
by Dover Wilson, and Muir in 1951,
though in 1984 he preferred 'time-
pleaser'), but not necessarily. The phrase
can simply mean that the farmer's entry
is timely. Harcourt's suggestion of 'Come
in, Time', as referring to the farmer
envisaged as carrying his scythe, and thus
'the immemorial symbol of Time' (394)
is attractive, but see Blake's defence of
the F punctuation (*Grammar*, 102.2a).
The farmer, equivocator and tailor turn
out to be parallel figures.

6 **napkins** handkerchiefs, to wipe away the
sweat, either from the heat of hell-fire or
perhaps from the sweating-tub used to
cure venereal disease

7–8 **th'other devil's name** He is too hung
over to remember another name. The one
he means is Lucifer, as spectators would
have known (TC). See *H5* 4.7.135–6
and n.

8–11 **equivocator ... heaven** Equivocating,
in the sense of saying one thing but
meaning another (*OED* equivocate *v.* 4),
was associated with Jesuits. This is
another reference to Father Garnet, whose
execution on 3 May 1606 for treasonous
complicity in the Gunpowder Plot showed
that he 'could not equivocate to heaven'.

3, 7, 12, 15, 19 SDs] [*Knocking*] *Ard²; Knock within Oxf*   4 Belzebub] Beelzebub *Collier*   5 time.] time
– *Oxf;* time-server *Cam¹*   8 Faith] 'Faith *Capell*

committed treason enough for God's sake, yet could 10
not equivocate to heaven. O, come in, equivocator.
(*Knock*) Knock, knock, knock. Who's there? Faith,
here's an English tailor come hither, for stealing out
of a French hose. Come in, tailor; here you may roast
your goose. (*Knock*) Knock, knock. Never at quiet. 15
What are you? But this place is too cold for hell. I'll
devil-porter it no further. I had thought to have let in
some of all professions that go the primrose way to
the everlasting bonfire. (*Knock*) Anon, anon, I pray
you, remember the porter. 20

13–14 **English tailor ... French hose** The tailor was a common type of cheating tradesman (Clark, *Pamphleteers*, 173), hence the Porter's joke about his skimping on the cloth in making up a pair of breeches. French hose could be either baggy or tight (Stubbes, *Anatomie of Abuses*, 1585, fol. 23b), but in either case skimping would be detrimental. 'Stealing' could also pun on 'staling' i.e. urinating (Braunmuller), which would look forward to the speech at 27–35 below. The tailor was also known as a 'tradesman-fornicator' (Williams, *Dictionary*, 'Tailor', citing *Tem* 2.2.52), and there may be other innuendoes: 'hose' could be slang for 'penis' (*TGV* 2.7.55), as could 'tail' (in 'tailor') for 'vagina' (*TS* 2.1.215–19).

14–15 **roast your goose** 'Goose' could mean a tailor's smoothing iron. See *OED* goose *n*. 5a, which gives this as its first citation, although it appears earlier in Thomas Lodge, *Euphues shadow, the battaile of the sences* (1592), and the Porter's surface meaning is 'heat your iron'. But it was also slang for 'prostitute' (esp. in the phrase 'Winchester goose', also referred to venereal disease, *OED* goose *n*. 3), thus continuing the Porter's strain of obscenity.

17 **devil-porter it** play my role as porter of Hell Gate

18 **primrose way** Compare *Ham* 1.3.49: 'The primrose path of dalliance'. Shakespeare seems to have coined this expression, and its association with the idea of an attractive course of action which leads to disaster and even damnation (*OED* primrose *n*. and *adj*. C2), though the idea of a smooth path which leads the traveller astray, as opposed to a rough one which goes the right way, is commonplace. See Spenser, *FQ*, 1.4.2–3, and *AW* 4.5.54–5. The origin of the idea may be Matthew, 7.13–14: 'It is the wide gate, and broad way that leadeth to destruction'.

20 **remember the porter** a request to Macduff and Lennox for a tip, but often delivered to the audience. There is also a more sinister sense of prophecy in these words.

20 porter.] porter. *Opens* / Capell; porter. *Opens the gate Ard²;* porter. *He opens the gate Oxf;* porter. [*Opens door*] *Oxf¹;* porter. (*Holding out his hand for a tip*) *(conj. GWW)*

Enter MACDUFF *and* LENNOX.

MACDUFF

Was it so late, friend, ere you went to bed,
That you do lie so late?

PORTER   Faith, sir, we were carousing till the second
cock; and drink, sir, is a great provoker of three things.

MACDUFF   What three things does drink especially   25
provoke?

PORTER   Marry, sir, nose-painting, sleep and urine.
Lechery, sir, it provokes and unprovokes: it provokes
the desire, but it takes away the performance. Therefore
much drink may be said to be an equivocator with   30
lechery: it makes him, and it mars him; it sets him
on, and it takes him off; it persuades him, and
disheartens him; makes him stand to, and not stand
to; in conclusion, equivocates him in a sleep and,
giving him the lie, leaves him.   35

---

22 **lie** lie in bed (referring to the Porter's
delay in opening the gate)

23–4 **the second cock** full dawn (Brooke)

24 **provoker . . . things** See Sir John Davies
of Hereford, *Microcosmos*: '3 Offices of
Drinke': 'Drinke hath three offices. The
first assists / Concoction, for in it is boil'd
the meate: / The Next, to mixe the foode
the first digests: / The Last, to bring it to
the Liver's heate' (955–8). Vickers, the
first to note Shakespeare's borrowing
here, comments on the Porter's 'comically
perverse display of rational argument'
(*Shakespeare*, 42). His dialogic technique
here recalls the Fool's in *KL*.

27 **nose-painting** 'the reddening of the sot's
nose' (Braunmuller)

28 **unprovokes** This line is *OED*'s only
citation for the negative of 'provoke' as a
verb, but other negative forms appeared
earlier, e.g. 'unprovoked' from 1534

(Erasmus, *A Plain and Goodly Exposi-
tion . . . of the Common Creed*: 'certayne
men haue vnprouoked and vncalled /
euen of theyr owne accorde runne forth
into the market').

31 **it makes . . . mars him** proverbial (Dent,
M48: 'To make, or (and) mar'). The
Porter's style of speech, with its 'repetitive doublings and triplings', has been
linked with that of the Witches (Krantz,
363).

31–2 **it sets . . . off** It arouses him sexually
and also disables him.

33 **stand to** have an erection (*OED* stand
v. 6c)

34 **equivocates . . . sleep** cheats him by
making him fall asleep, or by giving him
a wet dream

35 **giving . . . lie** tricking him; laying him
out (as in wrestling); making him urinate;
making him lose his erection

23–4] *Johnson; F lines* Cock: / things. /

MACDUFF   I believe drink gave thee the lie last night.

PORTER   That it did, sir, i'the very throat on me; but
I requited him for his lie, and, I think, being too
strong for him, though he took up my legs sometime,
yet I made a shift to cast him.   40

Enter MACBETH.

MACDUFF   Is thy master stirring?
Our knocking has awaked him; here he comes.

[*Exit Porter.*]

LENNOX
Good morrow, noble sir.

MACBETH   Good morrow both.

MACDUFF
Is the King stirring, worthy thane?

MACBETH   Not yet.

MACDUFF
He did command me to call timely on him;   45
I have almost slipped the hour.

MACBETH   I'll bring you to him.

MACDUFF
I know this is a joyful trouble to you;
But yet 'tis one.

---

37 **i'the ... throat** To lie in one's throat
meant to tell an outrageous lie. See *LLL*
4.3.10–11: 'I do nothing in the world
but lie, and lie in my throat'. The Porter
stresses the extent of his drinking.

39 **took ... legs** caused me to fall down, as
in a bout of wrestling

40 **made a shift** contrived. See Crystal
& Crystal, 'shift' *n.* 1, and *OED* shift
n. 6c.

cast throw to the ground (*OED v.* 12),
continuing the wrestling metaphor, but
also with play on 'vomit' (*v.* 25a)

42 SD *No exit is marked for the Porter in F,
but there is no theatrical reason for him to
remain on the scene once his duty is
performed.

44 **Not yet** Macbeth equivocates. 'Not yet'
can mean 'not as yet' and also 'no longer'.

45 **timely** early

46 **slipped** missed, overlooked

42 has] *(*ha's*)*   SD] *Oxf, Cam¹*

MACBETH

The labour we delight in physics pain;

This is the door.   50

MACDUFF

I'll make so bold to call, for 'tis my limited service.

Exit Macduff.

LENNOX

Goes the King hence today?

MACBETH

He does: he did appoint so.

LENNOX

The night has been unruly: where we lay

Our chimneys were blown down and, as they say,   55

Lamentings heard i'th' air, strange screams of death,

And prophesying, with accents terrible,

Of dire combustion, and confused events

New hatched to th' woeful time. The obscure bird

---

49 See Dent, D407: 'What we do willingly is easy'. Macbeth assumes his public, circumlocutory manner of speech.

51 **limited** appointed. See *MM* 4.2.163: 'Having the hour limited'.

53 **he ... so** In the second part of the line Macbeth corrects himself 'with an accuracy only the audience will pick up' (Wright, 145).

56–60 **Lamentings ... night** This description of the unnatural tumult on the night of Duncan's murder recalls other occasions when supernatural occurrences have accompanied portentous events, such as the assassination of Julius Caesar, demonstrating the sympathy between human and natural worlds. See *Ham* 1.1.114–27, and the accounts of Ross and the Old Man in 2.4. For contemporary comments on unusually violent weather in the spring of 1606, see Paul, 248–53.

57 **accents** See *OED* accent *n.* 4: 'the way in which anything is said: . . . sound . . . expressing feeling'.

58 **combustion** violent excitement or commotion (*OED n.* 5b) but perhaps with an echo of the less common meaning, 'the action or process of burning; consumption or destruction by fire' (*n.* 1a)

59 **New hatched** newly produced
    obscure bird the owl, bird of darkness, rarely seen and heard only at night, but also associated with prophecy. (See *OED* obscure *adj.* 1c, 'of, relating to, or frequenting the darkness', giving this line as its first citation.) If, as Johnson conjectured, there is a comma after *time* instead of a full stop (and concomitantly, a full stop after *events*), the bird becomes the subject of *prophesying* (*Miscellaneous*, Note XXI, 64–5).

---

54 has] *(*ha's)*   54–6] *Rowe; F lines* unruly: / downe, / i'th'Ayre / Death, /   59–61] *Hanmer; F lines* time. / Night. / feuorous, / shake. / Night. / ; *Rowe lines* time. / Night. / shake. / Night. /

Clamoured the livelong night. Some say the earth   60
Was feverous and did shake.

MACBETH   'Twas a rough night.

LENNOX

My young remembrance cannot parallel
A fellow to it.

Enter MACDUFF.

MACDUFF   O horror, horror, horror.
Tongue nor heart cannot conceive nor name thee.

MACBETH, LENNOX   What's the matter?   65

MACDUFF

Confusion now hath made his masterpiece.
Most sacrilegious murder hath broke ope
The Lord's anointed temple, and stole thence
The life o'th' building.

MACBETH   What is't you say? the life?

LENNOX

Mean you his majesty?   70

MACDUFF

Approach the chamber, and destroy your sight

---

60 **livelong** very long
61 **feverous** feverish. See *MM* 3.1.74: 'Lest
thou a feverous life shouldst entertain'.
64 The line is an example of the rhetorical
figure antimetabole, whereby the same
words or ideas are repeated in successive
clauses in reverse order: the pairings of
noun with verb are *tongue/name*, *heart/
conceive*. Macduff's distress is expressed
in elaborate speech, which becomes
increasingly hyperbolical.
66 **masterpiece** greatest achievement (a new
meaning at this time, first recorded in

Dekker, *Satiromastix*, 1602). See *OED
n.* 1a: 'in early use often applied to man as
the "masterpiece" of God or nature'.
68–9 **The Lord's ... building** Duncan's
body is imagined as a church which has
been desecrated by a robber. Muir suggests that 'The Lord's anointed temple'
is a mixed metaphor, derived from two
biblical passages, 1 Samuel, 24.10: 'the
Lordes annoynted', and 2 Corinthians,
6.16: 'ye are the temple of the lyving
God', referring to David's inability to lay
hands on King Saul.

64–5] *Capell lines* heart, / thee /

With a new Gorgon. Do not bid me speak –
See, and then speak yourselves.

Exeunt Macbeth and Lennox.
Awake, awake!
Ring the alarum bell! Murder and treason.
Banquo and Donalbain, Malcolm, awake,   75
Shake off this downy sleep, death's counterfeit,
And look on death itself. Up, up, and see
The great doom's image. Malcolm, Banquo,
As from your graves rise up, and walk like sprites   79
To countenance this horror. Ring the bell!   *Bell rings.*

Enter LADY.

LADY
What's the business,
That such a hideous trumpet calls to parley
The sleepers of the house? Speak, speak.

---

72 **Gorgon** mythical female monster with snakes for hair, whose look turned beholders into stone

74 **alarum bell** recalling the bell at the end of 2.1, which invited Macbeth to the act of murder and sounded Duncan's death knell

76 **downy** soft, referring to the down with which pillows were stuffed
sleep, death's counterfeit Death's resemblance to sleep was a commonplace. See Dent, S527: 'Sleep is the image of death', and Daniel, *Delia*, 45: 'Care-charmer sleep, son of the sable night, / Brother to death'.

78 **great doom's image** representation of the Last Judgement, a scene from Christian iconography often depicted on medieval wall paintings in English parish churches. The Last Judgement signified the end of

the world. See *KL* 5.3.261–2: 'Is this the promised end? / Or image of that horror?'

79 Macduff urges Malcolm and the rest to rise like the dead from their graves, as if the Last Judgement were really taking place.

80 **countenance** keep in countenance, be in keeping with (*OED v.* 6, which gives this as the first usage in this sense)

82 **trumpet** The Lady refers here to the alarm bell, but her choice of term is consonant with Macduff's images of the Last Judgement. See 1 Corinthians, 15.51–2: 'Beholde, I shewe you a misterie. We shall not all slepe: but we shall all be chaunged. In a moment, in the twynklying of an eye, at the last trumpe. For the trumpe shall blowe, and the dead shall ryse incorruptible, and we shall be changed.'
parley conference, as with an enemy (*OED n.*[1] 2a)

---

73 yourselves.] *(your selues:)* SD] *Dyce; after* Awake, awake! *F*   80 Ring the bell] *om. Theobald, Cam*[1]
81 business] *(business?)*

MACDUFF

 O gentle lady,
 'Tis not for you to hear what I can speak: 85
 The repetition in a woman's ear
 Would murder as it fell.

      Enter BANQUO.

       O Banquo, Banquo,
 Our royal master's murdered.

LADY   Woe, alas.

 What, in our house?

BANQUO   Too cruel anywhere.

 Dear Duff, I prithee contradict thyself   90
 And say it is not so.

  Enter MACBETH, LENNOX *and* ROSS.

MACBETH

 Had I but died an hour before this chance,
 I had lived a blessed time, for from this instant
 There's nothing serious in mortality;
 All is but toys; renown and grace is dead,   95

---

87 **fell** was spoken (*OED* fall *v.* 6)

91.1 Ross is often omitted by editors, following Rowe, for two reasons: he plays no part in the scene and he appears at the start of the next scene. However, he is present in F, and there are 12 lines between the general exeunt at 135 and the end of the scene. As a silent onlooker he could be involved in the group response to the news of Duncan's murder. He is retained by Oxf.

92–7 Bradley's summary of the paradox in these lines is succinct: 'This is . . . meant

to deceive, but it utters at the same time his profoundest feeling' (300–1). The sentiment anticipates 5.5.18–27.

92 **chance** mishap, but implying Macbeth's wish to present the death as nothing to do with him

93 **blessed** blessèd

94 **mortality** the condition of being mortal and subject to death (*OED n.* 1)

95 **toys** trifles, insubstantial things
 is dead For a plural subject followed by an apparently singular verb, see Abbott, 333.

87–9] *Theobald; F lines* fell. / murther'd. / alas: / House? / any where. /

The wine of life is drawn, and the mere lees
Is left this vault to brag of.

Enter MALCOLM *and* DONALBAIN.

DONALBAIN

What is amiss?

MACBETH   You are, and do not know't:
The spring, the head, the fountain of your blood
Is stopped, the very source of it is stopped.   100

MACDUFF

Your royal father's murdered.

MALCOLM   O, by whom?

LENNOX

Those of his chamber, as it seemed, had done't.
Their hands and faces were all badged with blood;
So were their daggers, which unwiped we found
Upon their pillows. They stared, and were distracted;   105
No man's life was to be trusted with them.

MACBETH

O, yet I do repent me of my fury,

---

96 **drawn** drained away (*OED* draw *v.* 40a.)
96–7 **lees . . . left** For a plural subject
with the singular form 'is', see Blake,
Grammar, 4.2.2.1. 'Lees' are the dregs
left at the bottom of a bottle of wine.
97 **vault** the apparent concave surface
formed by the sky (*OED n.*¹ 1, citing *KL*
5.3.256–7: 'Had I your tongues and eyes,
I'd use them so / That heaven's vault
should crack'.
brag boast
99 **spring . . . head** Braunmuller cites
Thomas More's *Utopia* here: 'From the
monarch, as from a never-failing spring,
flows a stream of all that is good or
evil over the whole nation' (More, 4.57).
Rosencrantz and Guildenstern express

the idea of the monarch's centrality to the
lives of his subjects with different metaphors (*Ham* 3.3.7–23). But Shakespeare
is also expressing the enormity of the
sons' loss of their father.
100 **stopped** blocked up. Compare 1.5.44.
103 **badged** marked, identified as with a
badge. Retainers wore heraldic emblems
or 'badges' to show the identity of their
master. The grooms wear bloody markings which identify them as Duncan's
servants (and, to Lennox, his murderers).
It appears that the Lady's plan to
incriminate the grooms has worked.
105 **stared** opened their eyes wide in
amazement (*OED* stare *v.* 3b)
distracted confused, mentally troubled

193

That I did kill them.

MACDUFF   Wherefore did you so?

MACBETH

Who can be wise, amazed, temperate and furious,
Loyal and neutral, in a moment? No man.   110
The expedition of my violent love
Outran the pauser, reason. Here lay Duncan,
His silver skin laced with his golden blood,
And his gashed stabs looked like a breach in nature
For ruin's wasteful entrance; there, the murderers,   115
Steeped in the colours of their trade, their daggers
Unmannerly breeched with gore. Who could refrain,

109–19 **Who . . . known**? Palfrey and Stern
analyse the rhythms of this speech, which
comes at 'a decisive moment in the
play' in terms of two different prosodic
models, soliloquy or 'failed dialogue',
suggesting that 'what is at stake . . . is
both a manner of acting . . . and . . . a
state of mind' (471–2). See also the
illuminating metrical analysis by Wright,
232–4.

110 **Loyal and neutral** i.e. loyal to Duncan,
neutral, or objective, towards his apparent
killers

111 **expedition** speedy enacting
violent love Macbeth's phrase is an
oxymoron. Compare *joyful trouble*, 47.

112 ***Outran** F's 'Out-run' is an archaic past
tense. See *OED* run *v*. A14.
pauser one who pauses; a Shakespearean
coinage

113 **silver . . . golden** Macbeth contrasts the
white of Duncan's skin with the red of his
blood (see 2.2.57–8n.). His metaphorical
language of precious metals turns the
body into a holy relic.
laced patterned, as if with lacework;
trimmed

114–15 **breach . . . entrance**   Duncan's
wounded body is imagined as a shoreline
broken up by the entrance of sea water, or
as a castle or fortification broken into by
invaders who enter to lay it waste. The
notion of the widespread devastation of
his land and people caused by the king's
murder permeates the scene.

115 **wasteful** destructive (*OED adj*. 1)

116 **Steeped** soaked or saturated

117 **Unmannerly . . . gore** clothed in blood
in an indecent way. 'Breeched' means
clothed in breeches, and may refer to the
breeching of boys when they were first
clothed in breeches, signifying their
potential manhood, rather than the long
gowns worn by both sexes. Hence the
phrase may carry the underlying implication that the daggers have attained
maturity through use. *Unmannerly* may
pun on 'unmanly', implying the cowardly
use of the daggers. The two words could
be easily confused in contemporary
handwriting. Mullaney comments aptly
here: 'The breach that is opening in
Duncan's flesh – allowing what is outside to intrude, spilling all that should

108 them.] them – *Rowe*   112 Outran] *Johnson;* Out-run *F*

That had a heart to love, and in that heart
Courage to make 's love known?

LADY   Help me hence, ho.

MACDUFF

Look to the lady.   120

MALCOLM

Why do we hold our tongues, that most may claim
This argument for ours?

DONALBAIN   What should be spoken
Here, where our fate, hid in an auger hole,
May rush and seize us? Let's away,
Our tears are not yet brewed.

MALCOLM   Nor our strong sorrow   125
Upon the foot of motion.

---

remain within – returns to the mind's eye
when "breech'd" succeeds it so closely'
('Lying', 41).

119 **make 's** make his
   Help . . . ho F gives no SD here for
   the Lady's action, perhaps repeated or
   intensified at 126. Davenant introduced
   the direction '*Faints*', while Rowe's was
   '*seeming to faint*'. For stage traditions at
   this point see Sprague, *Actors*, 246–7,
   Carlisle, *Greenroom*, 320–5, and Furness's
   long note. Jones, *Scenic*, 213, compares
   King Henry's swoon in *2H6* 3.2.32. See
   also Appendix 1.

121–6 **Why . . . motion** This exchange
   between the fearful brothers must take
   the form of an aside although F, in line
   with its current practice elsewhere in
   the text, does not mark it as such.
   Braunmuller (and others) have regarded
   it as a later insertion on the grounds that
   the repetition of the line 'Look to the
   lady' is an error (Braunmuller, 276–7).

But in the confusion of the action at
this point, it is not unlikely that attention
has to be drawn to the Lady's unusual
behaviour (whatever it may be) by two
different speakers.

121–2 **that . . ours** 'thus allowing others to
   impute Duncan's death to us'

122 **argument** subject of contention (*OED*
   argument *n*. 5b)

123 **hid . . . hole** lurking in a tiny space,
   almost totally concealed. An auger is
   a tool for boring holes. Donalbain is
   afraid that in this atmosphere of secret
   treachery their own fate, i.e. their deaths,
   may come upon them without warning.
   Greenblatt argues strongly that this use of
   auger hole recalls Scot's *Discovery* (Bk
   1, ch. 4) on the ability of witches to 'go in
   and out at awger holes', and contributes
   to a proof that Shakespeare did know this
   work (125).

125 **brewed** brought to maturity, ready
126 **Upon . . . motion** ready for expression

121–6] *Ard²; F lines* tongues, / ours? / here, / hole, / away, / brew'd. / Sorrow / Motion. / Lady: /   121 Why]
[*Aside to Don.*] Why *Ard², Oxf, Cam¹*   122 What] [*Aside to Mal.*] What *Ard², Oxf, Cam¹*   125 Nor] [*Aside
to Don.*] Nor *Ard², Oxf, Cam¹*

BANQUO   Look to the lady.   [*Exit Lady.*]
And when we have our naked frailties hid,
That suffer in exposure, let us meet
And question this most bloody piece of work
To know it further. Fears and scruples shake us.   130
In the great hand of God I stand, and thence
Against the undivulged pretence I fight
Of treasonous malice.

MACDUFF   And so do I.

ALL   So all.

MACBETH
Let's briefly put on manly readiness
And meet i'the hall together.

ALL   Well contented.   135

Exeunt [all but Malcolm and Donalbain].

MALCOLM
What will you do? Let's not consort with them.
To show an unfelt sorrow is an office
Which the false man does easy. I'll to England.

DONALBAIN
To Ireland, I; our separated fortune

Look . . . lady F gives no exit for the Lady at this point, but most editors provide one, and in production she invariably leaves the stage, either here or at 120 (e.g. Braunmuller). But see Mason for an argument that the 'openness of the text' is better preserved without an exit (343).

127 **naked frailties** Banquo may refer literally to the state of undress of all present, but more likely he means their distress at the situation, which is exacerbated by exposure.

130 **scruples** doubts, uncertainties

132 **undivulged pretence** undeclared design or intention (*OED* pretence *n.* and *adj.* 6). If Banquo has in mind Malcolm at this point, *pretence* could carry the undertone of 'claim to the throne'.

134 **briefly** quickly
put . . . readiness assume the garb appropriate to men, i.e. arm ourselves. Furness compares *1H6* 2.1.38 SD: '*Enter several ways, [the]* BASTARD *[of* ORLEANS], ALENÇON, REIGNIER, *half ready and half unready*'. See also Dessen & Thomson, 'ready'.

136 **consort** associate, keep company

138 **easy** easily

126 SD] [*Lady Macbeth is carried out*] Rowe; [*Exit Lady Macbeth attended*] Oxf; [*Exit Lady Macbeth, helped*] Oxf¹, Cam¹   135 SD *all . . . Donalbain*] Hanmer   136–42] Rowe; F *lines* doe? / them: / Office / easie. / England. / I: / safer: / Smiles; / bloody. / shot, /

196

Shall keep us both the safer. Where we are, 140
There's daggers in men's smiles; the near in blood,
The nearer bloody.

MALCOLM   This murderous shaft that's shot
Hath not yet lighted, and our safest way
Is to avoid the aim. Therefore to horse;
And let us not be dainty of leave-taking, 145
But shift away. There's warrant in that theft
Which steals itself, when there's no mercy left.   *Exeunt.*

2.4   *Enter* ROSS, *with an* Old Man.

OLD MAN

Threescore and ten I can remember well,
Within the volume of which time I have seen
Hours dreadful and things strange; but this sore night
Hath trifled former knowings.

ROSS   Ha, good father,
Thou seest the heavens, as troubled with man's act, 5
Threatens his bloody stage. By th' clock 'tis day,
And yet dark night strangles the travelling lamp.

141–2 **near ... bloody** Those nearest in blood (to Duncan) are most in danger. See Tilley, K38: 'The nearer in kin, the less in kindness'.

142–3 **This ... lighted** Malcolm conveys by metaphor his sense that the plan behind Duncan's murder is not yet fully carried out.

145 **dainty** scrupulous, careful (*OED a.* 5b)

146 **shift** slip off unobserved (*OED v.* 22a)
warrant justification

147 **steals itself** a pun on steal away, and theft

2.4.1 **Threescore and ten** i.e. 70 years, the natural limit of human life according to Psalms, 90.10: 'The dayes of our yeres be in all threescore yeres and tenne'.

3 **sore** violent, rough

4 **trifled** diminished, rendered insignificant (*OED* trifle *v.*[1] 6, for which this line is the only citation in this sense)
father honorific term applied to an old man

5–6 **heavens ... stage** The reflection of unnatural human activity in the cosmos is conveyed through images from the theatre: *heavens* (the canopy over the stage), *act* and *stage*.

6 **Threatens** a not uncommon use of a singular verb with a plural subject. See 2.3.95 and n.

7 **travelling lamp** periphrasis for the sun. F's spelling 'travailing' suggests effort or labour; the two spellings were interchangeable in early modern English.

141–2 near ... nearer] nea'er ... nearer *Oxf, Hunter, Cam*[1] 144 horse] house *F2–4* **2.4**] *Scena Quarta.*
4 Ha] Ah *Rowe* 6 Threatens] Threaten *Rowe* his] this *Theobald* 7 travelling] *F3–4;* trauailing *F1–2*

Is't night's predominance, or the day's shame,
That darkness does the face of earth entomb
When living light should kiss it?

OLD MAN   'Tis unnatural,   10
Even like the deed that's done. On Tuesday last
A falcon towering in her pride of place
Was by a mousing owl hawked at and killed.

ROSS

And Duncan's horses, a thing most strange and
    certain,
Beauteous and swift, the minions of their race,   15
Turned wild in nature, broke their stalls, flung out
Contending 'gainst obedience, as they would
Make war with mankind.

OLD MAN   'Tis said they eat each other.

ROSS

They did so, to th'amazement of mine eyes
That looked upon't.

Enter MACDUFF.

Here comes the good Macduff.   20
How goes the world, sir, now?

---

8 **predominance** strong influence, in an astrological sense. Compare *KL* 1.2.121–3: 'as if we were . . . knaves, thieves and treachers by spherical predominance'.
day's shame the day's sense of disgrace (at the deed – *man's act* – that has been committed, i.e. the murder of Duncan)

9 **entomb** bury, in the dark, as in a tomb

12 **towering** rising high in flight (*OED ppl. a.* 2)
pride of place a term in falconry, meaning the high point from which a bird

swoops down on its prey (*OED* pride *n.*¹ P3)

13 **mousing owl** owl hunting for mice. This is the first recorded use of 'mousing' (*OED* mousing *adj.* 1).
hawked at attacked on the wing (*OED* hawk *v.*¹ 2b). The owl flies lower than the hawk.

15 **minions** darlings, favourites

16 **broke** escaped from (*OED* break *v.* 19)

17 **Contending** struggling
as as if

18 **eat** ate; *eat* is an obsolete past tense

8 Is't] Is it *Capell*   day's] *F3–4;* dayes *F*   10 should] shall *F2*   14] *Pope; F lines* Horses, / certain) /   15 their] the *Theobald*   18 eat] ate *Singer*   19–20] *Pope; F lines* so: / vpon't / Macduffe. /

MACDUFF   Why, see you not?

ROSS

Is't known who did this more than bloody deed?

MACDUFF

Those that Macbeth hath slain.

ROSS   Alas, the day.

What good could they pretend?

MACDUFF   They were suborned.

Malcolm and Donalbain, the King's two sons,   25
Are stolen away and fled, which puts upon them
Suspicion of the deed.

ROSS   'Gainst nature still,

Thriftless ambition, that will raven up
Thine own life's means. Then 'tis most like
The sovereignty will fall upon Macbeth.   30

MACDUFF

He is already named, and gone to Scone
To be invested.

ROSS   Where is Duncan's body?

MACDUFF

Carried to Colmekill,
The sacred storehouse of his predecessors
And guardian of their bones.

ROSS   Will you to Scone?   35

---

24 **What ... pretend?** 'What good intention could they allege?' (*OED* pretend
v. 1)
   suborned bribed, illicitly induced
26 **stolen** pronounced as a monosyllable
   puts upon imputes to
28 **raven** swallow voraciously (*OED v*. 2)
29 **life's means** the means to sustain life

31 **Scone** (pronounced 'Skoon') ancient
royal city, two miles north of Perth,
longtime residence of Scottish kings, and
site of an abbey where the coronation
stone was held
32 **invested** installed as king
33 **Colmekill** the island of Iona, where the
kings of Scotland were traditionally buried

21 Why,] *Pope;* Why *F*   28 will] wilt *Warburton*   raven up] *(*rauen up*);* raven upon *F2–4;* ravin up
Theobald   29 life's] *Pope;* liues *F*   33 Colmekill] Colmeskill *Pope;* Colme-kill *Capell;* Colmkill
Cam¹

MACDUFF

No, cousin, I'll to Fife.

ROSS   Well, I will thither.

MACDUFF

Well may you see things well done there. Adieu,

Lest our old robes sit easier than our new.

ROSS

Farewell, father.

OLD MAN

God's benison go with you, and with those   40

That would make good of bad and friends of foes.

Exeunt omnes.

3.1   *Enter* BANQUO.

BANQUO

Thou hast it now, King, Cawdor, Glamis, all,

As the weïrd women promised, and I fear

Thou played'st most foully for't. Yet it was said

36 **Fife** district on the east coast of Scotland, and Macduff's domain. His assertion at this point is the first indication of his resolution to act as challenger to Macbeth's regime.

36–7 **Well ... Well ... well** Macduff's echo of Ross comments ironically on his decision.

36 **I will thither** I will go there (i.e. to Scone). Ross appears at least temporarily to be accepting Macbeth as king.

38 i.e. in case the old regime is more tolerable than the new. For another example of clothing imagery used to refer to regime change, see *2H4* 5.2.44–5: 'This new and gorgeous garment, majesty, / Sits not so easy on me as you think'.

40 **benison** blessing

41 The Old Man may be implying that Ross is a time-server (a view well utilized in

Polanski's film), or he may be innocently hoping for a future of reconciliation. For different views of Ross, see Furness, 172–3.

3.1.1–10 This ambiguous speech does not show Banquo as one of Macbeth's 'trustie friends', as he is in Holinshed (2.171). But his failure to voice his suspicions of Macbeth openly, and his entertaining of the possibility that the Witches' predictions may give him grounds for optimism, make him something more complex than Macbeth's virtuous adversary. See also Bradley, who considers that Banquo succumbs to evil and is punished for it (319–25).

2–3 **fear ... foully** The homophone of *fear/fair* produces a pun, and recalls 1.1.9 and 1.3.38.

37 Well] Well, *Theobald*   41 SD] *Exeunt severally Oxf; 38* new. [*Exit Macduff*]. *40* you, [*Exit Ross*]. *41* foes. [*Exit Old Man*]. *(GWW conj.)*   **3.1**] *Actus Tertius. Scena Prima.*   0.1] *Enter Banquo* [*dressed for riding.*] *Cam¹*   2 As] *om. Pope*   weïrd] *Theobald;* weyard *F;* weyward *Rowe*   women] woman *F3–4*   3 foully] *F2, F4;* fowly *F;* foulely *F3*

It should not stand in thy posterity,
But that myself should be the root and father   5
Of many kings. If there comes truth from them,
As upon thee, Macbeth, their speeches shine,
Why, by the verities on thee made good,
May they not be my oracles as well
And set me up in hope? But hush, no more.   10

Sennet sounded. Enter MACBETH *as King,* LADY,
LENNOX, ROSS, Lords *and Attendants.*

MACBETH
Here's our chief guest.

LADY   If he had been forgotten,
It had been as a gap in our great feast
And all thing unbecoming.

MACBETH
Tonight we hold a solemn supper, sir,
And I'll request your presence.

BANQUO   Let your highness   15
Command upon me, to the which my duties

---

4 **stand ... posterity** carry on in your descendants
5 **root** in the sense of origin. King James believed himself descended from Banquo. See pp. 37–8.
7 **shine** look favourably (*OED v.* 1d)
8 **made good** rendered true
10 **set ... hope** raise me up with royal expectations (*OED* set *v.*¹ PV 10a to set up)
10.1 ***Sennet sounded*** direction for a trumpet signal to denote a ceremonial entrance. Thomson, 149, calls this 'Macbeth's

confident assertion of his kingship', and suggests he might have had a throne lowered from the heavens. Wilson and Calore, 'sennet', note that the uses of the term in Shakespeare (which with one exception occurs only in F) indicate 'the company's awareness of the latest [musical] trends emanating from Italy'.
13 **all thing** completely (*OED* all thing *adv.* 2b)
16 **Command upon me** i.e. I am at your disposal. Banquo responds to the Macbeths' elaborate politeness in similar style.

---

7 shine] show *Collier*   10 hope?] *F4;* hope. *F*   10.1 *Sennet] (Senit)*   10.1–2 *Enter* . . . LADY, LENNOX,
ROSS . . . *Attendants*] *(Enter . . . Lady Lenox, Rosse, . . . Attendants.); Enter . . . Lady Macbeth, Lennox,
Ross, . . . Attendants / Rowe; Enter . . . Lady Macbeth Queen; Rosse, Lenox, Lords, Ladies / Capell*   13 all
thing] *Collier;* all-thing *F;* all-things *F2;* all things *F3–4*   14 MACBETH] MACBETH *(to Banquo) Oxf¹*
15 Let your highness] Lay your highness's *Rowe;* Lay your highness' *Pope*

Are with a most indissoluble tie
For ever knit.

MACBETH

Ride you this afternoon?

BANQUO   Ay, my good lord.

MACBETH

We should have else desired your good advice,   20
Which still hath been both grave and prosperous,
In this day's council: but we'll take tomorrow.
Is't far you ride?

BANQUO

As far, my lord, as will fill up the time
'Twixt this, and supper. Go not my horse the better,   25
I must become a borrower of the night
For a dark hour or twain.

MACBETH   Fail not our feast.

BANQUO

My lord, I will not.

MACBETH

We hear our bloody cousins are bestowed
In England and in Ireland, not confessing   30
Their cruel parricide, filling their hearers
With strange invention. But of that tomorrow,
When therewithal we shall have cause of state,

---

21 **still** always. Rosenberg, 387, draws
attention to this as an indication of the
passing of time since the preceding scene.
grave weighty, influential
prosperous leading to a successful
outcome, bringing prosperity

22 **take tomorrow** make use of tomorrow
instead; *take* is sometimes emended to
'talk', but need not be.

25 **Go . . . better** 'if my horse does not go
better' (than I hope). Banquo responds to
Macbeth's all-too-evident interest in his
movements non-committally.

27 **twain** two

31 **parricide** crime of killing their father

32 **strange invention** improbable fictions

33 **cause of state** state business, perhaps
with legal connotations (*OED* cause *n.* 8b)

22 council] *Rowe;* Councell *F;* councel *F3–4*   take] talk *Malone, Oxf*   29 cousins] *F3–4;* Cozens *F*

Craving us jointly. Hie you to horse. Adieu,
Till you return at night. Goes Fleance with you? 35
BANQUO
Ay, my good lord; our time does call upon's.
MACBETH
I wish your horses swift, and sure of foot;
And so I do commend you to their backs.
Farewell. *Exit Banquo.*
Let every man be master of his time 40
Till seven at night; to make society
The sweeter welcome, we will keep ourself
Till supper time alone. While then, God be with you.
Exeunt [all except Macbeth and a Servant].
Sirrah, a word with you: attend those men our
pleasure?
SERVANT
They are, my lord, without the palace gate. 45
MACBETH
Bring them before us. *Exit Servant.*
To be thus is nothing, but to be safely thus:
Our fears in Banquo stick deep,

34 **Craving us jointly** requiring us both
43 **While** until. *OED adv.* 3a notes this
usage ('while that') as 'now dialect,
chiefly north'. See also Blake, *Grammar*,
5.3.2.4f.
43 SD **all ... Servant* This is Muir's
clarifying replacement for F '*Lords*'.
45 **without** outside
47 Macbeth drops his pose of urbanity,
acknowledging that it is not worth having

the throne unless he can feel secure.
Brooke compares the Lady at 3.2.5–8.
48 Macbeth's speech is typically compressed.
He means that his fears about Banquo are
profound and not easily removed, but
also implies that these fears will penetrate
or pierce Banquo. For *stick*, see 1.7.61,
4.3.85, and *OED* stick *v.*[1] 2: 'To thrust (a
dagger, a spear, a pointed instrument) in,
into, through'.

34–5] *Pope; F lines* Horse: / Night: / you? / 34 you] *om. Pope* 36 upon's] upon us *Pope* 38 I do] do I
F3–4 41–2 night; to] night; / To *Ard²* 42–3] *Rowe; F lines* welcome: / alone: / you. / 43 SD] *Ard²;
Exeunt Lords F; Exeunt Lady Macbeth and Lords* / *Rowe; Exeunt all but Macbeth and an Attendant* / *Globe*
44] *Capell; F lines* men / pleasure? / 46–50] *Rowe lines* us. / nothing, / Banquo, / nature / dares, / ; *Pope
lines* nothing, / thus: / deep, / that, / dares / 47 nothing, but] nothing. But *Pope;* nothing; but *Theobald*

And in his royalty of nature reigns that
Which would be feared. 'Tis much he dares,   50
And to that dauntless temper of his mind,
He hath a wisdom that doth guide his valour
To act in safety. There is none but he,
Whose being I do fear; and under him
My genius is rebuked, as it is said   55
Mark Antony's was by Caesar. He chid the sisters
When first they put the name of king upon me,
And bade them speak to him. Then, prophet-like,
They hailed him father to a line of kings.
Upon my head they placed a fruitless crown   60
And put a barren sceptre in my gripe,
Thence to be wrenched with an unlineal hand,
No son of mine succeeding. If't be so,
For Banquo's issue have I filed my mind;
For them, the gracious Duncan have I murdered;   65

49 **royalty** metaphorically, fine or kingly quality, but also literally, royal potential
51 **dauntless temper** fearless temperament. The first recorded use of 'dauntless' is in Kyd, *The Tragedye of Solyman and Perseda* (1592), 1.5.10: 'Call home my hardy, dauntless Janissaries'.
54 **being** existence
55 **genius** tutelary or guardian spirit; see 56n.
56 **Mark ... Caesar** See *AC* 2.3.18–22, where the Soothsayer warns Antony to stay away from Octavius: 'Thy daemon – that thy spirit which keeps thee – is / Noble, courageous, high unmatchable, / Where Caesar's is not. But near him, thy angel / Becomes afeard, as being o'erpowered; therefore / Make space

enough between you.' For the source in Plutarch, see Bullough, 5.280.
60–1 **fruitless ... sceptre** Paul, 174–5, suggests that Shakespeare in this passage was following Leslie, *De Origine ... Scotorum*, and the family tree showing James VI and I's descent from Banquo (see Fig. 8). Bullough observes that 'Shakespeare must have read [*De Origine*], if at all, in Latin' (7.441), but includes some passages from the work as a 'possible source'. For Macbeth, the royal symbols metaphorically represent his own condition.
61 **gripe** grasp
62 **wrenched** torn away
   unlineal not in the line of descent
64 **filed** rendered foul, polluted (a now obsolete form of 'defile')

58 bade] *Theobald;* bad *F*   61 gripe] grip *Hunter*   62 with] *F;* by *Capell*   63 If 't be] If 't is *Pope;* If it be *Capell*   64 filed] fill'd *F3–4;* 'fil'd *Hanmer*

Put rancours in the vessel of my peace
Only for them; and mine eternal jewel
Given to the common enemy of man,
To make them kings, the seeds of Banquo kings.
Rather than so, come fate into the list,   70
And champion me to th'utterance. Who's there?

Enter Servant *and two* MURDERERS.

Now go to the door and stay there till we call.

Exit Servant.

Was it not yesterday we spoke together?

MURDERERS

It was, so please your highness.

66 **rancours** 'malicious enmity' (Dover Wilson, Glossary, 'rancour'). See *OED* rancour *n.* 1.
vessel . . . peace Macbeth's expression may suggest the communion chalice being defiled, as in 1.7.11: 'th'ingredience of our poisoned chalice'.

67 **eternal jewel** i.e. immortal soul

68 **common enemy** enemy of everyone, i.e. Satan. Macbeth already understands the full implications of what he has done.

69 **seeds** descendants. The plural use is unusual, but Brooke suggests it stresses 'the endless succession', as does the show of kings in 4.1.

70 **list** enclosed space between barriers where knights competed in tournaments, or, as in *R2* 1.3, to settle a dispute by armed combat (*OED n.*[3] 9a).

71 **champion** This is the only use of 'champion' as a verb in Shakespeare, and *OED*'s earliest citation for it in the sense of 'challenge to a contest'. *EEBO* records none earlier. As a noun it could mean 'acknowledged defender of a cause' (*OED n.*[1] 3). It makes more sense here for Macbeth to be inviting Fate to fight on

his side against the likelihood of Banquo's sons taking over the throne, though Johnson thought of Fate as Macbeth's challenger (*Miscellaneous*, 64–5).
to th'utterance to the death. Muir cites Cotgrave's definition of '*Combatre à oultrance*' as 'to *fight it out, or to the uttermost*'.

71.1 *two* MURDERERS Hired assassins are usually designated in this way (compare *R3* 1.4.83 SD), though these are not professional killers, as their speeches make clear. Granville Barker (85) insists that they are not 'gutter bred'. For more on the status of such men, see Wiggins, ch. 1.

73–85 **Was . . . Banquo** This passage has commonly been relineated by editors and sometimes set as prose (e.g. by Braunmuller), but the analysis of the lines by Palfrey and Stern in terms of F lineation (474) makes an effective point about the speech as 'a series of unanswered prompts' in which the short lines are indicative of Macbeth's 'communicative isolation'.

69 seeds] seed *Pope*   70 list] lists *Keightley*   71] *Pope; F lines* vtterance: / there? /   71.1 *Enter* Servant] *Re-enter Attendant / Capell*   72 Now] *om. Pope*   74 SP1] *(Murth.);* 1 Mur. *Steevens, Ard*[2]*; First Mur. Dyce*

MACBETH   Well then,
    Now have you considered of my speeches?   75
    Know, that it was he, in the times past,
    Which held you so under fortune,
    Which you had thought had been our innocent self.
    This I made good to you, in our last conference,
    Passed in probation with you: 80
    How you were borne in hand, how crossed;
    The instruments, who wrought with them,
    And all things else, that might
    To half a soul, and to a notion crazed,
    Say, 'Thus did Banquo'.

1 MURDERER   You made it known to us.   85

MACBETH
    I did so; and went further, which is now
    Our point of second meeting. Do you find
    Your patience so predominant in your nature
    That you can let this go? Are you so gospelled

74–5 **Well then, / Now** Olivier's repunctuation of these words in performance ('Well? Then, / Now') attracted much comment. Evans used it to illustrate Olivier's ability 'for giving life and purpose to short, apparently trivial phrases . . . which most other actors throw away' (39). Rosenberg (399–400) describes other actors' handling of this moment.

76 **he** i.e. Banquo. Macbeth's omission of Banquo's proper name at this point stresses his intimacy and collusion with the Murderers.

77 **held . . . fortune** kept you down, beneath your proper standing in life (*OED* fortune *n*. 5)

80 **Passed in probation** demonstrated with proofs

81 **borne in hand** deluded with false promises (*OED* bear *v*.[1] 3e). See *MA* 4.1.302–3: 'What, bear her in hand until they come to take hands'.
crossed thwarted

82 **instruments** agents
wrought worked, in the sense of shaped or moulded

84 **notion** mind, understanding

89 **gospelled** imbued with gospel teaching

74–85] *Rowe, Ard*[2] *line* now / Know / you / been / you, / you: / instruments, / might / crazed, / Banquo. / 74–92 Well . . . liege] *prose Oxf*[1]*, Cam*[1] 75 have you] you have *F3–4* speeches?] *F2;* speeches: *F* 78 self.] self? *Ard*[2] 85 You . . . us] True, you made it known *Pope* 86–92 I . . . ever?] *Rowe; F lines* so: / now / meeting. / predominant, / goe? / man, / hand / begger'd / euer? /

To pray for this good man, and for his issue,   90
Whose heavy hand hath bowed you to the grave,
And beggared yours for ever?

1 MURDERER   We are men, my liege.

MACBETH

Ay, in the catalogue ye go for men:
As hounds and greyhounds, mongrels, spaniels, curs,
Shoughs, water-rugs and demi-wolves are clept   95
All by the name of dogs. The valued file
Distinguishes the swift, the slow, the subtle,
The housekeeper, the hunter, every one
According to the gift which bounteous nature
Hath in him closed, whereby he does receive   100
Particular addition, from the bill
That writes them all alike: and so of men.
Now, if you have a station in the file
Not i'th' worst rank of manhood, say't,

---

91 **bowed you** bent you down
92 **yours** your families and descendants
93–102 Suggested sources for this passage include Erasmus' colloquy *Philodoxus* (Rea) and John Caius, *Of English Dogs, the diversities, the names, and the properties*, trans. Abraham Fleming (1576), though neither has any close similarities. See also Topsell, *The History of Four-Footed Beasts* (1607), whose extensive section on dogs (Topsell, *Beasts*, 139–90) incorporates Caius, and Braunmuller's long note on the passage (257–8).
93 **catalogue** list, roll-call
94 **curs** A 'cur' could mean a watch-dog or sheep dog without being pejorative, but Shakespeare often uses the term contemptuously (e.g. in *MND* 3.2.65 and *Cor* 3.3.119).
95 **Shoughs** long-haired pet dogs

water-rugs assumed to be rough-haired water dogs (Brooke) but otherwise unknown
demi-wolves cross-breed dogs, half wolf, half dog
clept archaic for 'called'
96 **valued file** list, with values attached (Braunmuller)
98 **housekeeper** The 'village dog or house-keeper' is mentioned in Topsell, *Beasts*, 160, as a kind of guard dog.
100 **closed** enclosed
101 **Particular addition** specific attribute
bill written list, inventory (*OED n.*³ 5a)
103 **station** metaphorical standing-place or position (*OED n.* 15, the first recorded usage in this sense)
file list, as above, but also in the military sense of a series of men in line (*OED n.*² 7)
104 **worst rank** lowest order, taking up the military metaphor

95 clept] *Capell;* clipt *F;* cleped *Theobald;* clep'd *Hanmer*   101 bill] quill *Collier*   104 Not i'th'] And not in the *Rowe*   say't] say it *Rowe*

And I will put that business in your bosoms   105
Whose execution takes your enemy off,
Grapples you to the heart and love of us,
Who wear our health but sickly in his life,
Which in his death were perfect.

2 MURDERER   I am one, my liege
Whom the vile blows and buffets of the world   110
Hath so incensed, that I am reckless what I do
To spite the world.

1 MURDERER   And I another
So weary with disasters, tugged with fortune,
That I would set my life on any chance,
To mend it, or be rid on't.   115

MACBETH
Both of you know Banquo was your enemy.

MURDERERS
True, my lord.

MACBETH
So is he mine; and in such bloody distance
That every minute of his being thrusts
Against my near'st of life: and though I could   120
With bare-faced power sweep him from my sight

---

105 **put . . . bosoms** give you that mission to
execute privately
106 **execution** carrying out, but with a pun on
execution as killing
takes . . . off gets rid of. Compare 1.7.20:
'The deep damnation of his taking off'.
107 **Grapples** attaches firmly. Compare *Ham*
1.3.62: 'Grapple them unto thy soul with
hoops of steel'.
108 **wear our health** Macbeth's elaborate
phrasing draws attention to the idea of
health as a garment and clothing metaphors
in his life while he lives

109 **perfect** sound, flawless
111 **incensed** enraged
113 **tugged** handled roughly, mauled (*OED*
tug *v*. 4b)
114 **set my life** risk my life
115 See the proverb 'Either mend or end'
(Dent, M874).
118 **distance** discord, disagreement (*OED n.*
1a)
119 **thrusts** strikes
120 **near'st of life** things most closely
affecting me (*OED near adj.* (and *n.*) 10)
121 **bare-faced** open, undisguised

105 that] the *F3–4* 107 heart] *Pope;* heart*; F* 109 my liege] *om. Pope* 111–12] *Ard² lines* what /
another, / 111 Hath] Have *Rowe* 113 weary] weary'd *Capell* with disasters, tugged] with disastrous
tugs *Warburton* 117, 141 SPs] *Dyce; Murth. F;* 2 Mur. *Malone*

And bid my will avouch it, yet I must not,
For certain friends that are both his and mine,
Whose loves I may not drop, but wail his fall
Who I myself struck down. And thence it is,   125
That I to your assistance do make love,
Masking the business from the common eye
For sundry weighty reasons.

2 MURDERER   We shall, my lord,
Perform what you command us.

1 MURDERER   Though our lives –

MACBETH

Your spirits shine through you. Within this hour
    at most,   130
I will advise you where to plant yourselves,
Acquaint you with the perfect spy o'th' time,
The moment on't – for't must be done tonight,
And something from the palace: always thought
That I require a clearness – and with him,   135
To leave no rubs nor botches in the work,

---

122 **bid . . . it** 'order that my will and pleasure be accepted as the justification of the deed' (Clarendon, cited by Furness); *avouch* is used in the sense of acknowledge, sanction, confirm (*OED* avouch *v.* 9a).

123 **For** because of

124 **but wail** must bewail ('must' understood from 122)

125 **thence** on that account

126 **make love** pay amorous attention (*OED* love *n.*[1] P 3a to make love). See *Ham* 5.2.57 (F reading): 'Why, man, they did make love to this employment'.

127 **Masking** concealing

130 **Your . . . you** Macbeth cuts off the First Murderer's protestations with an ironic compliment.
   at most at the latest

131 **plant** position

132 **the perfect . . . time** a problematic expression. Johnson took it to refer to the Third Murderer, and emended *the* to 'a'. But this seems too literal minded, and inconsistent with the Murderers' surprise when the Third Murderer appears in 3.3. *OED* spy *n.* 4 gives 'the action of spying, secret observation or watching', citing this passage. The sense of 'espial', observation, keeping watch, seems most appropriate to *spy*.

134 **from** away from
   always thought always bearing in mind

135 **clearness** freedom from suspicion
   with him in relation to him, i.e. Banquo

136 **rubs** impediments. See *Ham* 3.1.64: 'To sleep, perchance to dream – ay, there's the rub'.
   botches flaws or blemishes due to clumsy workmanship (*OED* botch *n.*[2] gives this as the first citation in this sense)

125 Who] Whom *Pope*   130] *Pope; F lines* you. / most, /   Within] In *Pope*

Fleance, his son, that keeps him company,
Whose absence is no less material to me
Than is his father's, must embrace the fate
Of that dark hour. Resolve yourselves apart;   140
I'll come to you anon.

MURDERERS   We are resolved, my lord.

MACBETH

I'll call upon you straight: abide within.

[Exeunt Murderers.]

It is concluded: Banquo, thy soul's flight
If it find heaven, must find it out tonight.   *Exit.*

3.2   *Enter Macbeth's* LADY *and a* Servant.

LADY

Is Banquo gone from court?

SERVANT

Ay, madam, but returns again tonight.

LADY

Say to the King I would attend his leisure
For a few words.

SERVANT   Madam, I will.   *Exit.*

LADY

Naught's had, all's spent,   5
Where our desire is got without content.

---

138 **absence** Macbeth's euphemism for death

140 **Resolve yourselves apart** 'Prepare yourselves elsewhere.' Macbeth is anxious to be rid of them.

142 **straight** at once
within inside

142 SD F gives no separate exit for the Murderers, but allows for a general exit at the end of the scene. Clearly, Macbeth orders them off, and his last words are spoken to himself alone.

143 **soul's flight** The soul, freed from the body, is imagined as a bird.

3.2.3 **attend his leisure** That Macbeth's Lady has now to send a servant to reach her husband may suggest their growing estrangement (Thomson, 149). This is the scene in which the ending of their partnership is signalled.

5 **spent** used up, squandered

140 apart] a-part *F3–4*   142 SD] *Theobald*   144 SD] *Theobald; Exeunt F*   **3.2**] *Scena Secunda.*
0.1 *Macbeth's* LADY] *Queen / Staunton; Lady Macbeth /Rowe*   Servant] *F; Seyton Booth*

'Tis safer to be that which we destroy,
Than by destruction dwell in doubtful joy.

Enter MACBETH.

How now, my lord, why do you keep alone?
Of sorriest fancies your companions making, 10
Using those thoughts which should indeed have died
With them they think on? Things without all remedy
Should be without regard: what's done, is done.

MACBETH

We have scorched the snake, not killed it:
She'll close, and be herself, whilst our poor malice 15
Remains in danger of her former tooth.
But let the frame of things disjoint, both the
    worlds suffer,
Ere we will eat our meal in fear, and sleep
In the affliction of these terrible dreams
That shake us nightly. Better be with the dead, 20
Whom we, to gain our peace, have sent to peace,

7 The use of *safer* recalls Macbeth at 3.1.47–8, where the feeling of frustration is similar.
8 **doubtful joy** an oxymoron, meaning joy which is fearful (*OED* doubtful *adj.* 4) as well as uncertain
10 **fancies** delusions, fantasies
11 **Using** pursuing
12–13 **Things . . . regard** See Dent, R71.1: 'Where there is no remedy, it is folly to chide'.
13 **regard** importance, estimation
14 **scorched** slashed or scored, as with a knife (*OED* scorch *v.*³). Theobald's emendation 'scotch'd' has often been adopted, and Shakespeare does use 'scotch' as a verb elsewhere (e.g. *Cor* 4.5.189–90: 'he scotched him and notched him'); but he

also uses 'scorch' meaning gashed or slashed in *CE* 5.1.183: 'to scorch your face and to disfigure you'. The snake is Duncan, who although dead lives on in his sons.
15 **close** join up (*OED v.* 11)
be herself resume her former strength
poor malice insufficient harmfulness. Macbeth is now openly conscious of the need to continue in wrongdoing.
17 **frame . . . disjoint** structure of the universe come apart. Macbeth is similarly reckless in his conjuration of the Witches at 4.1.49–60.
both the worlds this world and the next. See *Ham* 4.5.133: 'both the worlds I give to negligence'.

7 safer] better *Hanmer*   10 fancies] Francies *F2*   12 all] *om. Hanmer*   14 scorched] scotch'd *Theobald; but* scotch'd *Hudson*   17] *Pope; F lines* dis-ioynt, / suffer, /   21 peace] place *F2–4*

Than on the torture of the mind to lie
In restless ecstasy. Duncan is in his grave.
After life's fitful fever, he sleeps well;
Treason has done his worst: nor steel, nor poison,   25
Malice domestic, foreign levy, nothing,
Can touch him further.

LADY   Come on. Gentle my lord,
Sleek o'er your rugged looks, be bright and jovial
Among your guests tonight.

MACBETH

So shall I, love, and so I pray be you.   30
Let your remembrance apply to Banquo,
Present him eminence, both with eye and tongue.
Unsafe the while, that we must lave
Our honours in these flattering streams,
And make our faces vizards to our hearts,   35
Disguising what they are.

LADY   You must leave this.

---

22 **torture ... lie** 'The metaphor is from the rack' (Muir).

23 **ecstasy** state of being beside oneself, in anxiety or fear (*OED n.* 1)

24 **fitful** characterized by fits or paroxysms. *OED fitful adj.* 1 cites this as the first usage in this sense, and *EEBO* records none earlier. Life to Macbeth is a disease, only curable by death.

26 **Malice domestic** ill will or hatred on the home front
levy enlisting of soldiers

28 **Sleek** smooth
rugged rough or wrinkled with care (*OED* rough *adj.* 13b)

31 'Keep Banquo in mind.' For the contradictions in Macbeth's attitude to Banquo, having just arranged his murder yet apparently wishing him to be present at the banquet, see Jones, *Scenic*, 214. Harriet Walter gives an illuminating account of how she and Antony Sher as Macbeth dealt with this moment (Walter, 45–6).

32 **Present him eminence** 'Give him special honour.'

33–6 **Unsafe ... are** The syntax here is unclear, but the sense is that while the Macbeths are insecure, it is necessary for them to keep their honours clean by a deluge of flattery and continual deceit. *Unsafe the while* is perhaps an absolute construction, and *that* means 'so that'.

33 **lave** wash

35 **vizards** masks. For the sentiment, see 1.5.65–6.

23] *Rowe; F lines* extasie. / Graue: / 25 has] *(ha's)* 27–9 Come . . . tonight.] *Capell; F lines* on: / Lookes, / to Night. / 30–4] *Capell lines* love, / remembrance / both / we / streams, / 31 apply] still apply *F2–4* 34 flattering] so flattering *Rowe* 35 vizards] vizors *Theobald*

MACBETH

O, full of scorpions is my mind, dear wife:
Thou knowst that Banquo and his Fleance lives.

LADY

But in them nature's copy's not eterne.

MACBETH

There's comfort yet: they are assailable.   40
Then be thou jocund; ere the bat hath flown
His cloistered flight, ere to black Hecate's summons
The shard-born beetle, with his drowsy hums,
Hath rung night's yawning peal, there shall be done
A deed of dreadful note.

LADY   What's to be done?   45

MACBETH

Be innocent of the knowledge, dearest chuck,

---

39 **copy** pattern or reproduction, but with a play on the legal sense of copyhold tenure at the will of a landlord. (But see Sokol and Sokol, 'copy', who are doubtful about this meaning.)

eterne everlasting

40 **assailable** able to be disposed of. Macbeth takes his wife to mean that Banquo and Fleance are not immortal.

41 **jocund** cheerful

42 **cloistered** The bat was associated with ruins, and its flights are nocturnal. For superstitions associated with bats, see the entry in Werness.

black Hecate's Hecate is earlier thought of as *Pale* (2.1.52), but becomes *black* here in keeping with the mood of Macbeth's night-piece.

43 **shard-born** born in dung (*OED a.*, where this is the first citation). Editors have often emended to 'shard-borne' (borne up on scaly, or shard-like, wing-cases), following Steevens, who followed Hanmer, but Billings gives convincing

evidence to support *OED*. He suggests Whitney, *A Choice of Emblems* (1586), '*Turpibus excitium*', as a possible source, though there are no precise verbal parallels.

drowsy hums The dor-beetle flies with a loud humming sound.

44 **yawning** The image suggests the bell's 'mouth' (Braunmuller), but also connects with the humming beetle's inducement to sleep.

45 **note** distinction, notoriety

46–52 **Be ... wood** Mahood, 38–9, comments suggestively on the interlinked puns (between *deed*, *seeling*, *bond* and *pale*) in this passage.

46 **chuck** term of endearment, but according to Braunmuller unusual for an aristocratic couple (though Othello uses it to Desdemona, *Oth* 3.4.49 and 4.2.24, and Antony to Cleopatra, *AC* 4.4.2). It is always used by the more powerful character (in terms of gender or class) to the less powerful.

---

38 lives] live *Hanmer*   39 eterne] eternal *Pope*   43 shard-born] *F3;* shard-borne *F1–2*   44–5] *Rowe; F lines* Peale, / note. / done? /

Till thou applaud the deed. Come, seeling night,
Scarf up the tender eye of pitiful day
And with thy bloody and invisible hand
Cancel and tear to pieces that great bond   50
Which keeps me pale. Light thickens,
And the crow makes wing to th' rooky wood.
Good things of day begin to droop and drowse,
Whiles night's black agents to their preys do rouse.
Thou marvell'st at my words: but hold thee still;   55
Things bad begun, make strong themselves by ill.
So prithee, go with me.   *Exeunt.*

47 **seeling** blinding, a term from falconry, meaning sewing up the eyes of a young hawk or other bird as part of the taming process, and used metaphorically to mean hoodwinking. There is perhaps an underlying legal metaphor from the homophone 'sealing'.

48 **Scarf up** blindfold, cover up (recalling the clothing metaphor in 'the blanket of the dark', 1.5.53)

50 **Cancel** render null and void
that great bond ambiguous expression, perhaps signifying the contract or moral commitment which binds Macbeth to common humanity, or Banquo's 'bond' of life. Compare 4.1.82–3: 'But yet I'll make assurance double sure, / And take a bond of fate', where the term carries a stronger legalistic implication. See also *R3* 4.4.77: 'Cancel his bond of life, dear God, I pray'.

51 **pale** may mean fearful, cowardly, pallor being associated with lack of courage at 2.2.59 and 65–6, or perhaps confined within bounds (as in 'beyond the pale'). See *OED n.*[1] 4a and 5b.
Light thickens an oxymoron, meaning 'it grows darker', but recalling atmosphere created by the *fog and filthy air* of the Witches (1.1). Compare *Come thick night* (1.5.50). See Empson's suggestive

comments, 18–19, on the sound effects here.

52 **crow** large black bird that feeds on carrion (though it is solitary rather than gregarious, as editors point out)
rooky filled with rooks (*OED adj.*[1] gives this as the first citation in this sense, and *EEBO* has none earlier)

54 **rouse** start into action

55 **hold thee still** retain your composure. But see also Cordner, who suggests several other possible readings, including 'stay tight-lipped' and 'keep your behaviour normal, unemphatic' (91–2).

56 This is a rewording of the familiar Senecan aphorism (from *Agamemnon*, 115): '*Per scelera semper sceleribus tutum est iter*' – paraphrased by 'Crimes are made secure by greater crimes' (Dent, C826). Compare Hieronimo's use of the phrase in Latin in *The Spanish Tragedy*, 3.13.16. Miola comments that the use of this maxim 'serves instantly to characterize the speaker . . . as passionate in will and grimly dedicated to evil' (*Classical*, 93).

57 SD This may be their last exit as a united couple. Rosenberg (422–3) records contrasting styles of exit for them, sometimes hand in hand or even embracing, sometimes alienated.

47 seeling] sealing *Rowe*   51 Light] Night *Warburton*

3.3   *Enter three* MURDERERS.

1 MURDERER

But who did bid thee join with us?

3 MURDERER   Macbeth.

2 MURDERER

He needs not our mistrust, since he delivers
Our offices, and what we have to do,
To the direction just.

1 MURDERER   Then stand with us.

The west yet glimmers with some streaks of day.   5
Now spurs the lated traveller apace
To gain the timely inn, and near approaches
The subject of our watch.

3 MURDERER   Hark, I hear horses.

BANQUO (*within*)

Give us a light there, ho!

2 MURDERER   Then 'tis he: the rest,

That are within the note of expectation,   10
Already are i'th' court.

3.3.01 Speculations as to the identity of the Third Murderer have included Ross and Macbeth himself. Directors (e.g. Irving, Nunn) have favoured Seyton. Macbeth's anxiety in 3.4 seems to rule him out, and as Dover Wilson says, the introduction of a further assassin shows that Macbeth, 'tyrant-like, feels he must spy even upon his own chosen instruments' (137). Furness reviews the several candidates, Williams, 'Third', dismisses the idea that Macbeth himself was the Murderer, and Wiggins discusses the relations between the three (77–8).

2 **He ... mistrust** We need not mistrust him (i.e. the Third Murderer).

3 **offices** duties

4 **To ... just** precisely according to Macbeth's directions (as referred to at 3.1.131–6)
   stand take a position

6 **lated** belated

7 **timely** opportune, appearing in good time

8 **hear horses** This sound effect, not uncommon in the theatre at this time, helps build up the atmosphere of tension in the darkness.

10 **within ... expectation** on the list of expected guests

3.3] *Scena Tertia.*   1 SP1] *Rowe;* 1. *F;* First Murd. *Dyce*   SP2] *Rowe;* 3. *F;* Third Murd. *Dyce*   2 SP] *Rowe;* 2. *F;* Second Murd. *Dyce*   our] to *Pope*   6 lated] latest *Rowe*   7 and] *F2;* end *F*   near] here *Collier*   9 a light] light *Pope*   'tis] it is *Pope*   9–10] *Pope; F lines* hoa. / hee: / expectation, /

1 MURDERER   His horses go about.

3 MURDERER

Almost a mile; but he does usually,
So all men do, from hence to the palace gate
Make it their walk.

Enter BANQUO *and* FLEANCE, *with a torch.*

2 MURDERER   A light, a light.

3 MURDERER   'Tis he.

1 MURDERER

Stand to't.

BANQUO   It will be rain tonight.

1 MURDERER   Let it come down.   15

BANQUO

O treachery!

[*The Murderers attack. First Murderer strikes out the light.*]
Fly, good Fleance, fly, fly, fly.

Thou mayst revenge –   [*Exit Fleance.*]
O slave!   [*Dies.*]

3 MURDERER

Who did strike out the light?

1 MURDERER   Was't not the way?

---

11 **go about** take a longer route (being led by grooms to the castle, while Banquo walks)

14.1 *with a torch* It must be Fleance here who carries the torch, since no one else enters.

15 **Let . . . down** Braunmuller suggests this is a grim jest, since Banquo need not worry about the weather. The line also conveys the idea of the rain of blows on the defenceless victims.

16 SD *F has no SD here, but it seems from 18 that the First Murderer is the one to strike out the light.

17 **Thou mayst revenge** Hawkins comments that although Fleance doesn't seek revenge, he does, indirectly, get it (164).

18 **way** plan, intention. The First Murderer in the confusion feels the need to defend his actions, the darkness having permitted Fleance's escape.

14.1] *Enter B. and F. Servant, with a Torch before them.* / *Capell*   16 SD] *Cam¹; They fall upon Banquo and kill him; in the scuffle Fleance escapes.* / *Rowe; They assault Banquo.* / *Theobald; The First Murderer strikes out the light, while the others assault Banquo. Ard²*   17 SD1, 2] *Pope; Dies. Fleance escapes. F* / *Dies.* / *Rowe; Dies Fl. and ser. fly.* / *Capell*

3 MURDERER
　There's but one down: the son is fled.

2 MURDERER　　　　　　　　　　　We have lost
　Best half of our affair.

1 MURDERER　　　　　　Well, let's away,　　　　　20
　And say how much is done.　　　　　　　　　*Exeunt.*

3.4　　*Banquet prepared. Enter* MACBETH, LADY, ROSS,
　　　LENNOX, Lords *and Attendants*.

MACBETH
　You know your own degrees, sit down. At first and last,
　The hearty welcome.

LORDS　　　　　　　　Thanks to your majesty.

MACBETH
　Ourself will mingle with society
　And play the humble host. Our hostess keeps her state,

20　**Best half** Macbeth has made clear at
3.1.135–40 the importance of Fleance's
death. Thomson notes that Fleance's
survival is of the greatest significance:
'The escaping Fleance carries Macbeth's
doom with him' (150).

3.4 This scene is often regarded as a turning-
point in the play, when Macbeth achieves
the tragic insight that he is living in 'a
world over which he has no control'
(Dyson, 370).

0.1　*Banquet prepared* A banquet in this
period could signify a light dessert course,
but here is a state dinner. (See Meads, 2,
and on this scene specifically, 143–5.)
The symbolic role of the banquet representing harmony and fellowship, and the
irony of its usage here, has long been

noted (e.g. by Wilson Knight, *Imperial*,
135–41). As Jones observes, Macbeth
is putting on a performance 'intended to
ratify the new social order, but is 'put out
of his part' (*Scenic*, 216).

0.1–2　*Enter . . . Attendants* a grand formal
entry, appropriate to Macbeth's first public
appearance as king, with his entourage

1　**degrees** social ranks, and hence, appropriate positions at the table. Macbeth
draws attention to the formality of the
occasion in his opening words on the
observance of hierarchical order.
　At . . . last to one and all (*OED* first *a*. 5e)

3　**society** the guests. Macbeth will not keep
his place at the head of the table.

4　**state** chair of state (*OED n*. 20a). See *1H4*
2.4.371: 'This chair shall be my state'.

---

19 We have] We've *Pope*　20–1 Well . . . done] *one line F*　21 SD] *Exeunt with Banquo's body. Oxf*
3.4] *Scaena Quarta.*　0.1–2] *Banquet prepared. Enter Macbeth as King, Lady Macbeth as Queen, Ross,
Lennox, Lords, and attendants.* [*Lady Macbeth sits.] Oxf; Banquet prepared.* [*Two thrones are placed on
stage.] Enter* MACBETH [*as King*], LADY [MACBETH *as Queen*], ROSS, LENNOX, LORDS, *and Attendants.*
[*Lady Macbeth sits.] Cam[1]*　1–7] *prose Braunmuller*　1–2 You . . . welcome] *Oxf; F lines* downe: / welcome. / ;
Capell (Johnson) lines first / welcome. /　1 At] *and Rowe*　2 welcome.] welcome. [*The Lords sit.] Cam[1]*
4–5] *Oxf; F lines* Host: / time / welcome. /

But in best time we will require her welcome.   5

LADY

Pronounce it for me, sir, to all our friends,
For my heart speaks, they are welcome.

Enter First MURDERER.

MACBETH

See, they encounter thee with their hearts' thanks.
Both sides are even: here I'll sit i'th' midst.
Be large in mirth; anon we'll drink a measure   10
The table round. – There's blood upon thy face.

1 MURDERER

'Tis Banquo's then.

MACBETH   'Tis better thee without, than he within.
Is he dispatched?

1 MURDERER

My lord, his throat is cut; that I did for him.

MACBETH

Thou art the best o'th' cut-throats;   15
Yet he's good that did the like for Fleance.
If thou didst it, thou art the nonpareil.

1 MURDERER

Most royal sir, Fleance is scaped.

7.1 Editors sometimes move this entrance, unnecessarily, to 12, when Macbeth addresses the Murderer, who is seen by no one else. Muir adds '*to the door*'.

8   **encounter thee** meet you, respond to you, perhaps with a toast

9   **Both . . . even** There is the same number of people on each side of the table.
     i'th' midst half-way down one side. Braunmuller notes that in the period the

place of honour could be either at the head of the table or in the centre down one side. But Macbeth is ostentatiously not sitting in the place of honour.

10   **large** bountiful, lavish

10–11 **a measure . . . round** a toast round the whole table

12   **thee . . . within** 'outside you than inside him'. Macbeth's joke is forced.

17   **nonpareil** one without equal

5 best] the best *F2–4*   welcome.] welcome. [*They sit.*] / *Rowe*   7 they are] they're *Pope*   7.1] *Enter . . . to the door.* / *Capell*   11 round.] round. [*Approaching the door.*] / *White;* round. *Goes to door. Ard²*   face.] face. [*To the Mur.*] *Rowe*   12 he] him *Hanmer*   14 that I did] I did that *Pope*   15–17] *Rowe lines* good / it, / non-pareil. /

MACBETH

Then comes my fit again: I had else been perfect;
Whole as the marble, founded as the rock,   20
As broad and general as the casing air:
But now I am cabined, cribbed, confined, bound in
To saucy doubts and fears. But Banquo's safe?

1 MURDERER

Ay, my good lord: safe in a ditch he bides,
With twenty trenched gashes on his head,   25
The least a death to nature.

MACBETH   Thanks for that.
There the grown serpent lies; the worm that's fled
Hath nature that in time will venom breed,
No teeth for th' present. Get thee gone, tomorrow
We'll hear ourselves again.   *Exit [First] Murderer.*

LADY   My royal lord,   30
You do not give the cheer: the feast is sold

19 **fit** attack or seizure
  perfect fully satisfied, whole and sound.
  Compare 3.1.109, and *Tim* 1.2.84–6:
  'Might we but have that happiness . . . we
  should think ourselves forever perfect'.
  Mahood suggests adding 'a nuance of the
  grammatical meaning (the perfect tense
  describes an action which is completed,
  that is *done* . . .)' (138).
20 'As hard as marble' and 'as fixed as rock'
  were proverbial. See Dent, M638.1, R151.
  founded secure, firmly based (*OED ppl.
  a.* gives this as the first citation for this
  meaning)
21 **broad and general** free and uncon-
  strained. See Dent, A88: 'As free as air'.
  casing encasing or enclosing (*OED ppl.
  a.* gives this as the first citation for this
  meaning and *EEBO* has none earlier.) But
  Macbeth really seems to mean encompassing or surrounding.

22 **cabined** confined, as in a cabin
  cribbed shut up, as in an animal's stall or
  crib
23 **saucy** insolent, presumptuous (*OED a.*[1] *2a*)
  safe Macbeth's euphemism for 'dead'.
  Compare 3.1.47, 3.2.7.
25 **trenched** trenchèd; deeply cut (*OED*
  cites this line under trench *v.* 4d, meaning
  encroached upon). See *TGV* 3.2.6–7: 'a
  figure / Trenched in ice'.
27 **worm** young snake. Compare 3.2.14–16.
30 **hear ourselves** hear each other, i.e. talk
  together
31 **give the cheer** give a kindly welcome
  (*OED* cheer *n.*[1] 5), raise a toast
31–3 **feast . . . welcome** The Lady again
  assumes the formal idiom of courtesy. She
  justifies elaborately her call to Macbeth to
  demonstrate hospitality. The feast that is
  not frequently pledged (*vouched*) is like
  a commercial transaction (*sold*). Brooke

19] *Pope; F lines* againe: / perfect; /   23 saucy] *(sawcy)*   30 We'll] Well *F3–4*   hear ourselves] *(our
selves);* hear't ourselves *Theobald;* hear thee ourselves *Hanmer;* hear, ourselves *Malone;* hear, ourselves,
Dyce; hear't, ourself, *Hudson*   31 sold] cold *Pope*

That is not often vouched, while 'tis a-making,
'Tis given with welcome. To feed were best at home:
From thence, the sauce to meat is ceremony,
Meeting were bare without it.

Enter the Ghost of BANQUO, *and sits in Macbeth's place.*

MACBETH   Sweet remembrancer.   35
Now good digestion wait on appetite,
And health on both.

LENNOX   May't please your highness sit.

MACBETH

Here had we now our country's honour roofed,
Were the graced person of our Banquo present,
Who may I rather challenge for unkindness   40
Than pity for mischance.

ROSS   His absence, sir,
Lays blame upon his promise. Please't your highness
To grace us with your royal company?

cites the proverb 'Welcome is the best cheer' (Dent, W258).

32 **a-making** in the making, going on

33 **To ... home** 'It is better to eat at home' (if one is not properly welcomed).

34 **From thence** away from there
   sauce ... ceremony 'Food is made special by courtesy or social ritual.' There is a pun on *meat* and *Meeting*.

35 SD **Enter... BANQUO** For discussion of the staging of the Ghost's entrances, and of the fact that no exits are given for him in F1, see Worster. Editors (e.g. Muir) sometimes move the Ghost's entrance forward, to 39, to create the effect of the Ghost appearing when summoned. Dessen, *Recovering*, 76–7, defends the F placing of the entry. Thomson, 151–2, connects this moment to *The Knight of the Burning Pestle*, 5.1.22–8, and

suggests a tradition of stage business initiated by Burbage. See also p. 14. For discussion of whether the Ghost is 'real', and a range of stagings of it, see Rosenberg, 441–6. Simon Forman saw a ghost on the stage in 1611.

35 **remembrancer** one who reminds. But it can also refer to an official responsible for the collection of debts (*OED n.* 1b), and this secondary meaning has an ironic resonance spoken in the presence of the (as yet unseen) Ghost.

36 **wait on** attend on

38 **roofed** under one roof

39 **graced** favoured, gracious

40 **may I** I hope I may
   challenge reprove, reprehend (*OED v.* 2a)

41 **mischance** misfortune, accident

42 **blame** blameworthiness (cited as archaic in *OED n.* 3)

32 a-making] making *F2–4* 33 given with] *F3–4;* given, with *F* 35 SD] *after 37 Capell; after 39 Ard²*

MACBETH
    The table's full.

LENNOX   Here is a place reserved, sir.

MACBETH   Where?

LENNOX
    Here my good lord. What is't that moves your
        highness?   45

MACBETH
    Which of you have done this?

LORDS   What, my good lord?

MACBETH
    Thou canst not say I did it: never shake
    Thy gory locks at me.

ROSS
    Gentlemen, rise; his highness is not well.

LADY
    Sit, worthy friends; my lord is often thus,   50
    And hath been from his youth. Pray you, keep seat,
    The fit is momentary; upon a thought
    He will again be well. If much you note him
    You shall offend him, and extend his passion.
    Feed, and regard him not. [*to Macbeth*] Are you
        a man?   55

MACBETH
    Ay, and a bold one, that dare look on that
    Which might appal the devil.

---

44 **The table's full** Macbeth does not register the Ghost as such initially.

46 **Which ... this**? As Brooke notes, this suggests at first that Macbeth suspects a practical joke, but his next line seems to confirm that he means, 'Who has murdered Banquo?'

48 **gory locks** bloody hair

51 **keep seat** remain seated

52 **upon a thought** right away

54 **passion** fit, outburst of feeling (*OED n.* 6c)

45] *Capell; F lines* Lord. / Highnesse? /   49 ROSS] ROSS (*rising*) *Oxf;* ROSS [*Lady Macbeth joins the Lords.*] *Cam¹*   52 momentary] momentary *F2–4*   55 SD] *Rowe; To Macb. aside* / *Pope; Coming to M. and aside to him.* /*Collier; She speaks apart with Macbeth. Oxf*   55–81 Are . . . is] *aside Capell*

LADY   O, proper stuff.
This is the very painting of your fear:
This is the air-drawn dagger which you said
Led you to Duncan. O, these flaws and starts,   60
Imposters to true fear, would well become
A woman's story at a winter's fire,
Authorized by her grandam. Shame itself.
Why do you make such faces? When all's done
You look but on a stool.
MACBETH   Prithee see there.   65
Behold, look, lo, how say you?
[*to Ghost*] Why, what care I? If thou canst nod,
    speak too.
If charnel-houses and our graves must send
Those that we bury back, our monuments   69
Shall be the maws of kites.   [*Exit Ghost.*]

---

57 **proper stuff** complete nonsense
58 **very** veritable, true (*OED adj.* 3)
   painting image, false creation. Compare
   2.2.56.
60 **flaws** bursts of feeling (*OED* flaw *n.*² 2,
   citing this example as the earliest usage)
61 **Imposters** fraudulent pretences
63 **Authorized** confirmed, given authority
   (with the stress on the second syllable)
   (*OED* authorize *v.* 4)
65 **stool** seat, but perhaps referring literally
   to a stool, these being more common
   items of household furniture than chairs,
   which were then expensive
67 **Why . . . I?** Macbeth appears to be challenging the Ghost, which, unlike other
   Shakespearean ghosts, seems incapable
   of giving voice to any accusation.
   nod like 47–8, an implicit SD for the
   Ghost, indicating how it addresses itself
   to Macbeth

68 **charnel-houses** vaults in which to bury
   the bones of the dead
69–70 **monuments . . . kites** 'the only safe
   way with corpses is to let the vultures
   bury them' (Dover Wilson)
70 **maws** stomachs
   kites birds of prey, which eat carrion.
   The fact that they disgorge undigested
   material does not appear relevant here,
   since, in Macbeth's hyperbole, corpses
   must be thrown for birds of prey to
   devour, for their stomachs to replace
   the graves that no longer retain their
   function. Dover Wilson compares Scot,
   Discovery, Bk 5, Ch. 6: 'Some write that
   after the death of Nabuchadnezzar his son
   Eilumorodath gave his body to the ravens
   to be devoured, least afterwards his father
   should arise from death'.
70 SD * F1 has no exit for the Ghost, but
   F2's positioning is appropriate.

59 air-drawn dagger] *Capell;* air-drawn-dagger *F*   61 Imposters to] Imposters of *Hanmer;* Impostures of
Capell   70 SD] *F2–4; Ghost vanishes. / Rowe; Recovers himself. / Hudson; Ghost disappears. Ard²*

LADY

What? Quite unmanned in folly.

MACBETH

If I stand here, I saw him.

LADY   Fie, for shame.

MACBETH

Blood hath been shed ere now, i'th' olden time,
Ere humane statute purged the gentle weal;
Ay, and since too, murders have been performed   75
Too terrible for the ear. The times have been,
That when the brains were out, the man would die,
And there an end. But now they rise again
With twenty mortal murders on their crowns,
And push us from our stools. This is more strange   80
Than such a murder is.

LADY   My worthy lord,

Your noble friends do lack you.

MACBETH   I do forget.

Do not muse at me, my most worthy friends,
I have a strange infirmity, which is nothing

---

71 **unmanned** weakened, made timid. See *OED* unman *v.* 3: 'To deprive of manly courage or fortitude; to make weak or effeminate'. The earliest example in *OED* of the participial form is 1694.
folly foolish behaviour. Editors usually replace F's full stop with a question mark here, but this line can just as well be a disgusted comment as a rhetorical question.

72 **If . . . here** as surely as I stand here (Blake, *Grammar*, 5.3.2.5)

74 **humane statute** benevolent or compassionate law. 'Humane' was not distinguished from 'human' in this period, and 'man-made' is another possible meaning here.

gentle weal civilized state (*OED* weal *n.*[1] 3b); *purged* is used here with proleptic force, in that the state becomes civilized when it has been purged. Contrast 5.2.27–8: 'Meet we the medicine of the sickly weal, / And with him pour we in our country's purge'.

78 **And . . . end** proverbial. See Dent, E113.1: 'And there's an end'.

79 **twenty** a round number, recalling *twenty trenched gashes*, 25
mortal fatal
crowns heads

80 **push . . . stools** take over our seats at the feast, but also take over our place in succession to the crown

---

71] *(*unmann'd*)*; What quite unmanned in Folly? *Capell;* What! quite unmann'd in folly! *Keightley*
73 olden] olde *Rowe*   74 humane] human *Theobald*   statute] statue *F3–4*   gentle] gen'ral *Warburton*
76 times have] *F2–4;* times has *F;* time has *White*

223

To those that know me. Come, love and health to all,   85
Then I'll sit down. Give me some wine, fill full.

Enter Ghost.

I drink to the general joy o'the whole table,
And to our dear friend Banquo, whom we miss –
Would he were here. To all, and him we thirst,
And all to all.
LORDS   Our duties, and the pledge.   90
MACBETH
Avaunt, and quit my sight! Let the earth hide thee.
Thy bones are marrowless, thy blood is cold;
Thou hast no speculation in those eyes
Which thou dost glare with.
LADY   Think of this, good peers,
But as a thing of custom; 'tis no other,   95
Only it spoils the pleasure of the time.
MACBETH
What man dare, I dare.

86.1 Editors often move this direction further on, regarding it as anticipatory, but the Ghost's entry before Macbeth sees it offers an opportunity for irony.

89 **thirst** long for (*OED v.* 4)

90 **duties** respects
pledge toast

92 **marrowless** without substance, lacking what is essential to life. This is the earliest usage in *OED*, which also cites *The Revenger's Tragedy* (1607), 1.1.5–6: 'O that marrowless age / Would stuff the hollow bones with damned desires'.
blood . . . cold The Ghost is an oxymoron, an example of the living dead.

93 **speculation** the power of seeing, esp. 'intelligent or comprehending vision' (*OED n.* 1). The effect of this Latinate

polysyllable is reminiscent of 2.2.63. Shakespeare's interest in the eyes of a murdered man remembered after his death is evident in *2H6* 3.2.169–70 and 3.3.14. In that play, 3.3, where Cardinal Beaufort on his death-bed is haunted by the memory of the Duke of Gloucester whom he has murdered, has similarities with this scene.

94 **glare** look fixedly and fiercely (*OED v.* 2). *OED*'s first example of this meaning is 1609, but it appears earlier in *Hamlet*, also in an address to a ghost: 'O do not glare with looks so pitiful' (Q1, 11.62) and in Q2: 'Look you how pale he glares' (3.4.121).

97 As Brooke notes, this line metrically completes 94, and it is as if Macbeth

86.1] *As he is drinking the Ghost rises again just before him.* / Rowe; *The Ghost rises again.* / Pope; *after 88 Malone; after 90 Pope*

Approach thou like the rugged Russian bear,
The armed rhinoceros, or the Hyrcan tiger,
Take any shape but that, and my firm nerves   100
Shall never tremble. Or be alive again,
And dare me to the desert with thy sword;
If trembling I inhabit then, protest me
The baby of a girl. Hence, horrible shadow,
Unreal mockery, hence.   [*Exit Ghost.*]
                                    Why so, being gone   105
I am a man again. [*to Lords*] Pray you, sit still.

LADY

You have displaced the mirth, broke the good meeting
With most admired disorder.

takes no notice of his wife's intervention, but continues his own address to the Ghost. This line stresses his desperation to be thought manly.

98–101 **Approach . . . tremble** The verbs *Approach* and *Take* are best understood as conditional not imperative ('If you approach . . . if you take').

98 **rugged Russian bear** Braunmuller, citing Muir and giving examples from Dekker, *The Whore of Babylon*, 2.1.42–3, and *The Roaring Girl*, 3.3.50–1, suggests that the Russian bear may be proverbial for rough strength.

99 **armed** i.e. by its horn and tough skin
Hyrcan tiger Hyrcania was a district by the Caspian Sea, according to Pliny, *Natural History*, 8.18 (translated by Philemon Holland, 1601) the haunt of wild beasts including tigers. Tigers were proverbial for fierceness. See *3H6* 1.4.154–5: 'you are more inhuman, more inexorable, / O, ten times more,

than tigers of Hyrcania'. See also *Ham* 2.2.388: 'The rugged Pyrrhus, like th'Hyrcanian beast', and Thompson and Taylor's note where they also compare Marlowe and Nashe, *Dido, Queen of Carthage*, 5.1.159.

102 **dare . . . desert** 'challenge me to a deserted place' (to fight unimpeded)

103 **If . . . then** ambiguous expression. It may mean either 'If I, trembling, stay indoors' or 'If I take on trembling as a habit' (punning on 'habit' as clothing). See *AYL* 3.3.8–9: 'O knowledge ill-inhabited, worse than Jove in a thatched house'.
protest pronounce, proclaim (*OED v.* 5, an obsolete sense)

104 **baby . . . girl** girl's doll (*OED baby n.* 2)

105 **being gone** No exit is marked for the Ghost in F, but Macbeth's line indicates that it disappeared, rapidly and to order.

108 **admired** astonishing, amazing

99 Hyrcan] *F3–4;* Hircan *F;* Hyrcanian *Pope*   101 Or be] O be *Rowe;* Be *Pope*   103 I inhabit then,] I inhabit, then *F2–4;* I inhabit, then *Pope;* I inhabit then, *Capell;* I inhabit thee *Malone*   protest] protect *F4*   104 horrible] terrible *Theobald*   105 SD] *Ard² (Ghost disappears)*   being] be *F3–4*   gone] gone. [*Ghost vanishes.*] *Rowe;* gone. [*Ghost disappears*] *Malone;* gone. [*Spectre is supposed to vanish*] *Booth*   106 still.] still. [*The Lords rise*] *Rowe*   107–8 You . . . disorder] *Rowe; F lines* mirth, / disorder, /

225

MACBETH   Can such things be,
  And overcome us like a summer's cloud,
  Without our special wonder? You make me strange   110
  Even to the disposition that I owe,
  When now I think you can behold such sights
  And keep the natural ruby of your cheeks
  When mine is blanched with fear.
ROSS   What sights, my lord?
LADY
  I pray you speak not; he grows worse and worse;   115
  Question enrages him. At once, goodnight.
  Stand not upon the order of your going
  But go at once.
LENNOX   Goodnight, and better health
  Attend his majesty.
LADY   A kind goodnight to all.   *Exeunt Lords.*
MACBETH
  It will have blood they say: blood will have blood: 120
  Stones have been known to move, and trees to speak;

---

109 **overcome** take by surprise (*OED v.* 5b, citing this line)

110 **make me strange** estrange me (from)

111 **the disposition . . . owe** the nature or character which I possess, my true self

113 **ruby** redness, indicative of health. For Macbeth's dislike of pallor, compare 5.3.11 and 14–17.

114 **blanched** whitened

117 **Stand . . . going** 'Do not raise nice considerations of precedence in your leave-taking' (*OED* stand *v.* 74g). The Lady's urgency to be rid of her guests as quickly as possible contrasts with the formality at the beginning of the scene.
  order precedence, according to rank

120 **blood will have blood** proverbial, deriving from Genesis, 9.6: 'Whoso sheddeth man's blood, by man shall his blood be shed'. See Dent, B458. Macbeth's recourse to this familiar saying indicates weariness and resignation.

121 **Stones . . . move** Gaskill, 214–17, gives examples of providential revelations of secret murders by such means from contemporary accounts.
  trees to speak Vergil, *Aeneid*, 3.22–68, gives an example of a speaking tree which revealed a murder. See also Scot, *Discovery*, Bk 8, ch. 6, and Bk 9, ch. 18.

---

111 to] at *Hanmer*   owe] know *Johnson*   112 When now] Now when *Hanmer*   113 cheeks] cheek *Hanmer*   114 is] are *Malone*   sights] signs *F2–4*   115 and worse;] *Theobald;* and worse F; and worse. *Cam¹*   120] *Rowe;* F lines say: / Blood: /   blood they say:] blood, they say *Pope;* blood, they say; *Theobald;* blood. – They say, *Johnson*

Augures, and understood relations, have
By maggot-pies and choughs and rooks brought forth
The secret'st man of blood. What is the night?

LADY

Almost at odds with morning, which is which.   125

MACBETH

How sayst thou that Macduff denies his person
At our great bidding?

LADY   Did you send to him, sir?

MACBETH

I hear it by the way; but I will send.
There's not a one of them but in his house
I keep a servant fee'd. I will tomorrow,   130
And betimes I will, to the weïrd sisters.
More shall they speak: for now I am bent to know
By the worst means, the worst; for mine own good,

122 **Augures** auguries, predictions
  understood relations connections
  between incidents properly interpreted.
  Macbeth is perhaps thinking of the power
  of augurs or diviners to understand, as
  Johnson (*Miscellaneous*, 70) put it, 'how
  those things relate to each other, which
  have no visible combination or dependence' (cited by Muir).
123 **maggot-pies** magpies
  choughs birds of the crow family. These,
  like magpies and rooks, were birds used
  in sacrificial augury (Brooke) and also
  birds of ill omen.
124 **secret'st . . . blood** most carefully concealed murderer. Dover Wilson compares
  James VI and I's *Daemonologie*, 80–1:
  'As in a secret murther, if the deade
  carcase be at any time thereafter handled
  by the murtherer, it wil gush out of bloud,
  as if the blud were crying to the heaven
  for revenge of the murtherer, God having

appoynted that secret super-naturall
signe, for tryall of that secrete unnaturall
crime'.
  night time of night. Macbeth echoes
  Banquo's enquiry at 2.1.1.
125 **at odds** at variance, competing (*OED*
  odds *n*. 4)
126 **How sayst thou** how do you interpret it
127 **great bidding** important summons
128 **by the way** by chance. Macbeth's source
  of information is indicated at 130.
130 **fee'd** paid a fee
131 **betimes** early
132–3 **for . . . good** Braunmuller suggests a
  combination of two proverbial expressions: 'To know the worst is good' (Dent,
  W915) and 'It is good to fear the worst'
  (Dent, W912).
133 **worst means** Macbeth seems to
  recognize the implications of consulting
  the Sisters of his own accord.

122 and understood] that understood *Rowe;* that understand *Warburton*   123 maggot-pies and] mag-pies,
and by *Pope*   129 one] Thane *Theobald*   130 I keep] I'll keep *Collier*   131 weïrd] *Theobald;* weyard *F;*
wizard *F2–4;* wayward *Pope;* weird *Capell*

All causes shall give way. I am in blood
Stepped in so far, that should I wade no more,   135
Returning were as tedious as go o'er.
Strange things I have in head, that will to hand,
Which must be acted, ere they may be scanned.

LADY

You lack the season of all natures, sleep.

MACBETH

Come we'll to sleep. My strange and self-abuse   140
Is the initiate fear, that wants hard use.
We are yet but young in deed.   *Exeunt.*

3.5 *Thunder. Enter the three* WITCHES, *meeting* HECATE.

1 WITCH

Why how now Hecate? You look angerly.

134–5 **I . . . far** Proverbial. See Dent, F
565.1: 'Having wet his feet he cares not
how deep he goes', and S379: 'Over
shoes, over boots'. See *R3* 4.2.63–4: 'I
am in / So far in blood that sin will pluck
on sin'. This may also refer back to the
well-known line from Seneca, *Agamemnon*,
115: *'Per scelera semper sceleribus
tutum est iter'.* See 3.2.56 and n.
137 **will to hand** will come to hand, i.e. will
be put into execution
138 Hunter perceives a theatrical metaphor:
'There is not time to con the part, it must
be put into performance at once'.
scanned examined closely
139 **season** seasoning (*OED n.* 19)
140 **strange and self-abuse** Macbeth refers
either to his self-deception, viewing
the Ghost as a hallucination, or to his
self-destructive behaviour. Braunmuller
paraphrases: 'My inexplicable violation
of who and what I am'.

141 **initiate fear** the fear of a beginner or a
novice
wants lacks
3.5 This scene has long been ascribed to
Thomas Middleton rather than Shakespeare, although some recent scholars
have cast doubt on this view. It is in a
metre (tetrameter couplets) not used
previously by the Witches. For further
discussion see Appendix 1.
0.1 The Witches and Hecate enter from
different directions. The form of this SD
is rare in early modern drama outside the
works of Middleton and Heywood, but
does occur four times in Shakespeare,
in addition to 1.2 above (and excluding
Tim). See Taylor & Lavagnino, *Textual
Culture*, 384, and Appendix 1.
1 **angerly** angry. 'Angerly' is a rare word,
but it appears in *TGV* 1.2.62: 'How angerly
I taught my brow to frown', and *KJ* 4.1.81:
'Nor look upon the iron angerly'. *OED*

135 Stepped] Spent *F2–4*   136 go] going *Hanmer*   138 scanned] *(scand)*   139 natures] Nature's
Theobald   142 in deed] *Theobald;* indeed *F;* in deeds *Hanmer*   **3.5**] *Scena Quinta.*   0.1 HECATE] *F3–4;*
Hecat F1–2.   1 Hecate? . . . angerly.] *Ard²; Oxf; Hecat, . . . angerly? F*

HECATE

Have I not reason, beldams as you are,
Saucy and over-bold? How did you dare
To trade and traffic with Macbeth
In riddles and affairs of death; 5
And I, the mistress of your charms,
The close contriver of all harms,
Was never called to bear my part
Or show the glory of our art?
And, which is worse, all you have done 10
Hath been but for a wayward son,
Spiteful and wrathful, who, as others do,
Loves for his own ends, not for you.
But make amends now; get you gone,
And in the pit of Acheron 15
Meet me i'th' morning; thither he
Will come, to know his destiny.
Your vessels and your spells provide,
Your charms, and every thing beside.
I am for th'air: this night I'll spend 20
Unto a dismal and a fatal end.

records it mainly as an adverb, though in
Mac it appears to be an adjective.
2 **beldams** hags, unpleasant old women
4 **traffic** deal or conspire with (*OED* n. 2)
6 **charms** spells
7 **close** hidden, secret
11 **wayward** perverse, self-willed. Dover
Wilson considers that this description is
of 'no relevance to Macbeth; but seems
to echo jealous speeches by Hecate in
1.2 of Middleton's *Witch*'. The Sisters
are termed 'weyward' in the spelling of
Compositor A. See 1.3.32n.
15 **pit of Acheron** hell. Acheron was one of
the seven rivers of Hades.

18 **vessels** utensils
20 **for th'air** perhaps an indication that
Hecate exits flying. There is debate as to
whether 'flying' machinery was available at the Globe, where Simon Forman
saw *Macbeth* in 1611, although it was
at the Blackfriars (Smith, 414–18).
Braunmuller, 273, fn. 1, reviews the most
recent evidence. Astington considers that
it was almost certainly available in public
theatres well before this time.
spend use
21 **dismal** sinister, malign
fatal destined, but also causing death

2+ SP] *F3–4; Hec. F* reason, beldams] *Knight;* reason (Beldams) *F;* reason, Beldams, *Rowe* 2–3 are, . . .
over-bold?] *Capell;* are? . . . ouer-bold, *F;* are? . . . overbold! *Theobald* 11 wayward] weyward *Pope*
12 Spiteful] *Capell;* Spightfull *F* 21 dismal and a fatal] *F;* dismal, fatal *Pope;* dismal-fatal *Steevens*

> Great business must be wrought ere noon.
> Upon the corner of the moon
> There hangs a vaporous drop profound,
> I'll catch it ere it come to ground;   25
> And that, distilled by magic sleights,
> Shall raise such artificial sprites
> As by the strength of their illusion,
> Shall draw him on to his confusion.
> He shall spurn fate, scorn death, and bear   30
> His hopes 'bove wisdom, grace and fear;
> And you all know, security
> Is mortals' chiefest enemy.   *Music, and a song*
> Hark, I am called: my little spirit, see,   34
> Sits in a foggy cloud, and stays for me.   [*Exit.*]
> *Sing within.* 'Come away, come away, *etc.*'

1 WITCH

> Come, let's make haste, she'll soon be back again.   *Exeunt.*

---

24 **vaporous drop** assumed to mean the *virus lunare* (Lucan, *Pharsalia*, vi.669), 'a foam which the moon was supposed to shed on particular herbs, or other objects, when strongly solicited by enchantment' (Steevens). In Lucan, this foam is used by the witch Erictho for a spell. For *vaporous* compare *Luc* 771: 'O hateful, vaporous and foggy Night', and *MM* 4.1.58: 'The vaporous night approaches'.
profound with deep or hidden qualities

26 **sleights** tricks

27 **artificial** either cunning, artful (*OED adj.* 9) or produced by art rather than nature (*adj.* 1)

28 **illusion** deceptive impression

29 **confusion** overthrow or ruin (*OED n.* 1)

31 **'bove** in the sense of beyond. Macbeth's hopes will exceed those dictated by wisdom, etc.

32 **security** over-confidence. See Dent, W152: 'The way to be safe is never to be secure'. See *JC* 2.3.7: 'Security gives way to conspiracy', and *TC* 2.2.14–15: 'The wound of peace is surety, / Surety secure'.

35 SD2 The opening words of this song, sung offstage, are from a song given in full in Middleton's *The Witch*, and constitute one of the main pieces of evidence adduced for Middleton's authorship of the scene. Brooke, 162–5, includes the whole of the song in his text.

---

26 sleights] *Collier;* slights *F*   27 raise] rise *F2*   33 mortals'] *Theobald;* mortals *F;* mortal's *Rowe*
SD] SPIRITS (*singing dispersedly within*) Come away, come away, / Hecate, Hecate, Hecate, come away. *Oxf; Music, and a song* [, *'Come away, come away', within.*] *Cam¹*   35 SD] *Capell*   36] *Pope; F lines* be / againe. /   36 SD] *Oxf adds 'The Song' etc. from Middleton's 'The Witch' (35 lines)*

3.6   *Enter* LENNOX *and another* Lord.

LENNOX

My former speeches have but hit your thoughts
Which can interpret further. Only I say
Things have been strangely borne. The gracious Duncan
Was pitied of Macbeth; marry, he was dead.
And the right-valiant Banquo walked too late,   5
Whom you may say, if't please you, Fleance killed,
For Fleance fled: men must not walk too late.
Who cannot want the thought how monstrous
It was for Malcolm and for Donalbain
To kill their gracious father? Damned fact,   10
How it did grieve Macbeth! Did he not straight,
In pious rage, the two delinquents tear,
That were the slaves of drink and thralls of sleep?
Was not that nobly done? Ay, and wisely too:
For 'twould have angered any heart alive   15
To hear the men deny't. So that I say,

3.6 The role of Lennox in this sinister scene is ambiguous. He is often regarded as the observer of Macbeth's iniquities, exposing the conditions of tyranny in his indirect and ironic style of speech. But Kinney states that, having been Macbeth's most trusted thane, 'clearly he is spying for Macbeth' (*Lies*, 140). See also Muir's note on 14. For discussion of the question of narrative inconsistency between this scene and 4.1 see pp. 69–70.

1   **hit** agreed or coincided with (*OED v.* 16)
3   **borne** managed, conducted. Compare *Cor* 4.7.21: 'he bears all things fairly'.
5   **right-valiant** very valiant
8   **want** lack, fail to have. Lennox really means the opposite: 'Who can fail to think that . . . '. In early modern English two negatives normally intensify the meaning rather than cancelling it out (Crystal & Crystal, 295); here, the negative force of *want* (= lack) creates such intensification.

10   **Damned** damnèd
     fact crime (*OED n.* 1c)
12   **pious** dutiful, loyal. Lennox is ironically employing Macbeth's own perspective on his actions here.
     tear destroy
13   **thralls** slaves
15–16 **For . . . deny't** 'He killed them so that men should not be angered by hearing them deny it' (Hunter). This sentence illustrates the double-talk and equivocation that become the language of tyranny.

3.6] *Scaena Sexta.*   1] *Rowe; F lines* Speeches, / Thoughts, /   2 further] *Johnson;* farther *F*   3 borne] born *F4*   5 right-valiant] *Theobald;* right valiant *F*   6 if 't] if it *Capell*   8 Who] You *Hanmer*   monstrous] monstrous too *Pope;* monsterous *Capell*   11 . . . Macbeth!] *Capell;* it did greeue *Macbeth? F;* did it grieve Macbeth? *Pope*   14 not that] that not *F3–4*

He has borne all things well, and I do think
That had he Duncan's sons under his key,
As, an't please heaven, he shall not, they should find
What 'twere to kill a father; so should Fleance.   20
But peace; for from broad words, and 'cause he failed
His presence at the tyrant's feast, I hear
Macduff lives in disgrace. Sir, can you tell
Where he bestows himself?

LORD   The son of Duncan,
From whom this tyrant holds the due of birth,   25
Lives in the English court, and is received
Of the most pious Edward with such grace
That the malevolence of fortune nothing
Takes from his high respect. Thither Macduff
Is gone, to pray the holy king, upon his aid   30
To wake Northumberland, and warlike Siward,
That by the help of these, with Him above
To ratify the work, we may again
Give to our tables meat, sleep to our nights,
Free from our feasts and banquets bloody knives;   35
Do faithful homage, and receive free honours,
All which we pine for now. And this report

---

19 **an't** if it. For 'and' used as a synonym for 'if', see *OED* and *conj. formerly prep.* C 1a.

21 **broad** outspoken, unrestrained. Braunmuller compares 3.4.21.

21–2 **failed ... feast** Compare Macbeth's injunction to Banquo at 3.1.27.

24 **bestows** locates (*OED* bestow *v.* 1)

25 **holds** witholds
   due of birth birthright

27 **pious Edward** Edward the Confessor (King of England 1042–66), pious in the modern sense

28–9 **nothing / Takes** does not derogate

30 **upon** with (the use of) (*OED* upon *prep.* 11i)

31 **Northumberland ... Siward** Northumberland was (and is) a county in the north of England. Siward was the family name of the earls of Northumberland; *warlike Siward*, who enters the play in 5.4, was an earl of Northumberland who, historically, died in 1055, two years before Macbeth. For an account of Malcolm and Macduff gaining support from Edward, see Holinshed, 2.175.

33 **ratify** validate

35 'free our feasts and banquets from bloody knives'

---

17 has] *(ha's)*   18 his] the *F2–4*   19 should] shall *F2–4*   24 son] *Theobald;* Sonnes *F;* sons *F4*   26 Lives] Live *F2–4*   is] are *Rowe*   30 upon] on *Capell*   31 Siward] *Theobald;* Seyward *F*   36 free] fair *Collier*

Hath so exasperate their king, that he
Prepares for some attempt of war.

LENNOX

Sent he to Macduff?   40

LORD

He did. And with an absolute, 'Sir, not I'
The cloudy messenger turns me his back
And hums, as who should say, 'You'll rue the time
That clogs me with this answer'.

LENNOX   And that well might

Advise him to a caution, t'hold what distance   45
His wisdom can provide. Some holy angel
Fly to the court of England and unfold
His message ere he come, that a swift blessing
May soon return to this our suffering country,
Under a hand accursed.

LORD   I'll send my prayers with him.   50

Exeunt.

38 **exasperate** exasperated, enraged. Muir
compares *TC* 5.1.29: 'Why art thou then
exasperate?'
    their king often emended to 'the king',
because Lennox's reply clearly refers to
Macbeth. But since Edward is the king
discussed throughout the Lord's speech,
and in Act 4 is preparing for war, it makes
more sense for him to be referred to here,
although the transition to Macbeth by
Lennox is abrupt. Brooke, 52–3, and
Braunmuller, 277, both retain *their* and
discuss the reading in relation to textual
problems in the play.
39 **attempt** attack, warlike assault (*OED
n.* 3a, citing this line)
41 **absolute** unconditional, uncompromising
(*OED a.* 12a). Compare *MM* 3.1.5: 'Be
absolute for death'.
    Sir, not I Macduff's words

42 **cloudy** sullen, scowling (*OED adj.* 6b).
See *1H4* 3.2.81–3: 'But rather drowsed
and hung their eyelids down . . . As
cloudy men use to their adversaries'.
    turns . . . back *me* is an ethical dative,
used for emphasis. The Lord is amazed at
Macduff's behaviour.
43 **hums** as from embarrassment (*OED* hum
v.[1] 2c). See *Cor* 5.1.48–9: 'to bite his
lip / And hum at good Cominius much
unhearts me'.
44 **clogs** burdens, obstructs (*OED* clog *v.* 3),
perhaps referring to the idea that a messenger
will suffer for bringing bad news (as in 5.3)
    that refers to the messenger's response
45 **him** i.e. Macduff
    distance i.e. between himself and Macbeth
49–50 **suffering country** / **Under** *suffering*
may qualify *country* and also govern
Under, i.e. 'suffering under an accursed
hand' (Brooke).

38 exasperate] exasperated *Rowe;* exasp'rated *Pope*   their] the *Hanmer*   39 of war] *om. Pope*   41 'Sir, not I']
Pope subst.; Sir, not I *F;* Sir-not-I *Capell*   45 t'hold] t hold *F*   49 suffering country] country suffering *Capell*

4.1   *Thunder. Enter the three* WITCHES.

1 WITCH
Thrice the brinded cat hath mewed.
2 WITCH
Thrice, and once the hedge-pig whined.
3 WITCH
Harpier cries, ''Tis time, 'tis time.'
1 WITCH
Round about the cauldron go;
In the poisoned entrails throw.   5
Toad, that under cold stone
Days and nights has thirty-one,
Sweltered venom sleeping got,
Boil thou first i'th' charmed pot.

4.1 This scene, the most spectacular in the play, has often been set '*in a dark Cave*' (Rowe), where the Witches concoct a spell in their cauldron and summon up apparitions who prophesy in enigmatic terms. This action has been seen as an 'anti-feast' (Hawkins, 166), an inversion of the banquet in 3.4. Ide (349) discusses the Witches' spell as bringing together the concepts of feasting and slaughter. The iambic lines of Hecate and the First Witch (39–43, 124–31) and the Song (43) may well be interpolations by Middleton. For full discussion see Appendix 1.

1   **brinded** tawny, but marked with streaks of a different colour, perhaps a kind of tabby

2   **hedge-pig** hedgehog (the earliest citation in *OED* for this rare word). Elsewhere Shakespeare uses 'hedgehog', in *R3* 1.2.104, *MND* 2.2.10 and *Tem* 2.2.10, always in a derogatory sense.

3   **Harpier** another familiar, like Gray-Malkin and Paddock in 1.1

4   **cauldron** a familiar cooking utensil in the period. Fitzpatrick draws attention to the

'fusion of the familiar and the exotic' (47) in the ingredients. The cauldron might have been raised by mechanical means through the stage trapdoor. Macbeth's question at 105 suggests this.

6–8 **Toad ... venom** In *News from Scotland* Agnes Tompson claimed to have 'collected and gathered' a toad's venom in her attempt to bewitch the King to death (16). Toads were popularly believed to be poisonous (and some species are, but not generally those native to Britain), perhaps because their skins secrete a substance which can sting anyone handling them. See *AYL* 2.1.13: 'the toad, ugly and venomous', and Topsell, *Serpents*, 'Of the Toade', 187.

7   **thirty-one** perhaps referring to the length of a month

8   **Sweltered** exuded like sweat, oozing (*OED ppl. a.* 1 gives this as the first citation and a Shakespearean coinage, though there are many earlier uses of 'sweltered' to mean 'bathed in, or oppressed with, great heat')

9   **charmed** charmèd

4.1] *Actus Quartus. Scena Prima.*   1 brinded] brindled *Cam¹* 2 Thrice] Twice *Theobald*   hedge-pig] *(*Hedge-Pigge*)* ; Hedges Pigge *F2–4*   3 ''Tis . . . time.'] *Cam;* 'tis . . . time. *F*   5 throw.] *Rowe;* throw *F* 6 cold] the cold *Rowe;* coldest *Steevens*   7 has] *(*ha's*);* hast *Capell*   8 Sweltered] *(*Sweltred*)*

ALL

> Double, double, toil and trouble; 10
> Fire burn, and cauldron bubble.

2 WITCH

> Fillet of a fenny snake,
> In the cauldron boil and bake;
> Eye of newt and toe of frog,
> Wool of bat and tongue of dog, 15
> Adder's fork and blind-worm's sting,
> Lizard's leg and howlet's wing,
> For a charm of powerful trouble,
> Like a hell-broth boil and bubble.

ALL

> Double, double, toil and trouble; 20
> Fire burn, and cauldron bubble.

3 WITCH

> Scale of dragon, tooth of wolf,
> Witch's mummy, maw and gulf

10 **Double, double** Fitzpatrick, 49, suggests an allusion to 'double beer', which was especially strong because boiled twice. According to her, Queen Elizabeth attempted to ban the practice of brewing extra strong beer.

12 **Fillet** thick slice
fenny from the fens, or muddy

13 **boil and bake** both cooking processes done in cauldrons. Ovens were owned only by bakers and great houses.

14 **newt** small lizard-like amphibian

15 **Wool** soft under-hair, or down. See *OED n.* 1c. *EEBO* records the word used in this sense from 1555 (Pietro Martire d'Anghiera, *The decades of the new world or west India*).

16 **fork** forked tongue
blind-worm's referring to a slow-worm, a snake-like legless lizard. See *MND* 2.2.11: 'Newts and blind-worms, do no wrong'. Both creatures were believed to be poisonous. See Topsell, *Serpents*, 'Of the Neute or Water-Lizard', 212, 'Of the Scytal', 232.

17 **howlet's** young owl's

22 **Scale ... dragon** example of an exotic ingredient, as cited in 4n.

23 **mummy** medicinal substance, made from mummified (embalmed) flesh, usually that of human beings (*OED n.* 1). Fitzpatrick, 48, cites the London *Pharmacopoeia* (1618) on its quasi-miraculous medicinal properties. The use of exhumed bodies for witchcraft was a capital offence in the witchcraft statute of 1604 (1 Jac. 1, c.12). See also James VI and I's *Daemonologie* on how the devil causes witches to 'joynt dead corpses & to make powders thereof' (43). For mummy as an ingredient in magical recipes, see *Oth* 3.4.75–7.
maw throat or gullet (*OED n.*[1] 3a)

10, 20, 35 double, toil] double toil *Steevens* 23 Witch's] *(* Witches*);* Witches' *Theobald*

Of the ravined salt-sea shark,
Root of hemlock digged i'th' dark,   25
Liver of blaspheming Jew,
Gall of goat and slips of yew
Slivered in the moon's eclipse,
Nose of Turk and Tartar's lips,
Finger of birth-strangled babe   30
Ditch-delivered by a drab,
Make the gruel thick and slab.
Add thereto a tiger's chawdron,
For th'ingredience of our cauldron.

gulf whirlpool, used figuratively for that which swallows up anything (*OED n.* 3), but perhaps a hendiadys for 'gulf-like maw' (Braunmuller).

24 **ravined** glutted with prey. See 2.4.28.
shark regarded as a creature of voracious appetite. See *STM* 6.95–8: 'other ruffians . . . Would shark on you, and men, like ravenous fishes, / Would feed on one another'.

25 **hemlock** well-known poisonous plant, used medically as a powerful sedative
digged i'th' dark because the time when such ingredients are collected was believed to affect their efficacy. See *Ham* 3.2.250–1: 'Thou mixture rank, of midnight weeds collected, / With Hecate's ban thrice blasted, thrice infected'.

26 **blaspheming Jew** because Jews, like Turks and Tartars, denied the divinity of Christ

27 **Gall** bile, the secretion of the liver, then thought to be poisonous
slips of yew twigs from the yew tree, poisonous and commonly associated with death

28 **Slivered** cut or torn off as a sliver or thin slice. See *KL* 4.2.35–6: 'She that herself will sliver and disbranch / From her material sap'.

moon's eclipse regarded as an unlucky time for lawful activities. Compare Milton, *Paradise Lost*, 1.594–8: 'As when the sun . . . from behind the moon / In dim eclipse disastrous twilight sheds'.

29 **Turk . . . Tartar's** Turks and Tartars are infidels, commonly associated together. See *MV* 4.1.31–2: 'stubborn Turks, and Tartars never trained / To offices of gentle courtesy'. Their characterizing body parts would be especially potent in a spell, since, like the *Jew* (26) and the *birth-strangled babe* (30) they were not protected by baptism.

30 **birth-strangled** killed at birth, hence unbaptized

31 **Ditch-delivered** born in a ditch, without the presence of a midwife or assistant, and hence likely to be illegitimate
drab slut or prostitute

32 **gruel** broth of oatmeal to which other ingredients can be added
slab semi-solid (*OED a.*[1], the first citation in this sense), but perhaps with suggestions of wet, dirty (as in *OED* slabby *a.*[1], with citations from 1542) or befouled, as with saliva (*OED* slabber *v.* 1 and 2)

33 **chawdron** entrails of an animal, especially as used for food (*OED n.* 2)

34 **th'ingredience** See 1.7.11n.

24 salt-sea] *Capell;* salt Sea *F*   28 Slivered] *(*Sliuer'd*);* Silver'd *Rowe*   33 chawdron] chaudron *Ard²*
34 th'ingredience] th'ingredients *Rowe*   cauldron] *(*Cawdron*)*

ALL

   Double, double, toil and trouble;   35
   Fire burn, and cauldron bubble.

2 WITCH

   Cool it with a baboon's blood,
   Then the charm is firm and good.

       Enter HECATE *and the other three* WITCHES.

HECATE

   O, well done. I commend your pains,
   And everyone shall share i'th' gains.   40
   And now about the cauldron sing,
   Like elves and fairies in a ring,
   Enchanting all that you put in.
     Music and a song. 'Black spirits, *etc.*'
       [*Exeunt Hecate and the three other Witches.*]

2 WITCH

   By the pricking of my thumbs,
   Something wicked this way comes.   45
   Open locks, whoever knocks.

38.1 This SD and Hecate's speech are often thought to be later interpolations into the text made before F was printed (see Appendix 1). The SD has sometimes been emended to '*Enter Hecate to the other three witches*', so as not to overcrowd the stage with witches. Hecate, however, is not a witch, and the extra three may be needed for the song.

43 **Enchanting** casting a spell over

43 SD1 ***Music . . . song*** The full lyrics to this song ('Black spirits and white') appear in Middleton, *The Witch*, 5.2.63–79, though, as Muir says, 'It is to be hoped that this song was altered for *Macbeth*, as some lines are relevant only to the plot of Middleton's play.' Brooke prints the whole song. No SD is given in F for the exit of Hecate and the extra witches, but they have no more lines, and it makes more sense to have them leave. Rowe's engraving of this scene (1703) does not show them present.

44 **pricking** tingling (probably an established superstition; *OED* notes the phrase 'pricking of . . . one's thumbs' as 'an intuitive feeling or hunch; a premonition or foreboding' with reference to this line)

44–5 Though editors (e.g. Muir, Oxf) sometimes add a SD such as '*Knocking*' after *comes*, this is unnecessarily literalistic. The Second Witch's intuition of Macbeth's arrival is more uncanny without it.

38.1] *Enter* HECATE *to the other three Witches.* / Globe HECATE] *(Hecat)* 39 SP] *F3–4; Hec.* F
43 SD2] Ard²; *Hecate retires.* / Globe; *Exit Hecate.* / Dyce 45 comes.] comes. – *Knocking* Ard²; comes.
[*Knock within*] Oxf

Enter MACBETH.

MACBETH

How now, you secret, black and midnight hags?
What is't you do?

ALL   A deed without a name.

MACBETH

I conjure you, by that which you profess,
Howe'er you come to know it, answer me;   50
Though you untie the winds and let them fight
Against the churches, though the yeasty waves
Confound and swallow navigation up,
Though bladed corn be lodged and trees blown down,
Though castles topple on their warders' heads,   55
Though palaces and pyramids do slope
Their heads to their foundations, though the treasure

49–60 **I . . . you** Macbeth's speech, crediting
the Witches with great powers of black
magic, has been compared to Medea's
claims for powers she can exercise with
Hecate's assistance, in Ovid, *Met.*, 7.192–
209, in Seneca, *Medea*, 759–68, and
also in Jonson, *The Masque of Queens*,
213–20, in that it consists of a list of
adynata (feats beyond natural causation).
Wills (63–5) discusses these parallels.

49 **conjure** constrain, by appealing to something sacred (*OED v.* 3), entreat solemnly
profess claim to have knowledge of or
skill in (*OED v.* 6)

52 **yeasty** foamy, frothy (*OED adj.* 3, where
this is the first citation for this meaning,
though Marston uses the word to mean
'froth-covered' in *The History of Antonio
and Mellida* (?1599), Ind.: 'as slovenly as
the yeasty breast of an ale-knight')

53 **navigation** shipping, vessels collectively
(*OED n.* 5a)

54 **bladed corn** new corn, when the blade
protects the ear. Muir notes a reference in
Scot, *Discovery*, Bk 1, ch. 4. to the power

of witches to 'transferre corne in the
blade from one place to another' (10).
lodged beaten down, flattened

55 **warders'** Warders are guardians or keepers.

56 **pyramids** Braunmuller notes that 'Shakespeare and other contemporary writers
probably confused pyramids with obelisks'.
Obelisk or pillar seems to be meant in
TNK 5.3.79–80: 'Palamon had Arcite's
body / Within an inch o'th' pyramid'. But
either sense would work here.
slope bend down (*OED v.*[1] 3, where this
is the first citation for the verb in a
transitive sense). The word is not found
elsewhere in Shakespeare.

57–9 **though . . . sicken** i.e. though the
wealth of creation is so utterly ruined that
destruction itself falls ill through excess.
Macbeth's hyperbolical recklessness here
has often been compared with Lear's all-
encompassing rage at 3.2.1–9, esp. 8–9:
'Crack nature's moulds, all germens spill
at once / That make ingrateful man'.

57 **treasure** may mean treasury, store-house
(*OED n.* 3)

---

47 hags?] hags! *Ard²*   48+ SP] ALL THE WITCHES *Oxf*   52 yeasty] *(yesty)*   55 warders'] *(warders)*

Of Nature's germen tumble altogether
Even till destruction sicken, answer me
To what I ask you.

1 WITCH   Speak.

2 WITCH   Demand.

3 WITCH   We'll answer.   60

1 WITCH

Say, if thou'dst rather hear it from our mouths,
Or from our masters?

MACBETH   Call 'em, let me see 'em.

1 WITCH

Pour in sow's blood that hath eaten
Her nine farrow; grease that's sweaten
From the murderer's gibbet, throw   65
Into the flame.

ALL   Come, high or low,
Thy self and office deftly show.   *Thunder*

---

58 **germen** collective noun, meaning seed or
'life-forming elements' (Crystal & Crystal).
Curry (30–49) suggests, with reference
to St Augustine, *De Trinitate*, 3.8, that
this refers to the *rationes seminales*,
'the material essences which correspond
to the exemplars in God's mind' (31).
St Augustine's discussion concerns the
power of demons to work magic. Hankins
(34–8) uses this reference in a discussion of Renaissance conceptions of the
material composition of life. Compare
Banquo's reference to the 'seeds of time'
(1.3.58).
altogether completely, utterly
59 **sicken** become ill through over-
consumption. Brooke compares Donne,
Holy Sonnet 10: 'Death, thou shalt die'.
60 **Speak … answer** Palfrey and Stern, in
their discussion of short-line cues, comment on the 'metrical struggle' in this

line and those following, suggesting that
Macbeth has to be 'prompted into words'
by the First Witch at 61–2 (145).
62 **masters** evidently, the Apparitions, or
the powers that govern them. Kermode
compares *Tem* 5.1.41: 'Weak masters
though ye be', and Spenser, *FQ*, 3.8.4:
'Where she was wont her Sprights to
entertaine / The maisters of her art'.
'The term is technical and applies to the
helpers of magicians' (Kermode, 213).
63–4 **eaten … farrow** Sows (and other
animals) on occasion eat their young.
64 **farrow** litter of young pigs
sweaten exuded. This is an irregularly
formed word, to rhyme with *eaten*.
65 **gibbet** gallows, or the structure from
which the bodies of executed criminals
were suspended for public display
67 **office** duty, or the performance of a duty
(*OED n.* 3b)

---

58 germen] *(Germaine)*; germains *Pope*; germins *Theobald*; germen *Globe*   altogether] all together
Pope   61 thou'dst] *Capell*; th'hadst *F*   62 masters?] *Pope*; Masters. *F*; masters'? *Capell*   65 murderer's]
*(*Murderers)*   67 SD1, 2] *Thunder* / 1. *Apparition, an Armed Head. F; Thunder.* [*Enter*] FIRST APPARITION,
an armed Head. Cam[1]

239

[*Enter*] FIRST APPARITION: *an armed head.*

MACBETH

Tell me, thou unknown power –

1 WITCH   He knows thy thought:

Hear his speech, but say thou nought.

1 APPARITION

Macbeth, Macbeth, Macbeth. Beware Macduff,   70

Beware the Thane of Fife. Dismiss me. Enough.

He descends.

MACBETH

Whate'er thou art, for thy good caution, thanks;

Thou hast harped my fear aright. But one word more –

1 WITCH

He will not be commanded. Here's another,   74

More potent than the first.   *Thunder*

[*Enter*] SECOND APPARITION: *a bloody child.*

2 APPARITION

Macbeth, Macbeth, Macbeth.

67.1 *an armed head* a head wearing a helmet. This may represent Macbeth's head, as cut off by Macduff at the end of the play, or the head of Macdonald, former thane of Cawdor, executed by Macbeth at the beginning of the play, both the heads of traitors, or Macduff himself, Macbeth's own executioner. But as Brooke says, the three Apparitions 'remain, as they undoubtedly should, cryptic'. Rosenberg, 514–15, describes some ways in which the Apparitions have been staged, for instance emerging from the steam of the cauldron, as optical illusions created by mirrors or projections, or as puppets, effigies or dolls. See also Dessen, *Rescripting*, 156–8, on more recent stagings.

69 The insistence on Macbeth's silence may create a heightened sense of expectation,

and also stress the mysterious power of the Apparitions.

71 SD Thomson suggests that SDs requiring descents refer to the 'more elaborate trap-doors' at the Blackfriars or the second Globe, rather than the first Globe (153). A descent to hell may be suggested. See also Dessen & Thomson, 'descend'.

73 **harped** guessed, given voice to (*OED* harp *v.* 7, the first citation in this sense and Shakespeare's only such use). The sense of a harp string having been plucked is close behind this usage. Macbeth's fear (about Macduff's loyalty) has not hitherto been expressed, but the Witches have sounded out his innermost secrets.

75.1 *a bloody child* This Apparition has multi-ple resonances, and may represent, as Braunmuller suggests, Macduff, *Untimely*

68 power –] *Rowe*; power. *F*   70] *Rowe*; *F lines* ³*Macbeth:* / *Macduffe,* /   71 SD] *Descends* / *Rowe*
73 more –] *Rowe*; more. *F*   75 SD1, 2] *Thunder* / 2 *Apparition, a Bloody Childe. F; Thunder.* [*Enter*]
SECOND APPARITION, *a bloody Child. Cam¹*

MACBETH

Had I three ears, I'd hear thee.

2 APPARITION

Be bloody, bold and resolute: laugh to scorn
The power of man, for none of woman born   79
Shall harm Macbeth.   *Descends.*

MACBETH

Then live, Macduff: what need I fear of thee?
But yet I'll make assurance double sure,
And take a bond of fate: thou shalt not live,
That I may tell pale-hearted fear it lies
And sleep in spite of thunder.   *Thunder*

[*Enter*] THIRD APPARITION: *a child crowned,
with a tree in his hand.*

What is this,   85

That rises like the issue of a king
And wears upon his baby-brow the round
And top of sovereignty?

ALL   Listen, but speak not to't.

ripped from his mother's womb (5.8.16), Fleance, threatened with murder, Banquo's potential children who will succeed Macbeth, and any children who threaten Macbeth. It also recalls Macbeth's Lady at 1.7.54–9.

82 **assurance double sure** Macbeth will double the assurance that (as he believes) Macduff cannot harm him by killing him. His longing for certainty reflects back on Hecate's mocking words at 3.5.32–3, and the reiteration of *double* relates his language to the idiom of the Witches and their incantation earlier in the scene. See pp. 49–50.

83 **bond** contract, legal guarantee. Sokol and Sokol, 'bond', see an allusion to the 'double bond', a deed of obligation ensuring timely repayment: 'a typical penalty for a money bond was forfeiture of property worth twice as much as the amount of the debt'. See also Kinney, *Lies*, 151–2, on the 'bond of manrent', and Macbeth at 3.2.49–50.
   thou referring to Macduff

84 **it** fear personified

85.1–2 *a child . . . hand* This seems to refer to Malcolm, advancing with a branch from Birnam Wood.

86 **issue** descendant

87–8 **round . . . sovereignty** hendiadys for crown

77 I'd] *(Il'd)*   82 assurance] *Pope;* assurance: *F*   85 SD1, 2] *Thunder / 3 Apparition, a Childe Crowned, with a Tree in his hand. F; Thunder. [Enter]* THIRD APPARITION, *a Child crowned, with a tree in his hand. Cam¹*   85–6 What . . . king] *Rowe; one line F*   87 baby-brow] *(Baby-brow)*

3 APPARITION

Be lion-mettled, proud, and take no care
Who chafes, who frets, or where conspirers are. 90
Macbeth shall never vanquished be, until
Great Birnam Wood to high Dunsinane Hill
Shall come against him.   *Descend*[*s*].
MACBETH   That will never be.
Who can impress the forest, bid the tree
Unfix his earth-bound root? Sweet bodements, good. 95
Rebellious dead, rise never till the Wood
Of Birnam rise, and our high-placed Macbeth
Shall live the lease of nature, pay his breath
To time, and mortal custom. Yet my heart
Throbs to know one thing: tell me, if your art 100

89 **lion-mettled** with the temperament of
a lion, i.e. courageous
92 **Birnam Wood** F spells this name
Byrnam, Byrnan, Byrnane, Birnane and
Birnan. 'Birnam' is the usual modern
form. Birnam is 'a hill opposite Dunkeld
on the Tay, visible from Dunsinane 12
miles off' (Dover Wilson).
Dunsinane Hill a peak in the Sidlaw
Hills, north-east of Perth, on which
now stand the ruins of an ancient fort.
Dunsinane is here accented on the second
syllable, but elsewhere on the first.
93–100 **That . . . art** Macbeth, completing
the Third Apparition's line and seemingly
absorbed into its world, speaks for the
first time in the play in a long series
of rhymed couplets. Palfrey and Stern
comment on Shakespeare's 'new manner'
in these rhymes, which do not complete
the thought of the couplet (480). Kittredge
notes that Macbeth 'in eager acceptance
of the oracle, continues it in the same
rhymed form', thus identifying himself
with the spirits he has consulted.

94 **impress** conscript, enlist for military
service
95 **Sweet bodements** happy or fortunate
omens. *OED* bodement *n.* 1 gives this as
the first citation in this sense, though it also
appears in *TC* 5.3.79–80: 'This foolish,
dreaming, superstitious girl / Makes all
these bodements'.
96 **Rebellious dead** sometimes emended (e.g.
by Dyce, Hudson and Kittredge, following Theobald) to 'rebellion's head'. But
Macbeth's recollection of Banquo's ghost
and his horror of those who 'rise again / With
twenty mortal murders on their crowns'
(3.4.78–9) justifies the retention of F.
97 **our high-placed Macbeth** Macbeth's
curious use of the third person may imply
the supreme self-confidence of tragic
hubris. Oxf's emendation, 'on's high place',
is ingenious, but not strictly necessary.
98 **lease of nature** allotted term of natural
life, continuing the legal imagery from
bond of fate (83)
99 **mortal custom** normal length of mortal
life (Braunmuller)

89 lion-mettled] *(* lyon metled*)*   92 Dunsinane] *(*Dunsmane*)*; *Dunsinan Oxf¹*   93 SD] *Rowe*   95 bodements, good] *(*boadments, good:*)*; boadments! good! *Rowe;* bodements! good! *Oxf*   96 Rebellious dead]
Rebellious head *Theobald;* Rebellion's head *Hanmer*   97 our high-placed] on's high place *Oxf*

Can tell so much, shall Banquo's issue ever
Reign in this kingdom?

ALL   Seek to know no more.

MACBETH

I will be satisfied. Deny me this,
And an eternal curse fall on you. Let me know.
Why sinks that cauldron, and what noise is this?   105

Hautboys

1 WITCH

Show.

2 WITCH

Show.

3 WITCH

Show.

ALL

Show his eyes, and grieve his heart;
Come like shadows, so depart.   110

A show of eight kings, the last with a glass
in his hand; and BANQUO.

MACBETH

Thou art too like the spirit of Banquo; down:

105 **sinks that cauldron** clear evidence that a cauldron was among the props for this scene, and could be lowered into the trap area
105 SD For a description of the hautboy, see 1.6.01n. As in *AC* 4.3.12, where '*Music of the hautboys is under the stage*' as a prelude to the God Hercules' desertion of Antony, the sound is ominous, and suggestive of the underworld. See Wilson & Calore, 'hoboy'.
110.1–2 *This is the most elaborate spectacle in the play, expressing 'a vision of order and power, of the continuity Macbeth

has violated' (Leggatt, 164). Rosenberg, 522–5, describes stagings designed to produce a 'ritual aura of ceremonial awe' (522) by means of gauzes, backlighting, reflecting mirrors and masks. The dumb-show depicts the eight kings who had ruled Scotland at the time of the play's composition, but excludes Mary, Queen of Scots, executed on Elizabeth's implicit order in 1587, perhaps because her appearance here would have recalled this. For the political implications of this dumb-show, see Brooke, 73–4. For an exploration of the problems created by

105 SD] *Hautboys.* [*Cauldron descends*] / Rowe; *Hautboys. The Cauldron sinks. Oxf* 110.1–2] *Oxf; A shew of eight Kings, and Banquo last, with a glasse in his hand. F;* [*Enter*] *a show of eight kings, and* [*the*] *last with a glass in his hand* [*; Banquo's Ghost following.*] *Cam¹*

243

Thy crown does sear mine eyeballs. And thy hair,
Thou other gold-bound brow, is like the first.
A third is like the former. Filthy hags,
Why do you show me this? – A fourth? Start, eyes!   115
What, will the line stretch out to th' crack of doom?
Another yet? A seventh? I'll see no more;
And yet the eighth appears, who bears a glass
Which shows me many more; and some I see
That twofold balls and treble sceptres carry.   120

its image of royal lineage, see Kastan, 'Name', 168–9, 178–81. F's SD needs emendation, because 118 makes it clear that it is the eighth king bearing the glass, not Banquo.

110.1 *glass* There are different views as to what this might have been: a 'magic crystal permitting visions of the future' (Braunmuller, citing *OED n.* 8e), a perspective glass in which the monarch (if present) might have seen his own reflection (Stern, *Making*, 32–3), or a mirror reflecting the other seven kings. Thomson, 154, is properly sceptical of this latter view. The magic glass used for divination seems most likely. See *MM* 2.2.95–6: 'a prophet / Looks in a glass that shows . . . future evils'. Clark relates the show of kings and particularly the glass to the play's preoccupation with 'the workings of human vision' (*Vanities*, 236). James Shapiro (in correspondence) suggests a reference to the royal mirror on display at Richmond Palace which supposedly had magical properties (described in several entries in William Brenchley Rye, ed., *England as Seen by Foreigners in the Days of Elizabeth and James the First* (1865), 128, 134, 172, 272 n. 133).

111 **Thou . . . Banquo** Macbeth does not yet see Banquo's ghost, but already he recognizes in the first king the truth of the Witches' prophecy.

112 **sear** burn (*OED v.* 3a)

hair F 'hair' has sometimes been emended to 'heir' which could be spelt 'hair' in the period, and Macbeth's preoccupation with succession makes 'heir' fit. But as Braunmuller points out, the address to the second king in *thy* and *thou* makes 'heir' less likely. 'Air', proposed by Johnson (*Miscellaneous*, Note XXXVI, 74), is also a possibility. For a modern listener, all these meanings could be entertained, though Cercignani, 332–5, is not certain that pre-vocalic *h-* would have been unvoiced in these instances.

113 **gold-bound** i.e. with a crown

116 **crack of doom** crack of thunder announcing the Last Judgement. See 2.3.78n.

120 **twofold . . . sceptres** a much disputed phrase, perhaps referring to James's unification of the thrones of England and Scotland. The *balls* may be orbs, golden globes with a crown on top held in the hand, or the 'mounds' (orbs) on top of the English and Scottish royal crowns. Cases can be made for the twofold balls as symbolic of James's double coronation (in both England and Scotland) and treble sceptres as referring to the kingdoms of England, Scotland and Wales, but there are many possibilities. See Lyle, who makes a persuasive case for *twofold* as referring to England and Scotland and *treble* either to England, Scotland and Wales or to Britain, France and Ireland ('Twofold', 516–90), and Braunmuller's long note, 259.

112 hair] *(*haire*)*; air *Johnson*   113 gold-bound brow] *(*Gold-bound-brow*)*   118 eighth] *F3–4*; eight *F1–2*

Horrible sight. Now I see 'tis true;
For the blood-boltered Banquo smiles upon me
And points at them for his.   [*Exeunt kings and Banquo.*]
                                What? Is this so?

1 WITCH

Ay, sir, all this is so. But why
Stands Macbeth thus amazedly?   125
Come, sisters, cheer we up his sprites,
And show the best of our delights.
I'll charm the air to give a sound,
While you perform your antique round,
That this great king may kindly say   130
Our duties did his welcome pay.

Music. The Witches dance and vanish.

MACBETH

Where are they? Gone? Let this pernicious hour
Stand ay accursed in the calendar.
Come in, without there.

---

122 **blood-boltered** having the hair matted or clotted with blood. See *OED* blood *n*. 21, which refers to 'balter', an obsolete verb meaning to clot or clog with anything sticky, or to form tangled knots.

123 **his** i.e. his descendants

124–31 For the view that this passage is not by Shakespeare, or else a later interpolation, see Appendix 1.

125 **amazedly** dumbfounded, 'as in a maze' (Braunmuller)

129 **antique round** ancient dance, in a ring. See *OED* antique *adj*. and *n*. 1: 'Belonging to former times, ancient, olden'. F 'antique' is often emended to antic, meaning fantastic or bizarre, but need not be.

130–1 If these lines are a later interpolation, this may be a meta-theatrical reference to the king present in the audience. If not, *great king* in reference to Macbeth may be tinged with irony, an interpretation effectively put across at the production at the Everyman Theatre, Liverpool, 2011.

131 **duties** expressions of duty, tributes
did . . . pay 'showed him the respect due to a monarch' (Braunmuller)

133 'be perpetually regarded as an unlucky day'. Early modern almanacs set out 'good' and 'evil' days (Capp, 210).
accursed accursèd

134 **without there** from outside, where Lennox has presumably been keeping guard. On the role of Lennox, see 3.6n.

122 blood-boltered] blood-baltered *Oxf*   123 SD] *Oxf*   What?] What, *Pope*   124 SP] HECATE *Oxf*
129 antique] antic *Theobald*   131 SD vanish.] vanish [*with Hecate.*] *Oxf¹*   132] *Rowe; F lines* Gone? /
houre, /

Enter LENNOX.

LENNOX   What's your Grace's will?

MACBETH

Saw you the weïrd sisters?

LENNOX   No, my lord.   135

MACBETH

Came they not by you?

LENNOX   No indeed, my lord.

MACBETH

Infected be the air whereon they ride,

And damned all those that trust them. I did hear

The galloping of horse. Who was't came by?

LENNOX

'Tis two or three, my lord, that bring you word   140

Macduff is fled to England.

MACBETH   Fled to England?

LENNOX

Ay, my good lord.

MACBETH

Time, thou anticipat'st my dread exploits.

The flighty purpose never is o'ertook

---

137 'Let the air on which they ride be tainted with disease.' The line is suggestive of flying effects used on stage. See 1.3.78 SDn., 3.5.20n. Scot, *Discovery*, refers frequently to the belief that witches could fly; see Bk 1, ch.1: 'The Imperial law (saith *Brentius*) condemneth to death them that trouble and infect the air: but I affirm . . . that it is neither in the power of Witch nor Devil to do so, but in God only'.

138 **damned . . . them** Macbeth unwittingly includes himself.

139 **horse** collective plural for 'horses'

141 **fled to England?** Macbeth's ignorance of Macduff's movements seems inconsistent with 3.6. For discussion, see pp. 69–70.

143 **anticipat'st** deal with beforehand, forestall (*OED* anticipate *v.* 3, the first citation for this meaning)

144–5 **The flighty . . . it** Macbeth seems to mean that 'our deeds never keep pace with our purposes unless we act at once' (Dover Wilson, citing Grierson & Smith) but in this case *purpose* is not (and cannot logically be) overtaken by *deed*. The gap between intention and deed is imagined as one between a pair of racing horses.

flighty swift (*OED adj.* 1a). Crystal and Crystal suggest 'swiftly conceived, quickly vanishing'.

135 weïrd] *Theobald;* Weyard *F;* wizard *F2–3;* wizards *F4*   143 Time] *Aside.* Time *Johnson*

Unless the deed go with it. From this moment   145
The very firstlings of my heart shall be
The firstlings of my hand. And even now,
To crown my thoughts with acts, be it thought and
    done.
The castle of Macduff I will surprise,
Seize upon Fife, give to th'edge o'th' sword   150
His wife, his babes and all unfortunate souls
That trace him in his line. No boasting like a fool;
This deed I'll do before this purpose cool.
But no more sights. Where are these gentlemen?   154
Come, bring me where they are.   *Exeunt.*

4.2   *Enter Macduff's* WIFE, *her* SON *and* ROSS.

WIFE
     What had he done, to make him fly the land?
ROSS
     You must have patience, madam.
WIFE   He had none;
     His flight was madness. When our actions do not,
     Our fears do make us traitors.
ROSS   You know not
     Whether it was his wisdom or his fear.   5

146 **firstlings** first productions or conceptions (*OED* firstling *n.* a), here implicitly suggestive of children
148 **crown** add the finishing touch (*OED v.* 9) **be ... done** let it be done as soon as thought of. See Dent, S117: 'No sooner said than done'.
152 **trace** follow after, succeed (*OED v.*¹ 5) **line** line of descent
154 **no more sights** i.e. such as he has just been shown
4.2 This is the play's only scene of family life. In Holinshed, 2.174, Macduff does

not flee to England, where he laments 'the unhappy necessity of his flight' to Malcolm, until after he knows of the murders of his wife and children. He goes there specifically to raise support to revenge them. Adelman discusses the problems created by Macduff's fatal abandonment of his family in relation to 'unresolved contradictions' (143) around the character.
4 **Our ... traitors** The Wife recognizes that fears which prompt flight can give the impression of guilt.

146 firstlings] firstling *Rowe*   154 sights] sights – *Capell;* sights! *Ard²;* sights. [*To Lennox.*] *Oxf*
4.2] *Scena Secunda.*   0.1 *Macduff's* WIFE] LADY MACDUFF *Rowe*   1+ SP] LADY MACDUFF *Rowe*

WIFE

Wisdom? To leave his wife, to leave his babes,
His mansion and his titles in a place
From whence himself does fly? He loves us not;
He wants the natural touch. For the poor wren,
The most diminutive of birds, will fight,   10
Her young ones in her nest, against the owl.
All is the fear and nothing is the love;
As little is the wisdom, where the flight
So runs against all reason.

ROSS   My dearest coz,
I pray you, school yourself. But for your husband,   15
He is noble, wise, judicious, and best knows
The fits o'th' season. I dare not speak much further;
But cruel are the times when we are traitors
And do not know ourselves; when we hold rumour
From what we fear, yet know not what we fear,   20
But float upon a wild and violent sea

6   **babes** The single child who appears in this scene seems to represent a larger family, as indicated here, at 70 and in Macduff's outburst at 4.3.219–22. Directors commonly provide the Wife with two or more children (e.g. at the Globe, London 2010, and Rosenberg, 533, gives other examples), but Holinshed does not indicate how many children the couple had. The survival (or not) of sons is important to Macbeth.

7   **titles** entitlements

9   **wants . . . touch** lacks the feeling of natural affection. This contrasts ironically with Macbeth's Lady's criticism of her husband, 1.5.17, for having too much of the 'milk of human kindness'.

9–11 **wren . . . nest** Harting, 144, corrects this view of the wren. It is not the very smallest of British birds (though prover-

bial among the Elizabethans for smallness), and does not behave in this way.

11 **Her . . . nest** an absolute construction, meaning 'when (or if) her young ones are in the nest'

12 a reversal of normal word order in the Wife's summary of her husband's behaviour

14 **coz** cousin, here a term of friendship rather than kinship

15 **school** control
    for as for

17 **fits o'th' season** disorders of the times. Compare *Cor* 3.2.34: 'The violent fit o'th' time craves it as physic'.

19–20 **hold . . . fear** entertain rumours derived from our fears. Muir compares *KJ* 4.2.144–6: 'I find the people strangely fantasied, / Possess'd with rumours, full of idle dreams, / Not knowing what they fear, but full of fear'.

6 Wisdom?] Wisdom! *Ard²*   10 diminutive] *(diminitive)*   19 know] know't *Hanmer*   20 not . . . fear,] not . . . fear; *Theobald*   21 sea] sea, *Ard¹*

Each way and move. I take my leave of you;
Shall not be long but I'll be here again.
Things at the worst will cease, or else climb upward
To what they were before. My pretty cousin,   25
Blessing upon you.

WIFE
Fathered he is, and yet he's fatherless.

ROSS
I am so much a fool, should I stay longer,
It would be my disgrace and your discomfort.
I take my leave at once.   *Exit Ross.*

WIFE Sirrah, your father's dead. And what will you do   31
now? How will you live?

SON As birds do, mother.

WIFE What, with worms and flies?

---

22 **move** Many editors including Dover
Wilson and Braunmuller have emended
to 'none', assuming a minim misreading.
But F 'move' may be retained, especially
if, following Johnson (*Miscellaneous*,
Note XXXVIII, 75), Ross breaks off in
the middle of his sentence, afraid of
saying too much. See also Sisson, who
accepts *move*, paraphrasing, 'We float,
tossed by contrary winds and currents'
(2.202). Compare a similar idea in *AC*
1.4.44–7: 'This common body / . . . Goes
to and back, lackeying the varying tide, /
To rot itself with motion'. Brooke takes
move as a noun in the sense of motion or
movement, suggesting aimless drifting,
but *OED* does not record such a sense in
the period.

23 **Shall** It shall

25 **cousin** addressed to the Son

27 The child is *Fathered* in the sense of
having a father who engendered him, but
fatherless as he is without a father present

to protect him. Braunmuller, 22, relates
the Wife's wry paradox about her son to
his father, who by the circumstances of
his birth is 'mothered/motherless'.

28 **so . . . fool** i.e. as to cry. Furness gives
many instances where Shakespeare connects crying with foolishness, e.g. *Tem*
3.1.73–4: 'I am a fool / To weep at what
I am glad of'.

31–65 Recent editors (e.g. Oxf, Hunter,
Brooke, Braunmuller) have set this
passage wholly or partially in prose. For
those who have set it as verse, there is no
consensus as to where the breaks should
come. The tone of the scene, which is
sandwiched between sections of verse,
changes at Ross's exit, and prose better
captures the informality and intimacy of
the mother/son exchange. The succession
of short lines has something of the quality
of stichomythia.

31 **Sirrah** familiar, playful form of address

34 **with** by eating

22 Each . . . move.] Each way and wave, *Theobald;* And move each way *Capell;* Each way and move
– *Johnson;* Each way and none *Cam¹;* Each way and move. *Oxf¹*   27] *Rowe; F lines* is, / Father-lesse /
31 father's] *(fathers)*

249

SON With what I get, I mean; and so do they.   35

WIFE Poor bird. Thou'dst never fear the net nor lime,
    the pitfall nor the gin.

SON Why should I, mother? Poor birds they are not set
    for. My father is not dead, for all your saying.

WIFE Yes, he is dead. How wilt thou do for a father?   40

SON Nay, how will you do for a husband?

WIFE Why, I can buy me twenty at any market.

SON Then you'll buy 'em to sell again.

WIFE Thou speak'st with all thy wit, and yet, i'faith,
    with wit enough for thee.   45

SON Was my father a traitor, mother?

WIFE Ay, that he was.

SON What is a traitor?

WIFE Why one that swears and lies.

SON And be all traitors, that do so?   50

WIFE Every one that does so is a traitor and must be
    hanged.

SON And must they all be hanged that swear and lie?

WIFE Every one.

SON Who must hang them?   55

36–7 **net . . . gin** forms of traps for birds; *lime* is birdlime, a sticky substance for catching small birds, *pitfall* is a trap in which a cover falls over a hole, and *gin* a snare for catching game.

38–9 **Poor . . . for** *Poor* in the sense of low quality (*OED adj.* 2a). The boy, punning on his mother's use of *Poor* to mean unfortunate, means that he is too worthless to be trapped.

43 **buy . . . again** The Wife will only buy twenty husbands if she is to resell (or deceive) them. See Dent, B787: 'To be bought and sold', also *OED* sell *v.* 2a, and Crystal & Crystal, 'buy and sell'.

Compare *R3* 5.3.305: 'Dickon thy master is bought and sold'.

44–5 'You speak with all the (minimal) cleverness that you are capable of, yet in fact you have some understanding, given your age.' She puns on *wit* as verbal dexterity and as mental acumen.

46–56 This conversation about treachery is sometimes used to stress the play's topicality in the aftermath of the Gunpowder Plot. See p. 17.

49 **swears and lies** swears an oath and breaks it. Hunter suggests that the Wife has in mind both the marriage vows and the oath of allegiance to the monarch.

35 I mean] *om. F2–4*   36–7] *Cam*[1]*; F lines* Bird, / Lime, / Gin. / *; Theobald lines* Lime, / Gin. /   44 with all] *F2;* withall *F*   50 so?] *F3;* so. *F*   51–2] *Pope; F lines* Traitor, / hang'd. /

WIFE Why, the honest men.

SON Then the liars and swearers are fools, for there are
liars and swearers enow to beat the honest men, and
hang up them.

WIFE Now, God help thee, poor monkey. But how wilt   60
thou do for a father?

SON If he were dead, you'd weep for him; if you would
not, it were a good sign that I should quickly have
a new father.

WIFE Poor prattler, how thou talk'st.   65

Enter a Messenger.

MESSENGER

Bless you, fair dame. I am not to you known,
Though in your state of honour I am perfect.
I doubt some danger does approach you nearly.
If you will take a homely man's advice,
Be not found here; hence, with your little ones.   70
To fright you thus, methinks I am too savage;
To do worse to you were fell cruelty,
Which is too nigh your person. Heaven preserve you.
I dare abide no longer.   *Exit Messenger.*

WIFE

Whither should I fly?   75
I have done no harm. But I remember now
I am in this earthly world, where to do harm

58 **enow** enough
60 **monkey** then as now, a term of
endearment
65 **prattler** chatterbox
67 'Though I am fully conversant with your
high status and reputation' (*OED* perfect
adj., *n.* and *adv.* 4a)

68 **doubt** fear (*OED v.* 5b)
nearly close by (*OED adv.*, *adj.* 4a)
69 **homely** unsophisticated, simple (*OED*
adj. 4b, citing this line)
71 **methinks** it seems to me
72 **fell** terrible. See *TA* 5.3.99: 'For their fell
faults our brothers were beheaded'.

56 the] *om. F4*   62 you'd] *(*youl'd*)*   70–1 ones. . . . thus, methinks . . . savage;] *F2–4;* ones . . . thus. Me
thinkes . . . sauage: *F*   72 worse] less, *Hanmer;* less *Capell*

251

Is often laudable, to do good sometime
Accounted dangerous folly. Why, then, alas,
Do I put up that womanly defence,   80
To say I have done no harm?

Enter MURDERERS.

                                                What are these faces?

1 MURDERER
Where is your husband?

WIFE
I hope in no place so unsanctified
Where such as thou mayst find him.

1 MURDERER   He's a traitor.

SON
Thou liest, thou shag-haired villain.

1 MURDERER   What, you egg!   85
Young fry of treachery!

SON   He has killed me, mother.
Run away, I pray you.   *Exit [Wife] crying* 'Murder'.
                                              [Exeunt Murderers.]

80 **womanly** womanish, ineffectual
81 **What . . . faces?** Braunmuller suggests that the Wife may rebuke her son, presumably for showing fear, but it seems more likely that she is commenting on the appearance of the Murderers.
83 **unsanctified** unholy, unprotected
85 *****shag-haired** with long shaggy hair. Wiggins, 67, compares shag-haired assassins in *King Leir* (2277) and *The Fair Maid of Bristol* (1604, sig. E1ᵛ).

Cercignani, 335, suggests that F's 'shagge-ear'd' 'may be due to a misreading of an original *shagheard* as *shaggeard*'.
85–6 **egg . . . fry** offspring, spawn, used pejoratively; *egg* links back to the prevalent images of birds in this scene.
87 SD *F's SD does not allow for the exits of the Son and Murderers. A SD that is non-prescriptive in the case of the Son allows directors to make their own decisions about the removal of the body.

81 SD] *Cam¹; after* villain. *85 F*   82 SP, 84 SP, 85 SP2] *Capell; Mur. F; First Mur. Cam*   85 shag-haired] *Steevens, Ard², Cam¹;* shagge-ear'd *F*   86 treachery!] *(Treachery?);* treachery. *[Stabbing him] / Rowe, Ard²;* treachery! *[Kills him] Oxf¹, Cam¹* has] *(ha's)*   87 SD] *this edn; Exit crying Murther. F; Son dies. Exit Wife crying 'Murder' / Hunter; [He dies] Exit Macduff's Wife crying 'Murder!' followed by Murderers [with the Son's body.] Oxf; Exit [Lady Macduff] crying 'Murder' [, pursued by Murderers with her son.] Oxf¹*

4.3 *Enter* MALCOLM *and* MACDUFF.

MALCOLM

Let us seek out some desolate shade and there
Weep our sad bosoms empty.

MACDUFF   Let us rather

Hold fast the mortal sword, and like good men
Bestride our downfall birthdom. Each new morn
New widows howl, new orphans cry, new sorrows   5
Strike heaven on the face, that it resounds
As if it felt with Scotland and yelled out

4.3 For the first part of this scene, the
longest in the play, Shakespeare follows
Holinshed (2.174–5, Bullough, 7.501–2)
more closely than anywhere else. The
rationale for Malcolm's testing of
Macduff is clearly explained: 'Though
Malcolme was verie sorrowfull for the
oppression of his countriemen the Scots,
in maner as Makduffe had declared; yet
doubting whether he were come as one
that ment unfeinedlie as he spake, or else
as sent from Makbeth to betraie him,
he thought to have made some further
triall . . . thereupon dissembling his mind
at the first'. The scene has been condemned for dullness by many critics (e.g.
Booth, *'King Lear'*, 108–10), and is
sometimes shortened in production, but it
fulfils many important functions, especially in enlarging the roles of the main
speakers and characterizing the nature
and effects of tyranny. See Braunmuller's
fine discussion of it, 88–93; also
Campbell on the testing of Macduff,
challenged by Ribner, 255–9; Ide, 356
and fn. 30, on Malcolm's 'symbolic
awakening to kingship', contrasted with
the reading of Riebling, esp. 277–8 on
Malcolm's 'virtuoso display of politic
dissimulation'. Bruckner, 199–202, discusses Malcolm's emotional manipulation

of Macduff. Palfrey, 212–20, discusses
Macduff's role as a 'mirror opposite'
to Macbeth (218). The setting is now
England, and near to the court of King
Edward the Confessor, whose appearance
is expected at 140–2. The details are
gradually revealed in the text as the scene
progresses.

1–4 **Let . . . birthdom** The initial contrast
between Malcolm's defeatism and
Macduff's more positive attitude is
striking, but is soon replaced by a more
complex dynamic. By the end of the
scene, Malcolm is the readier for action
against the common enemy, Macbeth.

3   **mortal** lethal, deadly (compare 'mortal
enemy')

4   **Bestride . . . birthdom** take action to
protect our downfallen country. The
metaphor is from the idea of standing
protectively over the body of a fallen
comrade. See *1H4* 5.1.121–2 when
Falstaff says to Prince Henry: 'if thou see
me down in the battle and bestride me, so;
'tis a point of friendship'.
     birthdom birthright, inheritance, native
land (apparently a Shakespearean coinage
and *OED*'s only citation for this word.
EEBO records none earlier.)

6   **that** so that

4.3] *Scaena Tertia.*   4 downfall] down-fall'n *Johnson*

Like syllable of dolour.

MALCOLM   What I believe, I'll wail;

What know, believe; and what I can redress,

As I shall find the time to friend, I will.   10

What you have spoke, it may be so, perchance.

This tyrant, whose sole name blisters our tongues,

Was once thought honest: you have loved him well;

He hath not touched you yet. I am young, but
    something

You may discern of him through me, and wisdom   15

To offer up a weak, poor, innocent lamb

T'appease an angry god.

MACDUFF

I am not treacherous.

MALCOLM   But Macbeth is.

A good and virtuous nature may recoil

In an imperial charge. But I shall crave your pardon;   20

8   **Like syllable** a similar sound (*OED*
      syllable *n.* 1)
      dolour woe, lamentation

8–11 **What ... perchance** Malcolm speaks
      formally and cautiously, uncertain of
      Macduff's sincerity.

8   **wail** bewail, lament

10   **time to friend** opportune moment

12   **sole name** name alone

14   **He ... you** He has not yet harmed you
      (as he has me).

14–17 **I ... god** Malcolm appears to be
      suggesting that Macduff might regard
      him as expendable and therefore sacrifice
      him so as to ingratiate himself with
      Macbeth.

14–15 **something ... me** 'You may see
      something of him in me.' Malcolm may
      be preparing for his elaborate self-
      incrimination later in the scene, or he
      may be referring to his suffering at
      Macbeth's hands. Theobald's emendation

of 'deserve' for *discern* is plausible,
although it follows less well from *I am
young*.

15   **and wisdom** it is wisdom

16   **innocent lamb** In Christian tradition the
      lamb is emblematic of innocence. The
      proverb 'As innocent as a lamb' (Dent,
      L34.1) appeared around this period.
      Compare 'Esteem him as a lamb' at 54.

19–20 **A good ... charge** Malcolm appears
      to refer indirectly to the possibility that
      Macduff may have been corrupted under
      Macbeth's command.

19   **recoil** fall away, degenerate, shrink back
      (*OED v.*[1] 3b, citing this line). Compare
      Cym 1.7.126–8: 'Be reveng'd / Or she
      that bore you was no queen, and you /
      Recoil from your great stock'. Dover
      Wilson, taking *charge* in a military sense,
      sees a suppressed image from gunnery.

20   **charge** office, commission (*OED n.* 12),
      or command

15 discern] deserve *Theobald*   and] 'tis *Hanmer*

That which you are, my thoughts cannot transpose.
Angels are bright still, though the brightest fell.
Though all things foul would wear the brows of grace,
Yet grace must still look so.

MACDUFF   I have lost my hopes.

MALCOLM

Perchance even there where I did find my doubts.   25
Why in that rawness left you wife and child –
Those precious motives, those strong knots of love –
Without leave-taking? I pray you,
Let not my jealousies be your dishonours,
But mine own safeties. You may be rightly just,   30
Whatever I shall think.

MACDUFF   Bleed, bleed, poor country.
Great tyranny, lay thou thy basis sure,
For goodness dare not check thee. Wear thou thy
    wrongs;

21 **transpose** change, transform. Malcolm means that whatever Macduff is really like cannot be affected by what he thinks of him.
22 **the brightest** reference to Satan, whose alternative name, Lucifer, means 'bearer of light'
23–4 **Though . . . so** 'Though evil things want to take on the appearance of good, goodness must retain its appearance of virtue.' Andrews suggests an allusion to 2 Corinthians, 11.13–14 ('For such false Apostles [are] disceiptfull workers, transfourmed into ye Apostles of Christe. And no maruayle, for Satan himselfe is transfourmed into an angel of lyght'). The thought echoes Duncan at 1.4.11–14.
23 **brows** countenance (*OED* brow *n.*¹ 5c)
25 **there** i.e. either in Scotland, or under Macbeth's tyranny
26 **rawness** unprotected condition (Dover Wilson cites *H5* 4.1.140–1: 'children rawly left')

28 Brooke comments helpfully on this short line: 'The missing foot . . . is supplied by the natural pause after "leave-taking?", before a change in tone in "I pray you" – especially if Macduff reacts violently'.
29–30 **Let . . . safeties** 'Don't regard my suspicions as aspersions on your honour, but as my own self-protection.'
30 **safeties** safeguards (*OED* safety 3). Crystal and Crystal compare *2H6* 5.3.23: 'I know our safety is to follow them'.
32 **Great . . . thou** Macduff apostrophizes Macbeth.
   basis foundation, support. This is the first citation given by *OED* (*n.* 8) for this sense.
33 **goodness** i.e. Malcolm
   check curb, control (*OED* v.¹ 14a)
   Wear . . . wrongs perhaps 'wear as a title' (deriving from *OED* wear v.¹ 4)

23 wear] bear *F4*   25] *Rowe; F lines* there / doubts. /   26 child –] *(*Childe?*);* children? *F2–4*

The title is affeered. Fare thee well, lord.
I would not be the villain that thou think'st   35
For the whole space that's in the tyrant's grasp
And the rich East to boot.

MALCOLM   Be not offended;
I speak not as in absolute fear of you.
I think our country sinks beneath the yoke;
It weeps, it bleeds, and each new day a gash   40
Is added to her wounds. I think withal
There would be hands uplifted in my right;
And here from gracious England have I offer
Of goodly thousands. But for all this,
When I shall tread upon the tyrant's head,   45
Or wear it on my sword, yet my poor country
Shall have more vices than it had before,
More suffer, and more sundry ways than ever,
By him that shall succeed.

MACDUFF   What should he be?

34 **title is affeered** ambiguous expression, depending on whether *thou* (*Wear thou thy wrongs*) refers to Macbeth or to Malcolm. The ambiguity is increased by F's colon (sometimes modernized to a semi-colon) after *thee* in 33, but a reference to Macbeth seems the most likely. 'Affeered' (emended from F's 'affear'd') means 'confirmed', originally a legal term, perhaps suggested by *check* (Dover Wilson). *OED* affeer *v.* 2, 'to settle, confirm', cites this line. In reference to Macbeth, the line means, 'Your claim to the title (of tyrant) is confirmed', which makes the best sense. But 'affear'd' as in F may refer to Malcolm, meaning something like 'both the title and its claimant are afraid'.

Fare ... lord Macduff may be offering to leave, offended by Malcolm's apparently critical attitude towards him.
37 **to boot** in addition
38 **absolute fear** complete distrust
39 **yoke** state of subjection
41 **withal** in addition
43 **England** the King of England, Edward the Confessor
44 **thousands** i.e. of soldiers
44–117 **But ... honour** Malcolm's testing of Macduff. This passage, based closely on Holinshed, 2.174–5, has received considerable commentary, much of it adverse. See Braunmuller, 88–93, esp. 91–2, and Dover Wilson, 156. Malcolm, as Rosenberg, 546, says, must be totally credible here.
48 **sundry** various

34 The] Thy *Malone*   affeered] *Hanmer;* affear'd *F*   Fare] *F2–4;* Far *F*   44 thousands.] thousands.
[*Showing a paper*] / *Collier*

MALCOLM

It is myself I mean, in whom I know 50
All the particulars of vice so grafted
That, when they shall be opened, black Macbeth
Will seem as pure as snow, and the poor state
Esteem him as a lamb, being compared
With my confineless harms.

MACDUFF   Not in the legions 55
Of horrid hell can come a devil more damned
In evils to top Macbeth.

MALCOLM   I grant him bloody,
Luxurious, avaricious, false, deceitful,
Sudden, malicious, smacking of every sin
That has a name. But there's no bottom, none, 60
In my voluptuousness. Your wives, your daughters,
Your matrons and your maids could not fill up
The cistern of my lust; and my desire
All continent impediments would o'erbear

---

51 **grafted** implanted. Contrast the use of botanical terms in a positive sense by Duncan and Banquo, 1.4.28–33.

52 **opened** either opened like a bud, following the botanical metaphor in *grafted*, or in the sense of dissection (Braunmuller)

55 **confineless** boundless, unlimited (*OED*'s only citation for this word, and its only use by Shakespeare. *EEBO* has nothing earlier.)
   legions hosts, multitudes (*OED* legion *n*. 3a suggests this term is frequently used of 'angels or spirits, with reminiscence of Matthew 26.53'.)

57 **top** surpass

57–60 **I ... name** Not all of these sins obviously apply to Macbeth, and Brooke calls the catalogue 'conventional'. See also Bushnell, 140–2, for a discussion of this scene in relation to early modern concepts of tyranny.

58 **Luxurious** lecherous, lustful (*OED adj.* 1)

59 **Sudden** hasty, rash, impetuous (*OED adj.* 2b)
   smacking of savouring, having the flavour of. See *MM* 2.2.5: 'All sects, all ages smack of this vice'.

61 **voluptuousness** lust, addiction to the pleasures of the flesh (*OED n.* 1), used in a more censorious sense than nowadays

63 **cistern** tank, reservoir, large vessel; used by Shakespeare as a metaphor for insatiable lust. See *Oth* 4.2.62–3: 'keep it as a cistern for foul toads / To knot and gender in'.

64 **continent** confining, restraining (*OED a.* 3), but also self-restraining in the sense of chaste (*a.* 1)

57 evils] ills *Pope*   59 smacking] smoaking *F2–4*

257

That did oppose my will. Better Macbeth   65
Than such an one to reign.

MACDUFF   Boundless intemperance
In nature is a tyranny. It hath been
Th'untimely emptying of the happy throne,
And fall of many kings. But fear not yet
To take upon you what is yours. You may   70
Convey your pleasures in a spacious plenty
And yet seem cold. The time you may so hoodwink.
We have willing dames enough; there cannot be
That vulture in you to devour so many
As will to greatness dedicate themselves,   75
Finding it so inclined.

MALCOLM   With this there grows
In my most ill-composed affection such
A stanchless avarice that, were I king,
I should cut off the nobles for their lands,
Desire his jewels and this other's house,   80

66–7 **Boundless . . . tyranny** 'Uncontrolled appetite constitutes tyranny in the microcosmic kingdom of man's nature.'

68 'the downfall of an otherwise successful dynasty before its time'

70–6 **You . . . inclined** Macduff's cynical attitude towards the sexual conduct of monarchs follows Holinshed. Bushnell, 141, n. 59, citing James VI and I, *The Trew Law of Free Monarchies* (in McIlwain, 66), notes that Macduff's tolerance of Malcolm's intemperance 'is entirely in accordance with the ideas of James himself'.

71 **Convey** manage, carry on, with connotations of secrecy (*OED v.* 12). See *KL* 1.2.101–2: 'I will . . . convey the business as I shall find means'. In Holinshed, Macduff says: 'There are women enow in Scotland, and therefore follow my counsel, Make thy selfe king, and I shall

conveie the matter so wiselie, that thou shalt be so satisfied at thy pleasure in such secret wise, that no man shall be aware thereof' (2.175, Bullough, 7.502).

   in . . . plenty pleonasm (the use of more words than strictly necessary) for 'in abundance'

72 **hoodwink** blindfold, deceive

74 **vulture** metaphor here for an indiscriminately voracious nature

75 **to . . . themselves** surrender themselves to serve a great man. Macduff's expression is dryly misogynistic.

77 **affection** disposition (*OED* affection *n.*[1] 5)

78 **stanchless** unstoppable, limitless. *OED* (stanchless *a.*) gives this as the first citation for this word, but it appears earlier in Drayton, *Matilda* (1594): 'A stanchless heart, dead wounded'.

79 **cut off** put to death

66 an] a *Capell*   72 cold.] cold, *Theobald;* cold – *Ard*[2]   hoodwink.] *(* hoodwink:*)*   74 you] *Collier;* you, *F*

And my more-having would be as a sauce
To make me hunger more, that I should forge
Quarrels unjust against the good and loyal,
Destroying them for wealth.

MACDUFF   This avarice
Sticks deeper, grows with more pernicious root   85
Than summer-seeming lust, and it hath been
The sword of our slain kings. Yet do not fear;
Scotland hath foisons to fill up your will
Of your mere own. All these are portable,
With other graces weighed.   90

MALCOLM

But I have none. The king-becoming graces,
As justice, verity, temperance, stableness,
Bounty, perseverance, mercy, lowliness,
Devotion, patience, courage, fortitude,
I have no relish of them, but abound   95
In the division of each several crime,

81–2 **my more-having . . . more** the more I had would encourage me to want more, as a sauce tempts the appetite. See Dent, M1144: 'The more a man has, the more he desires'.

82 **forge** fabricate, invent (*OED v.*[1] 4)

85 **root** See Holinshed, 2.175, where Macduff responds to Malcolm, 'Avarice is the root of all mischiefe'. The metaphor derives from 1 Timothy, 6.10: 'For loue of money, is the roote of all euyll'.

86 **summer-seeming** 'either summer-beseeming or summer-like' (Muir). Lust may be associated with summer in being hot but short-lived.

87 **sword** cause of death. See Holinshed, 2.175, where Macduff observes that 'for that crime [avarice] the most part of our kings have been slaine'.

88 **foisons** resources (*OED* foison *n.* 2)
will desire, wish

89 **mere own** very own (wealth)
portable bearable, endurable (*OED adj.* and *n.* 1). Compare *KL* 3.6.105: 'How light and portable my pain seems now'.

90 **graces** The main meaning is pleasing qualities, but there is also an underlying musical metaphor, taken up in *division* (96) and *concord* (98). Graces and divisions are categories of ornament, the first formal, the second improvised. See Wilson & Calore, 'grace'.
weighed counterbalanced

92 **verity** truthfulness

93 **lowliness** meekness, humility

95 **relish** taste, savour

96 **division** separate parts, variations, carrying on the musical metaphor from *graces* (90).
several individual

85 Sticks] Strikes *Theobald*   86 summer-seeming] summer-teeming *Theobald;* summer-seeding *Steevens*
88 foisons] poisons *F2–4*

Acting it many ways. Nay, had I power, I should
Pour the sweet milk of concord into hell,
Uproar the universal peace, confound
All unity on earth.

MACDUFF   O Scotland, Scotland.   100

MALCOLM

If such a one be fit to govern, speak.
I am as I have spoken.

MACDUFF   Fit to govern?

No, not to live. O nation miserable!
With an untitled tyrant bloody-sceptred,
When shalt thou see thy wholesome days again,   105
Since that the truest issue of thy throne
By his own interdiction stands accursed
And does blaspheme his breed? Thy royal father
Was a most sainted king; the queen that bore thee,
Oft'ner upon her knees than on her feet,   110
Died every day she lived. Fare thee well.
These evils thou repeat'st upon thyself

---

98 **milk of concord** For *milk* see 1.5.17 and
n.; *concord* means 'harmony' and follows
up the musical metaphors at 90 and 96.

99 **Uproar** throw into confusion. *OED v.* 1
calls this usage 'rare'.

104 **untitled** without legal right; *OED*'s only
citation for this meaning, and *EEBO*
gives none earlier

105 **wholesome** healthy, free from disease or
taint (*OED a.* 3b, citing this line)

106 **truest issue** most legitimate child, i.e.
Malcolm himself

107 **interdiction** legal term, meaning a
restraint imposed on a person incapable
of managing his own affairs (*OED n.* 3a)
accursed F 'accust' has been rendered
'accus'd' by many editors, and 'accused'
might well follow from the legal meaning
of *interdiction*, but as Braunmuller says,

'*OED* offers no evidence for F's accust as
a past tense of "accuse"', and *accursed*
goes better with the religious connotations of *blaspheme* and the tone of the
rest of the speech.

108 **blaspheme his breed** slander or defame
his heritage

111 **Died ... lived** mortified herself every
day of her life. See 1 Corinthians, 15.31,
where St Paul claims, 'I die daily'.
Fare thee well Macduff again makes
as if to depart, horrified by Malcolm's
account of himself.

112–13 **These ... Scotland** 'Enormities
such as you relate have caused me to
regard myself as banished from
Scotland.'

112 **repeat'st** relate, recount (*OED* repeat *v.*
2a, citing this line)

---

102 SP] *(Mac.)*   102–3 Fit ... miserable] *Pope; one line F*   104 bloody-sceptred] *Pope;* bloody Sceptred *F*
105 again,] *(againe?)*   107 accursed] *(accust);* accurst *F2*   109 sainted king] *(*Sainted-King*)*

Hath banished me from Scotland. O my breast,
Thy hope ends here.

MALCOLM   Macduff, this noble passion,
Child of integrity, hath from my soul   115
Wiped the black scruples, reconciled my thoughts
To thy good truth and honour. Devilish Macbeth
By many of these trains hath sought to win me
Into his power, and modest wisdom plucks me
From over-credulous haste. But God above   120
Deal between thee and me. For even now
I put myself to thy direction and
Unspeak mine own detraction. Here abjure
The taints and blames I laid upon myself,
For strangers to my nature. I am yet   125
Unknown to woman, never was forsworn,
Scarcely have coveted what was mine own,
At no time broke my faith, would not betray
The devil to his fellow, and delight
No less in truth than life. My first false speaking   130
Was this upon myself. What I am truly
Is thine and my poor country's to command.
Whither indeed, before thy here-approach,
Old Siward, with ten thousand warlike men
Already at a point, was setting forth.   135

---

113 **Hath** singular verb with plural subject.
See Abbott, 334.
115 **Child** product, issue
116 **scruples** doubts, uncertainties (*OED*
scruple *n.*² 1)
118 **trains** tricks, deceptive stratagems (*OED*
train *n.*² 1b)
119 **plucks** pulls back (*OED* pluck *v.* 3)
120 **over-credulous** too ready to believe
122 **put myself** submit
123 **Unspeak** retract
abjure renounce, retract

126 **Unknown to woman** i.e. a virgin
forsworn perjured
133 ***thy here-approach** your arrival here.
This is Pope's emendation for F 'they
heere approach'. Compare *my here-remain*
(148). See also Crystal & Crystal, 'Here,
there, and where', 220–1.
135 **at a point** in readiness, prepared (*OED*
point *n.*¹ P1 a). Compare *KL* 1.4.316–17:
'to let him keep / At point a hundred
knights'.

113 Hath] Have *Rowe*   126 woman]women *F2–4*   133 thy here-approach] *Pope;* they heere approach *F;*
thy here approach *F2*

Now we'll together, and the chance of goodness
Be like our warranted quarrel. Why are you silent?

MACDUFF
Such welcome and unwelcome things at once
'Tis hard to reconcile.

Enter a Doctor.

MALCOLM   Well, more anon.
Comes the King forth, I pray you?   140

DOCTOR
Ay, sir; there are a crew of wretched souls
That stay his cure. Their malady convinces
The great assay of art, but at his touch,

136–7 **chance ... quarrel** 'May our good
fortune be equal to the justification for
our cause.' 'Chance of goodness' means
possibility of success (*OED* chance *n.* 5a).
For 'goodness' meaning 'good fortune'
OED gives no citation after 1550, but
Crystal and Crystal cite *KL* 5.1.7: 'You
know the goodness I intend upon you',
and *TNK* 2.2.63–4: ''Tis a main goodness, cousin, that our fortunes / Were
twined together' with similar meanings.
'Warranted quarrel' means legally justified cause of complaint (*OED* quarrel
*n.*³ 1a).
139 SD This doctor, like the one in 5.1, is
probably identified as a medical doctor
by his costume to distinguish him from
a cleric. His arrival seems to cause
Malcolm to cut short his response to
Macduff.
139–59 **Well ... grace** This episode has
sometimes been regarded as an interpolation or revision, and it has been
conjectured (e.g. by Coghill, 230–4) that
there was originally a scene in which
Edward the Confessor appeared. Dover

Wilson calls the episode a '*bonne
bouche*' intended to flatter King James
(xxxiii). For discussion of the possibility
of cuts in the text, see Appendix 1.
142 **stay** await (*OED v.*¹ 19)
cure 'Touching' for the King's Evil by
the monarch, who was believed during
the medieval period and up to the eighteenth century in England and France to
possess miraculous powers of healing,
was ascribed first to Edward the Confessor, and also practised by King James.
Bloch gives the standard account of the
practice in its historical context, Furness
has a useful long note and Willis comments perceptively on this speech in
relation to Malcolm's kingship (157–61).
See Holinshed, 1.195 (Bullough, 7.508),
and Rosenberg, 551–2. Braunmuller, 15,
n. 2, cites Lee Bliss's suggestion that
Camden's *Remains*, 216, may also be a
source.
convinces overcomes (*OED* convince
v. 1)
143 **great ... art** utmost effort (*OED* assay
n. 14) of medical practitioners

139–40 Well . . . you?] *Ard²; one line F*   139 anon.] anon. – *Capell;* anon. [*To the Doctor*] *Oxf*

Such sanctity hath heaven given his hand,   144
They presently amend.

MALCOLM   I thank you, Doctor.   *Exit [Doctor]*.

MACDUFF

What's the disease he means?

MALCOLM   'Tis called the Evil:
A most miraculous work in this good king,
Which often, since my here-remain in England,
I have seen him do. How he solicits heaven,
Himself best knows; but strangely-visited people,   150
All swol'n and ulcerous, pitiful to the eye,
The mere despair of surgery, he cures,
Hanging a golden stamp about their necks
Put on with holy prayers; and 'tis spoken,
To the succeeding royalty he leaves   155
The healing benediction. With this strange virtue
He hath a heavenly gift of prophecy,
And sundry blessings hang about his throne
That speak him full of grace.

---

145 **amend** recover (*OED v.* 6b)

146 **the Evil** the King's Evil, scrofula, 'a tubercular infection of the lymph nodes, swollen or diseased glands of the neck' (Barlow, 3).

148 **here-remain** sojourn, stay. Compare *here-approach*, 133.

149 **solicits** entreats

150 **strangely-visited** afflicted in unusual ways (*OED* visit *v.* 3b). Pope introduced the hyphenated form to create a compound adjective.

152 **mere** complete, total

153 **golden stamp** coin or medal. Holinshed does not describe Edward the Confessor hanging a medal around the necks of those he cured, but later monarchs did

this. For further detail, see Bloch, 65–7, 210–12.

154 **holy prayers** Shakespeare stresses the aura of sanctity surrounding Edward in contrast to the diabolical qualities of Macbeth.
  spoken said, reported

155 **succeeding royalty** kings who followed him. The gift was believed to be hereditary.

156 **benediction** blessedness, grace (*OED n.* 2)
  strange rare, exceptional. See *R2* 5.5.65–6: 'love to Richard / Is a strange brooch in this all-hating world'.
  virtue ability (*OED n.* 5a) or divine power (*n.* 1a)

159 **speak** bespeak, manifest (*OED v.* 16a)

145 SD] *Capell;after* amend. *F*   *Doctor*] *Capell*   146 Evil] evil *Oxf*   148 here-remain] *Pope;* heere remaine *F*   150 strangely-visited] *Pope;* strangely visited *F*   151 swol'n] *(swolne)*

Enter ROSS.

MACDUFF   See who comes here.

MALCOLM

My countryman, but yet I know him not.   160

MACDUFF

My ever gentle cousin, welcome hither.

MALCOLM

I know him now. Good God, betimes remove

The means that makes us strangers.

ROSS   Sir, amen.

MACDUFF

Stands Scotland where it did?

ROSS   Alas, poor country,

Almost afraid to know itself. It cannot   165

Be called our mother, but our grave. Where nothing,

But who knows nothing, is once seen to smile;

Where sighs, and groans, and shrieks that rend the air,

Are made, not marked; where violent sorrow seems

A modern ecstasy. The deadman's knell   170

Is there scarce asked for who, and good men's lives

159–63 **See ... strangers** Macduff immediately recognizes Ross, although Malcolm does not, which is perhaps indicative of the mutual suspicion amongst the Scots in the early part of the scene.

162 **betimes** speedily, soon

163 **means** something interposed or intervening (*OED* mean *n.*³ 7). It has been suggested that Ross's costume reveals his nationality, and that he may be wearing a hat which Malcolm asks him to remove.

164 **Stands ... did?** 'Is Scotland in the same state as it was?'

166 **mother ... grave** For another instance of this paradox, Braunmuller cites *RJ* 2.3.5–6: 'The earth that's nature's mother is her tomb, / What is her burying grave, that is her womb'.

166–7 **Where ... nothing** 'where no one, except those who are completely ignorant'

167 **once** ever, at any time. Compare 5.5.14–15: 'Direness ... / Cannot once start me.'

168 **rend** F has 'rent', which is an obsolete form of 'rend'.

169 **marked** remarked on, noticed

170 **modern** commonplace (*OED adj.* 4) **ecstasy** abnormal state of mind (*OED n.* 2) **deadman's knell** bell ringing to announce a death. *OED* notes that 'deadman' was 'formerly written and pronounced as one word'. For *knell*, see 2.1.63 and n.

171 **scarce ... who** i.e. no one bothers to ask the question 'For whom does the bell toll?' Compare Donne, *Devotions*, Meditation 17: 'Never send to know for whom the bell tolls; it tolls for thee'.

160 not] *(nor)*   168 rend] *Rowe;* rent *F*   170 deadman's] Dead-man's *F3–4;* dead man's *Johnson*

Expire before the flowers in their caps,
Dying or ere they sicken.

MACDUFF

O, relation too nice, and yet too true.

MALCOLM

What's the newest grief?   175

ROSS

That of an hour's age doth hiss the speaker;
Each minute teems a new one.

MACDUFF   How does my wife?

ROSS

Why, well.

MACDUFF   And all my children?

ROSS   Well too.

MACDUFF

The tyrant has not battered at their peace?

ROSS

No, they were well at peace, when I did leave 'em.   180

MACDUFF

Be not a niggard of your speech. How goes't?

ROSS

When I came hither to transport the tidings,
Which I have heavily borne, there ran a rumour
Of many worthy fellows that were out,

173 **or . . . sicken** before they show any signs
of sickness
174 **relation** narration, recital, account (*OED
n.* 1a)
  nice precise, meticulous (*OED adj.* and
  adv. 7) but perhaps also over-refined
  in literary style (3a). Ross's elegantly
  phrased account is also accurate.
176 **of . . . age** i.e. told an hour ago
  hiss express disapproval of (by hissing)
177 **teems** breeds, gives birth to
178 **well . . . Well** Although Macduff does not
  recognize it, Ross draws on the proverb

'He is well since he is in heaven' (Dent,
H347), also alluded to in *AC* 2.5.32–3:
'we use / To say the dead are well'.
181 **niggard** hoarder, miser
182 **tidings** i.e. the news of the murders of
  Macduff's family, which Ross delays in
  telling
183 **heavily** sorrowfully (*OED adv.* 3)
184 **out** in active rebellion. Muir notes that
  'the followers of the two Pretenders were
  frequently spoken of as "out" in the '15
  and '45'. See *OED adv.* 20, 'revealed,
  made known, no longer a secret'.

181 goes't] *(gos't)*

Which was to my belief witnessed the rather   185
For that I saw the tyrant's power afoot.
Now is the time of help: your eye in Scotland
Would create soldiers, make our women fight
To doff their dire distresses.

MALCOLM   Be't their comfort
We are coming thither. Gracious England hath   190
Lent us good Siward, and ten thousand men;
An older and a better soldier, none
That Christendom gives out.

ROSS   Would I could answer
This comfort with the like. But I have words
That would be howled out in the desert air,   195
Where hearing should not latch them.

MACDUFF   What concern they:
The general cause? Or is it a fee-grief
Due to some single breast?

ROSS   No mind that's honest
But in it shares some woe, though the main part
Pertains to you alone.

MACDUFF   If it be mine,   200
Keep it not from me, quickly let me have it.

ROSS
Let not your ears despise my tongue for ever,

---

185 'which was confirmed to me the more'.
    Ross may mean either that seeing
    Macbeth's army on the move convinced
    him that his opponents were also
    mobilizing or that Macbeth's army was
    mobilizing in response to that of the
    'many worthy fellows'.
187 **your eye** the sight of you (i.e. Malcolm)
189 **doff** take off (an image from clothing),
    from 'do off', analogous to 'don'
192 **none** (there is) none

196 **latch** catch, take hold of (*OED v.*[1] 4a)
197 **fee-grief** a quasi-legal term, coined on
    analogy with 'fee-farm', 'fee-simple',
    etc. A fee was an estate in land, held
    on condition of homage to a feudal lord
    (*OED* fee *n.*[2] 1). Shakespeare coins this
    expression to mean a grief that comes to
    a single owner (as opposed to a *general
    cause*).
198 **Due** owed

196 they:] *this edn;* they, *F;* they? *Theobald*

266

Which shall possess them with the heaviest sound
That ever yet they heard.

MACDUFF   H'm: I guess at it.

ROSS

Your castle is surprised; your wife and babes   205
Savagely slaughtered. To relate the manner
Were on the quarry of these murdered deer
To add the death of you.

MALCOLM   Merciful heaven.
What, man; ne'er pull your hat upon your brows:
Give sorrow words. The grief that does not speak   210
Whispers the o'erfraught heart and bids it break.

MACDUFF

My children too?

ROSS

Wife, children, servants, all that could be found.

MACDUFF

And I must be from thence? My wife killed too?

203 **possess them with** take hold of them with, affect them strongly with (*OED* possess *v.* 3)
heaviest most sorrowful

204 **H'm** an inarticulate sound and not a word as such, replacing F's more archaic 'Humh', indicating Macduff's emotional response to Ross's news

205 **surprised** taken by surprise

207 **quarry** metaphorically, a collection of deer killed in a hunt (*OED n.*[1] 2a)
murdered deer Ross develops the metaphor, punning on *deer*/dear. Compare Hal's epitaph for Falstaff, *1H4* 5.4.106–7: 'Death hath not struck so fat a deer today, / Though many dearer in this bloody fray'.

209 **pull ... brows** apparently, a conventional gesture of sorrow or grief. Title-pages of plays usually show the actors wearing hats, although modern actors tend not to. The line was not cut in the

2010 production at Shakespeare's Globe, London, despite the actors being hatless. It can carry a metaphorical resonance.

210–11 **The grief ... break** Malcolm gives a variant on a favourite saying of the period, originating from Seneca, *Hippolytus*, 607: '*Curae leves loquuntur, ingentes stupent*'; Florio, translating Montaigne's *Essays*, 1.2, renders this: 'Light cares can freely speak, / Great cares heart rather break', using a rhyme that Shakespeare also employs. 'Break' was pronounced to rhyme with 'speak' (Cercignani, 161). See Dent, G449: 'Grief pent up will break the heart', and Ford, *The Broken Heart*, 5.3.76: 'They are the silent griefs which cut the heart-strings'.

211 **Whispers** whispers to, contrasted with speaking out loud
o'erfraught overburdened

214 **from thence** absent

204 H'm] *this edn;* Humh: *F;* H'm – *Oxf*[1], *Cam*[1]

ROSS

    I have said.   215

MALCOLM

    Be comforted.

    Let's make us medicines of our great revenge,

    To cure this deadly grief.

MACDUFF

    He has no children. All my pretty ones?

    Did you say all? O hell-kite. All?   220

    What, all my pretty chickens, and their dam

    At one fell swoop?

MALCOLM

    Dispute it like a man.

MACDUFF   I shall do so,

    But I must also feel it as a man:

    I cannot but remember such things were   225

    That were most precious to me. Did heaven look on,

    And would not take their part? Sinful Macduff,

217 **make ... revenge** Brooke suggests that revenge is to be seen as 'an outlet for silent grief', citing Dent, D125: 'To lament the dead avails not and revenge vents hatred'.

219 **He ... children** often assumed to refer to Macbeth, and key to recent readings of the play such as Adelman's (130–46). Muir cites *3H6* 5.5.63 in support of this reading: 'You have no children, butchers; if you had, / The thought of them would have stirred up remorse'. But some scholars (e.g. Malone, Bradley, and others cited by Furness, 297–8) have taken it to mean Malcolm, whom Macduff is implicitly reproving for want of sympathy. Compare *KJ* 3.3.91: 'he talks to me that never had a son', and see Dent, C341: 'He that has not children knows not what love is'.

220 **hell-kite** hellish predator. The kite and its voracious appetite are always referred to pejoratively in Shakespeare. See 3.4.70n.

221 **chickens ... dam** continuing the avian metaphor, and perhaps pathetically recalling the child/bird images from 4.2. 'Dam' (mother) can be used of birds as well as animals.

222 **one fell swoop** *fell* means savage or ruthless (*OED* fell *a.* and *adv.* 1), and *swoop* refers to the pounce of the kite falling on its prey. Dover Wilson suggests a subsidiary meaning from gambling of 'at one sweep of the stakes'. The expression 'At one fell swoop' was not proverbial before Shakespeare. Compare *Ham* 4.5.140–1: 'is't writ in your revenge / That swoopstake you will draw both friend and foe'.

223 **Dispute** argue against, contend with

223–4 **I ... man** Macduff's view of manliness may be compared with those of Macbeth and his Lady in 1.7. Adelman, 143–4, expands on this.

227 **part** side, cause

They were all struck for thee. Naught that I am,
Not for their own demerits, but for mine,
Fell slaughter on their souls. Heaven rest them now.   230

MALCOLM

Be this the whetstone of your sword. Let grief
Convert to anger; blunt not the heart, enrage it.

MACDUFF

O, I could play the woman with mine eyes,
And braggart with my tongue. But gentle heavens,
Cut short all intermission. Front to front   235
Bring thou this fiend of Scotland and myself;
Within my sword's length set him. If he scape,
Heaven forgive him too.

MALCOLM   This time goes manly.
Come, go we to the King: our power is ready,
Our lack is nothing but our leave. Macbeth   240
Is ripe for shaking, and the powers above

---

228 **Naught** wicked or sinful person (*OED n.* 2d)
229 **demerits** faults, offences
231 **whetstone** a shaped stone for giving a smooth edge to cutting tools; metaphorically, something that sharpens the wits or incites to action
232 **blunt ... enrage** Malcolm is eager to reshape Macduff's guilt and grief for his own purposes.
233 **play the woman** proverbial, Dent, W637.2: 'To play the woman'. For another man's demeaning association of women with tears, see *AC* 4.2.35–6, where Enobarbus fears to be 'onion-eyed' and begs Antony, 'For shame! / Transform us not to women'.
234 **braggart** boaster. Braunmuller compares Macbeth's dismissal of boasting and self-correction at 4.1.152.

235 **intermission** lapse of time, pause in action
Front to front face to face
237 **scape** escape
238 **too** 'because if he escapes, it will be a sign that my hatred is appeased' (Muir)
time very often emended to 'tune' following Rowe, e.g. by Kittredge, Dover Wilson, Muir, Oxf, Hunter, Braunmuller and Bate & Rasmussen. The two words were easily confused in early modern handwriting. However, *time* may here be used both in a musical sense, meaning a 'manly' rhythm that differs from a dirge, and also, more generally, the new mood brought on by Macduff's last speech.
239 **power** army
240 **Our ... leave** 'All we need is formal leave-taking.'
241 **ripe for shaking** ready to fall (like ripe fruit). Macbeth later sees his own life in autumnal terms (5.3.22–3).

228 struck] *(strooke)*   236 myself] *Capell;* my self *F*   238 time] tune *Rowe*

Put on their instruments. Receive what cheer
  you may,
The night is long that never finds the day.   *Exeunt.*

5.1   *Enter a* Doctor of Physic*, and a* Waiting
Gentlewoman.

DOCTOR   I have two nights watched with you, but can
perceive no truth in your report. When was it she
last walked?

GENTLEWOMAN   Since his majesty went into the field, I
have seen her rise from her bed, throw her nightgown   5
upon her, unlock her closet, take forth paper, fold it,
write upon't, read it, afterwards seal it, and again
return to bed, yet all this while in a most fast sleep.

---

242 **Put ... instruments** either don their
weapons (*OED* instrument *n.* 2a) or
instigate their agents (*OED* put *v.* 16a)

243 perhaps referring to the proverb 'After
night comes the day' (Dent, N164)

5.1 In contrast to 4.3 which is an open, public
scene set in England, this scene takes
place in a private domestic space in
Scotland. In her sleep, the Lady recalls
and re-enacts moments from 2.2. There
are specific recollections of the earlier
scene at 27–30, 51–2, 63–4 and 67.

0.1 **Doctor of Physic** probably identified as a
medical doctor by his costume, to distinguish him from a cleric. Compare the
Doctor at 4.3.139. For discussion of the
Doctor's role in this scene, see Pettigrew,
ch. 3.

0.1–2 **Waiting Gentlewoman** lady-in-
waiting, personal attendant to a queen or
princess, of genteel birth

1 **watched** kept watch or kept awake
intentionally (*OED* watch *v.* 1b)

3 **walked** sleepwalked. Helkiah Crooke,
Microcosmographia (1615), observes of
sleepwalkers that 'The imagination in

sleepe is stronger then when we are
awake, as appeareth in those that walke
and talke in their sleepe' (288). For other
early modern discussions of sleep disorders, see Timothy Bright, *A Treatise of
Melancholy* (1586), 131–2, and Lewes
Lavater, *Of ghostes and spirites walkynge
by nyght* (1572), 48–9. Compare Thomas
Tomkis, *Lingua* (1607), 5.18: '*Lingua
ariseth in her sleepe and walketh*'. Janowitz
discusses sleepwalking and other sleep
disorders in the Macbeths from a modern
medical perspective.

4 **went ... field** engaged in military
operations

5 **nightgown** dressing gown. Compare
2.2.71. Diehl identifies the nightgown
with reference to contemporary emblem
books as 'a traditional Renaissance icon
of human mortality' (196).

6 **closet** cabinet for valuables (*OED n.* 3a)

7 **seal** place a seal of hot wax, as a mark of
authenticity. The seal identified the sender
and ensured the privacy of the letter's con-
tents. The Lady's mind may be reverting to
the letter she received from Macbeth in 1.5.

5.1] *Actus Quintus. Scena Prima.*   1 two] *F2–4;* too *F*

DOCTOR   A great perturbation in nature, to receive at
    once the benefit of sleep and do the effects of   10
    watching. In this slumbery agitation, besides her
    walking and other actual performances, what, at any
    time, have you heard her say?
GENTLEWOMAN   That, sir, which I will not report after
    her.   15
DOCTOR   You may to me, and 'tis most meet you should.
GENTLEWOMAN   Neither to you, nor anyone, having no
    witness to confirm my speech.

Enter LADY, *with a taper.*

Lo you, here she comes. This is her very guise, and
upon my life, fast asleep. Observe her, stand close.   20
DOCTOR   How came she by that light?
GENTLEWOMAN   Why, it stood by her: she has light by
    her continually; 'tis her command.

9   **perturbation** disturbance. For other instances where Shakespeare associates perturbation with uneasy sleep, see Iyengar, 'perturbation'.
10   **do the effects** create the appearances or outward manifestations (*OED* effect *n.* 4a)
11   **watching** being awake
    slumbery sleepy
    agitation mental disturbance, perturbation (*OED n.* 4); 'slumbery agitation' is an oxymoron, suggestive of the Lady's strange condition.
12   **actual** active (*OED a.* 1)
16   **meet** appropriate, proper
17–18   The Gentlewoman is careful not to implicate herself in a potentially treasonous utterance (Pettigrew, 83).
18.1   *taper* candle. See Furness, 303–4, and Sprague, *Actors*, 268–72, on stage business

associated with this moment, which has often been illustrated, e.g. in Henry Fuseli's painting of Sarah Siddons (*Lady Macbeth Sleepwalking*, 1783). Siddons's preparations for this scene, and her innovation in setting down the taper in order to mime hand-washing, are discussed in McDonald, *Look*, 40–2. Diehl calls the taper 'an icon of man's life and the human soul' (196).
19   **guise** manner, way (*OED n.* 1)
20   **upon my life** an oath. The Act to Restrain Abuses of Players (1606) obliged players and playwrights to restrain the style of oaths on pain of a fine of £10 every time an actor 'jestingly or profanely' spoke the name of God or Christ. Texts published after this date reflect this legislation.
    close concealed from sight (*OED a.* and *adv.* 4a)

9 nature,] nature, – *Dyce*   11 watching.] watching! *Dyce*   14 report] repeat *Warburton*   18.1 SD LADY]
Lady Macbeth / *Rowe;* QUEEN *Staunton*   22 has] *(*ha's*)*

271

DOCTOR   You see her eyes are open.

GENTLEWOMAN   Ay, but their sense are shut.   25

DOCTOR   What is it she does now? Look how she rubs
her hands.

GENTLEWOMAN   It is an accustomed action with her,
to seem thus washing her hands. I have known her
continue in this a quarter of an hour.   30

LADY   Yet here's a spot.

DOCTOR   Hark, she speaks. I will set down what comes
from her, to satisfy my remembrance the more
strongly.

LADY   Out, damned spot: out, I say. One; two. Why   35
then 'tis time to do't. Hell is murky. Fie, my lord,
fie, a soldier and afeared? What need we fear? Who
knows it when none can call our power to account?
Yet who would have thought the old man to have
had so much blood in him?   40

---

25 **sense are shut** i.e. she cannot see. For
other instances of eyes that do not see
compare 2.2.55–6, 3.2.47–51, 3.4.93–4.
For this use of a plural verb with a singular
noun, see Muir's note. Braunmuller compares *Oth* 4.3.93: 'Their wives have sense
like them', where Shakespeare seems to
use 'sense' as a collective plural.

28–30 Compare her reference to *a little
water* at 2.2.68.

32 **set down** write down. This is an implicit
SD to the Doctor to produce a notebook.

33 **satisfy** meet (a wish or expectation),
content (*OED v.* 4b)

35 **One; two** She seems to hear a sound such
as the striking of a clock or tolling of
a bell (as at 2.1.62).

36 **murky** dark, gloomy. Compare *Tem*
4.1.25–8: 'the murkiest den, / The most

opportune place . . . shall never melt /
Mine honour into lust'.

37 **afeared** afraid. She recalls her conversation with Macbeth in 1.7.

37–8 **Who . . . account** No one can be said
to *know* what the Macbeths have done
when they are accountable to no one.
Editors often emend F's punctuation here,
removing the question mark after *fear*,
but the separation into two questions
emphasizes the Lady's reliance on the
self-authenticating power of tyrannical
rule. See Muir and Braunmuller on the
implications of the punctuation, and
Bishop's defence of F.

39–40 **Yet . . . him?** It was believed that the
supply of blood dried up with age. See
MA 4.1.193: 'Time hath not yet so dried
this blood of mine'.

25 sense are] sense' are *Dyce;* senses are *Keightley;* sense is *Davenant*   33 satisfy] *(*satisfie*);* fortifie
Warburton   34 strongly.] strongly. [*Taking out his Tables.*] / *Capell*   35 spot:] spot! *Steevens*   36 murky.]
murky! *Steevens*   37 afeard] afeard] *(*affear'd*);* afraid *Rowe*   37–8 fear? Who . . . account?] *(*fear? who . . . account*)*
F3–4; fear? who . . . accompt: *F;* fear who . . . account – *Rowe;* fear who . . . account? *Theobald*
40 him?] *Rowe;* him. *F*

DOCTOR   Do you mark that?

LADY   The Thane of Fife had a wife. Where is she now? What, will these hands ne'er be clean? No more o'that, my lord, no more o'that. You mar all with this starting.   45

DOCTOR   Go to, go to. You have known what you should not.

GENTLEWOMAN   She has spoke what she should not, I am sure of that. Heaven knows what she has known.

LADY   Here's the smell of the blood still. All the   50 perfumes of Arabia will not sweeten this little hand. Oh, oh, oh.

DOCTOR   What a sigh is there. The heart is sorely charged.

GENTLEWOMAN   I would not have such a heart in my   55 bosom, for the dignity of the whole body.

DOCTOR   Well, well, well.

GENTLEWOMAN   Pray God it be, sir.

42   **The Thane ... wife** The Thane of Fife is Macduff, and the implication may be that the Lady is aware of the murders of his wife and children. The doggerel rhyme suggests a song or nursery rhyme, though none is known.

43   **What ... clean** Webster imitated this line for Cornelia's mad scene in *The White Devil*, 5.4.82–3: 'here's a white hand: / Can blood so soon be wash'd out?'

45   **starting** flinching, moving nervously. Compare Macbeth's reactions at 1.3.51 and 3.4.60.

46   **Go to** Come, come (an exclamation of impatience or reproach). The Doctor comments on the Lady's revelatory speech.

48   **spoke** spoken (obsolete form)

51   **perfumes of Arabia** Arabia had been a source of perfumes to the West since the Middle Ages. The Lady's hyperbole recalls Macbeth's similar feelings about his bloody hands at 2.2.61–4.

52   **Oh, oh, oh** an indication to the actor to make an appropriate sound, such as a groan or sigh. Compare *KL* 5.3.308 (Q only).

53–4   **sorely charged** painfully overburdened (*OED* charge *v*. 9a)

56   **dignity** rank, status (*OED n*. 3). She means that she would not want the Lady's guilty conscience, even to be queen.

41 that?] that? [*Writing*] *Collier*   43 ne'er] *(*ne're*); neere *F2*   45 this] *om. Pope*   starting] stating *F2*
46–7] *Pope; F lines* too: / not. /   50 of the] of *F3–4*   52 Oh, oh, oh.] O, o, o. *Oxf*   56 the dignity] dignity
F3–4   57 well.] well – *Rowe*   58 Pray]'Pray *Steevens*

DOCTOR   This disease is beyond my practice: yet I have
    known those which have walked in their sleep, who   60
    have died holily in their beds.

LADY   Wash your hands, put on your nightgown, look
    not so pale. I tell you yet again, Banquo's buried; he
    cannot come out on's grave.

DOCTOR   Even so?   65

LADY   To bed, to bed: there's knocking at the gate. Come,
    come, come, come, give me your hand. What's done,
    cannot be undone. To bed, to bed, to bed.   *Exit Lady.*

DOCTOR   Will she go now to bed?

GENTLEWOMAN   Directly.   70

DOCTOR

Foul whisperings are abroad. Unnatural deeds
Do breed unnatural troubles. Infected minds
To their deaf pillows will discharge their secrets.
More needs she the divine than the physician.
God, God forgive us all. Look after her,   75
Remove from her the means of all annoyance,
And still keep eyes upon her. So, goodnight.

---

59   **practice** professional skill. See Pettigrew, 63–4, on the implications of the Doctor's refusal to treat the Lady's condition.

63   **pale** This recalls Macbeth's pallor at 2.2.59.

64   **on's** of his

66   **knocking** as during the latter part of 2.2

67–8   **What's . . . undone** See 1.7.1–2 and n., and 3.2.13. See Dent, T200: 'Things done cannot be undone'.

70   **Directly** at once

71–79   Bradley suggests that the return to blank verse 'lowers the tension towards that of the next scene' (337, fn. 1), and it could also create a return to the normality of Shakespeare's 'regular medium' (Palfrey, 107).

71   **whisperings** whisp'rings; rumours

74   **More . . . divine** The Doctor, acknowledging that the cause of the Lady's condition is spiritual rather than physical, recognizes his own limits. His view rests on a commonplace such as 'Where the Philosopher ends, the Physician begins; and he ends (they say) where the Divine begins' (*Purchas his Pilgrim*, 1619, sig. 2S1^V, as quoted in Dent, *Proverbial*, P252.11: 'Where the Philosopher ends the physition begins').
    the divine a priest to attend to her soul

76   i.e. so as to prevent her from committing suicide
    annoyance injury, harm (*OED n.* 1, citing this line)

64 on's] of his *Pope;* of 's *Capell*   71 whisperings] *(*whisp'rings*)*   75 God, God] Good God *Pope*

My mind she has mated and amazed my sight.
I think, but dare not speak.

GENTLEWOMAN   Good night, good doctor.

Exeunt.

5.2   *Drum and Colours. Enter* MENTEITH, CAITHNESS,
ANGUS, LENNOX, Soldiers.

MENTEITH

The English power is near, led on by Malcolm,
His uncle Siward and the good Macduff.
Revenges burn in them, for their dear causes
Would to the bleeding and the grim alarm

---

78 **mated** baffled (*OED* mate *v.*[1] 3)

79 **I think . . . speak** Like the Gentlewoman,
the Doctor fears to give voice to potentially treasonous utterance.

5.2.0.1 *Drum and Colours* A drummer with
his instrument, and a flagbearer; a common SD in the period. It signals here the
beginning of military conflict. See also
Dessen & Thomson, 'drum'.

0.1–2 MENTEITH, CAITHNESS, ANGUS names
possibly taken from Holinshed's list of
the earls created by Malcolm (2.176, in
Bullough, 7.506). See 5.9.27–9. Angus
has two speeches in 1.3, but neither he
nor the other two, who have not been
identified previously, say anything else
until this scene.

1 **power** army

2 **uncle Siward** According to Holinshed,
Siward was Malcolm's maternal grandfather, his daughter being Duncan's
wife. 'Nephew' could sometimes mean
'grandson' in the early modern period
(*OED* nephew *n.* 2a) and 5.6.2–3 supports this meaning, although it does not
appear to be the case that 'uncle' could
mean 'grandfather'.

good Macduff This evaluation of Macduff
contrasts markedly with his own (*Sinful
Macduff*) at 4.3.227, and contributes to a
simplification of the moral tone in the
play's last act.

3–5 **Revenges . . . man** The main meaning
of this ambiguously phrased sentence is
that the cause of Malcolm and Macduff is
powerful enough to bring the dead back
to life.

3 **dear** of great worth, precious (*OED a.*[1]
and *n.*[2] 4a), or 'most dear to them'. 'Dire'
or 'grievous' (*a.*[2] 2) may also be relevant
(Braunmuller).

causes may refer to the grounds for the
revenges, but 'cause' can also mean 'disease' (*OED* cause *n.* 12) and thus relate to
the other medical terms *bleeding* and *mortified*. Compare *AW* 2.1.109–10: 'touched
/ With that malignant cause', and *Cor*
3.1.236: 'Leave us to cure this cause'.

4 **bleeding** may be adjectival, meaning
'running with blood' (in the sense that a
dead man's wounds respond to the
presence of his murderer by bleeding), or
a noun meaning medical blood-letting
(thus implying that Scotland is like a

---

78 has] *(*ha's*)*   **5.2**] *Scena Secunda.*   0.1–2] *Enter* MENTEITH . . . *soldiers, with a drummer and colours.*
Oxf   0.2 LENNOX] *Lenx F2*   2 Siward] *Theobald; Seyward F*   3 them,] *Oxf;* them: *F;* them; *Collier*

Excite the mortified man.

ANGUS　　　　　　　　　　　Near Birnam Wood　　　5

Shall we well meet them; that way are they coming.

CAITHNESS

Who knows if Donalbain be with his brother?

LENNOX

For certain, sir, he is not; I have a file

Of all the gentry. There is Siward's son,

And many unrough youths, that even now　　　10

Protest their first of manhood.

MENTEITH　　　　　　　　　　What does the tyrant?

CAITHNESS

Great Dunsinane he strongly fortifies.

Some say he's mad; others, that lesser hate him,

Do call it valiant fury; but for certain,

He cannot buckle his distempered cause　　　15

Within the belt of rule.

ANGUS　　　　　　　　　　　Now does he feel

His secret murders sticking on his hands;

---

diseased patient in need of this procedure). Alternatively, it may form part of a phrase, 'the bleeding and the grim alarum', meaning 'bloody'.

grim cruel, formidable (*OED a.* and *adv.* 3b)

alarum call to arms

5 **Excite** rouse up, awaken (*OED v.* 2c)
　mortified dead or moribund
　Birnam Wood See 4.1.92 and n.
7 **Donalbain** at this time in exile in Ireland
8 **file** list, roll
10 **unrough** unbearded, i.e. untested (*OED* cites this line)
11 **Protest** claim, assert (*OED v.* 1b)
　first beginning, first part (*OED a.* (*n.*) and *adv.* 5c)

15–16 **He ... rule** For the metaphor, Muir compares *TC* 2.2.30–2: 'And buckle in a waist most fathomless / With spans and inches so diminutive / As fears and reasons'. The lines bring together images of clothing (e.g. 1.3.109–10, 1.7.32–5 and 20–2 below) and disease to indicate the extent of Macbeth's disordered condition.

15 **distempered** disordered, diseased, as in *2H4* 3.1.38–41: 'the body of our kingdom ... yet distempered', or immoderate, inordinate (*OED ppl. a.* 5)

16 **belt of rule** belt used as a metaphor for control

17 **sticking** as if with blood. See 3.1.48 and n., and also the image of bloody hands, and n., at 2.2.28.

---

5 Birnam] *F4;* Byrnan *F*　6 well] *om. F3–4*　8 I have] I've *Pope*　10 unrough] *Theobald;* unruffe *F;* unruff *F3–4;* unruff 'd *Pope;* untough *Collier*　11 tyrant?] *F4;* tyrant. *F*　13 hate] hates *F3–4*　15 cause] course *Collier*

Now minutely revolts upbraid his faith-breach;
Those he commands move only in command,
Nothing in love. Now does he feel his title   20
Hang loose about him, like a giant's robe
Upon a dwarfish thief.

MENTEITH   Who then shall blame
His pestered senses to recoil and start,
When all that is within him does condemn
Itself for being there.

CAITHNESS   Well, march we on,   25
To give obedience where 'tis truly owed.
Meet we the medicine of the sickly weal,
And with him pour we in our country's purge,
Each drop of us.

LENNOX   Or so much as it needs
To dew the sovereign flower, and drown the weeds.   30
Make we our march towards Birnam.   *Exeunt marching*.

---

18 **minutely** every minute (*OED adv.*²)
upbraid reproach, reprove (*OED v.* 2)
faith-breach breach of faith, treason (the
only citation for this compound word in
OED faith *n.* 14. *EEBO* records nothing
earlier.)

19–20 **only ... love** Braunmuller compares
AC 3.13.59–60: 'He knows that you
embrace not Antony / As you did love,
but as you feared him'.
in because of

20 **title** of king

22–5 **Who ... there** Macbeth's whole being
is so disordered that it is in a state of
internal insurrection.

23 **pestered** troubled, plagued (*OED* pester
*v.*¹ 4a) or entangled (*v.*¹ 1). Muir cites
Cotgrave: 'Empestrer. To pester, intricate,
intangle, trouble, incomber'.
recoil fall away, degenerate (*OED v.*¹ 4b).
See 4.3.19 and n.

27 **medicine** med'cine; physician, i.e.
Malcolm (*OED n.*²). See *WT* 4.4.584:
'Preserver of my father, now of me, / The
medicine of our house'.
weal commonwealth, state

28–9 **our country's ... drop** Caithness
envisages each of the soldiers as a drop of
medicine to rid Scotland of impurities,
but there is also a play on the idea of
drops of blood.

30 **dew** moisten as if with dew, though here
the 'dew' will be blood
sovereign royal, but with an underlying
meaning of supremely potent or medically efficacious (*OED n.* and *adj.* 3)
weeds metaphor for the state of disorder
in Scotland. See *R2* 3.4 for an extended
use of the commonwealth/garden analogy.

31 SD This direction may suggest order and
determination in contrast to the disorder
of Macbeth described in the scene.

---

25 there.] there? *Davenant*   27 medicine] *Knight;* med'cine *F;* medecin *Warburton;* med'cin *Hanmer*
31 we] me *Theobald*   Birnam] *F4;* Birnan *F*   SD] *Exeunt. / Rowe*

5.3   *Enter* MACBETH, Doctor *and Attendants.*

MACBETH

Bring me no more reports, let them fly all;
Till Birnam Wood remove to Dunsinane,
I cannot taint with fear. What's the boy Malcolm?
Was he not born of woman? The spirits that know
All mortal consequences have pronounced me thus: 5
'Fear not, Macbeth, no man that's born of woman
Shall e'er have power upon thee.' Then fly, false
      thanes,
And mingle with the English epicures;

5.3 In this scene Macbeth reappears after a long absence from the stage, and actors sometimes represent him as having aged. Rosenberg, 593–4, gives examples. Macbeth perceives himself as aged (22–6).

0.1 Although Macbeth enters with an entourage of the Doctor and Attendants, none of them has any interaction with him until he calls upon the Doctor at 37. It is not clear what they might be doing, or even if it is an attendant who is called upon at 48, 50 and 54. Macbeth's longer speeches, 1–10, 22–8, appear like quasi-soliloquies. The presence of these apparently superfluous onlookers may help to stress the loss of control conveyed by his lines.

3 **taint** lose courage, become weak (*OED* *v.*[1] C3b, where this line is the first citation). Perhaps there is also a hint of the meaning 'colour, dye, tinge' (*v.*[1] B1a), given the association of fear with pallor, e.g. at 1.7.37, and 11 below.
boy Malcolm For the experienced soldier's scorn of youth, compare Antony's attitude to 'the boy Caesar' (*AC* 3.13.17).

4 **spirits** referring to the Apparitions in 4.1, not to the Witches

5 Some editors (e.g. Dover Wilson, Muir) have emended *consequences* to 'consequence' on metrical grounds, and also because Shakespeare elsewhere only uses the singular form, but this does not produce a regular iambic line.
mortal consequences outcomes of human life. Andrews suggests 'all the causes and effects of mortal life', the kind of considerations Macbeth has in mind at 1.7.1–12.
me to me

8 **epicures** gluttons, pleasure-seekers. See Holinshed, 2.179–80: 'The Scottish people before had no knowledge nor understanding of fine fare or riotous surfet . . . those . . . superfluities . . . came into the realme of Scotland with the *English-men* . . . For manie of the people abhorring the riotous maners and superfluous gourmandizing brought in among them by the Englishmen, were willing inough to receiue this Donald for their King, trusting . . . they should by his severe order in gouernement recouer againe the former temperance of their old progenitors.' On English/Scots relations see also Floyd-Wilson.

5.3] *Scaena Tertia.*   0.1 Doctor] *the Doctor of Physic Oxf*   2 Birnam] *F3–4;* Byrnane *F;* Byrnam *F2*
4 The] *om. Pope*   7 upon] on *Steevens*   Then fly] Fly *Pope*

The mind I sway by, and the heart I bear,
Shall never sag with doubt, nor shake with fear.   10

Enter Servant.

The devil damn thee black, thou cream-faced loon.
Where got'st thou that goose-look?

SERVANT
There is ten thousand.

MACBETH   Geese, villain?

SERVANT   Soldiers, sir.

MACBETH
Go prick thy face, and over-red thy fear,
Thou lily-livered boy. What soldiers, patch?   15
Death of thy soul, those linen cheeks of thine

9–10 'The rhyme [in 9–10] lends finality and a touch of complacency which are immediately contradicted by what follows' (Dover Wilson).
9 **sway** move (*OED v.* 4b, citing this line), but also 'rule' (*OED v.* 9)
10 **sag** decline through lack of strength (*OED v.* 2a, citing this line)
11–12 Macbeth appears particularly offended with the Servant's pale face, betraying his fear (here and at 14, 16–17), perhaps because it is 'an unwelcome image of his own fear' (Tilmouth, 514). Compare his recourse to the proverb 'False face must hide what the false heart doth know' (1.7.83).
11 **cream-faced** having a face as pale as cream with fear. See 3n. on *taint*.
loon rogue, lout, clown, person of low status. F4 spells this word 'lown', as does *Oth* 2.3.88, where it rhymes with 'crown'. Braunmuller, citing William Patten, *The Expedicion into Scotlande of . . . Edward, Duke of Soomerset*, 1548 (sig. 18ᵛ, margin), calls this a Scotticism.

12 **goose-look** appearance which is foolish or stupid, geese being proverbially giddy (see Dent, G347.1) but perhaps also suggestive of pallor, geese being white, along with *cream-faced* and *lily-livered.*
14 **over-red** redden over, cover with blood (*OED*'s sole citation for this word. *EEBO* records nothing earlier.)
15 **lily-livered** cowardly. The liver was regarded as the organ of passion and courage, hence associated with red blood. See *2H4* 4.3.102–4: 'the liver white and pale, which is the badge of pusillanimity and cowardice', and the earlier use of the epithet in Kent's description of Oswald in *KL* 2.2.16–17: 'a lily-livered, action-taking [litigious] knave'.
patch fool, clown (*OED n.*² 1)
16 **Death . . . soul** an oath
linen white; a proverbial association. See Dent, L306.1: 'As white as linen', and also *VA* 589–90: 'whereat a sudden pale / Like lawn [linen] being spread upon the blushing rose / Usurps her cheek'.

10.1] *Enter an Attendant, hastily.* / *Capell*   11 loon] *(loone);* lown *F4*   12 goose-look?] *F4;* Goose-looke. *F*   13 is] are *Rowe*   thousand.] thousand – *Rowe*

279

Are counsellors to fear. What soldiers, whey-face?

SERVANT

The English force, so please you.

MACBETH

Take thy face hence.   [*Exit Servant.*]

Seyton, I am sick at heart,

When I behold – Seyton, I say – this push   20

Will cheer me ever, or disseat me now.

I have lived long enough: my way of life

Is fallen into the sere, the yellow leaf,

And that which should accompany old age,

17 **counsellors to fear** either associates of fear, or provokers of fear
whey-face face as pale as whey, the watery part of milk which remains when the curd is separated out by coagulation

19 **Seyton,** Most modern editors punctuate with an exclamation mark or a question mark at this point, but F's comma has been retained here to preserve its interpretative possibilities. Macbeth may believe Seyton is there, or perhaps he assumes he is close. He may be calling him. That Macbeth names him three times before he appears may indicate Macbeth's lack of authority and increasing isolation. Opinions differ as to whether the name Seyton was pronounced 'Satan', but we concur with Brooke and Braunmuller who accept it as a pun. Braunmuller gives evidence to support the claim (260). Brooke notes other punning names such as Lightborne (Marlowe, *Edward II*) and Mercadé (*LLL*).

20 **push** military advance (*OED n.²* 1b)

21 **cheer** comfort, encourage, but perhaps with a play on the near-homophone 'chair' meaning 'throne', which fits better with *disseat*
disseat unseat, dethrone. Under 'disseat' *OED* records uncertainty about this reading, noting that the word is printed as

'disease' in F2–4. But see *TNK* 5.4.70–3: 'he . . . seeks all foul means / Of boist'rous and rough jad'ry to disseat / His lord'.

22–8 **my . . . not** Miola, *Classical*, 117–18, compares Macbeth's lamentation for what he has lost with Seneca, *Hercules Furens*, 1258–61, Greville, *Alaham*, 5.3.106–7, and Chapman, *The Tragedy of Byron*, 5.4.69–72.

22 **way** Some editors, most recently Taylor (Taylor & Lavagnino, *Middleton*), have emended this to 'May' on the grounds that it strengthens the seasonal imagery and is used elsewhere by Shakespeare in this sense. See *MA* 5.1.76, *R2* 3.4.47–8, *H5* 1.2.120. Garrick said 'May' (Rosenberg, 599). But *way of life* suggesting course, path or journey fits the context and Macbeth's consciousness of progressive decline without invoking an idea of youth incongruous to him.

23 **sere** dry, withered. See *CE* 4.2.19: 'He is deformed, crooked, old and sere'.
yellow leaf metaphor for the last stage of life. See *Son* 73.1–4: 'That time of year thou mayst in me behold, / When yellow leaves, or none, or few do hang / Upon those boughs which shake against the cold, / Bare ruined choirs where late the sweet birds sang'.

17 counsellors] *F3;* Counsailers *F;* Counsailours *F2;* Counsellours *F4*   whey-face] *Davenant;* Whay-face *F*   19 SD] *Collier*   Seyton,] Seyton! – *Rowe*   21 disseat] *Capell;* dis-eate *F;* disease *F2–4;* dis-eat *Davenant;* dis-seat *Collier;* dis-ease *Furness*   22 way] May *Johnson*

As honour, love, obedience, troops of friends,   25
I must not look to have; but in their stead,
Curses not loud but deep, mouth-honour, breath
Which the poor heart would fain deny, and dare not.
Seyton?

Enter SEYTON.

SEYTON

What's your gracious pleasure?

MACBETH   What news more?   30

SEYTON

All is confirmed, my lord, which was reported.

MACBETH

I'll fight, till from my bones my flesh be hacked.
Give me my armour.

SEYTON   'Tis not needed yet.

MACBETH

I'll put it on.
Send out more horses, skirr the country round,   35
Hang those that talk of fear. Give me mine armour.
How does your patient, doctor?

DOCTOR   Not so sick, my lord,
As she is troubled with thick-coming fancies

26 **stead** place
27 **deep** profound, solemn
    mouth-honour i.e. lip-service (Brooke),
    as opposed to true *honour* (25). Muir
    compares Isaiah, 29.13: 'Foresomuch as
    this people, when they be in trouble, do
    honour me with their mouth and with
    their lippes, but their heart is farre fro
    me'.
28 **fain** gladly
35 **skirr** pass or ride rapidly through. See
    OED v. 3, where this line is the first
    citation. *EEBO* records nothing earlier in

this sense, though see *H5* 4.7.59– 61: 'we
will come to them / And make them skirr
away as swift as stones / Enforced from
the old Assyrian slings'.
37 **sick** physically ill
38 **thick-coming** frequently appearing, com-
    ing in crowds. Pettigrew, 88, suggests that
    thick-coming fancies may be the result of
    thickening of the blood, as called for by
    the Lady in 1.5.43, or psychological dis-
    turbance. 'Thick' appears in other sugges-
    tive contexts: *thick as tale* (1.3.98), *thick
    night* (1.5.50) and *thick and slab* (4.1.32).

26 stead] *F2–4;* steed *F*   29 Seyton?] *om. Rowe*   32 be] is *F2–4*   35 more] *F3–4;* moe *F*   36 talk of]
stand in *Rowe*

That keep her from her rest.

MACBETH   Cure her of that.

Canst thou not minister to a mind diseased,   40
Pluck from the memory a rooted sorrow,
Raze out the written troubles of the brain,
And with some sweet oblivious antidote
Cleanse the stuffed bosom of that perilous stuff
Which weighs upon the heart?

DOCTOR   Therein the patient   45
Must minister to himself.

MACBETH

Throw physic to the dogs, I'll none of it.
Come, put mine armour on; give me my staff;
Seyton, send out. Doctor, the thanes fly from me –
Come, sir, dispatch. – If thou couldst, doctor, cast   50
The water of my land, find her disease,

39–45 **Cure . . . heart** Muir suggests as a possible source Daniel, *The Queenes Arcadia* (1606), 1240–51, where Daphne consults a doctor about the insomnia caused by her guilty conscience, and 'those ougly formes of terror that affright / My broken sleepes, that layes upon my heart / This heavy loade that weighes it down with griefe'. This work was performed at Oxford in August 1605. Bullough calls this similarity 'a remarkable instance of that give-and-take often noted in the relations between Daniel and Shakespeare' (7.431).

42 **Raze out** erase, obliterate
written inscribed, permanent

43 **oblivious** associated with oblivion (*OED adj.* 3, citing this line), causing oblivion and forgetfulness

44 **stuffed . . . stuff** Editors have long been unhappy with this awkward-sounding repetition, but no emendation for *stuffed*

has ever been generally accepted. 'Stuffed' means 'clogged up' or 'obstructed' (*OED ppl. a.* 5). Furness gives a range of editorial suggestions, including 'foul', 'clogg'd' and 'fraught'.

45–6 **Therein . . . himself** The Doctor is studiedly neutral in his response, but the pronoun might imply that Macbeth's words apply to himself as well as his wife.

47 **physic** medicine

49, 50, 54 It is not clear to whom Macbeth's abrupt orders at these points are addressed. They may all be to Seyton, as at 49, or alternatively to the Attendants, who would otherwise be unoccupied.

48 **staff** spear, lance or similar weapon (*OED n.*¹ 3a), or baton of office (*n.*¹ 7)

49 **send out** i.e. for reinforcements or equipment, as at 35

50 **dispatch** make haste

50–1 **cast / The water** make a medical diagnosis as if by the analysis of urine

---

39 Cure . . . that.] *F2;* Cure of that: *F;* Cure her from that: *F3–4*   40 a mind] to minds *Pope*   42 Raze] Raise *F3;* Rase *F4;* 'Rase *Capell*   44 stuffed] *(stufft)*   46 to] unto *F2–4*   himself.] himself. *Seton returns with armour and an armourer, who presently begins to equip Macbeth. / Dover Wilson*   48 mine] my *F4*

And purge it to a sound and pristine health,
I would applaud thee to the very echo,
That should applaud again. – Pull't off, I say.
What rhubarb, senna, or what purgative drug   55
Would scour these English hence? Hear'st thou
   of them?

DOCTOR

Ay, my good lord: your royal preparation
Makes us hear something.

MACBETH   Bring it after me.
I will not be afraid of death and bane
Till Birnam forest come to Dunsinane.   60

                   [Exeunt all except Doctor.]

DOCTOR

Were I from Dunsinane away and clear,
Profit again should hardly draw me here.   *Exit.*

---

52 **pristine** pure

54 **Pull't off** an implicit SD to Seyton or to one of the Attendants, probably to remove the armour he put on at 48. Macbeth's disturbed state of mind is indicated by his vacillation.

55 **rhubarb** medicinal plant (rheum, Chinese rhubarb) imported from the far East, used as a purge. See Thomas & Faircloth, 'rhubarb'.

  ***senna** F's 'Cyme' is often taken, as in *OED*, as a misreading for 'cynne' and identified with senna, familiar from herbals such as Gerard, *The Herbal* (1597) as a popular purgative and emetic drug of the period. F2 and F3 read 'caeny', a spelling of 'sene' or 'senna', perhaps indicating that 'cyme' was unfamiliar. 'Cyme' does occur in English medical texts of the period, e.g. Thomas

Cartwright, *An hospital for the diseased* (1579), as part of a cure for 'the Collike in the side': 'take red sage, Camemell, Isope, Cyme, Peniriall, of like quantitie' (25), though here it is for external use on a poultice. 'Cynne' does not appear to be a current spelling in any of the herbals (Sujata Iyengar, personal communication).

56 **scour** clear out, remove (*OED v.*² 6a), perhaps also 'purge' (*v.*² 7a), continuing the medical metaphors

58 **Bring . . . me** another (unspecific) instruction to Seyton or one of the Attendants

59 **bane** death, destruction (*OED n.*¹ 3, citing this line)

62 Doctors were proverbially venal. His closing couplet is clearly not addressed to Macbeth.

---

52 pristine] *F2–4;* pristiue *F*   55 senna] *F4;* Cyme *F;* Caeny *F2–4;* cynne *Cam*¹   56 hence?] *Capell;* hence: *F*   Hear'st] Hearest *Capell*   thou] *F2–4;* yᵘ *F*   58 me.] me. – *Capell*   60 Birnam] *F2–4;* Birnane *F*   SD] *Dyce; Exit with his armourer and other followers. / Collier; Exit. Ard²; [Exeunt all but Doctor.] Cam*¹   61 Were] *Aside.* Were *Hanmer*   62 SD] Steevens; *Exeunt F*

5.4   *Drum and Colours. Enter* MALCOLM, SIWARD,
MACDUFF, *Siward's* Son, MENTEITH, CAITHNESS,
ANGUS *and* Soldiers *marching.*

MALCOLM

    Cousins, I hope the days are near at hand
    That chambers will be safe.

MENTEITH   We doubt it nothing.

SIWARD

    What wood is this before us?

MENTEITH   The Wood of Birnam.

MALCOLM

    Let every soldier hew him down a bough
    And bear't before him; thereby shall we shadow   5
    The numbers of our host, and make discovery
    Err in report of us.

SOLDIER   It shall be done.

SIWARD

    We learn no other but the confident tyrant

5.4.0.1 ***Drum and Colours*** See 5.2.0.1n.
Malcolm may now be combining the
colours of Scotland with those of England,
which would emphasize the union of England and Scotland under James VI and I.

0.1–2 SIWARD ... ***Siward's* Son** Malcolm's
English relations. See 5.2.2n. on *uncle
Siward.*

1   **Cousins** here, a term of familiarity, not
necessarily indicating kinship

2   **chambers** domestic rooms, especially
bedrooms

4   **hew ... bough** Holloway suggests a
reference to the Maying procession,

'celebrating the triumph of new life
over the sere and yellow leaf of winter'
(66).

5   **shadow** keep dark, conceal (*OED v.* 5a,
citing this line, though there are many
earlier uses)

6   **discovery** military reconnaissance (*OED
n.* 1b). Compare *KL* 5.1.53–4: 'Here is
the guess of their true strength and forces,
/ By diligent discovery'.

7   **Err** make a mistake, go astray

8   **no other** nothing else
    but except

5.4] *Scena Quarta.*   0.1 SIWARD] *(Seyward);* old Siward *Dyce*   1 Cousins] Cousin *F3–4*   3, 8, 16 SPs]
(Syew. 3, Syw. 8, Sey. 16)   3 Birnam] *F3–4;* Birnane *F;* Byrnam *F2*

Keeps still in Dunsinane, and will endure
Our setting down before't.

MALCOLM   'Tis his main hope.   10
For where there is advantage to be given,
Both more and less have given him the revolt,
And none serve with him but constrained things,
Whose hearts are absent too.

MACDUFF   Let our just censures
Attend the true event, and put we on   15
Industrious soldiership.

SIWARD   The time approaches,
That will with due decision make us know
What we shall say we have, and what we owe.
Thoughts speculative their unsure hopes relate,
But certain issue, strokes must arbitrate: 20
Towards which, advance the war.   *Exeunt marching.*

---

9   **endure** put up with, last out
10 **setting down** being encamped (so as to
     besiege). See *OED* set *v.*[1] PV 1b set
     down. Compare *AC* 3.13.173: 'Caesar
     sets down in Alexandria'.
11 **where ... given** when opportunity to
     escape is offered. Some editors, e.g.
     Dover Wilson, Muir, have emended *given*
     to 'gone', following Capell, but there
     may be play on *given* in 12.
     advantage favourable occasion, chance
     (*OED n.* 4)
12 **more and less** people of all ranks. See
     2H4 1.1.209: 'more and less do flock to
     follow him'.
     given ... revolt revolted from him
13 **constrained** constrainèd; enforced, act-
     ing under compulsion (*OED adj.* 1)

14–15 **Let ... event** 'Let our true judgement
     (of the state of Macbeth's support) await
     the final outcome (of the battle).' See
     TNK 1.2.113–15: 'Let th'event, / That
     never-erring arbitrator, tell us / When we
     know all ourselves'.
15 **event** outcome, issue (*OED n.* 3a)
18 'The difference between talk and true
     possession' (Hunter). Siward, like Macduff,
     tempers Malcolm's youthful optimism.
     owe own
19–20 Siward echoes Macduff. For a sure
     result (*certain issue*) (*OED* issue *n.* 8a),
     actual fighting (*strokes*) must be the
     decider (*arbitrate*).
21 **which** i.e. the *certain issue*

11 given] gone *Capell*   14–15 Let ... Attend] Let our best Censurers / Before *F2–4;* Set our best censures /
Before *Rowe*   20 arbitrate:] *Theobald;* arbitrate, *F;* arbitrate. *Pope*

5.5   *Enter* MACBETH, SEYTON *and* Soldiers,
with Drum and Colours.

MACBETH

Hang out our banners on the outward walls;
The cry is still, 'They come'. Our castle's strength
Will laugh a siege to scorn. Here let them lie,
Till famine and the ague eat them up.
Were they not forced with those that should be ours,   5
We might have met them dareful, beard to beard,
And beat them backward home.   *A cry within of women*
                         What is that noise?

SEYTON

It is the cry of women, my good lord.

MACBETH

I have almost forgot the taste of fears.
The time has been, my senses would have cooled   10

5.5.1 Macbeth's opening mood is defiant.

3 **lie** i.e. lie encamped

4 **ague** fever

5 **forced** reinforced (*OED* force *v.*[1] 13a). Muir suggests a pun on 'farced', meaning 'stuffed', which would fit with the food images in 4. Hunter adopts this as an emendation.
   that . . . ours who should be on our side

6 **dareful** full of daring or defiance. This rare word is first recorded in Lyly, *Euphues and his England* (1580): 'it behoveth us to be . . . of their country, more dareful to mark the natures of their men, then curious to note the situation of the place' (sig. B1).
   beard to beard face to face. See Dent, B143.1: 'To meet in the beard'.

8–16 Some editors, e.g. Muir, Brooke, give Seyton an exit at 8 and a re-entry at 16, assuming he needs to go offstage to discover the significance of the women's cry. But Dessen, *Elizabethan*, 5–7, objects to this as 'literal-mindedness' and makes a good case for retaining Seyton onstage, even though he 'has no normal (earthly?) way of knowing what he knows' (6), adding to the eerie quality of the character and the dramatic moment.

10 **cooled** become cold with fear (*OED* notes this usage as '*Obs. rare*' and cites only this line). Macbeth's reactions here contrast with his extreme sensitivity at 2.2.59.

5.5] *Scena Quinta. 0.1 Drum and Colours*] *Drum and Dolours. F3; Drums and Colours. F4*   2 'They come'] *Pope;* they come *F*   castle's] *(Castles)*   7 SD] *(after* noise?*)*   *within of women*] *of women within / Dyce*   8 lord.] lord. *Exit. / Dyce*   10 has] *(*ha's*)*   cooled] *(*cool'd*)*; quail'd *Collier*

To hear a night-shriek, and my fell of hair
Would at a dismal treatise rouse and stir
As life were in't. I have supped full with horrors;
Direness familiar to my slaughterous thoughts
Cannot once start me. Wherefore was that cry?   15

SEYTON

The Queen, my lord, is dead.

MACBETH   She should have died hereafter;
There would have been a time for such a word.
Tomorrow, and tomorrow, and tomorrow,
Creeps in this petty pace from day to day,
To the last syllable of recorded time;   20

---

11 **fell of hair** head or shock of hair (*OED* fell *n.*¹ 3), or perhaps hair on the skin. There may be an animal resonance in *fell*. See *AYL* 3.2.50–1: 'We are still handling our ewes, and their fells . . . are greasy'.

12 **dismal treatise** frightening or ominous story

13 **As** as if

14 **Direness** dreadful things, horror (*OED*'s first citation for this word, and *EEBO* has none earlier)

15 **start** startle (*OED v.* 15a)

16–27 **She . . . nothing** Miola, *Classical*, 97–8, suggests the influence of Studley's translation of the first chorus of Seneca's *Agamemnon* on this speech. See also Jones, *Origins*, 280, where the lines are related to Seneca, Letter 80 (Seneca, *Dialogues*).

16 **She . . . hereafter** Either she would have died at some point sooner or later, or she ought to have died at a future time (when there would have been a chance to mourn her, 17). The first interpretation, with *should* meaning 'certainly would', suits Macbeth's nihilistic mood; the second,

with *should* meaning 'ought', accords with the play's many references to things done out of time, e.g. 1.5.57–8, 1.7.4–7, 4.1.96–7, and leads more naturally into the rest of the speech. Booth aptly observes that ' "Hereafter" . . . echoes Lady Macbeth's first words to Macbeth', which are in turn an echo of the Third Witch's prophecy at 1.3.50 (*'King Lear'*, 95). Rosenberg, 611–14, relates an interestingly wide range of interpretations by both academics and actors of Macbeth's reception of Seyton's announcement.

17 **word** statement, utterance (*OED n.* 1a)

19 **petty** small, inadequate, insignificant
pace step, or possibly pass, a passage through difficult terrain (*OED n.*¹ 2a). For this second meaning and its implications, see Cummings, 'Metalepsis', 217–18.

20 **syllable** smallest trace, least hint or portion (*OED n.* 2a, citing this line), but picking up on *word* (17). There is also a sense of 'last utterance' (*OED* word *n.* 1a). **recorded** written (*OED v.*¹ 9a) or recollected, remembered (*v.*¹ 4). Muir cites Hudson: 'the last syllable of the *record* of time'.

---

11 night-shriek] *(*Night-shrieke*)*; Night-shrick *F3*   13 supped] *(*supt*)*   15 once] now *Hanmer*   me.] me.
– [*Re-enter Seyton*] / *Dyce*   16 my lord] *om. Pope*   died] *(*dy'de*)*   19 Creeps] *(*Creepes*)*; Creep *Capell*

287

And all our yesterdays have lighted fools
The way to dusty death. Out, out, brief candle,
Life's but a walking shadow, a poor player,
That struts and frets his hour upon the stage,
And then is heard no more. It is a tale   25
Told by an idiot, full of sound and fury
Signifying nothing.

Enter a Messenger.

Thou com'st to use thy tongue: thy story, quickly.

MESSENGER
   Gracious my lord,
   I should report that which I say I saw,   30
   But know not how to do't.

MACBETH   Well, say, sir.

---

21 **lighted** illuminated, shown (the way) (*OED* light *v.*² 4)

22–3 **dusty death ... walking shadow** These phrases recall the Order for the Burial of the Dead in the *Book of Common Prayer*: 'Man that is born of woman hath but a short time to live . . . he fleeth as it were a shadow . . . Earth to earth, ashes to ashes, dust to dust' (1599). See also Genesis, 3.19: 'For dust thou art, and unto dust shalt thou be turned'. 'Life is a shadow' was proverbial (Dent, L249.1).

23 **shadow** illusion, phantom. See *MND* 3.2.347: 'Believe me, king of shadows, I mistook'.
   player actor, perhaps suggested by *shadow*, as in *MND* 5.1.208: 'The best in this kind are but shadows' (Muir). 'Poor' may, but need not, mean 'bad'; as Kittredge suggests, Macbeth is contemptuous, not so much of the player as

of the transitory quality both of the player's art and of human life.

24 **struts ... stage** Shakespeare elsewhere applies such terms to actors in a derogatory sense. See *TC* 1.3.153–4: 'like a strutting player, whose conceit / Lies in his hamstring' and *Ham* 3.2.28–32: 'players ... that have so strutted and bellowed'. See also *3H6* 1.4.90–1: 'And I to make thee mad do mock thee thus. / Stamp, rave and fret'.
   frets worries away at (*OED* fret *v.*¹ 8)

25 **It ... tale** Muir cites Psalm 90, prescribed for the burial service: 'We bring our years to an end as a tale that is told' (v. 9).

28 Macbeth's address to the Messenger implies that the latter hesitates before delivering his unwelcome news.

30 'I ought to report what I claim to have seen.'

---

22 dusty] study *F2–4;* dusky *Theobald*   29 Gracious my] My gracious *F2–4*   30 I say] I'd say *Hanmer*   31 do't] *(*doo't*);* do it *Steevens*   say] say it *Pope*

MESSENGER

As I did stand my watch upon the hill,
I looked toward Birnam, and anon methought
The wood began to move.

MACBETH   Liar and slave.

MESSENGER

Let me endure your wrath, if't be not so.   35
Within this three mile may you see it coming.
I say, a moving grove.

MACBETH   If thou speak'st false,
Upon the next tree shalt thou hang alive
Till famine cling thee. If thy speech be sooth,
I care not if thou dost for me as much.   40
I pull in resolution, and begin
To doubt th'equivocation of the fiend,
That lies like truth: 'Fear not, till Birnam Wood
Do come to Dunsinane', and now a wood
Comes toward Dunsinane. Arm, arm, and out.   45
If this which he avouches does appear,
There is nor flying hence, nor tarrying here.

---

32 **stand** remain in (*OED v.* 38a)
39 **cling** shrivel, parch (OED *v.* ¹ 3)
   sooth truth
40 'I don't care if you do the same for me' (i.e. hang me).
41 **pull in** usually defined as 'rein in', as of a horse (see *OED* pull *v.* PV 4 pull in, where this is the first citation). But see the examples cited by Muir (Dekker, *Old Fortunatus* (1600), Prologue, 6–7, and Fletcher, *The Sea Voyage* (1622), 3.1.47, where 'pull in' clearly means 'retract', without any equine implications. Many editors, following Johnson, emend to 'pall', meaning fail. As Dover Wilson observes, 'pall' gives a better rhythm, and

is more emphatic in articulating Macbeth's moment of self-doubt.
42 **doubt** mistrust (*OED v.* 2)
   th'equivocation the ambiguous words, duplicity. See 2.3.8–11 and 30, and pp. 18–19, 50–1. Dover Wilson notes another example of equivocation by the devil in *2H6* 1.4.59–69, where a spirit conjured up at the behest of Eleanor, Duchess of Gloucester, produces riddling prophecies.
   fiend devil, with specific application to the Third Apparition in 4.1.
45 **out** i.e. out into battle
46 **avouches** claims (*OED* avouch *v.* 6)
   appear prove to be true

33 Birnam] *F4;* Byrnane *F;* Byrnam *F2–3*   34 slave.] slave. [*Striking him.*] / *Rowe*   36 may you] you may *F3–4*   38 shalt] *F2–4;* shall *F*   41 pull] pall *Johnson*   43–4 'Fear . . . Dunsinane',] *Pope;* Feare . . . Dunsinane, *F*   45 toward] towards *Warburton*   47 nor flying] *F1–2;* no flying *F3–4*

289

I 'gin to be aweary of the sun,
And wish th'estate o'th' world were now undone.
Ring the alarum bell. Blow wind, come wrack,   50
At least we'll die with harness on our back.   *Exeunt.*

5.6   *Drum and Colours. Enter* MALCOLM, SIWARD,
         MACDUFF *and their Army, with boughs.*

MALCOLM

Now near enough. Your leafy screens throw down,
And show like those you are. You, worthy uncle,
Shall with my cousin, your right noble son,
Lead our first battle. Worthy Macduff and we
Shall take upon's what else remains to do,   5
According to our order.
SIWARD   Fare you well.

48 **'gin** begin
49 **th'estate . . . world** the structure of the
   universe. For Macbeth's readiness to provoke total cosmic destruction, compare
   3.2.17 and 4.1.51–9.
   undone the last of many references to
   doing and undoing. See pp. 42–6.
50 **Ring . . . bell** Macbeth's command, probably a cue for a SD, recalls 2.3.74, when
   Macduff calls for the bell at the discovery
   of Duncan's murder.
   wrack ruin, destruction
51 **harness** i.e. armour. Macbeth is determined to die in a valiant and manly way.
5.6.0.1 *Drum and Colours* See 5.4.0.1n.
0.2 *with boughs* Dessen, *Recovering*, 82,
   considers the problems posed by the
   presence of the boughs in the scene, and
   the symbolic possibilities of their con-

tinuing presence for the remainder of the
play.
2 **show . . . are** The time for equivocation,
   by Malcolm himself in 4.3 and by
   Macbeth, is now over.
   uncle i.e. Siward. See 5.2.2 and n.
3 **right noble son** emphasis on father/son
   relationships may stress the childlessness
   of the Macbeths.
4 **battle** body of troops in battle array.
   According to Edelman, 'battle[4]', the leading of the 'first battle' was often given to
   a deserving captain, with the king or
   general leading the main engagement.
   Worthy Macduff a further instance,
   along with *tyrant* at 7 and 5.7.10, of the
   moral polarization suggested at 5.2.2.
   we Malcolm assumes the royal plural.
6 **order** disposition of the troops

48 aweary] *(a-weary); a weary F2–4;* weary *Johnson*   49 th'estate] the state *Pope;* the estate *Capell*
50 bell.] bell. [*Alarums*] *Oxf*   Blow wind, come wrack] blow, wind! come, wrack! *Theobald*   51 SD] *The
Alarum bell rings. Exit. / Collier*   **5.6**] *Scena Sexta.*   0.1 SIWARD] old SIWARD *Capell*   1 one line *Rowe; F
lines* enough: / down /   leafy] leauy *F*   2 are.] are. [*They throw down their boughs.*] *Oxf*   4 battle.
Worthy] battle: worthy *Capell*   5 upon's] upon us *Capell*

Do we but find the tyrant's power tonight,
Let us be beaten if we cannot fight.

MACDUFF

Make all our trumpets speak, give them all breath,
Those clamorous harbingers of blood and death.   10

Exeunt. Alarums continued.

5.7   *Enter* MACBETH.

MACBETH

They have tied me to a stake; I cannot fly,
But bear-like I must fight the course. What's he
That was not born of woman? Such a one
Am I to fear, or none.

Enter YOUNG SIWARD.

YOUNG SIWARD
What is thy name?
MACBETH   Thou'lt be afraid to hear it.   5

7   **power** army
10   **harbingers** forerunners. See 1.4.45n.
10 SD   The sounds of battle, first heard at the
      beginning of 5.2, continue intermittently
      until the final scene and enhance the
      continuity of the action.
5.7.1 tied ... stake Macbeth compares his
      entrapment to that of a bear chained to
      a post and baited by dogs for public
      entertainment, a common metaphor in the
      period. Some of the Bankside theatre
      arenas were also used for this practice.
      See *KL* 3.7.53: 'I am tied to the stake and
      I must stand the course', and *JC* 4.1.48–9:
      'we are at the stake / And bayed about

with many enemies'. See Palfrey, 162–4,
on the multiple possibilities for punning
in this line.
2   **course** each of a series of attacks (*OED*
      n. 27b, where this line is the first
      citation)
2–3 **What's ... woman** Macbeth still takes
      confidence from the prophecies of the
      Apparitions.
4.1 YOUNG 'Young' is commonly used in Shake-
      speare to differentiate son from father, e.g.
      young Fortinbras (*Ham*), young John Talbot
      (*1H4*), except in the curious instance of
      young Osric in *Ham*, for which see under
      'Osric' in the List of Roles, Ard[3], 144.

7 Do we] Let us *Pope*   **5.7**] *Scena Septima.; scene continued Rowe*   0.1 *Enter* MACBETH] *Alarums, as of*
a Battle join'd. Skirmishings. Capell   1 They have] They've *Pope*

YOUNG SIWARD

    No, though thou call'st thyself a hotter name

    Than any is in hell.

MACBETH   My name's Macbeth.

YOUNG SIWARD

    The devil himself could not pronounce a title

    More hateful to mine ear.

MACBETH   No, nor more fearful.

YOUNG SIWARD

    Thou liest, abhorred tyrant; with my sword   10

    I'll prove the lie thou speak'st.

    Fight, and Young Siward slain.

MACBETH

    Thou wast born of woman.

    But swords I smile at, weapons laugh to scorn,

    Brandished by man that's of a woman born.   *Exit.*

                Alarums. Enter MACDUFF.

MACDUFF

    That way the noise is. Tyrant, show thy face,   15

    If thou be'st slain, and with no stroke of mine,

    My wife and children's ghosts will haunt me still.

    I cannot strike at wretched kerns, whose arms

---

6 **hotter** more damnable (though there is no citation for this meaning in *OED*)

7 **is** which is

11 'I'll demonstrate that what you say is a lie.'

14 SD Some editors, e.g. Oxf, Braunmuller, direct Macbeth to remove Young Siward's body as he exits here, but F gives no such indication. It is perhaps odd that his father does not notice the body after entering at 24, and Ross later (5.9.10) does say it was 'brought off the field'. Swander argues that F's lack of a SD should be respected and that the body should remain onstage, as it sometimes does. See also Braunmuller, 265, n. 4.

18 **kerns** See 1.2.13n. Ironically, Macbeth now relies on the mercenaries who had fought with the traitor Macdonald.

6 hotter] *F2–4;* hoter *F*   10 abhorred] thou abhorred *F2–4*   11 SD *Siward*] *(Seyward); Seyward's F3–4*   14 SD] *Exit* [*with the body.*] *Oxf; Exit* [*with young Siward's body.*] *Cam¹*   15] *Marked as a new scene* [5.8] *Oxf*

Are hired to bear their staves. Either thou, Macbeth,
Or else my sword with an unbattered edge 20
I sheathe again undeeded. There thou shouldst be;
By this great clatter, one of greatest note
Seems bruited. Let me find him, Fortune,
And more I beg not. *Exit.*

Alarums. Enter MALCOLM *and* SIWARD.

SIWARD
This way, my lord, the castle's gently rendered. 25
The tyrant's people on both sides do fight;
The noble thanes do bravely in the war;
The day almost itself professes yours
And little is to do.
MALCOLM   We have met with foes 29
That strike beside us.
SIWARD   Enter, sir, the castle. *Exeunt.*

---

19 **staves** wooden poles, 'the crudest form of weapon' (Brooke). This is sometimes glossed as meaning the shafts of lances or spears, but the kerns, being foot-soldiers, would not have borne such arms.
19–21 **Either ... undeeded** 'Either I strike at you, Macbeth, or I will put away my sword unused.' Macduff will allow no one else to be Macbeth's antagonist.
20 **unbattered** undamaged
21 **undeeded** having performed no deeds (*OED*'s only citation for this word, probably a Shakespearean coinage)

22 **clatter** noisy din
23 **bruited** announced, proclaimed (*OED* bruit *v.* 1)
25 **gently rendered** surrendered without fighting; *gently* may also suggest 'nobly'.
26 **on both sides** The theme of equivocation underlies this account of the collapse of the opposition.
29–30 **foes ... us** either enemies who deliberately miss us, or enemies who fight on our side, in either case, a paradoxical expression

19 Either] *(either);* Or *Pope*   20 unbattered] unbatter'd *Rowe*   23 bruited] bruited there *Steevens*   find] but find *Steevens*   25] *marked as new scene* [5.9] *Oxf*   castle's] *(castles)*   28 itself professes] *(*it self professes*);* professes itself *Johnson*

5.8   *Alarum. Enter* MACBETH.

MACBETH

Why should I play the Roman fool, and die
On mine own sword? Whiles I see lives, the gashes
Do better upon them.

Enter MACDUFF.

MACDUFF   Turn, hell-hound, turn.

MACBETH

Of all men else I have avoided thee.
But get thee back, my soul is too much charged   5
With blood of thine already.

MACDUFF   I have no words.
My voice is in my sword, thou bloodier villain
Than terms can give thee out.   *Fight. Alarum.*

MACBETH   Thou losest labour;
As easy mayst thou the intrenchant air
With thy keen sword impress, as make me bleed.   10

5.8 F does not mark a scene division here, but
many editors, following Pope and Johnson,
give one, mainly because the stage has
been cleared before the entrance of a new
character, but also on the ground, less
relevant to a stage without scenery (like
the Globe), that Malcolm and the rest
enter the castle (5.7.30), and Macbeth's
appearance must be outside it.

1 **play . . . fool** Macbeth refers to the practice required by Roman military honour
of dying by suicide, rather than submitting
to capture, in what Cleopatra calls 'the
high Roman fashion' (*AC* 4.15.91) as
Brutus (*JC* 5.5) and Antony (*AC* 4.14)
do. In tragedies without classical settings,

such as *Ham* and *KL*, suicide is viewed
more equivocally. Compare Macbeth's
attitude at 27–9.

2 **lives** living beings
3 **upon them** i.e. than upon me
5 **charged** burdened, overloaded (*OED*
charge *v*. 9a)
8 **terms** words, language (*OED* term *n*. 14a)
losest labour waste effort
9 **easy** easily
intrenchant incapable of being cut
(*OED*'s only citation for this meaning,
and *EEBO* has none earlier). The positive
form of the word is more common. See
Tim 4.3.115: 'thy trenchant sword'.
10 **impress** make a mark on (*OED v*. 1a)

5.8] *marked as new scene* [VIII] *Dyce;* [5.10] *Oxf; not in F*   0.1 *Enter*] *Re-enter / Capell*   2 Whiles]
While *Davenant*   3.1 *Enter*] *Re-enter / Capell*   4 thee] the *F2*

Let fall thy blade on vulnerable crests;
I bear a charmed life, which must not yield
To one of woman born.

MACDUFF   Despair thy charm,
And let the angel whom thou still hast served
Tell thee, Macduff was from his mother's womb   15
Untimely ripped.

MACBETH

Accursed be that tongue that tells me so,
For it hath cowed my better part of man.
And be these juggling fiends no more believed
That palter with us in a double sense,   20
That keep the word of promise to our ear,
And break it to our hope. I'll not fight with thee.

MACDUFF

Then yield thee, coward,
And live to be the show and gaze o'th' time.

---

11 **vulnerable** capable of being wounded (*OED a.* 2a, where this is the first citation in this sense. The negative 'invulnerable' appears earlier. See *KJ* 2.1.251–2: 'Our cannons' malice vainly shall be spent / Against th'invulnerable clouds of heaven'. **crests** helmets, head-pieces (*OED* crest *n.* 4)

12 **charmed** charmèd

13 **Despair** despair of

14 **angel** evil spirit
   still always, continually (*OED adv.* 3a)

16 **Untimely ripped** torn from his mother's womb before the full term was up, which in early modern England was either just before or just after the mother's death. Macduff's announcement makes Macbeth aware that he has interpreted the Witches' prophecy to mean any man born from a woman, as in Matthew, 11.11: 'Among them that are born of women there hath not risen any greater than John the Baptist', but Macduff gives it a meaning

he had not considered, that of what is now called caesarean section. For the practice of this in early modern Europe, see Jaques Guillemeau, *Childbirth, or the Happie Deliverie of Women*, trans. Thomas Hatfield (1612), ch. 25, and also Iyengar, 'untimely ripped'. The shortness of the line may allow for a pause before he can respond, as Flatter, 28, suggests.

17 **Accursed** accursèd

18 **cowed** overawed, intimidated (*OED* cow *v.*[1], the first citation for this meaning, and *EEBO* has none earlier). Macduff perhaps puns on the word in 'Then yield thee, coward' at 23.
   better . . . man courage or manliness

19 **juggling** cheating, deceptive

20 **palter** deal evasively, use trickery (*OED v.* 3a)
   double sense ambiguous or equivocal meaning

24 **show and gaze** spectacle

23 thee, coward] *Rowe;* thee Coward *F*

We'll have thee, as our rarer monsters are,   25
Painted upon a pole, and underwrit,
'Here may you see the tyrant'.
MACBETH   I will not yield
To kiss the ground before young Malcolm's feet,
And to be baited with the rabble's curse.
Though Birnam Wood be come to Dunsinane,   30
And thou opposed, being of no woman born,
Yet I will try the last. Before my body
I throw my warlike shield. Lay on, Macduff,
And damned be him, that first cries, 'Hold, enough'.
                              Exeunt fighting. Alarums.

Enter fighting, and Macbeth slain. [_Exit Macduff
with Macbeth's body._]

25–7 **We'll . . . tyrant** Macduff insultingly evokes the idea of Macbeth exhibited as a fairground attraction, in the way that freaks and captured animals were. The prospect of becoming a public spectacle is also abhorred by Cleopatra (_AC_ 5.2.207–20).

26 **Painted . . . pole** painted on a cloth suspended from a pole, as in front of a booth

28 **kiss the ground** as a sign of abjection or complete surrender. See Dent, D651: 'To lick (kiss) the dust (ground)'.

29 **baited** taunted

30–1 Macbeth is now fully aware of how he has been tricked in both these respects.

31 **opposed** against me

32 **try the last** endure the ultimate

33 **Lay on** 'Make an attack' (_OED_ lay v.[1] 55).

34 **'Hold, enough'** 'Stop, I surrender' (Braunmuller). In the 2005 production at the Almeida Theatre, London, with

Simon Russell Beale as Macbeth, the line was repunctuated as 'Hold. Enough', with a pause for fighting between the two words. This reading creates a completely different, and novel, effect for Macbeth's demise, marking a change of mood from the rest of the speech. See the account by Sokolova, 282, and the discussions of the staging of this moment on pp. 117–8 above.

34.1 **_Enter fighting_** Sprague, _Actors_, suggests that this SD, immediately following _Exeunt_, may indicate that 'a change was made early in the play's history, and the fight fought out for all to see' (_Actors_, 278), so that Macbeth's death, like that of Richard III, takes place onstage. Garrick introduced a dying speech for Macbeth.

34.1–2 **_*Exit . . . body_** F has no SD here, but it is clear that Macduff must exit, and if he is to return with Macbeth's head in the next scene, the body must be removed.

27 'Here . . . tyrant.'] _Pope;_ Heere . . . Tyrant. _F_   30 Birnam] _F4;_ Byrnane _F;_ Byrnam _F2–3_   31 being] be _Theobald_   34 him] he _Pope_   'Hold, enough.'] _Pope;_ hold, enough. _F_   34.1–2 _Exit . . . body._] _Oxf, Cam[1]_

5.9   *Retreat and Flourish. Enter with Drum and Colours*
MALCOLM, SIWARD, ROSS, Thanes *and* Soldiers.

MALCOLM
I would the friends we miss were safe arrived.
SIWARD
Some must go off; and yet by these I see,
So great a day as this is cheaply bought.
MALCOLM
Macduff is missing, and your noble son.
ROSS
Your son, my lord, has paid a soldier's debt: 5
He only lived but till he was a man,
The which no sooner had his prowess confirmed,
In the unshrinking station where he fought,
But like a man he died.
SIWARD   Then he is dead?

5.9.0.1 *Retreat and Flourish.* The clearing of the stage from the previous action, the entry of a new set of characters and the movement into the play's final phase make a new scene division at this point logical. George Walton Williams, in correspondence, draws attention to the parallel with the last scene of *R3*, where the battle is concluded by a fight between the King and his opponent in which the King is slain, and the SD also contains the direction '*Retreat, and Flourish*' (*R3* 5.5 F text). A retreat, sounded by trumpets, signals the end of an engagement; a flourish is also sounded by trumpets or cornets, perhaps with drum accompaniment, to announce the entry of an important person. The trumpets for the '*Retreat*' may have been muted. See Wilson & Calore, 'retreat' and 'flourish', and Williams's discussion of scene divisions in Act 5 ('Scene', 33, 36).

2   **go off** die (*OED* go *v.* PV 4 go off). Muir suggests a metaphor from the stage.
3   **cheaply bought** i.e. without great loss of life
4–14 based closely on Holinshed, 1.192 (in Bullough, 7.507–8)
5   **soldier's debt** what a soldier owes, punning on *debt*/death. See *1H4* 5.1.126: 'Why, thou owest God a death', and the proverbs 'Death pays all debts' and 'To pay one's debt to nature' (Dent, D148 and D168).
6   **but till** until. Young Siward's youth is Shakespeare's invention, and not in Holinshed.
8   **unshrinking station** unyielding posture. For 'station' meaning posture, manner of standing (*OED* station *n.*[1] 1), see *Ham* 3.4.56: 'A station like the herald Mercury'.

5.9] *marked as new scene* [VIII] *Pope;* [5.11] *Oxf; not in F*   7 prowess] prow'ss *Pope*   9 he is] is he *Pope*

ROSS

   Aye, and brought off the field. Your cause of sorrow   10
   Must not be measured by his worth, for then
   It hath no end.

SIWARD   Had he his hurts before?

ROSS

   Aye, on the front.

SIWARD   Why then, God's soldier be he.
   Had I as many sons as I have hairs,
   I would not wish them to a fairer death.   15
   And so his knell is knolled.

MALCOLM   He's worth more sorrow,
   And that I'll spend for him.

SIWARD   He's worth no more;
   They say he parted well and paid his score,
   And so God be with him. Here comes newer comfort.

Enter MACDUFF *with Macbeth's head.*

10–19 A probable source for Siward's stoical reaction is Camden's *Remains Concerning Britain* (1605). When he hears that his son has died with wounds on his front he says, 'I am right glad, neither wish any other death to me or mine' (216). Paul, 156–7, gives a further account of Siward's heroic qualities.

10 **brought . . . field** removed from the battlefield (for burial)

12 **hurts before** wounds on the front of his body, signifying that he was not wounded as he ran away. Braunmuller cites Plutarch, 'Life of Pelopidas' (*Lives*, trans. Thomas North (1595), 315) as evidence that wounds to the front of the body were regarded as honourable.

14 **hairs** probable pun on 'heirs'. Compare 4.1.112.

16 **knell is knolled** bell rung to mark a death is ceremonially sounded. Siward's laconic polyptoton (repetition of words from the same root but with different endings) is in keeping with his response in Holinshed.

16–17 **He's . . . him** Compare Brutus' promise to spend more time on mourning the death of Cassius at a future date in *JC* 5.3.103.

18 **parted** departed, died. See *H5* 2.3.12: "A parted even just between twelve and one'. **score** reckoning, bill

19.1 **with Macbeth's head** Malone added '*on a pole*' to make sense of *stands* (20), but this can be a problem for modern directors. See Rosenberg, 651–2, for various stagings of this moment. In early modern England traitors' heads were publicly exhibited. Compare Macdonald's at 1.2.23.

19.1 *Enter*] *Re-enter* / Capell

MACDUFF

    Hail King, for so thou art. Behold where stands   20
    Th'usurper's cursed head: the time is free.
    I see thee compassed with thy kingdom's pearl,
    That speak my salutation in their minds;
    Whose voices I desire aloud with mine.   24
    Hail, King of Scotland.

ALL   Hail, King of Scotland.   *Flourish*

MALCOLM

    We shall not spend a large expense of time
    Before we reckon with your several loves
    And make us even with you. My thanes and kinsmen,
    Henceforth be earls, the first that ever Scotland
    In such an honour named. What's more to do,   30
    Which would be planted newly with the time,
    As calling home our exiled friends abroad,

---

21 **cursed** cursèd
   time is free Muir compares this to earlier references to time in equivocal contexts, e.g. 1.5.56–8 and 4.3.72. By contrast, Macduff expresses a sense of liberation.

22 **compassed** surrounded
   pearl collective noun, meaning the riches of the kingdom, its finest members (*OED n.*¹ 2b)

26–41 On the effect and significance of Malcolm's concluding speech, see Rosenberg, 652–4. Kittredge observes that 'The method of Elizabethan [meaning early modern] tragedy required that the closing speech should be uttered by the person of highest rank who survived, and this was seldom one of the characters in whom we have taken most interest. Such speeches, therefore, are always rather formal and serve as a kind of epilogue.' Perhaps for this reason, it has sometimes been abbreviated or even omitted in the theatre.

27 **reckon with** settle accounts with (*OED* reckon *v.* 5), add up what we owe. Thomas, *Political*, notes under 'reckon with' the abundance of economic vocabulary in this scene: *cheaply, debt, measured, worth, spend, expense.* Compare Duncan's language in 1.4.

28 **make . . . you** square things with you (so that we are no longer indebted to you). Thus Malcolm concludes a series of financial metaphors (*spend, expense, reckon*).

28–9 **thanes . . . earls** as in Holinshed. The new titles signify a new political establishment. On Shakespeare's anglicization of Malcolm, see Highley, 60–1.

31 'which should be newly established in keeping with a new age'; *planted newly* is an uneasy echo of Duncan's use of this metaphor at 1.4.28–9.

22 pearl] peers *Rowe*   25 SP] ALL BUT MALCOLM *Oxf*   26 expense] extent *Steevens*   28 My] *om. Pope*

That fled the snares of watchful tyranny,
Producing forth the cruel ministers
Of this dead butcher, and his fiend-like queen,   35
Who, as 'tis thought, by self and violent hands
Took off her life – this, and what needful else
That calls upon us, by the grace of grace,
We will perform in measure, time and place.
So thanks to all at once, and to each one,   40
Whom we invite to see us crowned at Scone.

Flourish. Exeunt omnes.

---

34 **Producing forth** bringing out of hiding
(Muir)
35 **dead . . . queen** Malcolm's bald summary
has often been found inadequate. See
Rosenberg, 652–4, and above, pp. 116–
21, on the staging of the play's end.
36 **self . . . hands** For 'self' meaning 'self-
same', see *OED* self *pron., adj.* and *n.* B1).

The suggestion that Macbeth's Lady
committed suicide is not in Holinshed.
Malcolm's description of her act takes on
the censorious attitude to suicide found
in 'Christian' rather than Roman plays.
38 **grace of grace** i.e. the grace of God
39 **measure** due proportion (*OED n.* 3a)
41 **Scone** See 2.4.31n.

37 what] what's *Hanmer*   38 of grace] of heaven *Pope;* of God *Warburton*

APPENDIX 1
The text of Macbeth

The following section is in two parts.[1] In the first, Pamela Mason discusses the text from the perspective of the editor. The editorial policy has as its lynchpin a respect for the Folio text and an allegiance to what it offers in the absence of coherent and compelling reasons to make emendations. Throughout this edition there has been a determined commitment to clarity and transparency in the way in which textual matters have been discussed and resolved. It is of crucial importance that readers of this, indeed of any, text are empowered to be able to engage with the means by which the particular text presented has been transmitted. In the second section, Sandra Clark focuses on the issue of the status of the Folio text in the light of debates about revision and authorship.

PART 1: EDITING THE TEXT

When Shakespeare died in 1616 fewer than half his plays had appeared in print. *Macbeth* belongs to the group of eighteen plays which were published for the first time in the First Folio in 1623. It is the sixth play in the section devoted to the tragedies and is placed between *Julius Caesar* and *Hamlet*, occupying just twenty pages (131–51), fewer than any other tragedy in the volume. Its division into acts and scenes is generally accepted, except in Act 5, where the Folio designation

---

1   The first section of this Appendix is a revised version of Pamela Mason's essay 'Sunshine in *Macbeth*' in Moschovakis, 335–49.

of seven scenes has been variously adjusted.[1] It is generally accepted that the underlying copy from which the text was set was a theatrical promptbook. In editorial terms it is judged to be a good text, clean and with a high degree of accuracy and clarity.

However, to read *Macbeth* in its Folio text is to see the play quite differently from the way it is presented to the modern reader. The editorial history has involved a process of reshaping and re-presenting the text which has in some ways prevented readers and actors from a direct engagement with the traces of the original play which the Folio text offers. Although systematic tidying, normalizing and regularizing has been judged to be a necessary and appropriate method of preparing and mediating the text for the modern reader, it may be that some of the irregularity, which it has been thought appropriate to regularize, may in fact contain rich material for consideration. It has been a primary concern of the editors of this edition to re-examine, consistently challenge and rethink the editorial tradition and practice surrounding the editing of *Macbeth* in an attempt to look at the text afresh, with new eyes, to reassess its particular qualities and characteristics.

The play needs to be allowed to make its case in its own terms, and Dogberry's view that 'comparisons are odorous' might perhaps be applied to the ways in which reference to a standard inhibits evaluation of the play. This is particularly true in relation to the play's comparative brevity. It has encouraged speculation about what might have been lost, censored or cut for theatrical reasons and has fuelled conjecture

1 Dover Wilson's New Shakespeare divides Act 5 into eight scenes; the Arden Shakespeare Second Series edition (Arden[2]) and New Cambridge (Cam[1]) give it nine scenes; the Oxford *Complete Works* (Oxf) manages eleven. In following Pope's inserted break after Macbeth's death Stanley Wells argues that it 'seems right, less for considerations of place (Muir) than because a time interval may be presumed' (Wells & Taylor, 544). This edition follows Braunmuller's New Cambridge edition in identifying nine separate scenes.

302

about what might be seen as evidence of collaboration with Middleton.[1]

Lineation and verse

Although *Macbeth* is acknowledged to be a good text, there has always been the qualification that there is a problem with its lineation. Discussion of the play's brevity and the concern about lineation have traditionally been considered separately, but it might be illuminating to consider them together. The language of the play can be seen as compressed and at times fragmented in a stylistic irregularity which mirrors the play's thematic concerns. Brooke dismisses the notion of such a correlation,[2] but it may be that assumptions about metrical conformity have interfered with an appreciation of the particular, even peculiar characteristics of the text of *Macbeth*.

It is, of course, accepted that as the Folio was set in formes[3] the process of casting off the text to enable simultaneous typesetting by two compositors presented problems in terms of layout. Any perusal of the pages of the Folio provides many examples of how the compositors struggled to accommodate either too little or too much text.[4] However, the text of *Macbeth* is fairly consistently spaced and does not contain any glaring example of either too little or too much text causing the compositors any major problems. It is not tenable, therefore, to use any 'white space' argument to justify editorial intervention in the case of the Folio text of *Macbeth*.

The style of *Macbeth* is frequently unconventional.[5] Blank verse predominates, but there is also the shorter, more rhythmic verse of the Witches, and some prose to accommodate the

1 See pp. 323–6.

2 Brooke, 55.

3 i.e. not in a linear process of successive pages. For a clear explanation of the way the pages of the Folio were configured in the printing process, see Hinman, xvi.

4 See Hinman, xvi–xvii.

5 See pp. 38–62.

naturalism of a Porter who has been drinking or the domestic exchange of mother and son. At times the blank verse is regular; and the fluency of dovetailed lines affirms the clarity of the Old Man's choric commentary (2.4) or establishes that, despite the apparent contradictions, Malcolm and Macduff do indeed speak the same language and share the same values (for most of their dialogue in 4.3 they complete each other's verse lines). Towards the end of the England scene (4.3) the taut regularity of the verse provides a secure framework to contain and offer reassurance to Macduff as he struggles to come to terms with the news of the murder of his family.

But elsewhere there is much that is fragmentary and unusual. It has been customary to designate the two compositors responsible for setting the text of the play (Compositors A and B) as the scapegoats for the irregularity. The text of *Macbeth* was divided between them, with A setting to the end of 3.3 and B setting from 3.4 to the end of the play.[1] The splitting of the play between the two compositors contributes to assertions about the perceived difficulties in the layout of the text. According to Charlton Hinman there were five compositors used in the process of printing the First Folio but more than two-thirds of the typesetting was done by A and B, and B set more text than any of his colleagues. Hinman's judgement is that while A sometimes misread his copy he was 'on the whole very faithful' while B was 'very much less accurate and characteristically took all manner of liberties with the text'.[2] Other scholars go further in defining the precise shortcomings of the compositors, concluding that A 'had a regrettable tendency to rearrange normal blank verse into a succession of irregular lines' and B 'had a tendency to set up prose as if it were verse'.[3] Braunmuller's conclusion is that 'the main difficulty partly created by A and B

---

1   B would seem to have helped A with two and a quarter pages before he began (Brooke, 50).

2   Hinman, xviii.

3   Wells & Taylor, 637, cited in Braunmuller, 267.

is the play's lineation, its setting out of verse and prose and the regularity of its verse.'[1] There needs, however, to be some caution in the face of what can seem like scientific precision.

There are, of course, some instances where it can be accepted that the physical constraints of the page layout enforce disruption of the lineation. The presence of the speech prefix often enforces a line break, which when coinciding with the caesura can create two short lines out of what can be readily accepted as one verse line:

Rosse. And *Duncans* Horses,
(A thing most strange, and certaine)

(F ll. 940–1 [2.2.14])

However, the relineation of longer passages is more problematical. English is naturally iambic, and it is fairly easy to organize utterances as blank verse. It is dangerous, therefore, to argue that because sections of text can be rearranged to offer more regular lines than appear in the Folio an editor should relineate. The belief that 'the text is disfigured by mislineation'[2] and that there are 'a number of lines which are obviously not correctly divided'[3] may deny the possibility that the play offers at times jagged and irregular verse. In some cases it can be argued that this is a means by which Shakespeare communicates the pressures, tensions and complexities which the characters are experiencing. Editorial tidying up may erase characteristics of the original play which might offer some clues and guidance to reader and actor.

It is disconcerting to realize that close reading which attends to aspects such as scansion, enjambement, use of short lines and metrical irregularity has been working on an adapted text. In the absence of any other textual evidence than that which

1 Braunmuller, 267.
2 Muir (9th edn, 1962), xiv.
3 Brooke, 50.

appears in the Folio it seems necessary to adopt a more cautious approach before tampering with the layout of a text which is in many ways unusual and unconventional. This is a complex and controversial issue, but it is appropriate to examine how extensive conjecture about the characteristics of Compositors A and B has paved the way for extensive relineation of this text. Having decided that they both display 'eccentricities' or what is also termed 'villainy' Brooke argues that: 'it follows inescapably that, wherever possible, eccentricities in [A's] setting of lines should be corrected'.[1] It is unfashionable to be in sympathy with the main thrust of Richard Flatter's argument in *Shakespeare's Producing Hand* (1948). Flatter argues a theatrical case for an awareness of pauses and action to challenge the insistence on setting out as many lines as possible in iambic pentameter. Although Brooke is not insensitive to such notions, he dismisses Flatter's case, on the grounds that Flatter has 'no understanding of the compositor's eccentricities'.[2] Most of Flatter's examples come from *Macbeth*: the best known is his case for letting the layout of the Captain's speech (1.2) stand. He argues that it represents 'the broken utterance of a seriously wounded man'[3] but his claim has been dismissed: as Brooke states: 'In fact, simple rearrangement shows it to be regular and rhetorically impressive in the manner of a Senecan messenger'.[4] Brooke's phrase 'simple rearrangement' is arguably a little disingenuous. In 3.1 Macbeth's edginess in conversation with Banquo is reflected in fragmented verse which sometimes dovetails and sometimes does not. Macbeth is then anxious to dismiss those around him (including his wife) in order to set up his meeting with the Murderers. The Folio text reads:

1   Brooke, 214.
2   Brooke, 215.
3   Brooke, 215.
4   Brooke, 215.

> *Macb.*   Bring them before us.   *Exit Servant.*
> To be thus, is nothing, but to be safely thus:
> Our feares in *Banquo* sticke deepe,
> And in his Royaltie of Nature reignes that
> Which would be fear'd. 'Tis much he dares

> (F ll. 1037–41 [3.1.46–50])

Both Brooke and Braunmuller relineate these lines:

MACBETH
>   Bring them before us.   *Exit Servant.*
>   To be thus is nothing,
>   But to be safely thus. Our fears in Banquo
>   Stick deep, and in his royalty of nature
>   Reigns that which would be feared. 'Tis much he
>   dares

Muir is quite sure that 'the Folio arrangement of these lines cannot be right' and confirms that 'all editors have made some changes'.[1] There has been no agreement, though, about the right, or even best, solution; as Brooke states there have been 'almost as many solutions as there have been editors'.[2] The problem in this section is judged to begin earlier with Macbeth's dismissal of Banquo, then the Lords (and there is also the question of no exit being marked for the Lady). But even when the earlier speech of Macbeth's is accepted as irregular (and printed as such), editors still insist upon imposing a new structure upon the following speech (as quoted above). It seems astonishing that no edition until Muir's and ours has kept intact the line 'To be thus is nothing, but to be safely thus'. It is a crowded, oppressively claustrophobic line where the thought can only be contained through elision and compression. In contrast, the missing foot in the following line makes it gape

1   Muir, 74.
2   Brooke, 221.

open, allowing the sharpness of 'stick' to jab against 'deep' in a powerfully effective demonstration of what Macbeth is about to propose to the Murderers. The decision to respect the layout of the Folio text presents rich and expressive lines for reader and actor; editorial practice seems to have gained nothing and lost a great deal.

Punctuation

Other editorial additions have shaped perceptions of the play, perhaps unhelpfully. No one would argue that it would make sense to follow the punctuation of the Folio text slavishly. To standardize the punctuation in order to help a modern reader is both a sensible and uncontested policy. However, there is an issue concerning the use of exclamation marks. Throughout the Folio they are used sparingly,[1] and in the Folio 1.14 *Macbeth* there are only three used; nonetheless, modern editions have conventionally been littered with them.

If the view is taken that greetings, warnings, cries, shouts, prophecies, announcements, exclamations, etc., need to be signalled by the addition of the exclamation mark, then all dramatic texts face the risk of being infested. The text of this play has been particularly distorted for its readers and by extension for its performance by such an approach. The particular characteristic of the Witches is repeated phrases of greeting (Hail, hail, hail) or prophecy. With exclamation marks added the appearance of the text encourages an eyebrow-raising, melodramatic delivery which may well have contributed to the perceived banality of much of the Witches' dialogue. It is no part of an editor's job to indicate that lines should be whispered or declaimed, enigmatically or winsomely, and liberal scattering of exclamation marks needs to be curtailed. *Fowler's Modern English Usage* urges restraint in the use of

---

1   See Antony Graham-White, *Punctuation and its Dramatic Value in Shakespearean Drama* (Newark, Del., 1995).

the exclamation mark. It acknowledges that the conventions for poetry are different from those for prose, but Robert Burchfield's remark that 'excessive use of exclamation marks . . . add[s] a spurious dash of sensation to something unsensational' is apposite.[1]

In recent years there has been a shift in editorial policy, and Braumuller's New Cambridge edition is significantly more restrained than earlier editions. But some issues and inconsistencies remain. After the discovery of Duncan's murder Macduff's utterance 'O horror, horror, horror' (2.3.63) looks and reads very differently if printed plainly. With editorial intervention it is fragmented, and the exclamatory markings imply an equality between the phrases and urge a regularity of delivery, 'O horror! horror! horror!' (Muir). The following twenty-four lines have a further eighteen exclamation marks in Muir's edition,[2] and traditionally this section has been heavily accented. In the New Cambridge edition there are only four exclamation marks (as against twenty-two in the Arden) but there seems to be some inconsistency. They are all grouped in the first part of Macduff's announcement:

> Awake, awake!
> Ring the alarum bell! Murder and treason!
> Banquo and Donalbain![3]

His speech continues in the same vein as he calls to Malcolm to 'awake' and later urges 'Up, up', but no marks are added to these commands. The editorial restraint is welcome but the inconsistency is puzzling. Mindful of Burchfield's warning about 'spurious sensation', editors might do well to return to the restraint of the Folio compositors in this matter (see Fig. 19).

1   R.W. Burchfield, *The New Fowler's Modern English Usage* (3rd edn, Oxford, 1996), 273.

2   2.3.64–88 (Muir).

3   2.3.67–9 (Braunmuller).

> *Enter Macduff.*
>
> *Macd.* O horror, horror, horror,
> Tongue nor Heart cannot conceiue,nor name thee.
>   *Macb. and Lenox.* What's the matter?
>   *Macd.* Confusion now hath made his Master-peece:
> Most sacrilegious Murther hath broke ope
> The Lords anoynted Temple,and stole thence
> The Life o'th' Building.
>   *Macb.* What is't you say,the Life?
>   *Lenox.* Meane you his Maiestie?
>   *Macd.* Approch the Chamber,and destroy your sight
> With a new *Gorgon.* Doe not bid me speake:
> See,and then speake your selues : awake,awake,
>   *Exeunt Macbeth and Lenox.*
> Ring the Alarum Bell : Murther,and Treason,
> *Banquo,*and *Donalbaine* : *Malcolme* awake,
> Shake off this Downey sleepe,Deaths counterfeit,
> And looke on Death it selfe : vp,vp,and see
> The great Doomes Image: *Malcolme,Banquo,*
> As from your Graues rise vp,and walke like Sprights,
> To countenance this horror. Ring the Bell.
>   *Bell rings. Enter Lady.*

19   *The Tragedie of Macbeth*, pp. 137–8, ll. 816–36, from *Mr William Shakespeare's Comedies, Histories, and Tragedies* (The First Folio) (1623)

William E. Cain argues similarly, persuasively demonstrating how the Folio text at l. 1194 [3.2.37], 'O, full of Scorpions is my Minde, deare Wife.', has been distorted by the imposition of an editorial exclamation mark at the end of the line, 'making a change that obliges the reader to hear a tone that is an editor's'.[1]

---

1   Cain, 17. Our edition preserves the Folio punctuation.

The significance of naming

Perhaps the most striking area of editorial and theatrical collusion which has distorted the play is in the matter of the character who has come to be known as Lady Macbeth. Quite simply, she does not exist in Shakespeare's play. The Folio stage direction for the fifth scene in the play reads '*Enter Macbeths Wife alone with a Letter*' and for 3.2 the stage direction reads '*Enter Macbeths Lady, and a Servant*'. She is consistently described simply as '*Lady*' in the speech prefixes. That designation distinguishes her from her counterpart, who is described as '*Macduffes Wife*' in the stage direction to 4.2 and is '*Wife*' throughout her speech prefixes. Shakespeare's text emphasizes the marital relationship for both women and makes a simple but clear distinction between them in the speech prefixes: Lady as against Wife. Nowhere in Shakespeare's play, therefore, is there any reference to the characters as they have become known both critically and theatrically: Lady Macbeth and Lady Macduff.

Simon Forman's account of seeing the play in April 1611[1] emerges from an experience of the play in performance, before the intervention of any editorial process. He does not see her as Lady Macbeth; to him she is 'his [Macbeth's] wife', a phrase which is used twice, and later in his account she becomes 'Mackbete's quen'. Stage directions and speech prefixes do not register verbally in the theatre, and Forman's account is a useful reminder of the need to consider what name and identity a character is granted within the text; either through their own words or through the comments of other characters.

'Lady' is used three times in the play; all three references occur in 2.3 within forty-four lines. It is Macduff who addresses Macbeth's wife as 'gentle lady' (84), and he again uses the term when he voices concern for her, 'Look to the lady' (120), a phrase exactly repeated by Banquo six lines later. 'Queen' is

---

1   See Appendix 2.

used three times in the play: there is one reference to Edward's wife in the England scene, but the other two both refer to Macbeth's queen. The announcement of her death grants her the title for the first time: 'The Queen, my lord, is dead' (5.5.16), and the play's final reference to the Macbeths defines them, in Malcolm's words, as 'this dead butcher, and his fiend-like queen' (5.9.35). 'Wife' is used thirteen times in the play: there is one reference to 'A sailor's wife' (1.3.4), but the other twelve are divided eight to four in favour of Macduff's wife. The spoken text of the play, therefore, confirms Shakespeare's depiction of the women and makes clear that the names Lady Macbeth and Lady Macduff have developed from outside not inside the play.

There is no list of characters in the Folio, but from Rowe onwards the women have almost without exception been designated Lady Macbeth and Lady Macduff. G.K. Hunter is unusual in resisting the renaming of Macduff's wife, whom he lists as such in 'The Characters in the Play'. Although he describes Macbeth's wife as Lady Macbeth in the same list he does follow the Folio speech prefixes in describing her as 'Lady' and her counterpart as 'Wife'. His edition restores the Folio readings against the general trend. However, acknowledgement must be made to John F. Andrews's edition, which breaks with the prevailing editorial tradition by following the Folio text very closely. Braunmuller in his edition refers to their names being 'moralised', but in his review John Jowett mused:

> In reading Braunmuller's edition I was reminded that the name Lady Macbeth is an unShakespearian invention by editors. Like Queen Elizabeth in *Richard III*, Lady Capulet in *Romeo and Juliet* and Prince Hal in *1 Henry IV*, the now familiar form of the name makes no appearance in the early printed texts.[1]

1   Jowett, 311.

Stage directions

Editorial intervention in the matter of stage directions is another contentious area. Gary Taylor argues that Shakespeare's texts have 'an invisible life-support system of stage directions' and that it is an editor's 'necessary' but 'hazardous' task to 'rectify the deficiency, by conjecturally writing for him the stage directions which Shakespeare himself assumed or spoke but never wrote'.[1] The process of clarifying the action through the addition or repositioning of stage directions is necessary and can be unproblematical, but objective indication of necessary action can become interpretative instruction. 'Lady Macbeth's faint' is a sequence which always excites interest in the way it is done onstage. Yet there is no textual support for the Lady's faint.[2]

She calls for assistance: 'Helpe me hence, hoa' [2.3.119], but the Folio text has no stage direction to indicate what, if any, action might accompany her words. Rowe inserted '*Seeming to faint*' and his addition was accepted by Pope, Theobald, Hanmer, Warburton and Capell. Collier, however, removed the indication of '*Seeming*' and preferred '*Lady Macbeth swoons*', which he inserted at Banquo's line 'Look to the lady' (126). Hunter emends that to '*swooning*'. Although Muir, Wells and Taylor, Brooke and Braunmuller all resist adding any stage direction, there is in their editions both an acknowledgment and an acceptance of the tradition of the faint.

First Macduff and then Banquo direct attention to her through the repeated command 'Look to the lady', but there is no stage direction in response. Rowe instructed '*Lady Macbeth is carried out*', and subsequent editors have modified the wording but not the sense of his suggestion: '*Lady Macbeth is taken out*', '*Exit Lady Macbeth, attended*', '*Exit Lady Macbeth, helped*'. Generally the exit is marked as following Banquo's

1   Wells & Taylor, 2–3.
2   See p. 195.

instruction, but Braunmuller inserts it after Macduff's comment (Braunmuller, 112 [120]).

The Lady's appeal for help has, therefore, traditionally been interpreted as preceding a swoon. Critical attention has focused upon whether it is real or feigned, and discussion focuses upon whether it is possible (or advisable) to seek to make such a decision apparent theatrically. However, it is not necessary for her to faint. The text indicates that she appeals for assistance to leave the stage, and more significant than her action is the fact that, although Macduff alerts the assembly to take note of her, six lines later his command is precisely echoed by Banquo. The absence of stage directions in the Folio text leaves this section interestingly open to interpretative choices about stage grouping, about Macbeth's inability or unwillingness to respond to his wife and about the positioning and the manner of the exit (see Fig. 20).

The textual additions and emendations reveal that interpretative assumptions about the Lady have been smuggled in here under the cloak of editorial impartiality. Rowe's '*Seeming*' established the moment as illustrative of the Lady's ability to dissemble. The combination of 'seeming' and 'fainting' is powerful in its indictment not only of her but in a wider sense of female duplicity and the exploitation of feminine traits for more sinister motives. It lies at the heart of the cultural anxiety about the character.

Where it is suggested that the faint might be genuine it serves to reveal her weakness in contrast to her husband's resilience under pressure, and in this respect she is judged to fail him. Braunmuller is brisk in his judgement that 'Whatever her action, she fails to perform the part she promised', and he cites her earlier words, 'we shall make our griefs and clamour roar, / Upon his death' (1.7.79–80).[1] The only major editorial enquiry that this sequence has prompted is Braunmuller's response to

---

1   Braunmuller, 172.

Macb. Who can be wife,amaz'd,temp'rate,& furious,
Loyall.and Neutrall,in a moment ? No man :
Th'expedition of my violent Loue
Out-run the pawfer,Reafon. Here lay *Duncan,*
His Siluer skinne,lac'd with his Golden Blood,
And his gafh'd Stabs,look'd like a Breach in Nature,
For Ruines waftfull entrance : there the Murtherers,
Steep'd in the Colours of their Trade ; their Daggers
Vnmannerly breech'd with gore : who could refraine,
That had a heart to loue ; and in that heart,
Courage,to make's loue knowne ?

 Lady. Helpe me hence ,hoa.

 Macd. Looke to the Lady.

 Mal. Why doe we hold our tongues,
That moft may clayme this argument for ours ?

 Donal. What fhould be fpoken here,
Where our Fate hid in an augure hole,
May rufh,and feize vs ? Let's away,
Our Teares are not yet brew'd.

 Mal. Nor our ftrong Sorrow
Vpon the foot of Motion.

 Banq. Looke to the Lady :
And when we haue our naked Frailties hid,
That fuffer in expofure; let vs meet,
And queftion this moft bloody piece of worke,
To know it further. Feares and fcruples fhake vs :
In the great Hand of God I ftand,and thence,
Againft the vndivulg'd pretence,I fight
Of Treafonous Mallice.

 Macd. And fo doe I,

 All. So all.

 Macb. Let's briefely put on manly readineffe,
And meet i'th' Hall together.

 All. Well contented.   *Exeunt.*

20 *The Tragedie of Macbeth*, p. 138, ll. 873–906, from *Mr William Shake-*
  speare's Comedies, Histories, and Tragedies (The First Folio) (1623)

Banquo's repetition of Macduff's line 'Look to the lady.' His edition includes extensive speculation about the kind of errors that this 'repetition bracket' might indicate by reference to the characterization of Macduff and Banquo.[1] If we strip away all the accumulation of masculine editorial interference the text is opened up for a range of interpretative possibilities to be explored.[2]

What does Macbeth's wife do to prompt the comments of Macduff and Banquo? Of course she might faint, but it is important to recognize that the text of the dialogue will work if she knocks over a table, tears her hair or even vomits. Crucially, she does something which draws attention to herself. It may or may not be a deliberate ploy to distract attention from her husband. It may or may not be related to illness, real or imagined. Most important is the recognition that her behaviour at this moment is undefined, and whatever choice is made here will have important consequences for the way in which her character is viewed. There is a need for transparency in the editorial, critical and theatrical choices that are made in order to enable readers and audiences to recognize that this is a moment of choice, not a moment in which the character is set down for us in Shakespeare's text.

The case for editorial restraint would seem to have been accepted in the matter of the faint in that modern editors have abstained from inserting a stage direction though annotation accepts the tradition. But all editions insert a stage direction to remove the Lady from the stage on or just before Banquo's line 'Look to the lady.'[3] And not only is the exit inserted but the

---

1 Braunmuller, 276–7.

2 There is an important parallel here with Julia's 'faint' at the end of *Two Gentlemen of Verona* where it is equally possible to argue against the assumption that the way in which she attracts attention is by fainting.

3 Editorially inserted exits in this edition (presented in square brackets) should be read as suggestions not instructions.

manner of it is generally indicated, e.g. '*taken out*', '*attended*', '*helped*'. But it is a decision that can be interrogated. It may be sensible but is not necessary to remove her before the '*Exeunt*'.

Banquo's words 'Look to the lady' are the beginning of a speech which might resonate more powerfully if allowed to be heard in the context of 'looking' at 'the lady'. They suggest that he is prompting a communal awareness of the need to recognize how 'our naked frailties' which 'suffer in exposure' need to be 'hid'. This action needs to take place before those he addresses meet again. When he states that 'Fears and scruples shake us' he is again drawing attention to a shared experience which might well register more strongly if the Lady remains onstage. Macbeth breaks his fifteen lines' silence by urging the assembly to 'put on manly readiness', which would certainly be capable of richer resonance if the Lady had remained. She could then leave the stage at the '*Exeunt*' for all but Malcolm and Donalbain. Of crucial importance is the need to preserve the openness of the text and ensure that readers know where editorial intervention has taken place. The issue in this particular instance is not simply that an earlier exit has been inserted by editors but that the manner of that exit has been prescribed.

Exits are frequently problematical for editors because although promptbooks will characteristically be fairly full and clear about entrances, the decision to leave the stage is not one in which the book-keeper, either in Shakespeare's theatre or in ours, can or need be involved. Consequently it is not unusual for an editor to have to supply indications for a character's exit. It is not always as straightforward as it might seem. A character's silence cannot always be assumed to indicate that they no longer play a role in a scene. In performance it can be possible for a character to fade from a scene without an audience noticing an exit. This might be effective, for example, in the case of the

Porter (2.3), for whom no exit is marked in the Folio text. In an acknowledgment of this interpretative richness and contrary to usual practice, many modern editions preserve the ambivalence of his role by not inserting an exit for him.[1] Editorial commentary can draw attention to possibilities that arise from what sometimes are simply assumed to be mistakes or omissions from the text. Fleance's exit in 2.1 is not indicated, and the assumption is that he leaves with his father, so '*Exit Banquo*' (at 30) is emended to '*Exeunt [and Fleance]*'. Such a suggestion is sensible, but it is also possible that Fleance leaves earlier, perhaps at 'All's well' (19).[2] Banquo's confession which follows, 'I dreamt last night of the three weïrd sisters', marks a significant shift to a confided intimacy. His words might seem awkward and inappropriate if spoken in the presence of his son. It seems proper for editors to open up discussion of the possibilities prompted by the incomplete nature of the text, rather than assume that the tidiest, most straightforward solution is necessarily the best one or the only one that should be offered to the reader.[3] Occasionally the richness of stage directions seems problematical. The matter of Macbeth's death is particularly interesting in this respect. The whole of the action from Macbeth's entrance at the start of 5.7 ('They have tied me to a stake') to the end of the play is presented as *Scena Septima* in the Folio. It is a scene of action and reflection, initially showing Macbeth's vigorous dispatch of Young Siward and illustrating his confidence in his invincibility by any except a man 'That was not born of woman'. Then Macduff replaces Macbeth, and his invocation 'Let me find him, Fortune' engages with the central prophecy of the play. The short pieces of dialogue and the repeated instructions in the stage directions

1   This edition suggests that he leave at l. 42.
2   This edition is the first to insert an exit for him at this point.
3   Brooke without comment deviates from Oxf's reading '*Exeunt Banquo and Fleance*' and offers simply '*Exit*'.

for '*Alarums*' creates the tension, excitement and unpredictability of battle. Malcolm is guided to the safety of the castle by Siward, whose reassurance that the 'noble thanes do bravely' is innocent of his son's death. His assertion that 'little is to do' is followed by Macbeth's entrance denouncing heroic suicide (5.8.1–2).

Macduff's command 'Turn, hell-hound, turn' (5.8.3) splendidly crafts the confrontation between the two who have been juxtaposed but so far kept apart onstage. After an exchange, Macduff declares, 'My voice is in my sword', and as described (F) there follows '*Fight: Alarum*'. Macbeth's confidence of his 'charmed life' is restated, to be defeated by Macduff's revelation of the manner of his birth ('Despair thy charm'). From confidence to withdrawal ('I'll not fight with thee') to defiance ('I will not yield') the action is graphically described. The climax to their combat is depicted in Macbeth's declaration 'Before my body, / I throw my warlike shield' and the stage direction which follows, '*Exeunt fighting. Alarums*'. In the Folio this text comes at the bottom of the left-hand column of print, and the next column is headed '*Enter Fighting, and Macbeth slaine*'. Immediately the text indicates how the repeated alarums are replaced by '*Retreat*' and '*Flourish*'. The stage picture is crafted in '*Enter with Drumme and Colours*' for Malcolm's entrance. Twenty-seven lines later the text instructs, '*Enter Macduffe; with Macbeths head*', and Macduff announces, 'Hail King, for so thou art. Behold where stands / Th'usurper's cursed head'; and with a directed '*Flourish*' Malcolm is acclaimed king.

Editors have always judged this section to need work. There has been general reluctance to let the action stand as one scene. Of modern editions only the Oxford single edition follows the Folio division, and Brooke argues lucidly for that decision:

> The fact is that scenes 2–6 represent the preparations
> for battle when the two armies must be understood to

be in separate locations (and Malcolm is marching), Scene 7 is the battle itself which is continuous, where a number of incidents happen before our eyes and the rest is off-stage. The Folio arrangement is therefore entirely rational, and any other forgets the reality of the theatre for an improbable series of mini-scenes designated 'Another part of the field'.[1]

Even more problematical is the matter of the stage directions relating to Macbeth's death. The lineation in the Folio is seen by some to support the case for emendation. Dyce had argued, 'The stage-directions given by the Ff in this scene are exquisitely absurd',[2] and all editions after Pope to the end of the nineteenth century kept the first and removed the second. So Macbeth pursued Macduff offstage and the Folio direction '*Enter Fighting, and Macbeth slaine*' was removed. Dover Wilson indulged in a characteristic flight of fancy and suggested '*they fight to and fro beneath the castle wall, until at length "Macbeth" is "slain"*'[3]

Modern editions include both but indicate reservations and qualifications through notes and additions, with editors evidently worrying a good deal about the practical arrangements for removing Macbeth's body. There has been no engagement with R.G. White's reasonable point that the stage direction which follows, '*Retreat, and Flourish*', might provide a solution. In 1883 he wrote:

It is possible that Shakespeare, or the stage-manager of his company, did not deny the audience the satisfaction of seeing the usurper meet his doom, and that in the subsequent 'retreat' his body was dragged off the stage for its supposed decapitation.[4]

1   Brooke, 206.
2   Furness, 345.
3   Dover Wilson, 84.
4   Furness, 345.

While modern editors (including those of this edition) feel the need to suggest that Macduff should remove Macbeth's body, it can be argued that such intervention betrays an insistent (even unhelpful) literal mindedness. It also might run the risk of denying theatrical inventiveness, militating against the essential openness of interpretative choices. Such additions are not, of course, prescriptive. Macbeth is killed onstage and then twenty-seven lines later Shakespeare's text instructs, '*Enter Macduffe; with Macbeths head*'. It is a vivid theatrical moment when, however the head is presented, an audience reads the iconography as Macbeth's final demise in a public display as a traitor. It defies naturalism in the most fundamental of ways.

PART 2: THE FOLIO TEXT AND ITS INTEGRITY

There are a number of current theories about the nature of the Folio text of *Macbeth* and the extent to which it shows a play that has been adapted from an earlier original by abridgement, interpolation and rearrangement. Many editors consider that there are problems with the integrity of the play as a whole, and although there is no intention here to discuss these in any detail, the position needs briefly to be reviewed. E.K. Chambers, in 1924, was dismissive of many of the claims of what he called the disintegrators of Shakespeare, mentioning especially Clark and Wright, editors of the Cambridge Shakespeare (1863–4) who 'elaborated Coleridge's heresy about *Macbeth* by ascribing substantial interpolations in that play to Middleton'.[1] Recently, theories of disintegration have been revived, and applied, not without opposition, to the text of *Macbeth*. Chambers concluded

---

1 E.K. Chambers, 'The disintegration of Shakespeare', in *Shakespearean Gleanings* (1944), 4. Clark and Wright's discussion of the authorship of *Macbeth* appeared in their edition of the play for the Clarendon Press Series (1869). They ascribed about 300 lines of the play to Middleton.

that there was 'probably' some interpolation in the play but confined to three passages (3.5, 4.1.39–43 and 4.1.124–31); he did however feel that the text was in other ways unsatisfactory, showing signs of abridgement and of 'some manipulation' in the final battle scene.[1] The Folio text of *Macbeth* has been found problematic or subject to question in respect of its length and apparent inconsistencies by many editors. Reasons have been offered to think that the playtext was changed between 1606, when it was written, and 1623, when it was first printed, but there is no stable basis on which to pare away any such changes and reconstruct what might have been Shakespeare's original text.[2] The brevity of the play has often been adduced as an indication that the text as it stands is a cut version of a longer one. It is certainly the shortest of Shakespeare's tragedies, at around 2,500 lines coming out less than two-thirds the average length of the other major tragedies.[3] There are, however, no clear indications of missing scenes or of cuts due to censorship (as Nosworthy, *Shakespeare's*, 23, conjectured) or for other reasons; and the play's compression and speed are often admired and regarded as integral to the dramatic effect.[4] On the other hand, Muir lists nine passages as possible

---

1 Chambers, *Shakespeare*, 1.472–3. Nosworthy, *Shakespeare's*, 24–5, after reviewing the history of disintegration, concludes similarly that only these passages need serious consideration in this context.

2 This is not to say that experimenting with possibilities for various recensions of the text, as Taylor has done in his edition of *Macbeth* (Taylor & Lavagnino, *Middleton*), is pointless. The result, misleadingly called a 'genetic text', is suggestive and fascinating. But whether it brings us any nearer to knowing what Shakespeare originally wrote is disputable.

3 See Taylor & Lavagnino, *Textual Culture*, 385, for further calculations. Dawson points out that *Macbeth* is not so anomalous in relation to all tragedies (19–20). In TLN numbering, based on F1, *Macbeth* has 2,528 lines, *Othello* 3,743, *King Lear* 3,519 and *Antony and Cleopatra* 3,849, but *Titus* 2,708 and *Timon* 2,307.

4 Greg considers that while the text has 'certainly' undergone cutting, 'there is no proof that *Macbeth* was ever anything but a short play' (390).

interpolations, but retains only those cited by Chambers for more discussion; he considers that 4.2.46–59 (on the hanging of traitors) and 4.3.140–6 are 'probably interpolations, but by Shakespeare himself', though without clarifying his reasons.[1] The sequence from 3.6 to 4.1 is the most serious example of inconsistency, in the handling of Macduff's flight to England and Macbeth's response to it. In 3.6 it is indicated that Macduff's flight and reception at the English court are known to Macbeth, but in 4.1 he is surprised and angered to hear this has happened. This discrepancy has often been ascribed to some kind of textual revision (as well as to deliberate dramatic strategy); but there is no consensus as to what may have happened to the text, and in any case it may be the kind of problem that troubles a reader (or editor), but goes unnoticed in the theatre. It is impossible to come up with any theory of cutting that would explain it.[2]

Attitudes towards the likelihood of *Macbeth*'s being a revised text, or one where another writer has a significant input, can be strongly subjective, influenced by the belief that the text is fragmentary or in other ways unsatisfactory. Hunter, a scrupulous and conservative editor, opposing the idea of a shortened text, states firmly, 'The text as we have it is entirely intelligible, orderly and coherent' (Hunter, 94), while Taylor, who includes *Macbeth* in his edition of the collected works of Middleton, finds 'compelling evidence' for the presence of another writer, Thomas Middleton, and considers him responsible for cutting 'one quarter or more' of the original text.[3] One example of changing attitudes towards the integrity of the text can be found in the fact that Muir found it necessary to devote

---

1 See Muir, xxxii. Nosworthy (*Shakespeare's*, 39–44) also considers Shakespeare responsible for interpolating the songs.

2 For further discussion, see pp. 69–72. Braunmuller's discussion, 261–2, offers various possible explanations for the inconsistencies while remaining aware that none of them solves all the problems.

3 Taylor & Lavagnino, *Textual Culture*, 384, 397.

six pages of his introduction to defending the authenticity of the Porter scene from Pope's and Coleridge's rejections of it as an interpolation by the players. No editor would feel the need to do this now.[1]

Discrepancies between the Folio text and Simon Forman's account of a performance of 1611 have been the basis for theories that there was a version of the play in existence before the one recorded in the Folio, what Taylor calls 'the original text'.[2] Much significance has been attached to the fact that Forman, who was an astrologer and known to be interested in witchcraft, does not mention Hecate or the cauldron scene. A great deal of attention has also been paid to his idiosyncratic descriptions of performances in his 'Bocke of Plaies and Notes thereof', largely because they are unique as contemporary eyewitness accounts of Shakespeare onstage. But his descriptions of the two other Shakespeare plays he saw in 1611 (*Cymbeline* and *The Winter's Tale*)[3] are far from complete, for example failing to mention the statue scene in *The Winter's Tale*. His main interests seem to have been in telling the stories and extracting moral lessons from them, jotting down random points that struck him rather than giving full accounts of the productions. His recollections were not always accurate: he says that the Sisters hailed Macbeth 'king of Codon' (rather than Thane of Cawdor) and that Duncan 'made Mackbeth forth with Prince of Northumberland' (instead of making Malcolm Prince of Cumberland), both of these being rather crucial slips as far as the narrative is concerned. What he says of Macbeth's reign and also the description of the Sisters as '3 women feiries

---

1 Muir's edition was first published in 1951, but he included the defence of the Porter scene in his last revision of 1984.

2 For Forman's account, see Appendix 2. It was at one time thought to be a forgery but is now generally accepted as authentic. See Paul, 409.

3 He also describes a performance of *Richard II* at the Globe, but this was clearly not Shakespeare's play.

or Nimphes' reads as if he had been remembering Holinshed.[1] Forman may give some clues to striking effects in a 1611 production of *Macbeth*, but his account does not constitute reliable evidence either of what was 'actually staged' (Scragg, 87) at the Globe in 1611, or of the existence of a pre-Folio version.

Given that many of the questions about the status of the Folio text and the extent to which it may have been subject to adaptation cannot be resolved from the evidence currently available, it seems most profitable to focus the discussion here on those areas where there is the greatest consensus about adaptation, that is, the Hecate scenes and the two songs that are cued into them. In 3.5, the stage direction '*Sing within. Come away, come away, etc.*' is given after 35, and in 4.1, '*Music and a Song. Black spirits, etc.*' after 43. In neither case are further words for the songs supplied. That the cues refer to songs which are present in full in another playtext, *The Witch*, by Middleton, raises several interconnected questions: (i) in which play did the songs first appear? (ii) if *The Witch*, are they by Middleton? Or might they be songs already in existence composed by some other hand? (iii) if they were subsequently inserted into *Macbeth* then why? (iv) how far do they relate to the view that 3.5 and the parts of 4.1 involving Hecate are not by Shakespeare?

The history of the two songs – or at least, what is known of it – is worth rehearsing. It is often stated that they first appeared in print in the Davenant adaptation, written probably in 1663/4[2] and printed in 1674. 'Come away', however (though not 'Black spirits'), had been printed in full in a quarto of *Macbeth* in

---

1 See Leah Scragg's detailed examination of the relationship of Forman's account to Holinshed and of both to *Macbeth*.

2 Spencer, 225–9, argues convincingly that *Macbeth* was adapted by Davenant around 1663, because of imitations of it in *The Rivals* (1664), and that this was the version used in the first recorded performance of the play after 1660 on 5 November 1664.

1673.[1] Since *The Witch* was not then in print, it would appear either that someone had access to a manuscript of it or that versions of the song were then available in a theatrical context. Greg's view is that the Duke of York's Men, who performed the Davenant adaptation (and, it appears, the 1673 quarto version), obtained the words from a 'stage-copy' of *Macbeth* rather than from a manuscript of *The Witch*.[2] He does not speculate about the origins or date of this copy. *The Witch* was not printed until 1778, when Steevens, one of the great eighteenth-century editors of Shakespeare, acquired the manuscript of it, an undated transcript by Ralph Crane, who worked for the King's Men.[3] Steevens noticed that it contained the full texts of the two songs cued into the witch scenes of Shakespeare's play, and believing that *The Witch* was an Elizabethan play, he assumed that Shakespeare had taken over the songs that were part of it (though not necessarily that they were by Middleton). He copied the play out and had it printed in 1778. Malone, in his Variorum of 1821, argued that *The Witch* was written after 1613 (as is now accepted). It is generally agreed to allude to, and even dramatize, aspects of the court scandals involving the divorce of Frances Howard, Countess of Suffolk, from Robert Devereux, Earl of Essex, in 1613, her subsequent remarriage to Robert Carr in the same year, and the Overbury murder trials in

1   This quarto of *Macbeth*, printed without any author's name, is based on the Folio text, but with additional scenes for the Witches, who sing and dance. After 2.2, there are fifteen lines apparently derived from Davenant, and after 2.3 sixteen more; 3.5 includes the words for 'Come away' largely as in *The Witch*. It includes a cast list, so must have been performed at some point. Odell speculates that it was this version that Pepys saw in 1664, when he called it 'a pretty good play, but admirably acted', whereas it was the Davenant version which he saw in 1666, describing it as 'a most excellent play for variety' (Odell, 1.28). See also Brooke's discussion of the variants in the song texts (Appendix B, 226–7).

2   Greg & Wilson, x. Davenant worked for the King's Men in the 1630s, so conceivably had access to a playhouse manuscript of *Macbeth*, as Schafer notes in her edition of *The Witch*, xv.

3   The manuscript is held in the Bodleian Library, MS Malone 12.

1615 and 1616.[1] Those who regard Middleton as having a significant role in *Macbeth* consider the songs to be a 'decisive link' with him.[2]

In which play did the songs first appear? Most scholars assume that it was *The Witch*, and it is believed that since Middleton's play was either a 'stage flop' or else suppressed because of its political content the songs were rescued for reuse in another play also belonging to the King's Men, that is, in a version of *Macbeth* revised to accommodate them.[3] The relationship between the two plays is open to different interpretations. Edward J. Esche, a recent editor of *The Witch*, has suggested that this play quotes from *Macbeth* in several places, and observes that Middleton might be drawing on the audience's knowledge of it as a prior play by the same company.[4] He does not discuss the songs, but seems to assume that the Folio text of *Macbeth* was a revision made by Middleton to include them. Brooke in his edition of *Macbeth* takes the radical line that Middleton wrote the songs for *Macbeth* when he revised it in 1609–10, and reused them later for *The Witch*.[5] Taylor, in his edition of *Macbeth* included in the works of Middleton, argues that the songs were taken from *The Witch* and interpolated in

1 See Marion O'Connor's account in Taylor & Lavagnino, *Textual Culture*, 382–3. She dates the play at mid-1616. Esche proposes early 1616 (25). Schafer (xi–xii) supports 1615–16.

2 Brooke, 58.

3 See discussions in Lancashire, 161–81, also Brooke, 64–6, Esche, 21–6, Schafer, xiv–xv, Hutchings & Bromham, 62–4, and Taylor, 'Empirical', forthcoming.

4 Esche, 60–4, discusses parallels between *The Witch* and *Macbeth*, some of which are more convincing than others. His view that Middleton's flying witches in 3.3 and the knocking in 4.3 (which also features 'a bawdy joking servant' and the use of posset by an evil woman to drug the servants) refer back to *Macbeth* is persuasive, as is his reference to the cauldron in *The Witch*, 5.2, as 'a direct iconic quotation' (62). His sense of the intertextual relation between the two plays is influenced by Ewbank's discussion of the two plays in 'Middle', 156–72.

5 He proposes that the Hecate material was added soon after the King's Men had taken over the Blackfriars theatre and before Forman saw the play at the Globe, but allows that it is a 'tentative' conclusion (66).

Macbeth by Middleton when he was making extensive adaptations to the play for a revival to be put on soon after the suppression of *The Witch*.[1] What of the possibility that both playwrights used songs already in existence? Tiffany Stern gives much evidence to show that 'songs did not always belong as powerfully to a single play as did other aspects of the text', and that 'playwrights putting texts together at speed sometimes took whatever song was at hand', although she does believe that the songs originated in *The Witch* and were later used to 'bolster' *Macbeth*.[2] Versions of a song 'Come away, Hecate' exist in two collections of lute songs datable *c.* 1630, with no ascriptions to either a play or a composer.[3] William St Clair suggests that 'both Middleton and Shakespeare may have been using a song which had already been printed' and Peter Thomson (152) allows that the songs might have been 'part of a common stock'.[4] But that is as far as this line of argument seems to go. Inga-Stina Ewbank, however, feels that the songs are 'inextricably connected' with the Hecate passages, and hence unlikely to have originated independently of either play.[5] Her view is that they 'are almost bound' to have been originally written for *The Witch*.

That the songs were inserted into a version of *Macbeth* that did not originally contain them is an assumption that can find much support from within the text and is almost universally

1 Taylor, *Textual Culture*, 384–5.
2 Stern, *Documents*, 152, 134. (She does however believe that the songs originated in *The Witch*.)
3 See Brooke's Appendix B, 'Musical additions', 225ff., for a fuller account of the songs.
4 See St Clair, 154, Thomson, 152. Suhamy suggests that 'Come away' may have been 'a familiar and popular ditty' and not by Middleton. Bentley (140) makes the point that the songs were added but not necessarily by Middleton, 'since the manuscript of *The Witch* belonged to the King's Men and any reviser with access to the Blackfriars archives could have transferred the songs'.
5 Ewbank, Introduction to *The Tragedy of Macbeth: A Genetic Text*, in Taylor & Lavagnino, *Middleton*, 1166.

accepted. Apart from their appearance in another play, there is the fact that only brief cues are given, whereas songs in other Shakespeare plays are given in full. In the case of 'Come away, come away' there is no introduction for the song or reference to it in the surrounding dialogue or action. According to the stage direction, it is sung '*within*', so that the three spirits and the cat who sing the parts along with Hecate do not appear on the stage. 'Black spirits' is introduced by a five-line speech by Hecate, who has apparently made an appearance specifically to do this, because she has no more involvement in the scene.[1] Her lines, which seem to be interposed into a speech by the Second Witch, are thus usually assumed to be part of the interpolation. This song is sung onstage by '*the other three witches*' who have entered with Hecate. The songs are often considered to be out of place in *Macbeth* and stylistically unsuited to the play, whereas they fit more acceptably into the context of *The Witch*. When printed in full as part of *Macbeth*, as in the Oxford Shakespeare and in Brooke, it is impossible not to feel their incongruity.

It is a widely held view that not just the songs but the neighbouring sections of text, including the whole of 3.5, and 4.1.39–43 and 124–31, mar Shakespeare's play.[2] They do, as Ewbank puts it, make the play 'more of a show',[3] perhaps an ambiguous phrase to use about a play that ends with a display of its protagonist's head. But Bernice Kliman, following up this kind of reading, suggests that these 'problematic Hecate segments' may have been part of the play even in 1606; she believes that unity of tone, which is easier to create if Hecate

---

1 Brooke and the Oxford editors retain her (and the other three witches) onstage until 4.1.131, assigning her the speech beginning 'Ay, sir, all this is so' (124), although there is no textual warrant for this.

2 This is a reason used to support the idea that the interpolations were made by Middleton after Shakespeare's death, e.g. as implied by Egan in *The Struggle for Shakespeare's Text* and in private conversation.

3 Ewbank, 'Middle', 158.

along with the songs and dances is cut, would have been less desirable in Shakespeare's time than what she calls, the 'medieval disjunction' of generically mixed effects (Kliman, 15).[1] The authenticity of 3.5 has been questioned on several grounds: mainly, that Hecate is a new character, previously unmentioned by the Witches (though associated by Macbeth with witchcraft at 2.1.51–2 and with evil at 3.2.42); that most of the scene is in iambic couplets rather than the trochaic metre used earlier by the Witches; that what Chambers called 'the prettinesses of lyrical fancy' are alien to the conception of witchcraft elsewhere in the play.[2] Although the scene has long been regarded as spurious, and since the nineteenth century has rarely been staged,[3] these grounds are not conclusive. The different verse style has been justified in various ways, since, as Brooke says, '[Hecate] is a goddess from a machine and as such has a different verse from the Weïrd Sisters' (53). As he also notes, the gods and goddesses in *Cymbeline* and *The Tempest* are given different verse forms from other characters, and use iambic couplets. Similarities with the speeches of the fairies in *A Midsummer Night's Dream* have also been observed.[4] Stress has been placed by Taylor and others on the significance of the formula '*Enter . . . meeting . . .*' in the stage directions for 3.5 ('*Enter the three* WITCHES, *meeting Hecate*')

---

1 Kliman cites a production by Ron Daniels in New York, 1999, in which the Witches' dance in 4.1 was used 'to excellent effect' (15).

2 Chambers, *Shakespeare*, 1.472. But Vickers and Dahl, arguing for Shakespeare's authorship, aptly note Greg's comment that 'if "prettinesses of lyrical fancy" are alien to Shakespeare's treatment of the witches, they are still further removed from Middleton's coarse and caustic treatment'.

3 A major exception to this was Peter Hall's National Theatre production of 1978. His reasons for including Hecate are discussed in 'Directing "*Macbeth*" ', in Brown, 242–4. See p. 100.

4 E.g. by Vickers and Dahl. Nosworthy, *Shakespeare's*, 25–7, cites Wilson Knight's defence of Hecate in *The Shakespearian Tempest*, which rests on parallels with *A Midsummer Night's Dream*, calling it 'the only concrete evidence' in favour of Shakespeare's authorship.

as well as 1.2 ('*Enter* KING . . . *meeting a bleeding* Captain') as evidence of Middleton's presence, since it is uncommon in any plays other than his, and occurs only once in a scene undisputedly Shakespeare's.[1] Holdsworth ('Directions', 191–200) has shown that the form of early modern stage directions can constitute strong indications of authorship. This issue may contribute to the general uncertainty over 3.5, though this is not to say that the scene is totally redundant. While omission of the scene in performance is rarely noticed, it does have a dramatic function in preparing for the longer witchcraft scene, 4.1, and it makes the point that Macbeth has less control over events than he believes.[2] It can be theatrically spectacular, introducing a 'masque-like element' to the play.[3] Hunter notes that Hecate's speech 'catches at a principal theme of the whole play, the danger of security' and that it is 'poetically very accomplished'.[4] The scene has recently been subjected to computer-based tests using digital databases. Although experts in this field allow that 'no one type of testing can create absolute certainty' (Jackson,

---

1 See Braunmuller, 239. The other occurrence in Shakespeare is in *King Lear*, 1608 Q: '*Enter Bast*[*ard*] *and Curan meeting*', which Vickers and Dahl claim causes 'a large part' of Taylor's argument about Middleton and Macbeth to collapse. Egan, however, thinks that ' "*Enter X and Y meeting*" is not the same as "*Enter X meeting Y*" ', and that Vickers and Dahl's case is therefore weakened (reviewing Vickers & Dahl in Egan, 'Editions'). Taylor's discussions in '*Macbeth* and Middleton', 297–8, and 'Empirical', forthcoming, support Egan's point. Dessen and Thomson, 'meet', give a proliferation of variations on the basis of '*Enter . . . meet*'. While it may be difficult to gauge how much stress to put on the differences of wording, Holdsworth's close (and non-electronic) examination of the '*enter X meeting Y*' formula ('Directions', 191–200) strongly supports the case that it is one of Middleton's 'trademark mannerisms' (189).

2 Suhamy argues strongly for the scene as Shakespeare's on grounds of its functional relevance as well as the qualities of its verse and metrics. Bullough (7.424) gives reasons to support Shakespeare's authorship of the scene on similar grounds.

3 The phrase is Thomson's (152). Thomson calls the scene 'a splendid example of the "impurity" of popular drama'. Ewbank, in Taylor & Lavagnino, *Middleton*, 1167–8, develops this idea.

4 Hunter, 133.

'Reviewing', 154), it seems likely that Shakespeare was not its author.[1]

In 4.1 Hecate's appearance is briefer, and apparently necessary only to introduce the song 'Black spirits' and lead its performance.[2] While the Folio text gives no exit for her, editors usually supply one at 43, since otherwise she and the other three witches who have made their entrance with her must remain onstage without anything to do for nearly ninety lines until the exit marked at 131 (*'The Witches dance and vanish'*). This passage (39–43) seems to have no function other than introducing the song, and thus appears to be an interpolation; and if this song is accepted as an interpolation, then it seems logical to assume that the other song, which shares the same provenance, is also. This might apply to the whole of 3.5; here, the song, which is sung *'within'*, is not called for in the text and no reference is made to it.

The First Witch's last lines in 4.1 (124–31) have been suspected partly on the same grounds as 3.5 – the iambic metre and the more lyrical tone. Like the earlier passage, they serve to introduce music and a witches' dance, in this case, the prelude to their vanishing. The lines create a division between two speeches of Macbeth, which could without difficulty form a continuous whole. He makes no reference to the content of the passage, only to the Witches' sudden departure. After the show of kings, Macbeth reacts with horror: 'What? Is this so?' The

---

1 The data collected by Vickers and his colleague Marcus Dahl (Dahl *et al.*) shows evidence of Shakespearean diction throughout the scene. But Egan, Jackson, Taylor and others have questioned the methodology used to support their claims for Shakespeare, which derive from an incomplete database of the Middleton canon. Dawson is unconvinced by Vickers and Dahl's ascription of 3.5 to Shakespeare (18–19). See Jackson, 'Reviewing', 60, and Taylor, *'Macbeth* and Middleton', 301–3, and 'Empirical', forthcoming. In 'Empirical' Taylor describes and applies his own digital methodology specifically to 3.5, 4.1.39–43 and 124–31.

2 The Oxford editors ascribe the first forty-three lines (in Oxford, sixty) of the scene to Middleton, assuming that Shakespeare's part only begins at the Second Witch's line 'By the pricking of my thumbs', but they present no evidence to support this.

First Witch then dedicates the entertainment to him with a kind
of parodic irony:

> Ay, sir, all this is so. But why
> Stands Macbeth thus amazedly?
> Come, sisters, cheer we up his sprights,
> And show the best of our delights.
> I'll charm the air to give a sound,
> While you perform your antique round,
> That this great king may kindly say
> Our duties did his welcome pay.

$$(4.1.124–31)^1$$

This passage has been both praised and execrated. George
Fletcher says that it is

> not only remarkable as the final communication made
> by these evil beings to their wicked consulter, but is the
> most pointedly characteristic of their diabolical nature.
> It is the exulting mockery with which the fiend pays off
> the presumptuous criminal who has so insolently dared
> him.[2]

But Dover Wilson refers to it as 'an interpolation . . . which
ruins a fine theatrical effect' (152). There has been speculation
that the 'great king' might refer to King James, and that the
lines were perhaps inserted for a specific performance when he
was present,[3] but there is no evidence to support this claim, and
the whole speech, as Fletcher shows, can be directed with some

1 Ewbank (in Taylor & Lavagnino, *Middleton*, 1167), while assuming tentatively that the
   lines were written by Middleton for Hecate, draws attention to the use of 'welcome'
   as an ironic echo of the four uses of the word by the Macbeths in the banquet scene.
2 George Fletcher, *Studies of Shakespeare* (1847), 151.
3 Kernan (77) and Thomson (137, 154) among others hypothesize a performance at
   Hampton Court in August 1606. This would favour Shakespeare, not Middleton, as
   the interpolator.

point to Macbeth. The passage could be an interpolation, since Macbeth's question at 123, 'What? Is this so?', could be rhetorical and need not be answered, and could be followed by his further questions at 132, 'Where are they? Gone?' But the Witches need an exit at this point, and it makes sense for them to have some lines before they depart. The style and metre are similar to those in 3.5.

While there is no completely objective proof that any parts of these speeches and the songs in 3.5 and 4.1 were added to the first version of *Macbeth* at a later date, the position that seems likeliest is that the songs in all probability, and then perhaps also the suspect passages in 4.1, were interpolations. The two hundred years' history of their importance on the stage suggests that reasons for such interpolation are not difficult to find during periods when song, dance and spectacle were valued constituents of *Macbeth*, even if they have been rejected by both critics and theatre directors after the nineteenth century, when attitudes to what is authentically Shakespearean have changed. But who was responsible for interpolating them? The case for Middleton is strong and of long standing. It derives from the view that the songs originated in *The Witch*, and it can be supported by computer-based methodologies. Those who accept it generally assume that the interpolation was made after 1616.[1] Arguments that Shakespeare himself inserted them at an earlier date are counteracted by the general acceptance that *The Witch* dates from around 1616, and is connected with court scandals involving the Essex divorce case.[2] Assuming, then that the

1 Though Ewbank thinks it not unlikely that Shakespeare was still alive when Middleton 'adapted *Macbeth*' ('Middle', 157).

2 Nosworthy, *Shakespeare's*, 48, and Ioppolo, 121–4, argue for Shakespeare as the interpolator. But see O'Connor, the most recent editor of *The Witch*, who summarizes the position on the dating of the play (in Taylor & Lavagnino, *Textual Culture*, 382–3). Hutchings and Bromham, considering the issue from a Middletonian perspective, discuss reasons why Middleton might have wanted to reuse material from *The Witch* (62–4).

songs were added from *The Witch*, together with extra lines for Hecate in 4.1 (39–43), and possibly after Shakespeare's death, it might have been to increase the play's spectacular potential, which was something that Davenant clearly seized upon after the Restoration.[1] Kathleen McLuskie suggests that what she calls Middleton's 'tinkering additions' may have been made to keep the play up to date, as 'part of the process that all the theatre companies used to make the most of their back-list to extend their repertory'.[2] Whether Middleton was personally responsible for adding the songs and extra lines we cannot know. His involvement in Shakespeare's playwriting appears to have been spasmodic, consisting otherwise of no more than collaborating on *Timon of Athens* around 1607 and, according to Jowett and Taylor, adapting *Measure for Measure* much later, in 1621,[3] though this view is not widely accepted.

By comparison with the issues raised by the song cues, the case for adaptation elsewhere in the play is much less substantial. Taylor makes an extensive case for the inclusion of *Macbeth* in the Oxford edition of the works of Middleton, stemming from the premise that 'If Middleton contributed the Hecate passages, then it is obvious that he may also be present elsewhere'.[4] It does not seem to me that this premise alone is sufficient to justify what follows in the edition, although it is not Taylor's sole evidence. He finds Middleton responsible for both cuts and additions, assuming that the play's 'anomalous brevity' (385)

---

1 Diane Purkiss, in her challenging account of what she calls 'the Jacobean witch-vogue' in Jonson's *The Masque of Queenes*, *Macbeth* and *The Witch*, denounces the witch scenes in *Macbeth* for replacing 'any serious engagement with witchcraft' with 'a forthright rendering of witches as a stage spectacular' (207).

2 McLuskie, 104.

3 Taylor & Lavagnino, *Middleton*, 1544–6.

4 Taylor & Lavagnino, *Textual Culture*, 385. After examining 1.2, 1.3, 3.5, 3.6, 4.1 and 4.2 in considerable verbal detail he concludes that Middleton's presence can be detected in all these scenes, adding, cutting and transposing lines, affecting about 11% of the whole play. In addition, he may also have been responsible 'for cutting one quarter or more of the original text' (397).

must be accounted for by cuts and therefore that 'Middleton almost certainly abridged the original'. For cuts it is of course hard to find evidence; they might be indicated by 'metrical, syntactical and narrative strain' which Taylor finds in 1.2 (386), but this is a particular interpretation of speeches, the apparent oddities of which can be accounted for in other ways.[1] There may or may not have been an appearance of Edward the Confessor in 4.3, as Nevill Coghill thought,[2] but Edward's function in the play is clear enough without it, and the lack is not felt in performance. If the play was cut – which it is unlikely can ever be convincingly demonstrated – then there are many other possible explanations. For the additions, Forman's description is no solid foundation on which to build a theory of what the play he saw in 1611 did not contain. The Folio text of *Macbeth* is probably not the original version that Shakespeare wrote in 1606; but the extent to which it differs may well be very slight, and confined to 3.5 and two passages in 4.1.

---

1 See Dawson, 20–1. He considers the views of Brooke, Taylor and Braunmuller that the stage direction '*meeting . . . a bleeding* Captain' might indicate Middleton's presence, but regards it as 'insufficient to ground the evidence' (20) for any cutting in the scene.

2 Coghill, 230–4. The argument of Amnaéus, based mainly on Forman's account, that there was once a scene in which the Macbeths discussed Banquo's murder, is unconvincing. See also Thaler.

APPENDIX 2

Simon Forman, Bocke of Plaies *(?1611)*[1]

In Mackbeth at the Glob[e], 1610, the 20 of Aprill [Saturday],[2] ther was to be observed, firste, howe Mackbeth and Bancko, 2 noble men of Scotland, Ridinge thorowe a wod, the[re] stode before them 3 women feiries or Nimphes, And saluted Mackbeth, sayinge, 3 tyms unto him, haille Mackbeth, king of Codon; for thou shalt be a kinge, but shalt beget No kinges, &c. Then said Bancko, What all to Mackbeth And nothing to me. Yes, said the nimphes, haille to thee Bancko, thou shalt beget kinges, yet be no kinge. And so they departed & cam to the Courte of Scotland to Dunkin king of Scotes, and yt was in the dais of Edward the Confessor. And Dunkin bad them both kindly wellcome, And made Mackbeth forth with Prince of Northumberland, and sent him hom to his own castell, and appointed Mackbeth to provid for him, for he would sup with him the next dai at night, & did soe. And Mackebeth contrived to kill Dunkin, & thorowe the persuasion of his wife did that night Murder the kinge in his own Castell, beinge his guest. And ther were many prodigies seen that night & the dai before. And when Mack Beth had murdred the kinge, the blod on his handes could not be washed of by Any meanes, nor from his wives handes, which handled the bloddi daggers in hiding them, By which means they became both moch amazed & Affronted. The murder being knowen, Dunkins 2 sonns fled, the on to England, the [other to]

---

1   This version of Forman's text comes from Chambers, *Shakespeare*, 2.337–8. There is a facsimile and another transcription of the text, with discussion, in S. Schoenbaum, *William Shakespeare: Records and Images* (1981), 7–13. Schoenbaum's transcription is closer to Forman's almost unpunctuated text, but harder to read.

2   'Saturday' is represented in the MS by the astronomer's sign for Saturn, meaning Saturday. As 20 April did not fall on a Saturday in 1610, scholars assume that Forman meant 1611.

Walles, to save them selves, they being fled, they were supposed guilty of the murder of their father, which was nothinge so. Then was Mackbeth crowned kinge, and then he for feare of Banko, his old companion, that he should beget kinges but be no kinge him selfe, he contrived the death of Banko, and caused him to be Murdred on the way as he Rode. The next night, beinge at supper with his noble men whom he had bid to a feaste to the which also Banco should have com, he began to speak of Noble Banco, and to wish that he wer ther. And as he thus did, standing up to drincke a Carouse to him, the ghoste of Banco came and sate down in his cheier behind him. And he turninge About to sit down Again sawe the goste of Banco, which fronted him so, that he fell into a great passion of fear and fury, Utterynge many wordes about his murder, by which, when they h[e]ard that Banco was Murdred they Suspected Mackbet.

Then MackDove fled to England to the kinges sonn, And soe they Raised an Army, And cam into Scotland, and at Dunston Anyse[1] overthrue Mackbet. In the meantime while Macdovee was in England, Mackbet slewe Mackdoves wife & children, and after in the battelle Mackdove slewe Mackbet.

Observe Also howe Mackbetes quen did Rise in the night in her slepe, & walke and talked and confessed all, & the docter noted her wordes.

---

1   Dunsinane.

APPENDIX 3

Macbeth's genealogy

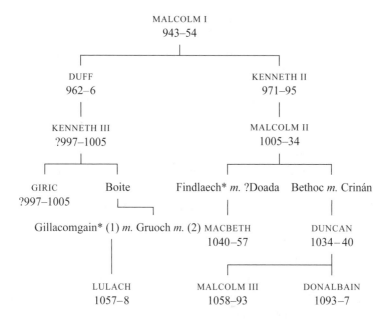

This table, adapted from those in Aitchison, 63, and Watson, xiii, demonstrates Macbeth's relationship to Duncan and his twofold claim to the throne of Scotland. The names of kings of Scotland are capitalized; the dates are those of their reigns. Kenneth III and Giric may have been joint rulers. Some of the lines of descent (i.e. from Kenneth III to Boite and from Malcolm II to Doada) are probable rather than certain.

*Indicates that both Findlaech and Gillacomgain were Mormaers of Moray, powerful regional magnates. Gillacomgain, Macbeth's cousin, murdered Findlaech in 1020.

APPENDIX 4
List of productions

This list consists only of productions referred to in the Introduction. Theatres are in London unless otherwise indicated; the location of the Shakespeare Memorial Theatre, the Swan Theatre and The Other Place is Stratford-upon-Avon.

1673	Thomas Betterton and Mrs Betterton	Dorset Garden
1748	David Garrick and Hannah Pritchard	Drury Lane
1773	Charles Macklin and Elizabeth Hartley	Covent Garden
1788	John Philip Kemble and Sarah Siddons	Drury Lane
1794	John Philip Kemble and Sarah Siddons	Drury Lane
1814	Edmund Kean and Sarah Bartley	Drury Lane
1820	William Charles Macready and Margaret Bunn	Covent Garden
1842	William Charles Macready and Helen Faucit	Drury Lane
1843	William Charles Macready and Charlotte Cushman	Drury Lane
1847	Samuel Phelps and Laura Addison	Sadlers Wells
1851	William Charles Macready and Mary Warner	Haymarket
1853	Charles Kean and Ellen Kean	Princess's
1858	Samuel Phelps and Helen Faucit	Her Majesty's
1864	Samuel Phelps and Helen Faucit	Drury Lane

1875	Henry Irving and Kate Bateman	Lyceum
1888	Henry Irving and Ellen Terry	Lyceum
1898	Johnston Forbes-Robertson and Mrs Patrick Campbell	Lyceum
1911	Herbert Beerbohm Tree and Violet Vanbrugh	His Majesty's
1917/18	Sir Frank Benson and Genevieve Townsend (dir. Benson)	Touring production
1928	Eric Maturin and Mary Merrell (dir. Barry Jackson)	Royal Court
1930	Sir John Gielgud and Martita Hunt (dir. Harcourt Williams)	Old Vic
1933	George Hayes and Fabia Drake (dir. Theodore Komisarjevsky)	Shakespeare Memorial Theatre
1934	Charles Laughton and Flora Robson (dir. Tyrone Guthrie)	Old Vic
1942	Sir John Gielgud and Gwen Ffrangçon-Davies (dir. Gielgud)	Piccadilly Theatre
1945	Donald Wolfit and Patricia Jessel (dir. Wolfit)	The Winter Garden
1948	Orson Welles and Jeanette Nolan (dir. Orson Welles)	Film
1949	Godfrey Tearle and Diana Wynyard (dir. Anthony Quayle)	Shakespeare Memorial Theatre
1952	Ralph Richardson and Margaret Leighton (dir. John Gielgud)	Shakespeare Memorial Theatre
1953	Donald Wolfit and Rosalind Iden (dir. Wolfit)	Kings Theatre, Hammersmith
1955	Laurence Olivier and Vivien Leigh (dir. Glen Byam Shaw)	Shakespeare Memorial Theatre
1957	Glynn Edwards and Eileen Keneally (dir. Joan Littlewood)	Theatre Royal, Stratford East

1957	Toshiro Mifune and Isuzu Yamada (*Throne of Blood*, dir. Akira Kurosawa)	Film
1967	Paul Scofield and Vivien Merchant (RSC, dir. Peter Hall)	Shakespeare Memorial Theatre
1971	Jon Finch and Francesca Annis (dir. Roman Polanski)	Film
1972	Anthony Hopkins and Diana Rigg (dir. Michael Blakemore)	National Theatre
1976	Ian McKellen and Judi Dench (RSC, dir. Trevor Nunn)	The Other Place
1978	Albert Finney and Dorothy Tutin (dir. Peter Hall)	National Theatre
1986	Jonathan Pryce and Sinead Cusack (RSC, dir. Adrian Noble)	Shakespeare Memorial Theatre
1992	Michael Pennington and Jenny Quayle (dir. Michael Bogdanov)	English Shakespeare Company, touring
1993	Derek Jacobi and Cheryl Campbell (dir. Adrian Noble)	Barbican
1999	Antony Sher and Harriet Walter (RSC, dir. Greg Doran)	Swan Theatre
2004	Greg Hicks and Sian Thomas (RSC, dir. Dominic Cooke)	Shakespeare Memorial Theatre
2004/5	Danny Sapani and Monica Dolan (dir. Max Stafford-Clark)	Touring production
2005	Simon Russell Beale and Emma Fielding (dir. John Caird)	Almeida Theatre
2005	Piotr Kazmierczak and Barbara Krasinska (Teatr Biuro Podrozy, dir. Pawel Szkotak)	Outdoor productions in Cork, 2005, Edinburgh, 2007, National Theatre, 2008

2007	Patrick O'Kane and Derbhle Crotty (RSC, dir. Conall Morrison)	Swan Theatre
2007/8	Patrick Stewart and Kate Fleetwood (dir. Rupert Goold)	Chichester Festival Theatre
2010	Will Keen and Anastasia Hille (Cheek by Jowl, dir. Declan Donnellan)	Barbican
2010	Elliot Cowan and Laura Rogers (dir. Lucy Bailey)	Shakespeare's Globe
2011	David Morrisey and Julia Ford (dir. Gemma Bodinetz)	Liverpool Everyman
2011	Jonathan Slinger and Aislin McGuckin (RSC, dir. Michael Boyd)	Shakespeare Memorial Theatre
2013	James McAvoy and Claire Foy (dir. Jamie Lloyd)	Trafalgar Studios

APPENDIX 5

Casting chart[1]

Actor(s)	1.1	1.2	1.3	1.4	1.5	1.6	1.7	2.1	2.2	2.3
Duncan		x		x		x				
Malcolm		x		x		x				x
Donalbain		x		x		x				x
Macbeth			x	x	x		x	x	x	x
Lady (Macbeth's wife)					x	x	x		x	x
Banquo			x	x		x		x		x
Fleance								x		
Macduff						x				x
(Macduff's) Wife										
(Macduff's) Son										
Lennox		x		x		x				x
Ross		x	x	x		x				
Angus		x	x	x		x				
Menteith										
Caithness										
Siward										
Young Siward										
1 Witch	x		x							
2 Witch	x		x							
3 Witch	x		x							
Hecate										
Three other Witches										
Apparitions										
Captain		x								
Seyton										
Porter										x
Old Man										
1 Murderer										
2 Murderer										
3 Murderer										
Other Murderers										
Doctor (in England)										
Doctor (in Scotland)										
Waiting Gentlewoman										

344

Actor(s)	2.4	3.1	3.2	3.3	3.4	3.5	3.6	4.1	4.2	4.3
Duncan										
Malcolm										x
Donalbain										
Macbeth		x	x		x			x		
Lady (Macbeth's wife)		x	x		x					
Banquo		x		x	x					
Fleance				x						
Macduff	x									x
(Macduff's) Wife									x	
(Macduff's) Son									x	
Lennox		x			x		x	x		
Ross	x	x			x				x	x
Angus										
Menteith										
Caithness										
Siward										
Young Siward										
1 Witch						x		x		
2 Witch						x		x		
3 Witch						x		x		
Hecate						x		x		
Three other Witches								x		
Apparitions								x		
Captain										
Seyton										
Porter										
Old Man	x									
1 Murderer		x		x	x					
2 Murderer		x		x						
3 Murderer				x						
Other Murderers									x	
Doctor (in England)										x
Doctor (in Scotland)										
Waiting Gentlewoman										

1   Messengers, Servants, Attendants, Lords, Thanes and Soldiers are not listed, but appear in a number of scenes, notably 1.2, 1.4, 1.5, 1.6, 1.7, 3.1, 3.2, 3.4, 3.6, 4.2, 5.2, 5.3, 5.4, 5.5, 5.6 and 5.9.

Actor(s)	5.1	5.2	5.3	5.4	5.5	5.6	5.7	5.8	5.9
Duncan									
Malcolm				X		X	X		X
Donalbain									
Macbeth			X		X		X	X	
Lady (Macbeth's wife)	X								
Banquo									
Fleance									
Macduff				X		X	X	X	X
(Macduff's) Wife									
(Macduff's) Son									
Lennox		X							
Ross									X
Angus		X		X					
Menteith		X		X					
Caithness		X		X					
Siward				X		X	X		X
Young Siward				X			X		
1 Witch									
2 Witch									
3 Witch									
Hecate									
Three other Witches									
Apparitions									
Captain									
Seyton			X		X				
Porter									
Old Man									
1 Murderer									
2 Murderer									
3 Murderer									
Other Murderers									
Doctor (in England)									
Doctor (in Scotland)	X		X						
Waiting Gentlewoman	X								

ABBREVIATIONS AND REFERENCES

Quotations from and references to Shakespeare's works other than *Macbeth* are from individual volumes of *The Arden Shakespeare*, Third Series, where available, otherwise from *The Arden Shakespeare*, Second Series. Biblical references are to the Bishops' Bible (1568). Unless otherwise stated, the place of publication is London.

ABBREVIATIONS

ABBREVIATIONS USED IN NOTES

*	precedes commentary notes involving readings altered from the Folio text
conj.	conjectured by
ESC	English Shakespeare Company
F	First Folio
om.	omitted
opp.	opposite
Q	Quarto
rev.	revised
rpt.	reprinted
RSC	Royal Shakespeare Company
SD	stage direction
SP	speech prefix
subst.	substantially
this edn	reading, SD or SP first adopted in this edition
TLN	through line numbering
trans.	translated by

WORKS BY AND PARTLY BY SHAKESPEARE

AC	*Antony and Cleopatra*
AW	*All's Well That Ends Well*
AYL	*As You Like It*
CE	*The Comedy of Errors*
Cor	*Coriolanus*
Cym	*Cymbeline*
DF	*Double Falsehood*
E3	*King Edward III*

Ham	*Hamlet*
1H4	*King Henry IV, Part 1*
2H4	*King Henry IV, Part 2*
H5	*King Henry V*
1H6	*King Henry VI, Part 1*
2H6	*King Henry VI, Part 2*
3H6	*King Henry VI, Part 3*
H8	*King Henry VIII*
JC	*Julius Caesar*
KJ	*King John*
KL	*King Lear*
LC	*A Lover's Complaint*
LLL	*Love's Labour's Lost*
Luc	*The Rape of Lucrece*
MA	*Much Ado About Nothing*
Mac	*Macbeth*
MM	*Measure for Measure*
MND	*A Midsummer Night's Dream*
MV	*The Merchant of Venice*
MW	*The Merry Wives of Windsor*
Oth	*Othello*
Per	*Pericles*
PP	*The Passionate Pilgrim*
PT	*The Phoenix and Turtle*
R2	*King Richard II*
R3	*King Richard III*
RJ	*Romeo and Juliet*
Son	*Sonnets*
STM	*Sir Thomas More*
TC	*Troilus and Cressida*
Tem	*The Tempest*
TGV	*The Two Gentlemen of Verona*
Tim	*Timon of Athens*
Tit	*Titus Andronicus*
TN	*Twelfth Night*
TNK	*The Two Noble Kinsmen*
TS	*The Taming of the Shrew*
VA	*Venus and Adonis*
WT	*The Winter's Tale*

REFERENCES

EDITIONS OF *MACBETH* CONSULTED

Andrews   *Macbeth*, ed. John F. Andrews, Everyman Shakespeare (New York, 1990, rev. edn 1993)

Ard²   *Macbeth*, ed. Kenneth Muir (1951, rpt. with corrections 1972, with a new introduction 1984). References are to the 1984 edition, unless otherwise indicated.

Barnet   *Macbeth*, ed. Sylvan Barnet, Signet (New York, 1998)

Bate & Rasmussen *The RSC Shakespeare*, ed. Jonathan Bate and Eric Rasmussen (2008)

Booth   *Shakespeare's Tragedy of Macbeth, the prompt-book*, prepared by Edwin Booth, ed. William Winter (New York, 1878)

Braunmuller   See Cam¹

Brooke   See Oxf¹

Cam   *Macbeth* in *The Works of William Shakespeare*, ed. W.G. Clark and W.A. Wright, 2nd edn, 9 vols (Cambridge, 1891–3), vol. 7 (1892)

Cam¹   *Macbeth*, ed. A.R. Braunmuller, New Cambridge Shakespeare (Cambridge, 1997, rev. edn 2008). References are to the 2008 edition.

Capell   *Mr William Shakespeare: His Comedies, Histories, and Tragedies*, ed. Edward Capell, 10 vols (1767–8), vol. 4

Clarendon   *Shakespeare Select Plays*: *Macbeth*, ed. W.G. Clark and W.A. Wright (Oxford, 1869)

Collier   *The Works of William Shakespeare*, ed. J. Payne Collier, 8 vols (1843), vol. 7

Davenant   See *Other works cited or used* below

Dover Wilson   *Macbeth*, ed. J. Dover Wilson, The New Cambridge Shakespeare (Cambridge, 1947, rpt. 1951)

Dyce   *The Works of William Shakespeare*, ed. Alexander Dyce, 6 vols (1857), vol. 5

F, F1   *Mr William Shakespeares Comedies, Histories, and Tragedies*, The First Folio (1623)

F2   *Mr William Shakespeares Comedies, Histories, and Tragedies*, The Second Folio (1632)

F3   *Mr William Shakespeares Comedies, Histories, and Tragedies*, The Third Folio (1663–4)

F4   *Mr William Shakespeares Comedies, Histories, and Tragedies*, The Fourth Folio (1685)

Furness   See *Var*

Globe	*The Works of William Shakespeare*, ed. W.G. Clark and W. Aldis Wright, Globe Edition (1865)
Grierson & Smith	*Select Plays of Shakespeare*, ed. H.J.C. Grierson and J.C. Smith (Oxford, 1914)
Halliwell	*The Works of William Shakespeare*, ed. J.O. Halliwell, 6 vols (1865), vol. 14
Hanmer	*The Works of William Shakespeare*, ed. Thomas Hanmer, 6 vols (1743–4), vol. 5
Hudson	*The Windsor Shakespeare*, ed. Henry N. Hudson, 20 vols (n.d., *c*. 1910), vol. 17
Hunter	*Macbeth*, ed. G.K. Hunter, introduced by Carol Chillington Rutter, Penguin Shakespeare (2005)
Johnson	*The Plays of William Shakespeare*, ed. Samuel Johnson, 8 vols (1765), vol. 6
Keightley	*The Plays of William Shakespeare*, ed. Thomas Keightley, 6 vols (1864), vol. 6
Kittredge	*The Tragedy of Macbeth*, ed. George Lyman Kittredge, revised by Irving Ribner (1967)
Knight	*The Pictorial Edition of the Works of Shakespeare*, ed. Charles Knight, 6 vols (1841), vol. 2, *Tragedies*
Malone	*The Plays and Poems of William Shakespeare*, ed. Edmond Malone, 10 vols (1790), vol. 5
Miola	*Macbeth*, ed. Robert Miola, Norton Critical Edition (New York, 2004, 2nd edn New York, 2014)
Muir	See Ard[2]
Oxf	*William Shakespeare: The Complete Works*, ed. Stanley Wells and Gary Taylor (Oxford, 1986)
Oxf[1]	*Macbeth*, ed. Nicholas Brooke, Oxford World's Classics (Oxford, 1994)
Pope	*The Works of Shakespear*, ed. Alexander Pope, 6 vols (1723), vol. 5
Riv	*The Riverside Shakespeare*, ed. G. Blakemore Evans (Boston, 1974)
Rowe	*The Works of Mr William Shakespear*, ed. Nicholas Rowe, 6 vols (1709), vol. 5
Rowe, Katherine	*Macbeth*, ed. Katherine Rowe (Boston, Mass., 2012)
Singer	*The Dramatic Works of William Shakespeare*, ed. S.W. Singer, 10 vols (4th edn, 1826), vol. 4
Staunton	*Routledge's Shakespeare*, ed. Howard Staunton, 50 parts in 3 vols (1858–60), parts 42–3 (September–October 1859)
Steevens	*The Plays of William Shakespeare*, ed. Samuel Johnson and George Steevens, 10 vols (1778), vol. 4

Theobald	*The Works of Shakespeare*, ed. Lewis Theobald, 8 vols (1740), vol. 6
Var	*Macbeth. A New Variorum Edition*, ed. Horace Howard Furness, Jr (New York, 1963)
Warburton	*The Works of William Shakespeare*, ed. William Warburton, 8 vols (1747), vol. 6
White	*The Complete Works of Shakespeare*, ed. Richard Grant White, 3 vols (Boston, 1883), vol. 3
Wilders	*Macbeth*, ed. John Wilders, Shakespeare in Production (Cambridge, 2004)

OTHER WORKS CITED OR USED

Abbott	E.A. Abbott, *A Shakespearian Grammar*, 2nd edn (1870)
Adamson *et al.*	Sylvia Adamson, Gavin Alexander and Katrin Ettenhuber (eds), *Renaissance Figures of Speech* (Cambridge, 2007)
Adelman	Janet Adelman, *Suffocating Mothers: Fantasies of Maternal Origin in Shakespeare's Plays* (London and New York, 1992)
Aitchison	Nick Aitchison, *Macbeth: Man and Myth* (Frome, 1999)
Alker & Nelson	Sharon Alker and Faith Nelson, '*Macbeth*, the Jacobean Scot, and the politics of the union', *SEL*, 47.2 (2007), 379–401
Allen	M.J.B. Allen, 'Toys, prologues and the Great Amiss: Shakespeare's tragic openings', in *Shakespearian Tragedy*, Stratford-upon-Avon Studies 20 (1984), 3–30
Amnaéus	Daniel A. Amnaéus, 'A missing scene in *Macbeth*', *Journal of English and Germanic Philology*, 60.3 (1961), 435–40
AN&Q	*American Notes & Queries*
Astington	John Astington, 'Descent machinery in the playhouses', *Medieval and Renaissance Drama in England*, 2 (1985), 119–33
Atkins	Brian Atkins, 'Heavy Seneca: his influence on Shakespeare's tragedies', *Classics Ireland*, 2 (1995), 1–16
Badawi	M.M. Badawi, 'Euphemism and circumlocution in *Macbeth*', *Cairo Studies in English* (1960), 25–46
Baldo	Jonathan Baldo, '"A rooted sorrow": Scotland's unusable past', in Moschovakis, 88–103
Barlow	Frank Barlow, 'The King's Evil', *English Historical Review*, 95 (1980), 3–27

Barnes	Jennifer Barnes, ' "Posterity is dispossessed": Laurence Olivier's *Macbeth* manuscripts in 1958 and 2012', *Shakespeare Bulletin*, 30.3 (2012), 263–97
Barroll	J. Leeds Barroll, *Politics, Plague, and Shakespeare's Theater* (Ithaca, NY, and London, 1991)
Bartholomeusz	Dennis Bartholomeusz, *Shakespeare and the Players* (Cambridge, 1969)
Bate	Jonathan Bate, *Shakespeare and the Romantic Imagination* (rpt. Oxford, 1992)
Bate & Jackson	Jonathan Bate and Russell Jackson (eds), *Shakespeare: An Illustrated Stage History* (Oxford, 1996)
Belsey	Catherine Belsey, 'Shakespeare's "vaulting ambition" ', *English Language Notes*, 10 (1972)
Benecke	Ingrid Benecke, 'Simon Forman's notes on *Macbeth* – the alternative reading', *N&Q*, 57.3 (2010), 389–93
Bentley	G.E. Bentley, *The Profession of Dramatist in Shakespeare's Time, 1590–1642* (Princeton, NJ, 1971, rpt. 1986, together with *The Profession of Player*)
Berger, 'Early'	Harry Berger, Jr, 'The early scenes of *Macbeth*: preface to a new interpretation', *ELH*, 47.1 (1980), 1–31
Berger, 'Text'	Harry Berger, Jr, 'Text against performance: the example of *Macbeth*', *Genre*, 15 (1982), 49–79
Berry	Francis Berry, *Poets' Grammar: Person, Time and Mood in Poetry* (1958)
Billings	Timothy Billings, 'Squashing the "shard-borne beetle" crux: a hard case with a few pat readings', *SQ*, 56.4 (2005), 434–47
Bishop	T.G. Bishop, 'Reconsidering a F reading in *Macbeth* 5.1', *SQ*, 46.1 (1995), 76–80
Blake, *Grammar*	N.F. Blake, *A Grammar of Shakespeare's Language* (Basingstoke and New York, 2002)
Blake, 'Study'	N.F. Blake, 'The study of Shakespeare's language: its implications for editors, critics and translators', *Sederi*, X (1999), 11–29
Bloch	Marc Bloch, *The Royal Touch: Sacred Monarchy and Scrofula in England and France*, trans. J.E. Anderson (1973)
Bloom	Harold Bloom, *Shakespeare: The Invention of the Human* (1999)
Blumenfeld-Kosinski	Renate Blumenfeld-Kosinski, *Not of Woman Born: Representations of Caesarean Birth in Medieval and Renaissance Culture* (Ithaca, NY, and London, 1990)

Boas   F.S. Boas, '*Macbeth* and *Lingua*', *Modern Language Review*, 4 (1909), 517–20
Boece   Hector Boece, *Scotorum Historiae* (Paris, 1526)
Boling   Ronald J. Boling, 'Tanistry, primogeniture, and the anglicizing of Scotland in *Macbeth*', *Publications of the Arkansas Philological Society*, 25.1 (1999), 1–14
Booth, *'King Lear'*   Stephen Booth, *'King Lear', 'Macbeth', Indefinition, and Tragedy* (New Haven, Conn., and London, 1983)
Booth,   Stephen Booth, 'Shakespeare's language and the
  'Shakespeare's'   language of Shakespeare's time', *SS 50* (1997), 1–18
Bradbrook   M.C. Bradbrook, 'The sources of *Macbeth*', *SS 4* (1951), rpt. in Muir & Edwards, 12–25
Bradley   A.C. Bradley, *Shakespearean Tragedy: Lectures on Hamlet, Othello, King Lear, Macbeth* (1904, rpt. 1963)
Bradshaw   Graham Bradshaw, *Shakespeare's Scepticism* (Brighton, 1987)
Brennan   Anthony Brennan, *Onstage and Offstage Worlds in Shakespeare's Plays* (1989)
Brome & Heywood   Richard Brome and Thomas Heywood, *The Late Lancashire Witches* (1633), ed. Laird H. Barber (New York, 1979)
Brooks   Cleanth Brooks, 'The naked babe and the cloak of manliness', in *The Well-Wrought Urn: Studies in the Structure of Poetry* (1947), 22–49
Brown   John Russell Brown (ed.), *Focus on 'Macbeth'* (1982)
Bruckner   Lynne Dickson Bruckner, '"Let grief convert to anger": authority and affect in *Macbeth*', in Moschovakis, 192–207
Bruster   Douglas Bruster, *Drama and the Marketplace in the Age of Shakespeare* (Cambridge, 1992)
Buchanan   George Buchanan, *Rerum Scoticarum Historia* (Edinburgh, 1582)
Bullough   Geoffrey Bullough, *Narrative and Dramatic Sources of Shakespeare*, 8 vols (1957–75), vol. 7
Bushnell   Rebecca Bushnell, *Tragedies of Tyrants* (1990)
Cain   William E. Cain, 'A new play by Shakespeare: making sense of *Macbeth*', *Shakespeare Newsletter*, 60.1 (2010), 17–22
Calderwood   James L. Calderwood, *If It Were Done: 'Macbeth' and Tragic Action* (Amherst, Mass., 1986)
Callaghan   Dympna Callaghan, 'Wicked women in *Macbeth*: a study of power, ideology and the production of motherhood', in Mario A. Di Cesare (ed.), *Reconsidering the Renaissance* (Binghampton, NY, 1992), 355–69

Camden	William Camden, *Remains Concerning Britain* (1605), ed. R.D. Dunn (1984)
Campbell	Lily B. Campbell, 'Political ideas in *Macbeth* IV.iii', *SQ*, 2 (1951), 281–6
Capp	Bernard Capp, *Astrology and the Popular Press. English Almanacs 1500–1800* (1979)
Carlisle, 'Faucit'	Carol Jones Carlisle, 'Helen Faucit's Lady Macbeth', *SSt*, 16 (1983), 205–33
Carlisle, *Greenroom*	Carol Jones Carlisle, *Shakespeare from the Greenroom* (Chapel Hill, NC, 1969)
Cavell	Stanley Cavell, *Disowning Knowledge in Seven Plays of Shakespeare* (new edn, Cambridge, 2003)
Cercignani	Fausto Cercignani, *Shakespeare's Works and Elizabethan Pronunciation* (1981)
Chambers	E.K. Chambers, *Shakespearean Gleanings* (1944)
Chambers, *ES*	E.K. Chambers, *The Elizabethan Stage*, 4 vols (Oxford, 1923)
Chambers, *Shakespeare*	E.K. Chambers, *William Shakespeare: A Study of Facts and Problems*, 2 vols (Oxford, 1930)
Charney & Charney	Maurice Charney and Hanna Charney, 'The language of madwomen in Shakespeare and his fellow dramatists', *Signs: Journal of Women in Culture and Society*, 3.2 (1977), 451–60
Clare	Janet Clare, *'Art made tongue-tied by authority': Elizabethan and Jacobean Dramatic Censorship* (Manchester, 1990)
Clark, *Murder*	Arthur Melville Clark, *Murder under Trust, or The Topical Macbeth and other Jacobean Matters* (Edinburgh, 1981)
Clark, *Pamphleteers*	Sandra Clark, *The Elizabethan Pamphleteers* (1983)
Clark, 'Passions'	Sandra Clark, '*Macbeth* and the language of the passions', *Shakespeare*, 8.3 (2012), 300–11
Clark, *Thinking*	Stuart Clark, *Thinking with Demons* (Oxford, 1997)
Clark, *Vanities*	Stuart Clark, *Vanities of the Eye: Vision in Early Modern Europe* (Oxford, 2007)
Coghill	Nevill Coghill, '*Macbeth* at the Globe, 1606–1616 (?): three questions', in J.G. Price (ed.), *The Triple Bond: Plays, Mainly Shakespearean in Performance* (Penn State, Pa., 1975), 223–39
Coleman	John Coleman, 'Facts and fancies about *Macbeth*', *The Gentleman's Magazine* (March 1889), 218–32
Coleridge	Samuel Taylor Coleridge, *Notes on Shakespeare's Tragedies*, in *Samuel Taylor Coleridge: Shakespearean*

	Criticism, ed. T.M. Raysor, 2 vols (2nd edn, 1960), vol. 1
Colombo & Guardamagna	Rosy Colombo and Daniela Guardamagna (eds), *Memoria di Shakespeare*, 8, special issue on authorship (Rome, 2012)
Cordner	Michael Cordner, ' "Wrought with things forgotten": memory and performance in editing *Macbeth*', in Peter Holland (ed.), *Shakespeare, Memory and Performance* (Cambridge, 2006), 87–116
Cotgrave	Randle Cotgrave, *A Dictionary of the French and English Tongues* (1611)
Coursen	Herbert R. Coursen, 'In deepest consequence: *Macbeth*', *SQ*, 18.4 (1967), 375–88
Craig, 'Accidents'	Hardin Craig, 'The shackling of accidents: a study of Elizabethan tragedy', *PQ*, 19 (1940), 1–19
Craig, *Of Philosophers*	Leon Harold Craig, *Of Philosophers and Kings: Political Philosophy in Shakespeare's 'Macbeth' and 'King Lear'* (Toronto, 2001)
Crystal	David Crystal, *Think on My Words: Exploring Shakespeare's Language* (2008)
Crystal & Crystal	David Crystal and Ben Crystal, *Shakespeare's Words: A Glossary and Language Companion* (2003)
Cummings	Brian Cummings, 'Metalepsis: the boundaries of metaphor', in Adamson *et al.*, 217–36
Cunliffe	J.W. Cunliffe, *The Influence of Seneca on Elizabethan Tragedy* (1925)
Curry	Walter Clyde Curry, *Shakespeare's Philosophical Patterns* (Baton Rouge, La., 1937)
Daemonologie	James VI and I, *Daemonologie* (1597), ed. G.B. Harrison, Bodley Head Quartos (1924)
Dahl *et al.*	Marcus Dahl, Marina Tarlinskaya and Brian Vickers, 'An enquiry into Middleton's supposed "adaptation" of *Macbeth*' (2010), at www.ies.sas.ac.uk/networks/london-forum-authorship-studies#Macbethmiddleton)
Daly	Peter M. Daly, 'Of Macbeth, martlets, and other "fowles of heaven" ', *Mosaic*, 12.1 (1978), 23–46
Daniel	Samuel Daniel, *The Queenes Arcadia* (1606)
Davenant	William Davenant, *Macbeth, A Tragaedy* (1674)
David	Richard David, 'The tragic curve', *SS 9* (1965), 122–31
Davies	Anthony Davies, *Filming Shakespeare's Plays* (1988)
Dawson	Anthony B. Dawson, 'Notes and queries concerning the text of *Macbeth*', in Ann Thompson (ed.), *'Macbeth': The State of Play* (2014), 11–30

Dean	Paul Dean, 'Murderous repetition: *Macbeth* as echo chamber', *English Studies*, 80 (1999), 216–23
Dekker	Thomas Dekker, *The Gull's Horn-book* (1609)
Dent	R.W. Dent, *Shakespeare's Proverbial Language: An Index* (Berkeley, Calif., and London, 1981)
Dent, *Proverbial*	R.W. Dent, *Proverbial Language in English Drama Exclusive of Shakespeare, 1595–1616* (Berkeley, Calif., and London, 1984)
De Quincey	Thomas De Quincey, 'On the knocking on the gate in *Macbeth*' (1823), in David Masson (ed.), *The Collected Works of Thomas De Quincey*, 14 vols (1889–90), vol. 10, 389–95
Dessen, *Elizabethan*	Alan C. Dessen, *Elizabethan Stage Conventions and Modern Interpreters* (Cambridge, 1986)
Dessen, *Recovering*	Alan C. Dessen, *Recovering Shakespeare's Theatrical Vocabulary* (Cambridge, 1995)
Dessen, *Rescripting*	Alan C. Dessen, *Rescripting Shakespeare: The Text, the Director, and Modern Productions* (Cambridge, 2002)
Dessen & Thomson	Alan C. Dessen and Leslie Thomson, *A Dictionary of Stage Directions in English Drama, 1580–1624* (Cambridge, 1999)
Diehl	Huston Diehl, 'Horrid image, sorry sight, fatal vision: the visual rhetoric of *Macbeth*', *SSt*, 16 (1983), 191–203
Dobson	Michael Dobson (ed.), *Performing Shakespeare's Tragedies Today: the Actor's Perspective* (Cambridge, 2006)
Dolan	Frances Dolan, *Dangerous Familiars: Representations of Domestic Crime in England 1550–1700* (Ithaca, NY, 1994)
Donaldson	Peter S. Donaldson, *Shakespearean Films/Shakespearean Directors* (1990)
Downer	Alan Downer, *William Charles Macready* (1966)
Doran	Madeleine Doran, 'The *Macbeth* music', *SSt*, 16 (1983), 153–73
Drakakis & Townshend	John Drakakis and Dale Townshend (eds), *Macbeth: A Critical Reader* (2013)
Dyson	J.P. Dyson, 'The structural function of the banquet scene in *Macbeth*', *SQ*, 14 (1963), 369–78
Edelman	Charles Edelman, *Shakespeare's Military Language: A Dictionary* (2000)
EEBO	*Early English Books Online* (eebo.chadwick.com)
Egan, 'Editions'	Gabriel Egan, 'Shakespeare, editions and textual matters', *YWES*, 91 (2012), 390–2

Egan, *Shakespeare* Gabriel Egan, *The Struggle for Shakespeare's Text* (Cambridge, 2010)

ELH *English Literary History*

Elliott G.R. Elliott, *Dramatic Providence in 'Macbeth': A Study of Shakespeare's Tragic Theme of Humanity and Grace* (1958)

Empson William Empson, *Seven Types of Ambiguity* (1930, 3rd edn 1965)

Esche Edward J. Esche (ed.), *A Critical Edition of Thomas Middleton's 'The Witch'* (New York and London, 1993)

Evans Gareth Lloyd Evans, '*Macbeth* in the twentieth century', *Theatre Quarterly*, 1.3 (1971), 36–9

Everett Barbara Everett, *Young Hamlet: Essays on Shakespeare's Tragedies* (Oxford, 1989)

Ewbank, 'Fiend-like' Inga-Stina Ewbank, 'The fiend-like Queen: a note on *Macbeth* and Seneca's *Medea*', *SS 19* (1966), 83–5, rpt. in Muir & Edwards, 53–65

Ewbank, 'Middle' Inga-Stina Ewbank, 'The middle of Middleton', in Murray Biggs *et al.* (eds), *The Arts of Performance in Elizabethan and Early Stuart Drama: Essays for G.K. Hunter* (Edinburgh, 1991), 156–72

Findlay Alison Findlay, *Women in Shakespeare: A Dictionary* (2010)

Finkenstaedt Thomas Finkenstaedt, *A Chronological English Dictionary* (Heidelberg, 1970)

Fitzpatrick Joan Fitzpatrick, *Food in Shakespeare* (Aldershot and Burlington, Vt, 2007)

Flatter Richard Flatter, *Shakespeare's Producing Hand* (1948)

Fletcher George Fletcher, *Studies of Shakespeare* (1847)

Flint Lorna Flint, 'The significance of rime in Shakespeare's plays: the example of *Macbeth*', *Cahiers Élisabéthains*, 43 (1993), 13–20

Floyd-Wilson Mary Floyd-Wilson, 'English epicures and Scottish witches', *SQ*, 57 (2006), 131–61

Foakes & Rickert R.A. Foakes and R.T. Rickert (eds), *Henslowe's Diary* (Cambridge, 1961)

Ford John Ford, *The Broken Heart*, ed. Donald K. Anderson, Jr (Lincoln, Nebr., 1968)

Fox Alice Fox, 'Obstetrics and gynaecology in *Macbeth*', *SSt*, 12 (1979), 127–41

France Richard France (ed.), *Orson Welles on Shakespeare: The W.P.A. and Mercury Theatre Playscripts* (New York, 1990)

357

Freud	Sigmund Freud, *Art and Literature*, Pelican Freud Library, vol. 1 (Harmondsworth, 1985)
Gardner	Helen Gardner, *The Business of Criticism* (Oxford, 1959)
Garrett	John Garrett (ed.), *Talking of Shakespeare* (1954)
Gaskill	Malcolm Gaskill, *Crime and Mentalities in Early Modern England* (Cambridge, 2000)
Gibson & Esra	Marion Gibson and Jo Esra, *Shakespeare's Demonology: A Dictionary* (2014)
Gillespie	Stewart Gillespie, *Shakespeare's Books: A Dictionary of Shakespeare Sources* (2001)
Goldberg	Jonathan Goldberg, 'Speculations: *Macbeth* and source', in Jean E. Howard and Marion F. O'Connor (eds), *Shakespeare Reproduced: The Text in History and Ideology* (New York, 1987), 242–64
Goldman	Michael Goldman, *Acting and Action in Shakespearean Tragedy* (Princeton, NJ, 1985)
Goodwin	James Goodwin, *Akira Kurosawa and Intertextual Cinema* (1994)
Granville Barker	Harley Granville Barker, *Preface to 'Macbeth'*, in *Prefaces to Shakespeare*, 6 vols (1974), vol. 6
Greenblatt	Stephen Greenblatt, 'Shakespeare bewitched', in Jeffery N. Cox and Larry J. Reynolds (eds), *New Historical Literary Study: Essays on Reproducing Texts, Representing History* (Princeton, NJ, 1993), 108–35
Greg	W.W. Greg, *The Shakespeare First Folio* (Oxford, 1955)
Greg & Wilson	W.W. Greg and F.P. Wilson (eds), *The Witch*, Malone Society Reprints (Oxford, 1950)
Guj	Louisa Guj, '*Macbeth* and the seeds of time', *SSt*, 18 (1986), 175–88
Gunter	J. Lawrence Gunter, '*Hamlet*, *Macbeth* and *King Lear* on film', in Russell Jackson (ed.), *Shakespeare on Film* (Cambridge, 200), 117–34
Gurr	Andrew Gurr, *The Shakespearean Stage, 1574–1642* (2nd edn, Cambridge, 1980)
GWW	George Walton Williams (private communication)
Hadfield	Andrew Hadfield, '*Hamlet*'s country matters: the 'Scottish play' within the play', in Maley & Murphy, 87–103
Hales	John W. Hales, *Essays and Notes on Shakespeare* (1884)
Hall	James Hall, *Dictionary of Subjects and Symbols in Art* (1974)

Hamilton	Thomas Middleton, *The Puritan Widow*, ed. Donna B. Hamilton, in Taylor & Lavagnino, *Middleton*
Hankins	John Erskine Hankins, *Backgrounds of Shakespeare's Thought* (1978)
Harcourt	John B. Harcourt, ' "I pray you, remember the porter" ', *SQ*, 12 (1961), 393–402
Harris	Jonathan Gil Harris, *Untimely Matter in the Time of Shakespeare* (Philadelphia, Pa., 2009)
Harting	James Harting, *The Ornithology of Shakespeare* (1864)
Hassel	R. Chris Hassel, Jr, *Shakespeare's Religious Language: A Dictionary* (2005)
Hattaway	Michael Hattaway, *Elizabethan Popular Theatre* (1982)
Hawkins	Michael Hawkins, 'History, politics and *Macbeth*', in Brown, 155–88
Hayes	Michael L. Hayes, *Shakespearean Tragedy as Chivalric Romance: Rethinking 'Macbeth', 'Hamlet', 'Othello', and 'King Lear'* (Woodbridge, 2003)
Hazlitt	William Hazlitt, *Characters of Shakespear's Plays* (1817, rpt. 1906)
Heal	Felicity Heal, *Hospitality in Early Modern England* (Oxford, 1990)
Heilman	Robert Heilman, 'The criminal as tragic hero: dramatic methods', in Muir & Edwards, 26–38
Highley	Christopher Highley, 'The place of Scots in the Scottish play: *Macbeth* and the politics of language', in Maley & Murphy, 53–66
Hinman	The Norton Facsimile, *The First Folio of Shakespeare*, prepared by Charlton Hinman (New York, 1968)
Holderness	Graham Holderness, ' "Come in, equivocator": tragic ambivalence in *Macbeth*', in Linda Cookson and Bryan Loughrey (eds), *Critical Essays on Macbeth* (Harlow, 1988), 61–71
Holdsworth, 'Directions'	Roger Holdsworth, 'Stage directions and authorship: Shakespeare, Middleton, Heywood', in Colombo & Guardamagna, 185–200
Holdsworth, *Littlewood*	Nadine Holdsworth, *Joan Littlewood's Theatre* (Cambridge, 2011)
Holdsworth, *Macbeth*	R.V. Holdsworth, '*Macbeth* and *The Puritan*', *N&Q*, 235 (1990), 204–5
Holinshed	Raphael Holinshed, *The Chronicles of England, Scotlande, and Ireland*, 2 vols (1577, 1587). *The Chronicle of Scotland* is in vol. 2. Quotations are taken from the 1587 edition.

Holland, 'Stands Scotland'	Peter Holland, ' "Stands Scotland where it did?" The location of *Macbeth* on film', in Miola, 357–80
Holloway	John Holloway, *The Story of the Night: Studies in Shakespeare's Major Tragedies* (1961)
Hope	Jonathan Hope, *Shakespeare's Grammar* (2003)
Hopkins	Lisa Hopkins, *Shakespeare on the Edge: Border-Crossings in the Tragedies and the Henriad* (2005)
Houston, *Rhetoric*	John Porter Houston, *The Rhetoric of Poetry in the Renaissance and Seventeenth Century* (Baton Rouge, La., 1983)
Houston, *Shakespearean*	John Porter Houston, *Shakespearean Sentences: A Study in Style and Syntax* (Baton Rouge, La., 1988)
Huggett	Richard Huggett, *The Curse of 'Macbeth' and Other Theatrical Superstitions: An Investigation* (Chippenham, 1981)
Hulme	Hilda Hulme, *Explorations in Shakespeare's Language* (1962)
Hutchings & Bromham	Mark Hutchings and A.A. Bromham, *Middleton and his Collaborators*, Writers and their Work (Horndon, Devon, 2008)
Ide	Richard S. Ide, 'The theatre of the mind: an essay on *Macbeth*', *ELH*, 42.3 (1975), 338–61
Innes	Paul Innes, *Class and Society in Shakespeare: A Dictionary* (2007)
Ioppolo	Grace Ioppolo, *Revising Shakespeare* (1991)
Iyengar	Sujata Iyengar, *Shakespeare's Medical Language: A Dictionary* (2011)
Jackson, *Companion*	Russell Jackson (ed.), *The Cambridge Companion to Shakespeare on Film* (Cambridge, 2000)
Jackson, 'Reviewing'	MacDonald P. Jackson, 'Reviewing authorship studies of Shakespeare and his contemporaries', in Colombo & Guardamagna, 149–67
Jacobs	Gerald Jacobs, *Judi Dench: A Great Deal of Laughter* (1985)
Jacobson	Howard Jacobson, '*Macbeth* 1.vii.7–10', *SQ*, 35 (1984), 321–2
Jameson	Anna Jameson, *Shakespeare's Heroines: Characteristics of Women, Moral, Poetical, and Historical* (1832, rev. edn 1913)
Janowitz	Henry Janowitz, 'Sleep disorders in the Macbeths', *Journal of the Royal Society of Medicine*, 93 (2000)
Jenkins	*Hamlet*, ed. Harold Jenkins, Arden Shakespeare, Second Series (1982)

JH	Jonathan Hope (personal communication)
Johnson, *Miscellaneous*	Samuel Johnson, *Miscellaneous Observations on the Tragedy of Macbeth* (1745), in Woudhuysen
Johnson, *Rambler*	Samuel Johnson, *The Rambler*, in Woudhuysen
Jones, *Origins*	Emrys Jones, *The Origins of Shakespeare* (Oxford, 1977)
Jones, *Scenic*	Emrys Jones, *Scenic Form in Shakespeare* (rev. edn, Oxford, 1985)
Jorgensen	Paul A. Jorgensen, *Our Naked Frailties* (1971)
Jowett	John Jowett, 'Editions and textual studies', *SS 51* (1998), 302–38
Kastan, 'Name'	David Scott Kastan, '*Macbeth* and the "name of king"', in *Shakespeare After Theory* (New York and London, 1999), 165–82
Kastan, *Shapes*	David Scott Kastan, *Shakespeare and the Shapes of Time* (1982)
Kermode	Frank Kermode, *Shakespeare's Language* (2000)
Kernan	Alvin Kernan, *Shakespeare, the King's Playwright: Theater in the Stuart Court 1603–1613* (New Haven, Conn., and London, 1995)
Kerrigan	John Kerrigan, *Archipelagic English: Literature, History and Politics 1603–1707* (Oxford, 2008)
Kinney, 'Bells'	Arthur Kinney, 'Shakespeare's bells', in *Shakespeare and Cognition: Aristotle's Legacy and Shakespeare's Drama* (2006), 94–117
Kinney, *Lies*	Arthur Kinney, *Lies Like Truth: Shakespeare, 'Macbeth' and the Cultural Moment* (Detroit, Mich., 2001)
Kinney, 'Scottish'	Arthur Kinney, 'Scottish history, the union of the crowns and the issue of right rule', in Jean R. Brink and William F. Gentrup (eds), *Renaissance Culture in Context* (Aldershot, 1993), 18–53
Kinsevik	Matthew J. Kinsevik, 'A sinister *Macbeth*: the Macklin production of 1773', *Harvard Library Bulletin*, 6 (1995), 51–76
Kirsch	Arthur Kirsch, 'Macbeth's suicide', *ELH*, 51.2 (1984), 269–96
Kliman	Bernice W. Kliman, *Shakespeare in Performance: Macbeth* (2nd edn, Manchester, 2004)
Knights, *Explorations*	L.C. Knights, *Explorations: Essays in Criticism Mainly on the Literature of the Seventeenth Century* (1946)
Knights, 'How many'	L.C. Knights, 'How many children had Lady Macbeth?', in *Explorations*, 15–24
Knights, *Themes*	L.C. Knights, *Some Shakespearean Themes* (1959)

Knutson	Rosalyn Lander Knutson, *The Repertory of Shakespeare's Company 1594–1613* (Fayetteville, Ariz., 1991)
Kökeritz	Helge Kökeritz, *Shakespeare's Pronunciation* (New Haven, Conn., 1953)
Krantz	David L. Krantz, 'The sounds of supernatural soliciting in *Macbeth*', *SP*, 100.3 (2003), 346–83
Kurland	Stuart M. Kurland, '*Hamlet* and the Scottish succession?' *SEL*, 34 (1994), 279–300
LaBelle	Jenijoy LaBelle, ' "A strange infirmity": Lady Macbeth's amenorrhea', *SQ*, 31.2 (1980), 381–6
Lancashire	Anne Lancashire, '*The Witch*: stage flop or political mistake?', in Kenneth Friedenreich (ed.), *'Accompaninge the Players': Essays Celebrating Thomas Middleton* (New York, 1983)
Leggatt	Alexander Leggatt (ed.), *William Shakespeare's 'Macbeth': A Sourcebook* (2006)
Leiter	Samuel L. Leiter *et al.*, *Shakespeare Around the Globe: A Guide to Notable Postwar Revivals* (New York and London, 1986)
Le Loyer	Pierre Le Loyer, *A Treatise of Specters* (1605)
Lemon	Rebecca Lemon, *Treason by Words: Literature, Law and Rebellion in Shakespeare's England* (Ithaca, NY, 2006)
Lerner	Laurence Lerner (ed.), *Shakespeare's Tragedies: An Anthology of Modern Criticism* (Harmondsworth, 1968)
Leslie	John Leslie, *De Origine, Moribus, et Rebus Gestis Scotorum* (1578)
Levin, 'Lady'	Joanna Levin, 'Lady Macbeth and the daemonologie of hysteria', *ELH*, 69.1 (2002), 39–55
Levin, 'New'	Richard Levin, 'The new refutation of Shakespeare', *Modern Philology*, 83.2 (1985), 123–41
Long	John H. Long, *Shakespeare's Use of Music: The Histories and the Tragedies* (Gainesville, Fla., 1971)
Loomis	E.A. Loomis, 'Master of the Tiger', *SQ*, 7 (1956), 457
Lucas	F.L. Lucas, *Seneca and Elizabethan Tragedy* (Cambridge, 1922)
Lyle, 'Number'	E.B. Lyle, 'Number of performers in the *Macbeth* dance', *AN&Q*, 12.5 (1974), 68–9
Lyle, 'Twofold'	E.B. Lyle, 'The "twofold balls and treble sceptres" in *Macbeth*', *SQ*, 28.4 (1977), 516–19
McAlindon	T. McAlindon, *Shakespeare's Tragic Cosmos* (Cambridge, 1991)

McCloskey	Susan McCloskey, 'Shakespeare, Orson Welles, and the "voodoo" *Macbeth*', *SQ*, 36.4 (1985), 406–16
McDonald, *Late*	Russ McDonald, *Shakespeare's Late Style* (Cambridge, 2006)
McDonald, *Look*	Russ McDonald, *Look to the Lady: Sarah Siddons, Ellen Terry, and Judi Dench on the Shakespearean Stage* (Athens, Ga., 2005)
McEachern	Claire McEachern, 'The Englishness of the Scottish play: *Macbeth* and the poetics of Jacobean union', in Allan I. Macinnes and Jane Ohlmeyer (eds), *The Stuart Kingdoms in the Seventeenth Century: Awkward Neighbours* (Dublin, 2002), 94–112
Macfarlane	A.D.J. Macfarlane, *Witchcraft in Tudor and Stuart England* (1970)
McIlwain	C.H. McIlwain (ed.), *The Political Works of James I* (Cambridge, Mass., 1918)
McLuskie	Kathleen E. McLuskie, *William Shakespeare: 'Macbeth'*, Writers and their Work (Horndon, Devon, 2009)
Macready	William Macready, *The Diaries of William Charles Macready 1833–51*, ed. William Toynbee, 2 vols (1912)
Magnus	Laury Magnus, 'Performance history', in Drakakis & Townshend, 55–94
Mahood	M. Mahood, *Shakespeare's Wordplay* (1957)
Maley & Murphy	Willy Maley and Andrew Murphy (eds), *Shakespeare and Scotland* (Manchester, 2004)
Marlowe	Christopher Marlowe, *Complete Plays and Poems*, ed. E.D. Pendry and J.C. Maxwell (1976)
Marshall	Tristan Marshall, *Theatre and Empire: Great Britain on the London Stages under James VI and I* (Manchester, 2000)
Marston	John Westland Marston, *Our Recent Actors*, 2 vols (1888)
Mason	Pamela Mason, 'Sunshine in *Macbeth*', in Moschovakis, 335–49
Meads	Chris Meads, *Banquets Set Forth: Banqueting in the English Renaissance* (Manchester, 2001)
Melchiori	*Edward III*, ed. Georgio Melchiori, New Cambridge Shakespeare (Cambridge, 1988)
Merchant	W. Moelwyn Merchant, ' "His fiend-like queen" ', *SS 19* (1966), rpt. in Muir & Edwards, 46–52
Middleton	*Thomas Middleton, The Collected Works*, ed. Gary Taylor and John Lavagnino (Oxford, 2007)
Middleton & Dekker	Thomas Middleton and Thomas Dekker, *The Roaring Girl*, ed. Andor Gomme (1976)

Miola, *Classical*	Robert Miola, *Shakespeare and Classical Tragedy* (Oxford, 1992)
Montaigne	*The Essays of Michael Lord of Montaigne*, trans. John Florio (1603), Everyman's Library, 3 vols (1910)
Moore	Edward M. Moore, 'William Poel', *SQ*, 23.1 (1972), 21–36
More	Sir Thomas More, *The Complete Works of Sir Thomas More*, ed. Edward Surtz, SJ, and J.H. Hexter, 15 vols (New Haven, Conn., 1965), vol. 4
Moschovakis	Nick Moschovakis (ed.), *'Macbeth': New Critical Essays* (New York and London, 2008)
Moulton	R.G. Moulton, *Shakespeare as a Dramatic Artist* (Oxford, 1885)
Muir, *Sources*	Kenneth Muir, *The Sources of Shakespeare's Plays* (1977)
Muir & Edwards	Kenneth Muir and Philip Edwards (eds), *Aspects of 'Macbeth'* (Cambridge, 1977)
Mullaney, 'Lying'	Steven Mullaney, 'Lying like truth: riddle, representation and treason in Renaissance England', *ELH*, 47.1 (1980), 32–47
Mullaney, *Stage*	Steven Mullaney, *The Place of the Stage* (1988)
Mullin, 'Augures'	Michael Mullin, 'Augures and understood relations: Theodore Komisarjevsky's *Macbeth*', *Educational Theatre Journal*, 26.1 (1974), 20–30
Mullin, 'Film'	Michael Mullin, '*Macbeth* on film', *Literature Film Quarterly*, 1 (1973), 332–42
Mullin, '*Macbeth*'	Michael Mullin, '*Macbeth* in modern dress: Royal Court Theatre, 1928', *Educational Theatre Journal*, 30.2 (1978), 176–85
Mullin, *Promptbook*	Michael Mullin, ed., *Macbeth Onstage. An Annotated Facsimile of Glen Byam Shaw's 1955 Promptbook* (Columbia, Mo., and London, 1976)
Mullin, 'Stage'	Michael Mullin, 'Stage and screen: the Trevor Nunn *Macbeth*', *SQ*, 38.3 (1987), 350–9
Mullin, 'Strange'	Michael Mullin, 'Strange images of death: Sir Herbert Beerbohm Tree's *Macbeth*, 1911', *Theatre Survey*, 17.2 (1976), 125–42
N&Q	*Notes & Queries*
Nagler	A.M. Nagler, *A Source Book in Theatrical History* (New York, 1952)
Nashe	*The Works of Thomas Nashe*, ed. R.B. McKerrow, rev. F.P. Wilson, 5 vols (Oxford, 1958)
Newes	*Newes from Scotland* (1591), in *Daemonologie*

Newstok & Thompson	Scott L. Newstok and Ayanna Thompson (eds), *Weyward Macbeth: Intersections of Race and Performance* (Basingstoke and New York, 2012)
Nielsen	Elizabeth Nielsen, '*Macbeth*: The nemesis of the post-Shakespearian actor', *SQ*, 16.1 (1965), 193–99
Norbrook	David Norbrook, '*Macbeth* and the politics of historiography', in Kevin Sharpe and Steven N. Zwicker (eds), *The Politics of Discourse* (1987), 78–116
Norgaard	Holger Norgaard, 'The bleeding captain scene in *Macbeth* and Daniel's *Cleopatra*', *RES*, n.s., 6.24 (1955), 395–6
Nosworthy, 'Bleeding'	J.M. Nosworthy, 'The bleeding captain scene in *Macbeth*', *RES*, 22.86 (1946), 126–30
Nosworthy, *Shakespeare's*	J.M. Nosworthy, *Shakespeare's Occasional Plays* (1965)
Odell	George C.D. Odell, *Shakespeare from Betterton to Irving*, 2 vols (New York, 1920)
ODNB	*Oxford Dictionary of National Biography Online* (www.oxforddnb.com)
OED	*Oxford English Dictionary Online* (www.oed.com)
Olivier	Laurence Olivier and Kenneth Tynan, 'The actor: Tynan interviews Olivier', *Tulane Drama Review*, 11.2 (1966), 71–101
Orgel	Stephen Orgel, '*Macbeth* and the antic round', *SS 52* (1999), 143–54
Ovid, *Met.*	*The xv Books of P. Ovidius Naso, entitled Metamorphoses*, trans. Arthur Golding (1567), ed. Madeleine Forey (Harmondsworth, 2002)
Palfrey	Simon Palfrey, *Doing Shakespeare* (2005)
Palfrey & Stern	Simon Palfrey and Tiffany Stern, *Shakespeare in Parts* (Oxford, 2007)
Park	Clara Claiborne Park, ' "Canst thou not minister to a mind diseas'd?" ', *American Scholar*, 56 (1987), 219–34
Parker	Patricia Parker, 'Hysteron proteron: or the preposterous', in Adamson *et al.*, 133–48
Parsons & Mason	Keith Parsons and Pamela Mason (eds), *Shakespeare in Performance* (1995)
Paul	Henry N. Paul, *The Royal Play of 'Macbeth'* (New York, 1950)
Pearson	Jacqueline Pearson, 'Shakespeare and *Caesar's Revenge*', *SQ*, 32.1 (1981), 101–4
Pettigrew	Todd H.J. Pettigrew, *Shakespeare and the Practice of Physic: Medical Narratives on the Early Modern Stage* (Newark, NJ, 2007)

Peyré	Yves Peyré, '"Confusion now hath made his master-piece": Senecan resonances in *Macbeth*', in Charles Martindale and A.B. Taylor (eds), *Shakespeare and the Classics* (Cambridge, 2004), 141–55
Players	Philip Brockbank, Russell Jackson and Robert Smallwood (eds), *Players of Shakespeare: Essays in Shakespearean Performance*, 5 vols (Cambridge, 1988–2005)
Pliny	*The Natural History of C. Plinius Secundus*, trans. Philemon Holland (1601)
Poole	Kristen Poole, *Supernatural Environments in Shake-speare's England: Spaces of Demonism, Divinity and Drama* (Cambridge, 2011)
PQ	*Philological Quarterly*
Prescott	Paul Prescott, 'Doing all that becomes a man: the reception and afterlife of the Macbeth actor', *SS 57* (2004), 81–95
Proudfoot	Richard Proudfoot, '*The Reign of King Edward III* (1596) and Shakespeare', in *British Academy Shakespeare Lectures 1980–89* (1993), 137–63
Purkiss	Diane Purkiss, *The Witch in History* (1996)
Rawson	C.J. Rawson, 'Macbeth on sleep: two parallels', *SQ*, 14 (1963), 484–5
Rea	John D. Rea, 'Notes on Shakespeare', *Modern Language Notes*, 35 (1920), 377–8
Read	Sophie Read, 'Puns: serious wordplay', in Adamson *et al.*, 81–96
RES	*Review of English Studies*
Rhodes	Neil Rhodes, 'Wrapped in the strong arms of the union: Shakespeare and King James', in Maley & Murphy, 37–52
Ribner	Irving Ribner, *The English History Play in the Age of Shakespeare* (Princeton, NJ, 1957)
Richards	Jeffery Richards (ed.), *Sir Henry Irving: Theatre, Culture and Society. Essays, Addresses and Lectures* (Keele, 1994)
Richardson	Brian Richardson, '"Hours dreadful and things strange": inversions of chronology and causality in *Macbeth*', *PQ*, 68.3 (1989), 283–94
Riebling	Barbara Riebling, 'Virtue's sacrifice: a Machiavellian reading of *Macbeth*', *SEL*, 31.2 (1991), 273–86
Rogers, 'Garnet'	H.L. Rogers, 'An English tailor and Father Garnet's straw', *RES*, n.s.16, 61 (1965), 44–9

Rogers, 'Scottish' Rebecca Rogers, 'How Scottish was 'the Scottish play'?
                    Macbeth's national identity in the eighteenth century',
                    in Maley & Murphy, 104–23
Rose   Mark Rose, *Shakespearean Design* (Cambridge, Mass.,
                    1972)
Rosen   Barbara Rosen (ed.), *Witchcraft* (1969)
Rosenberg   Marvin Rosenberg, *The Masks of 'Macbeth'* (Newark,
                    NJ, 1978)
Rutter   Carol Rutter, ed., *Clamorous Voices: Shakespeare's
                    Women Today* (1988)
Sackville & Norton Thomas Sackville and Thomas Norton, *Gorboduc, or
                    Ferrex and Porrex*, ed. Irby B. Cauthen, Jr (1970)
St Clair   William St Clair, *The Reading Nation in the Romantic
                    Period* (Cambridge, 2004)
Sanders   Wilbur Sanders, *The Dramatist and the Received Idea*
                    (Cambridge, 1968)
Schafer   Thomas Middleton, *The Witch*, ed. Elizabeth Schafer
                    (1994)
Schiffer   James Schiffer, '*Macbeth* and the bearded women',
                    in Dorothea Kehler and Susan Baker (eds), *In Another
                    Country: Feminist Perspectives on Renaissance Drama*,
                    (Metuchen, NJ, and London, 1991), 205–21
Schoenbaum   S. Schoenbaum, *William Shakespeare: Records and
                    Images* (1981)
Scot, *Discovery*   Reginald Scot, *The Discovery of Witchcraft* (1584)
Scragg   Leah Scragg, 'Macbeth on horseback', *SS 26* (1973),
                    81–8
SEL   *Studies in English Literature 1500–1900*
Seneca, *Dialogues* Lucius Annaeus Seneca, *Dialogues and Letters*, ed. and
                    trans. C.D.N. Costa (1997)
Seneca, *Tenne*   *Seneca, His Tenne Tragedies*, trans. John Studley
  Tragedies   (1581), ed. Thomas Newton, 2 vols (1927)
Seneca, *Tragedies* Lucius Annaeus Seneca, *Tragedies*, trans. John G. Fitch,
                    Loeb Classical Library, 2 vols (Cambridge, Mass., and
                    London, 2002–4)
Shaheen   Naseeb Shaheen, *Biblical References in Shakespeare's
                    Tragedies* (1987)
Shapiro   James Shapiro, '*The Scot's Tragedy* and the politics of
                    popular drama', *English Literary Review*, 23 (1993),
                    428–49
Sher   Antony Sher, *Beside Myself: An Actor's Life* (2001)
Sidney   Sir Philip Sidney, *An Apology for Poetry*, ed. Geoffrey
                    Shepherd, rev. R.W. Maslen (Manchester, 2002)

Sisson	C.J. Sisson, *New Readings in Shakespeare*, 2 vols (Cambridge, 1956)
Smallwood	Robert Smallwood (ed.), *Players of Shakespeare 4* (Cambridge, 1998)
Smith	Irwin Smith, *Shakespeare's Blackfriars Playhouse*: *its History and Design* (New York, 1964)
Sokol & Sokol	B.J. Sokol and Mary Sokol, *Shakespeare's Legal Language: A Dictionary* (2000)
Sokolova	Boika Sokolova, '"Who's there?": *Macbeth* on the London stage 2004–2005', in Marta Gibinska and Agnieszka Romanowska (eds), *Shakespeare in Europe: History and Memory* (Krakow, 2008), 277–90
SP	*Studies in Philology*
Spencer	Christopher Spencer, '*Macbeth* and Davenant's *The Rivals*', *SQ*, 20 (1969), 225–9
Spenser, *A View*	Edmund Spenser, *A View of the Present State of Ireland*, ed. W.L. Renwick (Oxford, 1970)
Spenser, *FQ*	*The Faerie Queene*, in Edmund Spenser, *The Poetical Works of Edmund Spenser*, ed. J.C. Smith and E. de Selincourt (Oxford, 1912)
Sprague, *Actors*	A.C. Sprague, *Shakespeare and the Actors* (Cambridge, Mass., 1945)
Sprague, *Shakespearian*	A.C. Sprague, *Shakespearian Players and Performances* (1954)
Spurgeon	Caroline Spurgeon, *Shakespeare's Imagery and What it Tells Us* (Cambridge, 1935)
SQ	*Shakespeare Quarterly*
SS	*Shakespeare Survey*
SSt	*Shakespeare Studies*
Stachniewski	John Stachniewski, 'Calvinist psychology in *Macbeth*', *SSt*, 20 (1988), 169–89
Stallybrass	Peter Stallybrass, '*Macbeth* and witchcraft', in Brown, 189–209
Stern, *Documents*	Tiffany Stern, *Documents of Performance in Early Modern England* (Cambridge, 2009)
Stern, *Making*	Tiffany Stern, *Making Shakespeare: From Stage to Page* (2004)
Stewart, *Cradle*	Alan Stewart, *The Cradle King: A Life of James VI and I* (2003)
Stewart, *Shakespeare's*	Alan Stewart, *Shakespeare's Letters* (Oxford, 2008)
Suhamy	Henri Suhamy, 'The authenticity of the Hecate scenes in *Macbeth*: arguments and counter-arguments', in

	Jean-Marie Maguin and Michèle Willems (eds), *French Essays on Shakespeare and his Contemporaries* (1995), 271–88
Swander	Homer Swander, 'No exit for a dead body: what to do with a scripted corpse?', *Journal of Dramatic Theory and Criticism*, 5 (1991), 139–52
Sypher	Wylie Sypher, *The Ethic of Time: Structures of Experience in Shakespeare* (New York, 1978)
TC	Tom Craik (in correspondence)
Taylor, 'Empirical'	Gary Taylor, 'Empirical Middleton: *Macbeth*, Adaptation and Microauthorship', *SQ*, 65.3 (2014), forthcoming
Taylor, 'Letters'	Mark Taylor, 'Letters and readers in *Macbeth*, *King Lear*, and *Twelfth Night*', *PQ*, 69 (1990), 31–53
Taylor, '*Macbeth* and Middleton'	Gary Taylor, '*Macbeth* and Middleton', in Miola, 2nd edn (2014), 296–305
Taylor & Lavagnino, *Middleton*	Gary Taylor and John Lavagnino (gen. eds), *Thomas Middleton: The Collected Works* (Oxford, 2007)
Taylor & Lavagnino, *Textual Culture*	Gary Taylor and John Lavagnino (gen. eds), *Thomas Middleton and Early Modern Textual Culture: A Companion to the Collected Works* (Oxford, 2007)
Thaler	Alwin Thaler, 'The "lost scenes" of Macbeth', in *Shakespeare and Democracy* (Knoxville, Tenn., 1941), 88–105
Thomas, *Political*	Vivian Thomas, *Shakespeare's Political and Economic Language: A Dictionary* (2008)
Thomas, *Religion*	Keith Thomas, *Religion and the Decline of Magic* (Harmondsworth, 1973)
Thomas & Faircloth	Vivian Thomas and Nicki Faircloth, *Shakespeare's Plants and Gardens: A Dictionary* (2014)
Thompson & Taylor	Ann Thompson and Neil Taylor (eds), *William Shakespeare, Hamlet* (2006)
Thomson	Peter Thomson, *Shakespeare's Theatre* (1983)
Thorndike	A.H. Thorndike, 'The relations of *Hamlet* to contemporary revenge plays', *Publications of the Modern Language Association*, 17 (1902), 125–220
Tillyard	E.M.W. Tillyard, *Shakespeare's History Plays* (rev. edn, Harmondsworth, 1969)
Tilmouth	Christopher Tilmouth, 'Shakespeare's open consciences', *Renaissance Studies*, 23.4 (2009), 501–15
TLS	*The Times Literary Supplement*
Topsell, *Beasts*	Edward Topsell, *The History of Four-footed Beasts* (1607)
Topsell, *Serpents*	Edward Topsell, *The History of Serpents* (1608)

Traversi	Derek Traversi, *An Approach to Shakespeare*, vol. 2 (rev. edn, 1969)
Turner	Frederick Turner, *Shakespeare and the Nature of Time* (Oxford, 1971)
Tynan, *Curtains*	Kenneth Tynan, *Curtains* (1961)
Tynan, *View*	Kenneth Tynan, *A View of the English Stage* (1975)
Vickers, *Critical*	Brian Vickers (ed.), *Shakespeare: The Critical Heritage*, 6 vols (1974–6)
Vickers, *Shakespeare*	Brian Vickers, *Shakespeare, A Lover's Complaint, and Sir John Davies of Hereford* (Cambridge, 2007)
Vickers, *Vivien Leigh*	Hugo Vickers, *Vivien Leigh* (1988)
Vickers & Dahl	Brian Vickers and Marcus Dahl, 'Disintegrated: did Thomas Middleton really adapt *Macbeth*?', *TLS*, 28 May 2010
Walker, R.	Roy Walker, *The Time is Free* (1949)
Walker, W.S.	W.S. Walker, *Shakespeare's Versification* (1854)
Waller	Gary F. Waller, *The Strong Necessity of Time* (The Hague, 1976)
Walter	Harriet Walter, *Actors on Shakespeare: 'Macbeth'* (2002)
Watson	Fiona Watson, *Macbeth: A True Story* (2010)
Webster	John Webster, *Three Plays*, ed. D.C. Gunby (Harmondsworth, 1972)
Wells & Taylor	Stanley Wells and Gary Taylor, with John Jowett and William Montgomery, *William Shakespeare: A Textual Companion* (Oxford, 1987)
Werness	Hope B. Werness, *The Continuum Encyclopaedia of Animal Symbolism in Art* (2004)
Wickham, 'Hell Castle'	Glynne Wickham, 'Hell Castle and its door-keeper', *SS 19* (1966), 68–74
Wickham, 'To fly'	Glynne Wickham, 'To fly or not to fly?', in Erica Hunnigher-Schilling (ed.), *Essays on Drama and the Theatre* (1973), 171–82
Wiggins	Martin Wiggins, *Journeymen in Murder: The Assassin in English Renaissance Drama* (Oxford, 1991)
Williams, *Dictionary*	Gordon Williams, *A Dictionary of Sexual Language and Imagery in Shakespearean and Stuart Literature*, 3 vols (1994)
Williams, 'Scene'	George Walton Williams, 'Scene individable: the battle of Birnam Wood', *Shakespeare Newsletter*, 55.2 (2005), 33, 36

Williams, 'Third'	George Walton Williams, 'The Third Murderer in *Macbeth*', *SQ*, 23.3 (1972), 261
Williams, 'Time'	George Walton Williams, '"Time for such a word": verbal echoing in *Macbeth*', *SS 47* (1994), 153–60
Willis	Deborah Willis, 'The monarch and the sacred: Shakespeare and the ceremony for the healing of the King's Evil', in Linda Woodbridge and Edward Berry (eds), *True Rites and Maimed Rites: Ritual and Anti-Ritual in Shakespeare and His Age* (1992)
Wills	Garry Wills, *Witches and Jesuits: Shakespeare's 'Macbeth'* (New York and Oxford, 1995)
Wilson	Richard Wilson, 'The pilot's thumb: *Macbeth* and the Jesuits', in *The Lancashire Witches. Histories and Stories*, ed. Robert Poole (2002), 126–45
Wilson & Calore	Christopher R. Wilson and Michaela Calore, *Music in Shakespeare: A Dictionary* (2005)
Wilson Knight, *Imperial*	G. Wilson Knight, *The Imperial Theme* (1931)
Wilson Knight, *Wheel*	G. Wilson Knight, *The Wheel of Fire* (1930)
Wormald	Jenny Wormald, 'Gunpowder, treason and Scots', *Journal of British Studies*, 24.2 (1985), 141–68
Worster	David Worster, 'Performance and pedagogy in *Macbeth*', *SQ*, 53 (2002), 362–78
Wortham	Christopher Wortham, 'Shakespeare, James I and the Matter of Britain', *English*, 45 (1996), 97–122
Woudhuysen	H.R. Woudhuysen, ed., *Samuel Johnson on Shakespeare* (1989)
Wright	George T. Wright, *Shakespeare's Metrical Art* (Berkeley and London, 1988)
YWES	*Year's Work in English Studies*
Zamir	Tzachi Zamir, 'Upon one bank and shoal of time: literature, nihilism, and moral philosophy', *New Literary History*, 31.3 (2000), 529–51

INDEX

This Index covers the Introduction, the commentary notes and Appendix 1; it excludes references to the OED and to Appendices 2, 3, 4 and 5. The abbreviation 'n.' is used only for footnotes in the Introduction and the Appendices; it is not used for commentary notes.